God and Knowledge

T&T Clark Studies in Systematic Theology

Edited by
John Webster
Ivor Davidson
Ian McFarland
Philip G. Ziegler

God and Knowledge

Herman Bavinck's Theological Epistemology

Nathaniel Gray Sutanto

LONDON • NEW YORK • OXFORD • NEW DELHI • SYDNEY

T&T CLARK
Bloomsbury Publishing Plc
50 Bedford Square, London, WC1B 3DP, UK
1385 Broadway, New York, NY 10018, USA
29 Earlsfort Terrace, Dublin 2, Ireland

BLOOMSBURY, T&T CLARK and the T&T Clark logo
are trademarks of Bloomsbury Publishing Plc

First published in Great Britain 2020
Paperback edition first published 2021

Copyright © Nathaniel Gray Sutanto, 2020

Nathaniel Gray Sutanto has asserted his right under the Copyright,
Designs and Patents Act, 1988, to be identified as Author of this work.

For legal purposes the Acknowledgements on p. ix constitute an
extension of this copyright page.

Cover design: Eleanor Rose
Cover image © Vince Cavataio/Getty Images

All rights reserved. No part of this publication may be reproduced or
transmitted in any form or by any means, electronic or mechanical,
including photocopying, recording, or any information storage or retrieval
system, without prior permission in writing from the publishers.

Bloomsbury Publishing Plc does not have any control over, or responsibility for,
any third-party websites referred to or in this book. All internet addresses given
in this book were correct at the time of going to press. The author and publisher
regret any inconvenience caused if addresses have changed or sites have
ceased to exist, but can accept no responsibility for any such changes.

A catalogue record for this book is available from the British Library.

Library of Congress Cataloging-in-Publication Data
Names: Sutanto, Nathaniel Gray, 1991-author.
Title: God and knowledge: Herman Bavinck's theological epistemology / Nathaniel Gray Sutanto.
Description: London; New York: T&T Clark, [2020] |
Series: T&T Clark studies in systematic theology; Volume 31 |
Includes bibliographical references and index.
Identifiers: LCCN 2019030578 (print) | LCCN 2019030579 (ebook) |
ISBN 9780567692283 (hardback) | ISBN 9780567692290 (adobe pdf) |
ISBN 9780567692306 (epub)
Subjects: LCSH: Bavinck, Herman, 1854-1921. | Reformed epistemology. |
Knowledge, Theory of (Religion)
Classification: LCC BX9479.B35 S88 2020 (print) |
LCC BX9479.B35 (ebook) | DDC 230/.42092–dc23
LC record available at https://lccn.loc.gov/2019030578
LC ebook record available at https://lccn.loc.gov/2019030579

ISBN: HB: 978-0-5676-9228-3
PB: 978-0-5676-9898-8
ePDF: 978-0-5676-9229-0
eBook: 978-0-5676-9230-6

Typeset by Deanta Global Publishing Services, Chennai, India

To find out more about our authors and books visit
www.bloomsbury.com and sign up for our newsletters.

As indicated in the body, parts of this work, in modified forms, have been published in:

Sutanto, Nathaniel. 'Herman Bavinck on the Image of God and Original Sin', *International Journal of Systematic Theology* 18 (2016): pp. 174–90.

Sutanto, Nathaniel. 'Herman Bavinck and Thomas Reid on Perception and Knowing God', *Harvard Theological Review* 111 (2018): pp. 115–34.

Contents

Acknowledgements		ix
1	Re-reading Bavinck's theological epistemology	1
	I Preliminary observations: Orthodox and modern	4
	II Theological epistemology and the organic motif: Reshaping the discussion	7
	III The way forward	13
2	Bavinck's organicism – God, anthropology and revelation	17
	I The organic motif	18
	II Organicism and the classical contours of Bavinck's doctrine of God	22
	III An organic anthropology: The individual, the relation and whole	30
	IV Revelation as organic	37
3	Organism and *Wetenschap* – the structure of Bavinck's epistemology	45
	I Organic knowing	47
	a. A 'unified worldview' – the organic and the mechanical	51
	b. Theology as the queen of the sciences and the theological character of the sciences	56
	c. An 'organism of science': *Principia* and unity-and-diversity	59
	II The kingdom of God and sphere sovereignty	68
	III Summary	71
4	Between Aquinas and Kuyper	75
	I Bavinck's Thomas and Roman Catholic epistemology	77
	II 'Bavinck's mistake': Re-situating Bavinck's account of Thomas within the current internal Thomist debates	83
	III On organisms and machines	93
	a. Re-articulating the difference between Bavinck and Kuyper	93
	b. Bodies and propositions	97
5	Bavinck, Thomas Reid, the 'gap' and the question of subjects and objects	101
	I Bavinck and world-directed beliefs: Two interpretations – reformed epistemology and post-Kantian trajectories	103

	II	Herman Bavinck and Thomas Reid on perception and the problem of the 'gap'	109
		a. A 'problem' in modern epistemology	110
		b. Reid's proposal	113
		c. Bavinck's proposal	115
	III	Towards Bavinck's use of Eduard von Hartmann	119
6		The Absolute and the organic – Bavinck and Eduard von Hartmann	123
	I	The 'mistake of idealism' and the immediacy of contact with the world: Bavinck's critical appropriation of Eduard von Hartmann	127
	II	Overcoming the gap: The absolute, revelation and the organic	134
		a. Philosophy of revelation	135
		b. The organic motif and the gap	141
	III	Holism and three implications: A (modified) Christian internalism, the question of subjectivism and nineteenth-century philosophical discourse – towards a development	145
7		Revelation, the unconscious, reason and feeling	151
	I	Revelation causing primordial awareness – innate and acquired knowledge	153
		a. Revelation that 'precedes' innate and acquired knowledge	154
		b. Organism, the psyche and feeling as unconscious knowing	158
		c. Concept formation and reason in the context of a primordial awareness	161
	II	Between *concursus* and *influentia*	164
	III	On 'unconscious knowledge' and primordial revelation: A revelational phenomenology as pre-predicative in broader neo-Calvinism	171

Conclusion	177
Bibliography	181
Index	194

Acknowledgements

This work began as a PhD thesis written at the University of Edinburgh. James Eglinton's support, enthusiasm, meticulous reading and encouragement have been of enormous value as he supervised this work at the time. He has been a model example in his commitment to academic rigour and a kind of winsome seriousness that attends his careful work as a theologian. I am thankful as well to David Fergusson, who also read numerous chapters and gave invaluable feedback that has redirected me in more than one occasion. Kevin Vanhoozer and Joshua Ralston were encouraging in their feedback and were insightful in drawing generative implications of this work. Brian Mattson, Henk van den Belt, Mark Garcia, Steven Duby and Christopher Cleveland, too, read substantive portions or chapters of the manuscript. I am grateful for their attention and excitement for the project. I am also thankful for the countless conversations I had with the faculty of theology at New College at the time: Lydia Schumacher, David Grumett and Zachary Purvis. I have also been helped from the daily engagement there with other researchers on Bavinck: Cory Brock, Gustavo Monteiro, Greg Parker, Bruce Pass and Cam Clausing.

I am thankful for the editors of this series – Philip Ziegler, Ian McFarland and Ivor Davidson – and Anna Turton for overseeing it to fruition – it's a privilege to be included in it. Their feedback was not only encouraging but also helpful for turning a thesis into a book. Thanks also are due to Oliver Crisp and Michael Allen, who gave some timely advice along the way.

Particular sections of the work were presented at Princeton Seminary's Kuyper Conference in 2016 and 2017, the advanced theological fellowship (2016) at Kampen Theological University (Holland), and at the Reformed Theology and History group at the 2016 meeting of the American Academy of Religion. Receiving the Puchinger prize in Spring 2017 at Princeton Theological Seminary allowed me to stay there and use their fine library. I have benefited from the feedback and support of those who participated in the presentation of the material. More specifically, George Harinck, Todd Billings, Dolf te Velde, James K. A. Smith and Ad de Bruijne all gave insights that I greatly appreciated. I am thankful too to the library of the Free University of Amsterdam for their patience and for granting me access to their archives, in which many of Bavinck's handwritten works reside. James Eglinton, Marinus de Jong, Andreas Jongeneel, Koos Tamminga and Bram van den Heuvel helped with the translations of various Dutch texts from Bavinck and others. I am responsible for shortcomings that remain in this work.

Friends at Edinburgh University, Biola University and Westminster Seminary (PA), Jakarta and Covenant City Church were also great sources of encouragement to me. It was Carl Trueman who first (strongly!) suggested that I study Bavinck, connecting me as well to James Eglinton. Brian Cox, the one who has guided me and mentored me through the faith, deserves special recognition. My wife, Indita Probosutedjo, fuels me with her kindness, patience and love – she's a daily reminder of God's grace towards me. This work would not be here without them.

Last, but certainly not least, is my family: my sisters, Novi (Christina), Mitzy, Cindy; my brothers in law, Adrian and Aryo; my niece and nephews, Ben, Mori, Maya, Max and Myra; Sumini, who had been labouring with our family faithfully; and my parents, Leo Sutanto and Elly Yanti Noor. I owe everything to their patience, love, support and generosity. It is to my parents that I dedicate this present work.

Nathaniel Gray Sutanto
June 2019

1

Re-reading Bavinck's theological epistemology

Christianity, Christian-theism has first laid the foundation and paved the way for this organic unity of science.[1]

If [a unified worldview] is possible, it can be explained only on the basis of the claim that the world is an organism and thus has first been thought of as such. Only then do philosophy and worldview have a right and ground of existence, as it is also on this high point of knowledge that subject and object harmonize.[2]

On 1 May 1903, *Friesche Kerkbode*, a Christian newspaper based in Friesland, printed a summary of a lecture that Herman Bavinck (1854–1921) delivered at a theological conference there on Thursday, 30 April of the same year. This lecture took place a year before the publication of Bavinck's *Christelijke wetenschap* and was on the same subject. Bavinck's theses in the lecture discussed the difference between positivistic (modern) and Christian views of science and how Christianity can help the academic disciplines flourish.[3] After remarking that Bavinck's lecture exposed the false assumptions underlying the opposition against Christian scholarship, the journalist wrote that Bavinck called for the indispensability of Christianity for scientific practice. The article ended with an encouragement to its readers:

> Therefore it is more necessary than ever for science to become practiced and taught in Christ, the spirit, to the support of the church, the blessing of society, the sanctity of the fatherland, the extension of God's kingdom, [and] the glory of his name. A high, sacred, delightful ideal desires us. May it inspire us all with courage and gird [us] with strength. It is a dedication and effort worth all of our strength.[4]

---

[1] Herman Bavinck, 'Christendom en Natuurwetenschap', in C. B. Bavinck (ed.), *Kennis en leven: Opstellen en artikelen uit vroegere jaren* (Kampen: Kok, 1922), p. 202. Dutch original: 'Het Christendom, het Christelijk Theisme heeft eerst den grond gelegd en den weg gebaand voor deze organische eenheid der wetenschap'. Unless otherwise noted, translations are my own.
[2] Bavinck, *Christelijke wereldbeschouwing*, 3rd edn (Kampen: Kok, 1929), pp. 32–3. Dutch original: 'Indien deze mogelijk is, dan kan dit alleen daaruit verklaard worden, dat de wereld een organisme is en dus eerst als zoodanig is gedacht. Dan alleen heeft philosophie en wereldbeschouwing recht en grond van bestaan, als ook op dit hoogtepunt der kennis subject en object samenstemmen'.
[3] Herman Bavinck, *Christelijke wetenschap* (Kampen: Kok, 1904).
[4] The author's name is only initialled as K. Jr, in *Friesche Kerkbode*, 1 May 1903, issue 809. Dutch original: 'Daarom is het meer dan ooit noodzakelijk, dat de wetenschap beoefend en onderwezen

The lecture prompted an intense enthusiastic response in the audience and the Christian commentator present there. But what, exactly, did Bavinck mean by this? What kind of resources would Christianity provide that might nurture the flourishing of the sciences?

The concern here is broader than the usual connotations that attend the English word 'science' – *wetenschap* refers not merely to matters of the empirical hard sciences but also to all higher learning and fields of knowledge in general. As such, it corresponds closely to the German *Wissenschaft*.[5] In this context, Herman Bavinck insisted on the medieval dictum that theology remains the queen of the sciences, though, as this study will show, he did this while considerably redefining the meaning of that queenship. In what sense, then, can he reassert theology's priority in the academy in this modern context? Is its material content to be siphoned off into its own sphere in distinction from the other sciences, or does it govern in such a way that it plays an influential role, reshaping how the other sciences are viewed? Bavinck's context amplifies the significance of his answers to these questions. Following the heels of the German debates concerning theology's place in the academy, and after the 1876 Higher Education Act in the Netherlands that significantly altered the character of theological and religious studies in an attempt to accommodate both modernist and traditionalist conceptions of the role of theology in higher education, Bavinck wrestled with these issues with acute urgency.[6]

The subject matter of this study consists in examining the meaning of his response to this situation – his characterization of science and knowledge as a 'single organism' and the concomitant claim that the placement of theology into a purely ecclesial sphere is to compromise the 'organism of science' (*organisme der wetenschap*).

This is amplified clearly in his parliament speech that addressed the 1876 Higher Education Act, which connected the act to the views of Utrecht University professor Cornelis Opzoomer (1821–92). Bavinck argued that a few decades earlier, Opzoomer had posited an entailment relationship between 'the principle of the separation between Church and State' and the consequence that the 'theological faculty must be removed

---

worde in Christ, geest, tot steun voor de kerk, tot zegen van de maatschappij, tot heil van het vaderland tot uitbreiding van Gods rijk, tot eere van zijn naam. Een hoog, heilig, heerlijk ideaal wenkt ons. Moge het ons allen bezielen met moed en aangorden met kracht. Het is de inspanning en toewijding van alle onze krachten waard'.

Bavinck delivered a lecture on the same points earlier that year in Utrecht on Thursday, 19 March 1903, as recorded on pages 83 and 84 of *Minerva: Algemeen Nederlandsch Studenten Weekblad*, 26 March 1903. Both of these items are archived at the Free University of Amsterdam under inventory number 353.

[5] Unless otherwise noted, I have the sense of *wetenschap* in mind when 'science' is used.

[6] See especially his speech in parliament which addresses the issue: *Verslag der Handelingen van de Eerste Kamer, 12 Maart 1913*, pp. 432–3. Cf. Jan Bank and Maarten van Buuren, *Dutch Culture in a European Perspective*, vol. 3: *1900: The Age of Bourgeois Culture*, Lynne Richards and John Rudge (trans.) (Hampshire: Palgrave Macmillan, 2004), pp. 311–35. Johannes Zachhuber, *Theology as Science in Nineteenth-Century Germany: From F.C. Baur to Ernst Troeltsch* (Oxford: Oxford University Press, 2013). Bavinck was clearly aware of the German discussions and their influence on his own Dutch context; see especially his speech in parliament which addresses the issue: *Verslag der Handelingen*, p. 433; see James Eglinton and Michael Bräutigam, 'Scientific Theology? Herman Bavinck and Adolf Schlatter on the Place of Theology in the University', *Journal of Reformed Theology* 7 (2013): pp. 27–50.

from the organism of science' that existed in the universities.[7] Opzoomer's argument to locate theology within the church rather than the academy was, to Bavinck, a splitting of a singular organism – it fails to do justice to the character of theology and the sciences as a whole.

In his perspective, the 1876 Act is the embodiment of the result of a series of modern movements that questioned the scientific (*wetenschappelijke*) character of theology and its relation to the other sciences. Propelled by the strict distinction erected by Immanuel Kant (1724–1804) between a knowledge that is 'limited to the circle of experience' and a faith that rests on 'personal, practical motives', dogmatics became gradually understood as the formal articulation of subjective mental states rather than a proper scientific study.[8] Under the pressures of these intellectual shifts, theologians who followed Friedrich Schleiermacher's (1768–1834) lead in seeking to justify theology's place within the academy at times posed an opposition between *Wissenschaft* and confessionalism, by arguing that the role of the theologian was concerned not with normative truths for all ages but 'with the interconnection of whatever doctrine has currency in a given social organization called a Christian church at a given time'.[9] Within this trajectory, too, others sought a mediating theology (*Vermittelungstheologie*) that attempted to fuse traditional Christian doctrines with the demands of the new *Weltanschauung*. The result of this was a 'tendency to replace all transcendent-metaphysical statements about God, his essence and attributes, his words and works, with descriptions of Christian experience and its content'.[10]

By 1876 in the Netherlands, the place of dogmatics and theological reflection in the academy was also reshaped. Religious studies, as the science of religion, would be included in the universities as an objective study that examines the phenomenon of religions, whereas the 'dogmatic and practical disciplines', Bavinck observed, 'would be taught under the auspices of the church'.[11]

---

[7] Bavinck, *Verslag der Handelingen*, pp. 432–3. Dutch original: 'Immers het lijdt geen twijfel, dat de theologische faculteit in het jaar 1876 is omgezet in een faculteit van godsdienstwetenschap. Het is met de regeling van de zaken der theologische faculteit in de vorige eeuw zeer eigenaardig toegegaan. Sedert de hoogleraar Opzoomer in 1848 het denkbeeld uitte, dat het beginsel van scheiding van Kerk en Staat ook medebracht de consequentie, dat de theologische faculteit uit het organisme der wetenschap verwijderd moest worden, en dat de opleiding van geestelijken in het algemeen aan de Kerken zelf moest worden toevertrouwd, heeft dit denkbeeld in steeds ruimer kring ingang gevonden.'

[8] Herman Bavinck, *Reformed Dogmatics*, vol. 1, *Prolegomena*, John Bolt (ed.), John Vriend (trans.) (Grand Rapids: Baker Academic, 2004), p. 233. Hereafter, *RD*. Where most relevant, I draw the original texts from Herman Bavinck, *Gereformeerde Dogmatiek*, 3rd edn, 4 vols (Kampen: Kok, 1918). Hereafter *GD*. The third to fifth editions are identical, except for pagination.

[9] Friedrich Schleiermacher, *Christian Faith: A New Translation and Critical Edition*, Catherine L. Kelsey and Terrence N. Tice (eds), Terrence N. Tice, Catherine L. Kelsey and Edwina Lawler (trans.) (Louisville: Westminster John Knox, 2016), §19. Cf. Bavinck, *RD*, 1: p. 48; Thomas Albert Howard, *Protestant Theology and the Making of the Modern German University* (Oxford: Oxford University Press, 2006), p. 131.

[10] Bavinck, *RD*, 1: p. 48.

[11] Bavinck, *RD*, 1: p. 49. Arie van Deursen included the act as one of the impetuses for the creation of the Free University of Amsterdam in *The Distinctive Character of the Free University in Amsterdam, 1880-2005: A Commemorative History*, Herbert Donald Morton (trans.) (Grand Rapids: Eerdmans, 2008), p. 6.

I Preliminary observations: Orthodox and modern

Herman Bavinck stood on the grounds of Reformed orthodoxy in response to these perceived challenges and devoted much of his career writing on these topics.[12] After writing his four-volume *Reformed Dogmatics*, he committed several works on the scientific character of theology, how human knowing is possible and the relationship between theology and the other sciences. Most of these works have remained untranslated. In 1904, he published two studies that tackled these issues directly: *Christelijke wereldbeschouwing* (*Christian Worldview*) and *Christelijke wetenschap* (*Christian Science*).[13] While the former work argues that the Christian faith provides more holistic answers concerning issues of epistemology, metaphysics and ethics, the latter work sets out a Christian understanding of scholarship in response to positivistic accounts of science. These two works, together, argue that Christianity offers unique resources to scholarship due to its distinctly organic vision of life. Bavinck's 1908 Stone Lectures at Princeton Seminary, the *Philosophy of Revelation*, continued this focus by arguing, inductively, that divine revelation rests behind every area of study.[14] Alongside other essays, his inaugural addresses at Kampen in 1883 and the Free University of Amsterdam in 1902 both tackle similar issues of how to relate and offer a Christian account of theology and the other sciences.[15] Relevant to our purposes here, too, is Bavinck's 1897 work *Beginselen der psychologie*, in which the inner workings of human cognition and its various faculties are parsed out.[16]

Bavinck challenged the charges against the orthodoxy of the post-Reformation period that came from modern theologians, which tended to report that Reformed scholasticism presented an arid form of rationalistic inquiry in their claim that a systematic knowledge of God was attainable.[17] In this sense, Bavinck's thought could be used to support some current trajectories that argue for the continuity that exists between the post-Reformation scholastics and the Reformers themselves.[18] The distinctive literary styles that often are noted to distinguish Calvin from the divines that came after him do not prove so much a difference of substance but a transition from a time of pioneering to confessionalization according to the needs of Reformation theology in the academies. Bavinck understood that the Reformation was rooted in

---

[12] Cf. *Een Leidse Vriendschap: Brieven van Christiaan Snouck Hurgronje aan Herman Bavinck*, George Harinck and J. Bruijn (eds) (Baarn: Ten Have, 1999), p. 100. Writing to his friend Christiaan Snouck Hurgronje, Bavinck expressed that he remained committed to Reformed theology, despite having completed his education at Leiden University.

[13] An English translation of *Christian Worldview*: Herman Bavinck, *Christian Worldview*, Nathaniel Gray Sutanto, James Eglinton and Cory Brock (eds and trans.) (Wheaton: Crossway, 2019).

[14] Herman Bavinck, *Philosophy of Revelation: A New Annotated Edition*, Cory Brock and Nathaniel Gray Sutanto (eds) (Peabody: Hendrickson, 2018).

[15] Herman Bavinck, *De wetenschap der H. Godgeleerdheid: Rede ter aanvaarding van het leeraarsambt aan de Theologische School te Kampen* (Kampen: Zalsman, 1883); Herman Bavinck, 'Religion and Theology', Bruce R. Pass (trans.), *Reformed Theological Review* 77 (2018): pp. 75–135.

[16] Herman Bavinck, *Beginselen der psychologie* (Kampen: Bos, 1897).

[17] Bavinck, *RD*, 1: pp. 83–4.

[18] See, for example, Richard A. Muller, *Post-Reformation Reformed Dogmatics: The Rise and Development of Reformed Orthodoxy, ca. 1520 to ca. 1725*, 4 vols (Grand Rapids: Baker Academic, 2003).

the medieval theology and that it drew from that heritage in a critical manner. He effectively resisted theologically motivated caricatures that introduce false binaries, for example, between being scholastic and biblical, or between Trinitarianism and federalism, into readings of Reformed scholasticism.

Indeed, his response to the intellectual currents that opposed the scientific character of theology is fundamentally attuned to these classical instincts. In particular, Bavinck insisted on two axiomatic principles: that God's revelation means that theology remains scientific and that theology can and should be related to other academic disciplines. This involved recovering the classical conviction that dogmatics must attend to the metaphysical implications of Scriptural revelation while obeying the obligation to relate all things back to their creator. 'A choice has to be made', he wrote. 'Either there is room in science for metaphysics and then positivism is in principle false, or positivism is the true view of science and metaphysics must be radically banished from its entire domain.'[19] 'Theology as a particular science', after all, 'assumes that God has unmistakably revealed himself.'[20] Insofar as a positivistic and modern definition of science precluded this conviction one must simply make a choice between two antithetical definitions of science.[21] Echoing a classical and Thomistic axiom, Bavinck affirmed that 'dogmatics is the knowledge that God has revealed in his Word to the church concerning himself and all creatures as they stand in relation to him.'[22]

Likewise, to excise the study of theology from the academy in order to relocate it strictly within the church is not to be considered an honour or service to theology itself. 'Scripture' remains 'a book for the whole of humankind and has meaning for all of human life',[23] and thus dogmaticians, too, have a responsibility to tease out the riches of divine wisdom in relation to the 'world of science [*erve der wetenschap*]'.[24] The relocation of dogmatics into a separate sphere would be to the detriment of both science and practice, rather than an improvement.[25]

Yet it would be a mistake to draw the conclusion from this that Bavinck sought a mere return to the orthodoxy that once was in an act of retreat. John Bolt's observation that Bavinck's serious interaction with modern philosophy is a 'hallmark of his exemplary work' remains apt.[26] Indeed, Bavinck's desire to set up an orthodox alternative to the intellectual challenges in his day preserved an understanding of the nuanced reciprocation that existed between modernity and orthodoxy. Despite all of the antithetical emphases of the modern intellectual currents, Bavinck still sought to appreciate its unique contributions and to highlight modernity's dependence upon the Christian milieu from which it came: 'Just as modern theology, in general, thinks and lives out of the Christian tradition much more than its practitioners themselves suppose,

---

[19] Bavinck, *RD*, 1: p. 37.
[20] Bavinck, *RD*, 1: pp. 37–8.
[21] Bavinck, *Christelijke wetenschap*, p. 9.
[22] Bavinck, *RD*, 1: p. 38.
[23] Bavinck, *RD*, 1: p. 46.
[24] Bavinck, *RD*, 1: p. 46; *GD*, 1: p. 26. *Erve* is a rather uncommon word and is a shortening of the word *erfgoed*, which could mean 'inheritance'. In that sense, Bavinck's meaning here can refer not merely to the sphere or environment of science but also to all that we've received and learned from it.
[25] Bavinck, *RD*, 1: p. 51.
[26] John Bolt, 'Editor's Introduction', in *RD*, 1: p. 14.

so is orthodoxy also – unless it entirely shut itself off from the environment – in [a] stronger or weaker degree under the influence of the spiritual currents of this century.'[27] Bavinck made a similar judgement a few years earlier in his 1908 Stone lectures: 'More than this, all our modern civilization, art, science, literature, ethics, jurisprudence, society, state, and politics, are leavened by religious, Christian, supranaturalistic elements, and still rest on the foundation of the old worldview.'[28] Christians, therefore, cannot afford to adopt a stance of complete opposition to modernism, and this is so for at least two reasons. First, it would naively assume that one is not already influenced by the dominant worldviews present in the contemporary culture. Second, one might miss the opportunity to showcase how Christian theism produced the ideals that modernity took for granted, such that, to the extent that it denies orthodox Christianity, it denies the very grounds on which it stands. Paul Tillich advocates the same kind of principle when he said this a few decades later: 'All theology of today is dependent in some way on the classical systems of orthodoxy.'[29]

There is, then, no desire in Bavinck to 'repristinate' the older conditions or to retrieve a 'dead conservatism'.[30] His appreciation of Reformed orthodoxy itself is not uncritical, as he would often note areas of disagreement with it.[31] It was of critical importance to him that dogmatics seeks development from generation to generation. To be sure, Bavinck's tendency to appreciate his contemporary intellectual scene is not sourced by a positive endorsement of enlightenment philosophy, according to which a disdain for the past is incubated along with an optimism placed on rational autonomy.[32] Rather, it is the desire to garner new insights generated by a reflection on the contemporary intellectual milieu while standing on the grounds of the great traditions of the ancient, medieval and reformed divines. In the 1895 foreword to the *Dogmatics*, he would argue that an aim to bring dogmatics forward by conversing with the present is implied in the very definition of Reformed catholicity: 'To cherish the ancient simply because it is ancient', he wrote, 'is neither Reformed nor Christian. A work of dogmatic theology should not simply describe what was true and valid but what abides as true and valid. It is rooted in the past but labors for the future.'[33] The result of this is a self-consciously irenic and eclectic approach – not as a tautological claim concerning the fact that all

---

[27] Bavinck, *Modernisme en Orthodoxie: Rede Gehouden bij de overdracht van het rectoraat aan de Vrije Universiteit op 20 oktober 1911* (Kampen: J.H. Kok, 1911), p. 15. Dutch original: 'Trouwens, niemand, die meeleeft met zijn tijd, kan in elk opzicht tegen al het moderne gekant zijn. Zooals de moderne theologie over het algemeen nog veel sterker uit de Christelijke traditie denkt en leeft dan zij zelve vermoedt, zoo staat ook de orthodoxie, tenzij zij zich geheel van hare omgeving afsluit, in zwakker of sterker mate onder den invloed van de geestesstroomingen dezer eeuw.'

[28] Bavinck, *Philosophy of Revelation*, p. 17. Bavinck expresses this same reasoning in a lecture (in English) on realism in art. The manuscript could be found in the Free University Bavinck Archive no. 346, box 19, folder 213, no date, 'Realism (nature) in de kunst'.

[29] Paul Tillich, *A History of Christian Thought*, Carl Braaten (ed.) (New York: Simon & Schuster, 1968), p. 277.

[30] Herman Bavinck, 'The Future of Calvinism', *The Presbyterian and Reformed Review* 5 (1894): p. 13.

[31] See, for example, Herman Bavinck, *The Certainty of Faith*, Harry der Nederlanden (trans.) (Ontario: Paideia Press, 1980), p. 41; Bavinck, *RD*, 2: p. 78.

[32] Cf. Immanuel Kant, 'An Answer to the Question: What is Enlightenment?' in H. S. Reiss (ed.), H. B. Nisbet (trans.), *Kant: Political Writings* (Cambridge: Cambridge University Press, 1991), p. 54.

[33] Herman Bavinck, 'Foreword to the First Edition (volume 1) of the *Gereformeerde Dogmatiek*', John Bolt (trans.), *Calvin Theological Journal* 45 (2010): p. 10.

thinkers are necessarily unique[34] but a self-conscious modus operandi grounded upon principled theological claims concerning the character of Christianity and the catholic scope of her witness.[35] Again, '[Theology] is not *per se* hostile to any philosophical system and does not, *a priori* and without criticism, give priority to the philosophy of Plato or of Kant, or vice versa.'[36] These convictions stem from the neo-Calvinistic tinge to Bavinck's theology, as he considered Calvinism to be more encompassing than the predicate 'Reformed' – in Calvinism there is a fecund power too momentous to be confined to the sphere of religion. The 'Calvinistic principle', he wrote, 'is too universal and accordingly too rich and fruitful' – it is generative not merely of a particular theology but of a 'specific view of the world and life as a whole; so to speak, a philosophy all its own.'[37]

II Theological epistemology and the organic motif: Reshaping the discussion

Bavinck's mode of operation informed his writing in a way that poses a considerable difficulty for interpreters. This is not a novel development – already in 1911 Bavinck complained that the neo-Calvinist movement was unfairly accused of adopting a 'double-minded standpoint' of being neither truly modern nor orthodox.[38] A cursory reading of the *Dogmatics* might provide an exculpatory explanation of these charges. Readers might find it taxing to locate Bavinck's own voice, as it is commonplace for him to describe his interlocutor's position for several paragraphs or pages on its own strongest terms, only to critique it in a single paragraph. It is difficult to know where Bavinck's voice begins or ends. Interlocutors invoked as foils for his own perspective in one area are deployed as a proponent of Bavinck's own claims in another. Here, readers of Bavinck can easily resonate with Wolter Huttinga's description of this phenomenon:

> The way [Bavinck] represents the opinions of others, even those with whom he obviously disagrees, always belies a deep sympathy which may cause the reader to

---

[34] 'For all theologians are "eclectic". None simply repristinates the thought of a single predecessor.' Robert Kolb, *Martin Luther: Confessor of the Faith* (Oxford: Oxford University Press, 2009), p. 31.

[35] 'But the Christian church and theology were, generally speaking, more sensible; adopted a critical, eclectic point of view; and tried, while investigating everything, to retain the good.' 'Christianity and Natural Science', in John Bolt (ed.), Harry Boonstra and Gerrit Sheeres (trans.), *Essays on Religion, Science and Society* (Grand Rapids: Baker Academic, 2008), p. 93. This is also recognized by Wolter Huttinga, *Participation and Communicability: Herman Bavinck and John Milbank on the Relation between God and the World* (Amsterdam: Buijten & Schipperheijn Motief, 2014), p. 23.

[36] Bavinck, RD, 1: p. 609. James Eglinton notes that this 'synthetic' character of Bavinck's intellectual method evidences the neo-Calvinistic paradigm of common grace in *Trinity and Organism: Toward a New Reading of Herman Bavinck's Organic Motif* (London: T&T Clark, 2012), pp. 37–44.

[37] Bavinck, 'The Future of Calvinism', p. 5.

[38] Bavinck, *Modernisme en Orthodoxie*, p. 5. 'Wel leidde zij tot eenige meerdere waardeering van ons bedoelen en streven, maar tenslotte liep zij toch uit op de ernstige beschuldiging, dat wij een *dubbelzinnig standpunt innamen*, noch modern noch orthodox, noch naturalistisch noch supranaturalistisch waren, en dat wij dus het best en het eerlijkst handelden, als wij naar het kamp der modernen verhuisden en daar onze tenten opsloegen'. Emphasis mine.

wonder to what extent Bavinck actually agreed with the author under discussion. When reading Bavinck, one often wonders: 'Whose voice is this?' In Bavinck's idiom, even the most obvious heresies sound tempting. He himself makes no secret of this, as he often confesses that 'there lies a great and deep truth' in this or that view – even if in the end it is not his own. The synthesizing character of Bavinck's mind makes it hard to ascertain what does and does not belong to the thread of his theology.[39]

As such, Bavinck interpreters often note the tensions that reside in his life and thinking: an inheritor of Reformed orthodoxy but a sympathizer of modern theology, educated within the pietistic and confessional heritage of Kampen and the mainline university in Leiden. He was a theologian who 'was part and parcel of modern culture and contributed to its character and direction'.[40] Past interpreters of Bavinck have pushed this duality to the point of contradiction, such that there were purportedly 'two Bavincks', the secondary literature claimed, each corresponding to an orthodox and modern side.[41] The positing of the modern–orthodox binary generated a source-critical hermeneutic according to which readers are exhorted to locate strands of Bavinck's thinking to a particular fabric: modern *or* orthodox.[42]

The secondary literature on Bavinck's epistemology is no exception to this trend. While these previous studies often make accurate observations about the sources behind Bavinck's epistemology, a failure to attend to the structural organicism in Bavinck's epistemology has produced significantly one-sided readings that force one to charge him with inconsistency when he allegedly deviates from a particular paradigm. These studies often identify Bavinck with his sources, such that his deployment of, for example, Thomas is taken to signify a rather committed subscription to Thomism, only to be frustrated by an encounter with significant sections of Bavinck in which he uses Kant, Schleiermacher or some other seemingly irreconcilable thinker. The other way around is also the case: that when Bavinck endorses an axiom of Kant or Romanticism he is charged for being susceptible to the same subjectivist tendencies of modernism. Indeed, it seems fruitful at this point to question the methodology of the whole process: instead of identifying Bavinck with his sources, one should attend to what Bavinck *does* with those sources in his deployment of the organic motif. The organic motif refers to

---

[39] Huttinga, *Participation and Communicability*, p. 78. Cf. S. Meijers, *Objectiviteit en Existentialiteit: Een onderzoek naar hun verhouding in de theologie van Herman Bavinck en in door hem beinvloede concepties* (Kampen: Kok, 1979), pp. 440–1

[40] George Harinck, 'The Religious Character of Modernism and the Modern Character of Religion: A Case Study of Herman Bavinck's Engagement with Modern Culture', *Scottish Bulletin of Evangelical Theology* 29 (2011): p. 62. See also James Bratt, 'The Context of Herman Bavinck's Stone Lectures: Culture and Politics in 1908', *The Bavinck Review* 1 (2010): pp. 4–24.

[41] See, for example, Valentine Hepp, *Dr. Herman Bavinck* (Amsterdam: W. Ten Have, 1921), pp. 317–18; Jan Veenhof, *Revelatie en Inspiratie: De Openbarings-en Schriftbeschouwing van Herman Bavinck in vergelijking met die der ethische theologie* (Amsterdam: Buijten en Schipperhejin, 1968), pp. 108–10, 250–68; E. P. Heidemann, *The Relation of Revelation and Reason in E. Brunner and H. Bavinck* (Assen: Van Gorcum, 1959), pp. 131–2, 156–7, 177–9. Recently, Sze Sze Chiew continues to characterize Bavinck's theology as exemplifying a 'striking duality' in *Middle Knowledge and Biblical Interpretation: Luis de Molina, Herman Bavinck, and William Lane Craig* (Frankfurt: Peter Lang, 2016), p. 77.

[42] Brian G. Mattson, *Restored to Our Destiny: Eschatology and the Image of God in Herman Bavinck's Reformed Dogmatics* (Leiden: Brill, 2012), p. 12.

the regularity with which Bavinck describes creation and other theological loci under organicist terms. Organic connectedness is the pattern of creation and doctrine because God himself is the original unity-in-diversity as the self-existent three-in-one. As this study will show, Bavinck's organic motif allowed him to reason principally under the conditions of the Reformed confessions while deploying an eclectic range of sources that span across the ancient, medieval, reformed and modern intellectual heritages. This study will also show that Bavinck's Trinitarian doctrine of God implicates not only his cosmology but also his epistemology. The Trinity *ad intra* implies an organic cosmology and epistemology *ad extra*.

My thesis, then, is to argue that Bavinck's unique organicism resulted in a theologically reinterpreted synthesis of classical and modern patterns of thought, between critical realism and absolute idealism, the emphasis on the specialization of the sciences on the one hand and its underlying unity on the other.[43] Attending to his organic epistemology not only eradicates ill-conceived constructions of the 'two Bavincks' but also further deepens our grasp of epistemology and the character of neo-Calvinism in distinction from other branches of Reformed theology. It offers a generative mode of inquiry to the Reformed tradition too, which, in many respects, often struggles to straddle the sensitive line between modernism and orthodoxy.

This reading also decisively reshapes the current discussions on Bavinck's epistemology while accommodating the best of their insights. Hence, the emphasis here is not to argue that either side is right or wrong. I contend that both are partially right insofar as there are, indeed, classical (Thomistic) *and* strongly post-Kantian elements in Bavinck's writings. But the point made by this thesis is that Bavinck's organic motif is able to resist contradicting these two strands and instead produces coherence. Insofar as that is true, the terms under which the secondary literature has been operating must be considerably reconfigured.

This study thus further supports the trajectory of the current scholarship that emphasizes the organic motif as that which accounts for Bavinck's eclectic use of modern and classical sources on principled theological grounds.[44] Brian Mattson argues that Bavinck deploys the organic motif for the purposes of persuasion, speaking into a nineteenth-century 'philosophical preoccupation with teleological concepts' by redefining that motif with resources that are 'internal' to the classical Reformed tradition.[45] James Eglinton, likewise, argues that the organic motif is Bavinck's preferred means of communicating a Trinitarian worldview. Creation displays an organic ontology of diversities in unity precisely because in God there is an archetypal unity and diversity: 'Theological organicism is the creation's triune shape.'[46] This conceptual apparatus allows Bavinck to preserve a worldview that includes a unity that does not imply uniformity, as well as a diversity that resists separation or analytic dissection; it

---

[43] As one shall see, Bavinck is aware of the important distinctions between kinds of realism and kinds of idealism.
[44] Mattson, *Restored to Our Destiny*; Eglinton, *Trinity and Organism*.
[45] Mattson, *Restored to Our Destiny*, p. 54.
[46] James Eglinton, 'Bavinck's Organic Motif: Questions Seeking Answers', *Calvin Theological Journal* 45 (2010): p. 66.

was used to 'facilitate, rather than to remove the tension between distinct elements in a system'.[47]

With the organic motif in place, then, it is no longer necessary to choose between an orthodox or modern Bavinck – the organic motif is Bavinck's means of negotiating the tensions he encountered, a uniting and conceptual catalyst for coherence: 'the outstanding agent of unity within Bavinck's worldview'.[48] Indeed, in Bavinck one sees a principled and orthodox theologian who incorporated contemporary philosophical grammars for the purposes of illumining and answering the serious intellectual problems he faced. He felt free to use classical, Thomistic and post-Kantian sources together as an application of his convictions concerning the catholicity of Christianity.

On the classical and orthodox side, interpreters have classified Bavinck's epistemology as a rehearsal of Thomism, despite Bavinck's many criticisms of Thomas. John Bolt has argued that Bavinck follows the tradition of Augustine and Aquinas, according to which a unified worldview is garnered by following the various principles of science (*scientia*) and a twofold truth according to which some truths are gained by a proper use of natural reason, and other truths by consulting special revelation.[49] An implication involves the call for a 'modest' recovery of natural theology, along with the claim that Christians should reason on publicly accessible and rational principles with regard to natural affairs.[50] Bolt further substantiates his claim that Bavinck's epistemology is 'Thomistic' by arguing that Bavinck's many criticisms of Thomas are mistaken because Bavinck 'too, was a child of his time, falling into the trap of reading Thomas through the lens … of neo-scholastic advocates'.[51]

Many others continue this interpretation. For Paul Helm, Bavinck and the classical Reformed tradition holds that there exists no revealed epistemology, such that reason plays a judicial role in natural matters.[52] David Sytsma further states that Bavinck's endorsement of Thomism is in direct response to the modern alternatives: 'Bavinck

---

[47] Eglinton, 'Bavinck's Organic Motif', p. 67.
[48] Eglinton, *Trinity and Organism*, p. 205.
[49] John Bolt, 'Bavinck's Recipe for Theological Cake', *Calvin Theological Journal* 45 (2010): pp. 11–17; John Bolt, 'Sola Scriptura as an Evangelical Theological Method?' in Gary Johnson and Ronald Gleason (eds), *Reforming or Conforming? Post-Conservative Evangelicals and the Emerging Church* (Wheaton: Crossway, 2008), pp. 79–81, 89. The term 'twofold truth' is from Bolt, 'Sola Scriptura as an Evangelical Theological Method?' p. 82. This is not to be confused with double truth, which affirmed that what might be true in philosophy might be false in theology or vice versa.
[50] John Bolt, 'An Opportunity Lost and Regained: Herman Bavinck on Revelation and Religion', *Mid-America Journal of Theology* 24 (2013): p. 96; John Bolt, 'Herman Bavinck on Natural Law and Two Kingdoms: Some Further Reflections', *The Bavinck Review* 4 (2013): p. 93.
[51] John Bolt, 'An Adventure in Ecumenicity: A Review Essay of *Berkouwer and Catholicism* by Eduardo Echeverria', *The Bavinck Review* 5 (2014): p. 79. Paul Helm, appealing to Henri de Lubac, has also claimed that Bavinck's reading of Thomas was mistaken. See Paul Helm, 'Religion and Reason from a Reformed Perspective', in Oliver D. Crisp, Gavin D'Costa, Mervyn Davies and Peter Hampson (eds), *Theology and Philosophy: Faith and Reason* (London: T&T Clark, 2012), p. 69. Paul Helm, *Calvin at the Centre* (Oxford: Oxford University Press, 2010), pp. 328–32. Steven J. Duby notes the natural realistic overtones of Bavinck's epistemology, but without pitting it against Bavinck's modern sources in 'Working with the Grain of Nature: Epistemic Underpinnings for Christian Witness in the Theology of Herman Bavinck', *The Bavinck Review* 3 (2012): pp. 62–74.
[52] Paul Helm, *Faith, Form and Fashion: Classical Reformed Theology and its Postmodern Critics* (Eugene: Cascade Books, 2014), pp. 57–9, 64–5.

was claiming the superiority of Thomistic epistemology as a handmaiden for theology over the contemporary philosophical trends of empiricism and rationalism.[53] From the statements of the above authors, one receives the impression that Bavinck was engaged in modernity only for the purposes of resisting it by a retrieval of classical epistemology – so much so that Bavinck's epistemology is unfortunately characterized at times as a 'reproduction' of that classical heritage.[54]

There are concessions in the above set of readings about Bavinck's irenic spirit and balanced handling of modern epistemology. Arvin Vos, however epitomizes the trajectory of the above readings, arguing that in Bavinck there are indeed undeniably Thomistic lines of thought.[55] However, by assuming that Bavinck's *use* of Thomistic motifs is indicative of Bavinck's advocacy of Thom*ism*, Vos's discovery of significant Kantian elements in Bavinck's writings forced him to question the consistency of Bavinck's epistemology.[56] This leads him to conclude that, despite Bavinck's desire to uphold Thomistic epistemology, his departure from other Thomistic tenets renders Thomas Aquinas as the superior realist who offered a more comprehensive account of the objectivity of knowledge.[57] On this point, one wonders if a more fruitful approach is to resist identifying deployment with systematic endorsement.

The readings above stand in contrast to the readings of Cornelis van der Kooi, Eugene Heideman and Henk van den Belt, each of whom identifies Bavinck's epistemology with the post-Kantian tradition.[58] Van der Kooi argues that Bavinck's distinction between the object-in-itself (*Ding an Sich*) and the object as they appear reflects a distinctly post-Kantian judgement on the nature of perception.[59] This epistemological picture questions whether Bavinck successfully evaded the subjectivist tendencies of modern epistemology, leading van der Kooi to argue that 'Bavinck cooperates in the turning towards the subject, and thereby (probably more than he likes) pays tribute to the anthropocentricism of modernity.'[60]

Henk van den Belt also argues that Bavinck's epistemology places priority on the subjective state of consciousness, with the result that Bavinck was self-aware

---

[53] David Sytsma, 'Herman Bavinck's Thomistic Epistemology', in John Bolt (ed.), *Five Studies in the Thought of Herman Bavinck, A Creator of Modern Dutch Theology* (Lewiston: Edwin Mellen Press, 2011), p. 47. The sense in which reason and philosophy are handmaidens to theology is that they prepare the way for its proper study.

[54] Sytsma, 'Bavinck's Thomistic Epistemology', p. 27.

[55] Arvin Vos, 'Knowledge According to Bavinck and Aquinas', *The Bavinck Review* 6 (2015): pp. 9–36.

[56] Vos, 'Bavinck and Aquinas', p. 30. Vos notes the strongly Kantian direction of Bavinck's *Beginselen der psychologie*.

[57] Arvin Vos, 'Knowledge According to Bavinck and Aquinas', *The Bavinck Review* 7 (2017): pp. 8–62.

[58] Post-Kantian epistemology is diverse and hard to define, but nonetheless the diversity shares similar characteristics. Among these are (1) the turn to the subject, (2) the focus on an attempt to resolve an assumed subject–object dichotomy and other potential oppositions and (3) the active acknowledgement of the role of consciousness in mediating knowledge. Cf. Frederick Beiser, *German Idealism: The Struggle against Subjectivism 1781-1801* (Cambridge: Harvard University Press, 2002), pp. 13–14; Andrew Bowie, *Schelling and Modern European Philosophy: An Introduction* (New York: Routledge, 1993), p. 33.

[59] Cornelis van der Kooi, 'The Appeal to the Inner Testimony of the Spirit, Especially in H. Bavinck', *Journal of Reformed Theology* 2 (2008): p. 108.

[60] Van der Kooi, 'The Appeal to the Inner Testimony', p. 107.

in his desire to curb his subjectivist tendencies.[61] In correspondence with this, van den Belt infers that Bavinck's epistemology is 'dominated' by the subject-object dichotomy.[62] In Bavinck one encounters not merely a rehearsal of Reformed orthodoxy but an attempt to apply classical conceptual tools in order to resolve distinctly modern epistemological problems – an attempt which further reshapes Bavinck's epistemology towards modern grounds. This close connection with which Bavinck relates subject and object, thought and being, leads Heideman to wonder whether Bavinck was too influenced by German idealism, rendering him unnecessarily vulnerable to charges of pantheism.[63] Nonetheless, Heideman, too, argues that Bavinck's epistemology puts a premium on the role of the subject and on self-consciousness.[64]

The incompatibility of the two strands of thinking between Bavinck's modernity and orthodoxy above becomes more explicit with John Bolt's review of van den Belt's *Authority of Scripture in Reformed Theology*. Though he commends the monograph, Bolt wonders if van den Belt was 'too preoccupied with the modern form of the subject-object discussion and whether this is a fruitful approach to Bavinck'.[65] Further, Bolt rejects that Bavinck's attention to the religious subject hints at the modern tendency towards subjectivism – for Bolt, Bavinck was simply articulating his endorsement of classical realism:

> But, is [the grounding of faith within the religious subject] not obviously necessary when we are trying to explain how religious subjects come to certainty of knowledge about God and the world? And why does Van den Belt consider this 'disappointing' and suggest Bavinck's tendency to subjectivism? (290ff.) Is Bavinck here not simply being a good Augustinian or Thomist in his realism?[66]

Again, one is pressed to decide between two competing claims: Bavinck the classical realist (and *not* modern), on the one hand, and Bavinck the modernist (and *not* classical), on the other. Is it possible to move beyond this impasse?

---

[61] Henk van den Belt, *The Authority of Scripture in Reformed Theology: Truth and Trust* (Leiden: Brill, 2008), pp. 249, 254, 266–7.

[62] Van den Belt, *The Authority of Scripture*, p. 294.

[63] Heideman, *The Relation of Revelation and Reason*, p. 144.

[64] Heideman, *The Relation of Revelation and Reason*, pp. 155–6. Jan Veenhof, in 'De God van de filosofen en de God van de bijbel: Herman Bavinck en de wijsbegeerte', in George Harinck and Gerrit Neven (eds), *Ontmoetingen met Herman Bavinck* (Barneveld: De Vuurbaak, 2006), pp. 221, 3, also argues that Bavinck was determined to work from within the post-Kantian trajectory even while he was standing on some tenets within the Thomistic tradition. Veenhof, though, is an exception in choosing not to pit Bavinck's use of classical and modern sources against each other.

[65] John Bolt, 'Review' of Henk van den Belt, *The Authority of Scripture in Reformed Theology: Truth and Trust* in *Journal of Reformed Theology* 4 (2010): p. 76. Laurence O'Donnell's review of another volume that included an essay by van den Belt also honed in on a similar issue: 'Review' of John Bowlin (ed.), *The Kuyper Center Review, Volume Two: Revelation and Common Grace*, in *The Bavinck Review* 3 (2011): p. 193. Cf. Henk van den Belt, 'An Alternative Approach to Apologetics', in John Bowlin (ed.), *The Kuyper Center Review*, vol. 2: *Revelation and Common Grace* (Grand Rapids: Eerdmans, 2011), pp. 43–60.

[66] Bolt, 'Review' of *The Authority of Scripture*, p. 76.

III The way forward

In each of the above interpretations Bavinck's organic motif is conspicuous by its absence.[67] I will argue that Bavinck's Trinitarian and organic worldview enabled him to utilize an eclectic range of sources such that a unified, organic epistemology emerges. The objective of this study is to investigate Bavinck's primary texts in order to examine his epistemology in relation to the organic motif. Indeed, a further exculpatory explanation for the inconsistencies that characterize the secondary literature in the Anglophone world is the lack of attention spent on the lesser known, and mostly untranslated, works of Bavinck in which epistemology is treated most comprehensively and in which the organic motif is prominent. The study unfolds Bavinck's understanding of what he considered to be the two important aspects of epistemology: the character of the sciences and the correspondence between subjects and objects, as predicated upon an organic worldview. The study elaborates on the two citations provided in the beginning of this introduction: the sciences form a single organism comprising of a unity-in-diversity, and subjects and objects correspond precisely because both are parts in an organically connected cosmos.

Reinterpreting Bavinck's epistemology in light of this motif should also provide some new insights concerning the current criticisms and appropriations of Bavinck by the various interpreters mentioned above while generating new avenues for contemporary epistemological reflection. Further, instead of reading Bavinck in light of the sources he cites, this study methodologically prioritizes ways in which Bavinck uses his sources by deploying the organic motif in line with the current readings offered by Eglinton and Mattson. In other words, it is a reading of Bavinck on his own terms. In this way, this study supports John Bolt's call to resist identifying 'a person's thought as "neo-Platonic" or "Thomist" or "Kantian" or "scholastic"' and to deem those identifications as reason enough 'to condemn' that person's thought.[68]

The next chapter furnishes the context in which this study takes place as it presents Bavinck's organicism in relation to the doctrines of God, anthropology and revelation. Building on the works of Mattson and Eglinton, it introduces the reader to the comprehensive scope of Bavinck's organic world view while seeking to develop that reading by noting the classical and modern sources of Bavinck's outlook. Bavinck's view of the creation's unity-in-diversity is rooted in his classical doctrines of God's simplicity and existence in three persons as modes of subsistence. His theological anthropology, shaped by organic language, consists not merely in conceiving the individual as an organic unity but in conceiving humanity as a whole as a singular organism grounded in the unity of a federal head. General and special revelation likewise form a single organism.

With this macro-level sketch of the organic worldview in place, one can now zoom in on Bavinck's characterization of the sciences and the structure of knowing as a single

---

[67] Bruce Pass, though admitting that in Bavinck's epistemology there is a complex mixture of modern and classical thinking, also does not comment on the significance of the organic motif in relation to Bavinck's epistemology. See his 'Herman Bavinck and the Problem of New Wine in Old Wineskins', *International Journal of Systematic Theology* 17.4 (2015): pp. 432–49.

[68] John Bolt, 'Following Bavinck's Lead', *Comment Magazine*, 28 November 2012.

organism. Chapters 3 and 4 elaborate on this point, focusing on Bavinck's *Dogmatics*, various addresses delivered by Bavinck and the three lesser known works that focus on epistemology: *Christelijke wetenschap* (*Christian Science*, 1904), *Christelijke wereldbeschouwing* (*Christian Worldview*, 1904) and *Kennis en leven* (published posthumously, 1922). Here it is articulated that Bavinck respects the integrity of the different fields of science, such that each enjoys a relative degree of independence, utilizing different methods and examining different objects. The differing *principia* of the sciences is correlative to the modern movement towards departmental specialization, influenced by Schleiermacher at the University of Berlin. In these contexts, the readings of Bavinck that emphasize the differing *principia* that function underlying the various sciences, as grounded in classical Thomistic elements, are to be appreciated. However, in Bavinck's characterization of science as a whole as a singular organism, there is an underlying unity that provides the overall grounds and shape of the diversity of the sciences, with Scripture, Christ and the triune God's glory constituting that methodological and teleological unifying centre that relativizes that diversity. This corresponds with Bavinck's neo-Calvinistic understanding of the kingdom of God and sphere sovereignty, according to which the diversity of the sciences correlates with the underlying unity of the organism of science and the Reformed orthodox conviction concerning the unity of truth and the harmony between general and special revelation. With these observations in place, Bavinck's similarities and differences with Thomas and Abraham Kuyper are also illumined. Chapter 4 locates the rationale for Bavinck's critiques of the epistemologies of Aquinas and Kuyper while locating Bavinck's critique of the former within the current debates on interpreting 'pure nature' Thomism. The differences between Bavinck and Kuyper, too, consist in the former's distinction between organic and mechanical knowing in reference to believing and unbelieving knowers. This chapter also sketches some preliminary implications of Bavinck's holistic epistemology, and I relate it constructively to the work of Charles Taylor and Hubert Dreyfus on *Gestalt Holism*.

Chapter 5 begins to probe the subject–object dichotomy in Bavinck while introducing the interpretations of Alvin Plantinga and Nicholas Wolterstorff that characterize Bavinck as a 'proto-Reformed epistemologist' and an advocate of a kind of Reidian common-sense realism. This chapter proceeds to examine the apparent similarities between Thomas Reid and Herman Bavinck, precisely because the interpretation of Bavinck as a Reidian poses a prima facie tension with the readings that locate Bavinck in the post-Kantian turn to the subject. It contends that the initial similarities that exist between Bavinck and Reid are really reflective of the accidental similarities between common-sense realism and the romantic and absolute-idealist tendency to affirm that subjects are always attuned (and organically connected) with their surroundings, especially as Reid denies a gap between mental ideas and the objects they represent, whereas Bavinck affirmed the gap between representations (*voorstellingen*) and things-in-themselves. This points to Bavinck's particular deployment of Eduard von Hartmann, which constitutes the subject matter of Chapter 6. An examination of Bavinck's deployment of von Hartmann will show their affinities: the acceptance of the gap between subjects and objects, a methodological prioritizing of sense perception in knowing and the participation of both subjects and objects in an Absolute whole.

The differences between the two are also highlighted, and those differences are determined precisely in Bavinck's understanding of the organic. Whereas von Hartmann's Absolute is an imminent, impersonal and unconscious reality that binds subjects and objects, Bavinck's Absolute is a Creator ontologically distinct from an organic creation that reflects that prior divine wisdom. Here, the organic motif's congeniality with the Thomistic understanding of perception grounded in the activity of the agent intellect is further demonstrated while showcasing the creative way in which Bavinck deployed both classical realist and absolute idealist moves through the lens of the organic.

Chapter 7, finally, examines the organic unity of the self in the locus of consciousness and the knowing faculties. There is an organic connection between reason and feeling, such that Bavinck affirms the existence of a knowing that takes place 'without concepts'. This revisits Bavinck's understanding of general revelation as a primordial and pre-predicative, non-conceptual reality that penetrates the unconscious *psyche*. His definitions of the innate and acquired knowledge of God are thus reshaped accordingly. This chapter also connects Bavinck's moves both to current studies on medieval epistemology, as a meshing of Bonaventure's *concursus* model and Thomas's *influentia* model of illumination, and to broader neo-Calvinist moves (in Kuyper, J. H. Bavinck and Gerrit Berkouwer) that tend to characterize general revelation as a kind of romantic and phenomenological presence in the locus of the *psyche*. Other than the *Dogmatics*, Chapters 5 to 7 focus on Bavinck's 1908 Stone lectures (*Philosophy of Revelation*) and his *Beginselen der psychologie* (1897).

The conclusion closes with some summative remarks and critical reflections on the fruitfulness and contextually determined nature of Bavinck's epistemology. This thesis demonstrates that it is no longer tenable to identify Bavinck with a particular source or thinker – whether Kantianism, Thomism, realism or absolute idealism. He was too eclectic to be identified with any particular '-ism', and his views of realism and idealism contribute to the emerging understanding that the relationship of the two cannot be characterized as a mere opposite. His advocacy of realism over subjective idealism did not hinder him from appreciating the insights of absolute idealism, and his affirmation of the critical importance of the role of the subject did not dissuade him from appreciating classically realist instincts. He did, however, advocate a holistic and organic epistemology that allowed him to use the varied array of sources the way he did. The organic motif, too, is not just a means by which Bavinck 'swallows' up insights with no regard to their overall systematic coherence. Indeed, it shall be displayed that he deploys the language of the organic to answer specific epistemological questions with acute precision.

This study will not only offer a unified interpretation of Herman Bavinck's epistemology. With the growing understanding of the diversities of the Reformed tradition and the distinctive characters of each, this study further highlights the particular characteristics that demarcate neo-Calvinism from the rest of the Reformed tradition. It also hopes further to stimulate studies that generate a greater understanding of Bavinck and the neo-Calvinistic tradition's conception of revelation and epistemology within the broader trajectories of the nineteenth to twentieth centuries, which tend towards holism and pre-conceptual understandings of revelation while also relating Bavinck to current trends within analytic and continental philosophy.

2

Bavinck's organicism – God, anthropology and revelation

The introduction displayed the various strands of the often conflicting interpretations of Bavinck's epistemology. It also shows how recent scholarship on Bavinck's organic motif promisingly delivers a unified, coherent interpretation that preserves the tensions in Bavinck's thought without having to introduce charges of inconsistency against him. Bavinck's sources do not reflect a bipolar theologian oscillating between his modern self and his classical, orthodox self – but rather a unified yet eclectic thinker who sought a coherent synthesis of the two milieus on Reformed orthodox grounds. In that vein, this study argues that Bavinck's epistemology is also shaped organically, much like his views on cosmology. In the next chapters, I shall observe that Bavinck describes knowledge (*kennis*) and science (*wetenschap*) as conforming to the organic shape of a unity in diversity, such that there is unifying centre that grounds and shapes the diverse fields of knowledge, and how the organic motif is Bavinck's means of reconciling the subject–object dichotomy.

Before embarking on the central epistemological concerns of this study, however, it is necessary first to highlight the major contours of Bavinck's organic vision of reality and its Trinitarian roots. This chapter, therefore, builds on the recent scholarship in sketching and developing Bavinck's organicism in relation to three key loci in an appreciative yet critical manner: the doctrine of God, anthropology and revelation. This organic worldview provides the context for the chapters that follow.

This chapter moves in four steps. First, I summarize the definition of Bavinck's organic motif and cosmology along with its Trinitarian roots. Second, I shall clarify and highlight the catholic shape of Bavinck's theology proper, emphasizing that the organic motif does not compromise but rather is resourced by a robust affirmation of the doctrines of divine simplicity and the immanent life of the divine persons as modes of subsistence. Third, I outline the way in which Bavinck's organicism shapes his theological anthropology. Finally, I sketch the way in which general and special revelation are considered to go together by Bavinck. As I cover each of the loci, the Bavinckian theme of grace restoring nature and the eclectic character of Bavinck's thinking shall also be displayed.

I The organic motif

For Bavinck, the Christian worldview is distinguished from that of non-theism by its capacity to see reality as organic rather than mechanistic. There are fundamentally two worldviews, 'the theistic and the atheistic', he claims.[1]

In Bavinck's perspective, the Christian view of the world goes against a narrow-minded mechanistic philosophy which imposes uniformity in an irreducibly complex universe. The mechanistic worldview demands in an aprioristic manner that 'life, consciousness, freedom, and teleology' should be explained under mechanistic terms, thus excluding all other explanations to be 'unscientific' as such.[2] Bavinck is arguing that the Christian view of all things provides a broader, more open-minded account of nature precisely because it recognizes that reality far eludes the human grasp and goes beyond the purely natural or mechanically verifiable. While the mechanical view is 'exclusive', the organic view 'recognizes' that mechanical explanations have their proper place but refuses to reduce the cosmos under its conditions.[3] The organic world view can account for the diverse phenomena one experiences within the world: 'There are the lifeless and the living, the inorganic and the organic, the inanimate and animated, the unconscious and the conscious, the material and spiritual creations, the mutually different in nature, yet all are included in the unity of the whole.'[4]

Bavinck's *Christelijke wereldbeschouwing*[5] provides the basic contours of his organicism, culled well by James Eglinton. First, unity-and-diversity marks the precise shape of the created order.[6] As it will be further clarified below, for Bavinck, God's triune character somehow necessitates that the creation he chooses to bring about will bear a triniform character; creation '*must* reflect his identity as three-in-one'.[7] The Trinity explains the diverse yet united phenomena encountered within God's creation more satisfactorily than rival ontologies.

Second, in the organism unity precedes diversity.[8] Bavinck shares with the German idealists the idea that the whole precedes the parts in such a way that they find their

---

[1] 'Eigenlijk zijn er dus maar twee wereldbeschouwingen, de theistsche en de atheistsche', Bavinck, *Christelijke wereldbeschouwing*, p. 51. Eglinton makes the same observation: 'In [*Christelijke wereldbeschouwing*, Bavinck] asserts that, at the most basic level, only two worldviews exist: the theistic and the atheistic.' *Trinity and Organism*, p. 67. Unless otherwise stated, all translations are my own.
[2] '[The organic worldview] komt alleen op tegen den aprioristischen eisch, dat leven, bewustzijn, vrijheid, doel zich mechanisch moeten laten verklaren, omdat elke andere verklaring onwetenschappelijk zou zijn.' Bavinck, *Christelijke wereldbeschouwing*, p. 50.
[3] 'De mechanische beschouwing is exclusief, zij eischt de gansche wereld voor zich op. Maar de organische beschouwing erkent ook het goed recht der mechanische verklaring, op haar terrein en binnen de door de natuur zelf haar gestelde grenzen.' Bavinck, *Christelijke wereldbeschouwing*, p. 50.
[4] Bavinck, *Christelijke wereldbeschouwing*, p. 50. Dutch original: 'Er zijn levenlooze en levende, anorganische en organische, onbezielde en bezielde, onbewuste en bewuste, stoffelijke en geestelijke schepselen, die onderlin in aard verschillend, toch alle opgenomen zijn in de eenheid van geheel'.
[5] Eglinton, *Trinity and Organism*, pp. 67–9.
[6] Bavinck, *Christelijke wereldbeschouwing*, p. 50.
[7] Eglinton, *Trinity and Organism*, p. 67. Emphasis mine.
[8] Bavinck, *Christelijke wereldbeschouwing*, p. 51.

existence and proper place by partaking in the whole.⁹ Bavinck makes this point by referring to the *Logical Investigations* [*Logische Untersuchungen*] of the German idealist Friedrich Adolf Trendelenburg (1802–72), as Bavinck claims that it is 'the idea that animates and governs the distinct parts in the organism'.¹⁰ Trendelenburg couples the Absolute-idealist organic view of the world with the Aristotelian emphasis on the primacy of sense perception and the modern, scientific, inductive method. In effect, Trendelenburg claimed that the absolute idealistic metaphysics he inherited from Hegel and Schelling needed to be methodologically updated with the claims and results of the new empirical sciences. These twin tendencies exemplified by Trendelenburg are appreciated well by Bavinck's own commitment to the epistemological significance of sense perception and the organic world view, though on different Christian-theistic grounds.¹¹ As such, Bavinck claims that all objects are knowable because all created things 'are still one [*toch één zijn*]' even as diversity is maintained. As Trendelenburg remarks, 'The individual only exists in the whole.'¹²

The rationale behind Bavinck's prioritizing of the unity of the parts stems from his belief in the unity of the God who creates the cosmos. Out of this principle the third naturally follows, which claims that the organism is bound by a common idea.¹³ The cosmos is unified in an orderly and harmonious manner which itself reflects the unity of God's thoughts. Following the Reformed scholastic Johann Alsted and the classical tradition here, Bavinck asserts that the 'thoughts of God [*gedachten Gods*]' are the 'exemplary causes of things' [*causae exemplares der dingen*]:¹⁴ 'It is the bond between God and the world, between the one and the many.'¹⁵ The divine ideas are the archetype for the things exemplified in creation, and because God is one, a single idea

---

[9] Eglinton, *Trinity and Organism*, p. 69: 'The notion that, within an organism, the whole precedes the parts is also found in Idealist organicism. Both were reacting against the mechanistic notion that the parts come first.' Frederick Beiser summarizes it this way: 'The idea of the whole contains and precedes all its parts, so that every part has its identity only in the whole.' *German Idealism: The Struggle against Subjectivism*, p. 517.

[10] Bavinck, *Christelijke wereldbeschouwing*, p. 52. Dutch original: 'Het is de idee die in het organisme de onderscheidene deelen bezielt en beheerscht.' Friedrich A. Trendelenburg, *Logische Untersuchungen* (Berlin: Bethge, 1840; 2nd edn., Leipzig: Hirzel, 1862; 3rd edn., Leipzig: Hirzel, 1870). Bavinck does not cite a particular line here, nor does he mention the edition with which he works, but points to pages 17, 19 and 124 onwards from the second volume. Bavinck cites the same work both positively and descriptively on pages 19, 32 and 67 of *Christelijke wereldbeschouwing*.

[11] Bavinck is well aware of the Romantic and idealist retrievals of Greek philosophy; on this and Bavinck's appropriation of Eduard von Hartmann (another German idealist who shares Trendelenburg's preference for sense perception and the absolute in the development of an organic worldview), see Chapters 4 and 6 of this work. See also Frederick Beiser, *Late German Idealism: Trendelenburg and Lotze* (Oxford: Oxford University Press, 2013), pp. 2–6, 30. On page 32, Beiser surmises that 'the phrase "organic worldview" sums up well Trendelenburg's entire philosophy'. However, this is not to suggest that Bavinck shares Trendelenburg's monism.

[12] Freiderich A. Trendelenburg, *Logische Untersuchungen* (3rd edn., reprint; Hildesheim: Georg Olms Verlagsbuchhandlung, 1964), II: p. 21. German original: 'Der Einzelne hat nur im Ganzen Bestand'.

[13] Bavinck, *Christelijke wereldbeschouwing*, p. 57.

[14] Bavinck, *Christelijke wereldbeschouwing*, p. 57. Elsewhere, however, Alsted is critiqued by Bavinck because of his decision to write an 'independent "natural theology"', signalling that Alsted was a sign of a decline that followed the Lutheran failure to uphold 'reformational principles' that bind together general and special revelation. Bavinck, *RD*, 1: pp. 306, 305.

[15] Bavinck, *Christelijke wereldbeschouwing*, p. 57. Dutch original: 'de band tusschen God en wereld, tusschen het ééne en het vele.'

orchestrates and organizes the cosmos into a single central locus: the Logos, who is God the Son.[16]

Fourth, characterizing creation as an organism means that it is driven towards a *telos*, which is the glory of the triune God.[17] The teleology inherent within the development of creation as an organism is not identical to a materialistic chain of cause and effect that leads to some deterministic end. Rather, the organism of creation tells the story of the God who seeks to dwell with humankind and the providence by which God sustains the world. It is a personal telos imbued with an eschatological specificity disclosed in Scripture and actualized by divine provision.

Bavinck's organic motif, therefore, is not a product of speculation concerning the nature of reality in order simply to account for the phenomenon one experientially encounters but rather Bavinck's way of articulating the implications of the Christian confession that the Creator is a non-monadic, triune God. This is summarized well in Eglinton's pithy statement that a 'theology of Trinity *ad intra* requires cosmology of organism *ad extra*'.[18] The theological assertion here involves the realistic claim that the nature of God *requires* that God's creation bear his marks. Yet, this is not to suggest that Bavinck is inferring that God is triune on the basis of the unities and diversities or the teleology embedded in creation – a 'bottom-up' move that would render Bavinck vulnerable to the critiques of Karl Barth.[19] The order is quite the other way around and is irreversibly so: creation is seen to be marked by unities and diversities precisely because the Christian views the world in light of the revelation of the triune God.[20] God is the archetype and creation is the ectype.[21] As Bavinck says in the *Reformed Dogmatics*,

> The Trinity reveals God to us as the fullness of being, the true life, eternal beauty. In God, too, there is unity in diversity, diversity in unity. Indeed, this order and

---

[16] Bavinck here cites Col. 1.15 to support his point. Bavinck claims that Christ is the 'organic centre' of all created history in *RD*, 1: p. 383.

[17] Bavinck, *Christelijke wereldbeschouwing*, pp. 65–7. Bavinck cites Trendelenburg, *Logische Untersuchungen*, II: pp. 29–30 on page 67.

[18] Eglinton, *Trinity and Organism*, p. 68.

[19] Cf. Karl Barth, 'Fate and Idea in Theology', in H. Martin Rumscheidt (ed.), *The Way of Theology in Karl Barth: Essays and Comments* (Allison Park: Pickwick, 1986), pp. 30–3. Cf. Keith Johnson, *Karl Barth and the Analogia Entis* (London: T&T Clark, 2010), especially chapters 4 and 5.

[20] 'The consistent tendency of Bavinck's work is to do the opposite [of interpreting God in light of the world]. He reads the cosmos in the light of its Creator, simultaneously guarding the uniqueness of God and the basic fact of general divine revelation in the universe.' Eglinton, *Trinity and Organism*, p. 112. Kevin Vanhoozer also offers a succinct articulation of this kind of approach in *Remythologizing Theology: Divine Action, Passion, and Authorship* (Cambridge: Cambridge University Press, 2012), pp. 8–23.

[21] The distinction between archetype and ectype has a strong pedigree within the Reformed tradition; it is articulated at length by Francis Junius's *Theologia Vera*, which was recently translated: Franciscus Junius, *A Treatise on True Theology*, David C. Noe (trans.) (Grand Rapids: Reformation Heritage, 2014). See also Willem J. van Asselt, 'The Fundamental Meaning of Theology: Archetypal and Ectypal Theology in Seventeenth-Century Reformed Thought', *Westminster Theological Journal* 64 (2007): pp. 289–306; Mattson, *Restored to Our Destiny*, p. 27; Eglinton, *Trinity and Organism*, p. 106; Nathaniel Gray Sutanto, 'Two Theological Accounts of Logic: Theistic Conceptual Realism and a Reformed Archetype-Ectype Model', *International Journal for the Philosophy of Religion* 79 (2016): pp. 239–60.

this harmony is present in him absolutely. In the case of creatures we see only a faint analogy of it. Either the unity or the diversity does not come into its own. ... But in God both are present: absolute unity as well as absolute diversity. It is one selfsame being sustained by three hypostases. This results in the most perfect kind of community, a community of the same beings; at the same time it results in the most perfect diversity, a diversity of divine persons.[22]

It is in this sense that Bavinck is defending and modifying the medieval notion that creation bears the vestiges of God. The theologian's task in seeking out vestiges of triniformity in creation does not consist in seeking proofs that God is triune as an exercise of the pre-dogmatic model of natural theology, nor should it result in seeking patterns of three-in-oneness in it.[23] With regard to the former, the vestiges of the triune God in creation are only visible to the one who re-investigates nature through the lenses of special revelation.[24] To the latter, Bavinck argues that the triunity of God is absolutely unique, such that creation's triniformity takes shape not as patterns of three-in-oneness but as non-numerical unities-in-diversities. Thus, in creatures, the diversity is not united in a perichoretic manner in a simple essence, as it is in the Godhead, yet the unity can be discerned by a 'profound physical unity [*physische eenheid*]' and also, in some, a 'moral unity [*zedelijke eenheid*]'.[25]

With these two moves Bavinck shows that a rejection of natural theology does not entail a rejection of an appropriate and modest account of the doctrine that creation displays the vestiges of God. Eglinton summarizes Bavinck's contribution thusly:

> In this respect, Bavinck's doctrine of God, by virtue of its outstanding emphases on the diversity and oneness of the Godhead, is the foundation for an important development in the Reformed tradition. It represents the neo-Calvinist redemption of the 'marks of the Trinity' concept. In doing so, Bavinck shows that one can be wholly against natural theology *and* wholly for the *vestigia trinitatis*. He moves away from the general post-Reformation aversion to the traditional terminology and, as such, reinvigorates the concept while asking profound questions on the consequences of God's Triunity for the Christian worldview. Whenever the *vestigia trinitatis* is referred to in relation to Bavinck's doctrine of God, it is therefore not used in the medieval sense. Rather, the phrase is qualified to mean that in Bavinck's understanding of the Trinity and the cosmos, *the Trinity is wholly unlike anything else, but everything else is like the Trinity*.[26]

---

[22] Bavinck, *RD*, 2: pp. 331–2. See also *RD*, 2: 555.
[23] The term 'triniformity' comes from Eglinton, *Trinity and Organism*, p. 54.
[24] Bavinck, *RD*, 1: p. 368. See also Eglinton, *Trinity and Organism*, pp. 86, 150–1. On the Reformed tradition's account of this, see Richard Muller, *Post-Reformation Reformed Dogmatics: The Rise and Development of Reformed Orthodoxy, ca. 1520 to ca. 1725*, vol. 4: *The Triunity of God* (Grand Rapids: Baker Academic, 2003), pp. 157–65.
[25] Bavinck, *RD*, 2: p. 331; *GD*, 2: p. 344. As it will become apparent, to express this ethical (or moral) unity, Bavinck consistently uses *zedelijk*, *moreel* and *ethisch* interchangeably and synonymously in his works.
[26] Eglinton, *Trinity and Organism*, p. 89. Emphases in original.

Bavinck's account should thus be situated within the classical affirmation of the Creator–creature distinction – an affirmation that excludes univocally identifying Bavinck's organic motif with that of his nineteenth-century idealist counterparts.[27] God's being is that of an absolute and unchangeable *being*, whereas creation is a mutable and developing *becoming*. While the latter is an obvious implication of creation's contingent and finite nature, the former corresponds with Bavinck's insistence on the aseity of God: 'God is exclusively from himself, not in the sense of being self-caused but being from eternity to eternity who he is, being not becoming.'[28] In Bavinck's view, Trendelenburg, von Hartmann and Hegel were inclined to tethering God's being with the becoming of history to the extent that God is often considered to be a being-in-becoming. In contrast to this, Bavinck maintains a strict separation between the two: God is being and all else is becoming. This ontological chasm explains in part the irreversibility of the Bavinckian claim that the Trinity is unlike everything else and yet everything else is like the Trinity.[29] Standing on Scripture, Bavinck demarcates the two in this way:

> Scripture's worldview is radically different. From the beginning heaven and earth have been distinct. Everything was created with a nature of its own and rests in ordinances established by God. ... The foundation of both diversity and unity is in God. It is he who created all things. ... Here is a unity that does not destroy but rather maintains diversity, and a diversity that does not come at the expense of unity, but rather unfolds its riches. In virtue of this unity the world can, metaphorically, be called an organism, in which all the parts are connected with each other and influence each other reciprocally.[30]

II Organicism and the classical contours of Bavinck's doctrine of God

Talks of there being an 'absolute diversity' or a perfect 'community' in God may raise alarm for those critical of current models of social Trinitarianism. However, the preceding discussion on the Trinity as the archetypal unity and diversity resulting in a creation marked by unities and diversities should not be misunderstood so as to imply that Bavinck advocates a form of social Trinitarianism, in which the diversity in the Godhead is meant to affirm a community of persons united in nature and by

---

[27] Bavinck, *RD*, 2: p. 30. Bavinck's rejection of Hegel's ontology is well documented, despite his adoption of organic language: see John Bolt, 'The Imitation of Christ Theme in the Cultural-Ethical Ideal of Herman Bavinck' (University of Toronto: unpublished PhD thesis, 1982), pp. 163–72; Mattson, *Restored to Our Destiny*, pp. 20–64; James Eglinton, 'To Be or to Become – That is the Question: Locating the Actualistic in Bavinck's Ontology', in John Bowlin (ed.), *The Kuyper Center Review*, vol. 2: *Revelation and Common Grace* (Grand Rapids: Eerdmans, 2011), pp. 104–24.
[28] Bavinck, *RD*, 2: p. 152.
[29] Eglinton, *Trinity and Organism*, p. 89.
[30] Bavinck, *RD*, 2: p. 71.

consent but not in being.³¹ Indeed, the affirmation of Bavinck's organicism *ad extra* rooted in the triune being of God must be set within Bavinck's catholic doctrine of God – a theology proper shared by the Reformed, medieval and ancient divines alike. Indeed, in theology proper Bavinck was content to inherit the vocabulary and grammar as confessed in the tradition of Nicaea, Augustine and Aquinas with little modification: 'Scholasticism, expanding this [Trinitarian] terminology, established a fixed scheme that was later taken over by theologians in general, including those of the Reformation.'³² This included the confession that the use of metaphysical and extrabiblical philosophical terminology does not hinder but rather bolsters the truths found in Scripture – words like substance, persons, essence and subsistence 'mark the boundary lines within which Christian thought must proceed in order to preserve the truth of God's revelation'.³³ In order to understand Bavinck's concerns, one must attend to the unity and simplicity of God and the relative properties that distinguish the persons within the Godhead as modes of subsistence. Then, I shall introduce some of the potential developments made by Bavinck in his theology proper.³⁴

Bavinck's treatment of the doctrine of God begins with the unity of the divine nature and its attributes, as shared by the three persons. Following this order, however, is not meant to imply that it is appropriate to demarcate between a theology based on reason alone and a theology as a reflection on divine revelation – such a 'procedure

---

[31] A paradigmatic and rather full-orbed model of social Trinitarianism is found in Richard Swinburne, *The Christian God* (Oxford: Clarendon Press, 1994). For a summary and critique of social Trinitarianism, see, for example, Karen Kilby, 'Perichoresis and Projection: Problems with Social Doctrines of the Trinity', *New Blackfriars* 81 (2000): pp. 432–45. See also Lewis Ayres, *Nicaea and Its Legacy: An Approach to Fourth Century Trinitarian Theology* (Oxford: Oxford University Press, 2004), pp. 408–9. It should be noted that Bavinck's tendency to see the unities-in-diversities in creation in light of an archetypal unity-in-diversity in the Godhead seems contrary to Ayres's argument that such a move is less than ideal: 'Thus the unity of the church is not to be primarily found in direct comparisons between unity and diversity in God and between human beings, but by reflection on the unity and diversity appropriate in the body of Christ during the process of purification and sanctification, a unity and diversity at this point in the drama of salvation.' *Nicaea and Its Legacy*, p. 417, n. 64. A useful survey of the current debate, along with a recent defence of social Trinitarianism, however, could be found in Gijsbert van den Brink, 'Social Trinitarianism: A Discussion of Some Recent Theological Criticisms', *International Journal of Systematic Theology* 16 (2014): pp. 331–50.
While Bavinck also emphasizes the importance of perichoresis in order to contemplate the unity that obtains within the Godhead, he does so as he affirms divine simplicity and the unity of the divine will, power and knowledge. Cf. Bavinck, *RD*, 2: p. 331.

[32] Bavinck, *RD*, 2: p. 298. Bavinck repeats this claim concerning the non-novelty of his inherited Reformed doctrine of God multiple times. On God's omnipresence, Bavinck would again observe that the 'thoughts of Augustine surface again later in the works of the scholastics. Catholic and Protestant theologians have not added anything essentially new.' Bavinck, *RD*, 2: p. 167. So, Eglinton: 'In terms of the basic priorities in its doctrine of God, *Reformed Dogmatics* stands in a most catholic tradition.' *Trinity and Organism*, p. 107. While Eglinton's study focused on the patterns of unity and diversity within the Godhead, this section highlights the catholicity of Bavinck's theology proper.

[33] Bavinck, *RD*, 2: p. 297. Cf. Matthew Levering, *Scripture and Metaphysics: Aquinas and the Renewal of Trinitarian Theology* (Oxford: Blackwell, 2004), pp. 1–46; Gilles Emery, 'Trinity and Creation', in Rik van Nieuwenhove and Joseph Wawrykow (eds), *The Theology of Thomas Aquinas* (Notre Dame: University of Notre Dame Press, 2005), pp. 58–77.

[34] Steven Duby comments that 'Herman Bavinck (1854-1921) is a rare example of a theologian at the turn of the twentieth century who unreservedly affirms a traditional doctrine of divine simplicity,' in his *Divine Simplicity: A Dogmatic Account* (London: Bloomsbury, 2015), p. 30.

would undoubtedly be objectionable'.[35] Rather, Bavinck's ordering reflects the pedagogical presentation of the 'tradition' on the triune God, which begins with the divine attributes as shared in common by the three persons, along with the ordering according to the redemptive-historical development of Scripture itself.[36] Further, Bavinck follows the lines of the classical mode of speech concerning the triune God which involves the twofold rule that distinguishes between essential and relative predication, that is, predication denoting the nature and essence of God in distinction from predication denoting the relative properties that properly belong to each person within the Godhead.[37] In so doing, Bavinck remains cognizant of the inappropriateness of prioritizing the oneness or the threeness of God, as if the divine essence exists in distinction from the three persons. God's divine essence exists *in* the divine persons and as such reminds creatures of the ontological distinction between them and God:

> Human nature as it exists in different people is never totally and quantitatively the same. For that reason people are not only distinct but also separate. In God all this is different. The divine nature cannot be conceived as an abstract generic concept, nor does it exist as a substance outside of, above, and behind the divine persons. It exists *in* the divine persons and is totally and quantitatively the same in each person. The persons, though distinct, are not separate. They are the same in essence, one in essence, and the same being. They are not separated by time or space or anything else. They all share in the same divine nature and perfections. It is one and the same divine nature that exists in each person individually and in all of them collectively. Consequently, there is in God but one eternal, omnipotent, and omniscient being, having one mind, one will, and one power.[38]

In this regard, one can develop James Eglinton's comment concerning Bavinck's decision to discuss divine diversity prior to the unity in the Godhead with greater precision.[39] Eglinton argues that Bavinck 'handles divine diversity and then, having established that God is non-uniform, explains the sense in which he is united' in reference to the manifold divine names and attributes of God as revealed in Scripture.[40] While it is true that Bavinck treats this diversity prior to considering the way in which these attributes or names are consonant with a robust affirmation of divine simplicity, it should be noted that Bavinck is still discussing the *divine nature* shared by the three persons of the Godhead prior to a treatment on the *personal properties* that distinguish

---

[35] Bavinck, *RD*, 2: p. 149. Likewise, Francis Turretin: 'Thus although theology treats of the same things with metaphysics ... the mode of considering is far different. It treats of God not like metaphysics as a being or as he can be known from the light of nature, but as the Creator and Redeemer made known by revelation.' *Institutes of Elenctic Theology*, 3 vols., James T. Dennison (ed.), George M. Giger (trans.) (Philipsburg: Presbyterian & Reformed, 1994), 1: p. 17.
[36] Bavinck, *RD*, 2: p. 150.
[37] This fundamental rule of Trinitarian speech can also be articulated as that which is 'common' as opposed to what is 'proper' to the persons of the Trinity.
[38] Bavinck, *RD*, 2: p. 300, emphasis in original. Hence, there is 'no genus to which he belongs as a member, and there are no specific marks of distinction whereby we can distinguish him from other beings in this genus'. *RD*, 2: p. 121.
[39] Eglinton, *Trinity and Organism*, pp. 104–6.
[40] Eglinton, *Trinity and Organism*, p. 104.

the three persons. So, while it is true that in treating the divine nature Bavinck begins with a discussion on the many names and attributes predicated of that divine nature, he is still following the classical pedagogical order of beginning with the unity of God's being prior to the threeness that unfold within that same being.[41]

God is independent, immutable and infinite, and his oneness consists in both 'the unity of singularity and the unity of simplicity [*de unitas singularitatis en de unitas simplicitatis*]'.[42] The unity of singularity denotes the essentially monotheistic faith of Christianity as set forth in the Old and New Testaments, whereas the unity of simplicity signals Bavinck's alignment with the traditional doctrine according to which God's attributes are 'identical with his essence'.[43] Bavinck self-consciously follows Augustine and the medieval scholastics, repeating once again his point that the Reformation faithfully receives this doctrine of God from them.

> Augustine again and again reverted to the simplicity of God. God, said he, is pure essence without accidents ... in God everything is one. God is everything he possesses. He is his own wisdom, his own life; being and living coincide in him. After Augustine we find this teaching in John of Damascus, in the work of the scholastics, and further in the thought of all Roman Catholic, Lutheran, and Reformed theologians.[44]

Divine simplicity follows God's naming of himself in Exod. 3.14. God is of himself, existing in divine fullness, needing nothing outside of who He is in order to be God. The doctrine of divine simplicity links with divine aseity: because God is not made of parts, there is no distinction between his essence and existence, between himself and his attributes, and as such he is the 'absolute fullness of being', the independent and fully self-sufficient God on whom every creature depends.[45] Bavinck further anticipates the objections from various corners of modern and Remonstrant theologies against the doctrine for its alleged dependence on abstract speculation. Against this, Bavinck argues that divine simplicity is squarely rooted in divine revelation and in the claim that God is the archetype of all creaturely perfections and cannot be identified with the gods of the philosophers. This is seen in these two statements culled from Bavinck's discussion on the name of God, on the one hand, and the incommunicable attributes of God, on the other:

> Hence, in that respect aseity may be called the primary attribute of God's being. We can even say – on the basis of God's revelation, not by means of a priori reasoning – that along with his aseity all those attributes have to be present in God

---

[41] This nuance remains in basic agreement with Eglinton's remark concerning Bavinck's consistent accent on the 'rich internal diversity pertaining to the Godhead'. *Trinity and Organism*, p. 110.
[42] Bavinck, *RD*, 2: p. 170; *GD*, p. 162. Though both are rendered into the English simply as 'simplicity' or 'divine simplicity', in the original text, Bavinck interchanges the Dutch 'eenvoudigheid Gods' with 'unitatis simplicitatis', signalling his adherence to the tradition on this point. For a recent defence of divine simplicity from a Protestant perspective, see Duby, *Divine Simplicity*.
[43] Bavinck, *RD*, 2: p. 173.
[44] Bavinck, *RD*, 2: p. 174.
[45] Bavinck, *RD*, 2: p. 175.

that nature and Scripture make known to us. If God is God, the only, eternal, and absolute Being, this implies that he possesses all the perfections. ... As One who exists of and through and unto himself, he is the fullness of being, the independent and supremely perfect Being.[46]

Further in the same volume, he writes:

All his attributes are divine, hence infinite and one with his being. For that reason he is and can only be all-sufficient, fully blessed, and glorious within himself. From this alone it is already evident that the simplicity of God is absolutely not a metaphysical abstraction. It is essentially distinct from the philosophical idea of absolute being, the One, the only One, the Absolute, or substance, terms by which Xenophanes, Plato, Philo, Plotinus, and later Spinoza and Hegel designated God.[47]

Divine simplicity is thus a revealed doctrine: the revealed God of Scripture is a simple God, with one will, power and wisdom. As such, Bavinck summarizes that God is 'absolute unity and simplicity, without composition or division; that unity is ... essential to the divine being'.[48] The persons within the Godhead do not therefore consist in a separation of wills but should be considered as an unfolding of the fullness and richness of the divine fecundity. 'The glory of the confession of the Trinity consists above all in the fact that that unity, however absolute, does not exclude but includes diversity ... whose diversity, so far from diminishing the unity, unfolds it to its fullest existence.'[49] Simplicity and Triunity are not opposed; the triune God exists as the simple God, and the simple God exists as triune.[50]

The persons are distinguished not by any essential properties, for they share equality in glory, power and divinity, existing in the divine nature in perfect unity. Hence, whatever is predicated of the divine nature is predicated of the three persons. Bavinck self-consciously follows Augustine in claiming that the distinction between 'the persons among themselves cannot lie in any substance but only in their mutual relations'.[51] In accord with Athanasius, the persons are modes of subsistence, a

---

[46] Bavinck, *RD*, 2: p. 124. Bavinck's descriptions of God's fullness of being in relation to divine aseity displays his awareness that aseity marks a *positive* doctrine that implies much more than the negation of the proposition that God is dependent on some external reality. 'God's fecundity is a beautiful theme, one that frequently recurs in the church fathers. God is no abstract fixed monadic, solitary substance, but a plenitude of life. ... God is an infinite fullness of blessed life.' Bavinck, *RD*, 2: p. 308. See also John Webster, 'Life in and Out of Himself: Reflections on God's Aseity', in Bruce McCormack (ed.), *Engaging the Doctrine of God: Contemporary Protestant Perspectives* (Grand Rapids: Baker Academic, 2008), pp. 107–24.

[47] Bavinck, *RD*, 2: p. 176.
[48] Bavinck, *RD*, 2: p. 300.
[49] Bavinck, *RD*, 2: p. 300.
[50] For some recent defences of the claim that Triunity and simplicity are not opposed, see Thomas Joseph White, O. P., 'Divine Simplicity and the Holy Trinity', *International Journal of Systematic Theology* 18 (2016): pp. 66–93; Scott Swain and Michael Allen, 'The Obedience of the Eternal Son', *International Journal of Systematic Theology* 15 (2013): pp. 114–34.
[51] Bavinck, *RD*, 2: p. 304.

distinction 'grounded in revelation and therefore objective and real'.[52] They are 'modes of existence within the being', which Thomas described in the analogy of the difference between an open palm and a closed fist.[53]

The Father, Son and Spirit exist with distinct proper names within the Godhead with personal properties proper to each: paternity, unbegottenness, active generation and spiration to the Father, filiation or sonship, passive generation and active spiration to the Son and procession or passive spiration to the Spirit.[54] The processions and relations are immanent to the Godhead and are identical to his being, uncompromising the simplicity of his nature; the relations between the persons are within 'that same being' that is God.[55] For Bavinck, a subsistent relation does not imply that two extrinsic objects are being linked or connected in some accidental fashion.[56] 'The "threeness" derives from, exists in, and serves the "oneness." The unfolding of the divine being occurs within that being, thus leaving the oneness and simplicity of that being undiminished.'[57]

The work of the economic Trinity *ad extra* is reflective of the immanent life of the Godhead. Because God is one, the works of God *ad extra* are common to the three persons – God in his unity is the author behind creation and re-creation. Yet the indivisibility of his works does not negate the proper distinctions that obtain by virtue of the immanent order of the persons. 'The "ontological Trinity" is mirrored in the "economic" Trinity.'[58] Just as there are personal or relative properties proper to the persons in the immanent Godhead, so there are economic distinctions in the works of God, in part signified by the diversity of prepositions applied in Scripture proper to the work of each person: 'The Father works *of* himself *through* the Son *in* the Spirit.'[59] The distinctions deployed here do not refer to historical phases or to some particular act, as if the work of creation, redemption or preservation corresponds to the work of only a single person without qualification. Bavinck is reiterating a classical axiom of Trinitarian theology that follows Augustine, who considered it paramount that 'according to the scriptures Father and Son and Holy Spirit in the inseparable equality of one substance present a divine unity ... although just as Father and Son and Holy Spirit are inseparable, so do they work inseparably. This is also my faith inasmuch as it is the Catholic faith.'[60] For Bavinck, the works

---

[52] Bavinck, *RD*, 2: p. 304.
[53] Bavinck, *RD*, 2: p. 304.
[54] Bavinck, *RD*, 2: p. 305. Later Bavinck notes that Aquinas and his followers further distinguished between generation and spiration by arguing that the former occurred in the manner of the intellect while the latter in the manner of the will, in relation to the association of generation with thought and the Spirit with love. However, Bavinck notes that 'though Protestant theologians did assume a distinction between "generation" and "spiration" – like the distinction between "Son" and "Spirit" – and also in part acknowledge the correctness of the above [Thomistic] distinctions, they were less inclined to speak with this degree of certainty and boldness and considered this distinction insufficiently scriptural and modest'. *RD*, 2: p. 314.
[55] Bavinck, *RD*, 2: p. 305.
[56] On this, see Aquinas *ST*, I, q. 28, a. 1–3.
[57] Bavinck, *RD*, 2: p. 306.
[58] Bavinck, *RD*, 2: p. 318.
[59] Bavinck, *RD*, 2: p. 319, emphasis in original.
[60] Augustine, *The Trinity*, Edmund Hill (trans.) (Brooklyn: New City Press, 1991), Bk. 1, para 7, see also para 11–22.

of God are works of the whole Trinity and only in an economic sense is some work properly predicated of a specific person:

> All the works *ad extra*: creation, providence, rule, incarnation, satisfaction (atonement), renewal, sanctification, and so on, are works of the Trinity as a whole. Yet in an 'economic' sense, the work of creation is more specifically assigned to the Father, the work of redemption to the Son, the work of sanctification to the Holy Spirit.[61]

What is highlighted is the priority on the unity of God in his works, such that all of God is involved in the creation to which he relates,[62] along with an equal emphasis on the ontological chasm that separates Creator and creature by virtue of the distinction between the immanent divine processions and the economic missions of God. 'The doctrine of the Trinity, accordingly, speaks of the generation of the Son and the procession of the Spirit. But of these are essentially distinct from the work of creation: the former are immanent relations, while the latter is work *ad extra*. The former are sufficient in themselves: God does not need creation.'[63]

Bavinck's adherence to these classical distinctions sheds light on his organic cosmology concerning the grounds on which he prioritizes the unity that precedes the diversity of God's creation as an organism. The unity of the Trinity in the work of creation, Bavinck reasons, is the reason why creation too is a unity, and the diversity proper to the work of the persons is further mirrored in the diversity displayed within creation.

> The doctrine of the Trinity provides true light here. Just as God is one in essence and distinct in persons, so also the work of creation is one and undivided, while in its unity it is still rich in diversity. It is one God who creates all things, and for that reason the world is a unity, just as the unity of the world demonstrates the unity of God. But in that one divine being there are three persons, each of whom performs a task of his own in that one work of creation.[64]

---

[61] Bavinck, *RD*, 2: p. 320. Bavinck reiterates this point later on: 'The confession of the essential oneness of the three persons has as its corollary that all the outward works of God (*opera ad extra*) are common and indivisible (*communia et indivisa*).' Bavinck, *RD*, 2: p. 422.

[62] 'Prominent in these works, therefore, is the oneness of God rather than the distinction of the persons.' Bavinck, *RD*, 2: p. 330.

[63] Bavinck, *RD*, 2: p. 332. Later Bavinck repeats the same point with different terminology.

> 'Scripture, and therefore Christian theology, knows both emanation and creation, a twofold communication of God – one within and the other outside the divine being; one to the Son who was in the beginning with God and was himself God, and another to creatures who originated in time; one from the being and another by the will of God. The former is called generation; the latter, creation. By generation, from all eternity, the full image of God is communicated to the Son; by creation only a weak and pale image of God is communicated to the creature.' *RD*, 2: p. 420.

Implicit in Bavinck's language is the distinction between immanent activities and transitive acts.

[64] Bavinck, *RD*, 2: p. 422. Cf. Ian McFarland, *From Nothing: A Theology of Creation* (Louisville: Westminster John Knox, 2014), pp. 67–83.

If there is a potential and modest point of uniqueness in Bavinck's treatment of theology proper (outside of the organic motif as a characterization of reality in light of God's triune being), it is Bavinck's predication of the divine being as the 'absolute personality' in response to modern theology's emphasis on the psychological depth that attends talk of personality.[65] Bavinck responds to two trends in modern theology: the first involves the total lack of attribution of consciousness or personality to God such that he is described as an absolute 'unconscious force', while the second fails to acknowledge the total uniqueness of the term 'person' that does properly refer to the Godhead.[66] In response to both, Bavinck argues that personality can be attributed to God, but its definition 'in no way lies on the elements of rationality and self-consciousness' as found in human beings.[67] Such a move improperly applies human categories to God, transgressing our epistemic jurisdiction in theological predication. Personhood, when applied to God, bears a radical discontinuity from how it is predicated to human creatures; 'all three persons have the same being, and attributes and hence the same knowledge and wisdom.'[68] Bavinck further argues that it is not that we attribute a definition of personality taken from the human experience and apply it to God, but the reverse. Humans have their experience as persons precisely because God is the archetypal absolute personality: 'The persons are not three revelational modes of the one divine personality; the divine being is tripersonal, precisely because it is the absolute divine personality.'[69] Bavinck then argues that personality and its concomitant psychological features, as found in human creatures, are a mere analogy to the absolute personality in God:

> In humans we witness only a faint analogy of divine personality. Personality in humans arises only because they are subjects who confront themselves as object and unite the two (subject and object) in an act of self-consciousness. Hence three moments (constituents) constitute the essence of human personality. ... In God, however, because he is not subject to space or time, to extension or division, these three are not moments but 'hypostases', modes of existence of one and the same being. ... This self-differentiation results from the self-unfolding of the divine nature into personality, thus making it tri-personal ... the unfolding of his being into personality coincides with that of his being unfolding into three persons. The three persons are the one divine personality brought to complete self-unfolding, a self-unfoldment arising out of, by the agency of, and within the divine being.[70]

---

[65] Bavinck, *RD*, 2: p. 302. Ayres, like Bavinck, remarks that modern theology introduces a 'psychological density' into the definition of persons that is taken from the experience of human consciousness in *Nicaea and Its Legacy*, p. 408. Hence: 'Modern notions of personhood here do not simply introduce too much division into the Trinity, they run the risk of corrupting the basic pro-Nicene sense of the mysterious and incomprehensible union of the Godhead'. *Nicaea and Its Legacy*, p. 412.
[66] Bavinck, *RD*, 2: p. 302.
[67] Bavinck, *RD*, 2: p. 302.
[68] Bavinck, *RD*, 2: p. 302.
[69] Bavinck, *RD*, 2: p. 302. As he recognizes elsewhere, 'To put it in modern theological language, in Scripture the personality and absoluteness of God go hand in hand.' Bavinck, *RD*, 2: p. 34.
[70] Bavinck, *RD*, 2: p. 303. Bavinck's characterization of psychology here is consonant with what he says in his *Beginselen der psychologie* [*Foundations of Psychology*], pp. 1–2.

In this rather provocative line of reasoning, and drawing critically from modern psychology, Bavinck argues that human personality is analogous to the divine being as defined by classical Trinitarian theology. However, in arguing that there is an unfolding into the three persons in the simple God (not as moments in a series but as coinciding with God's eternal nature as pure actuality), which flows from his essence as absolute personality, he makes the interesting move of predicating personality to the divine essence. The question of whether this should be seen as Bavinck unwittingly adopting the innovative modern theology he sought to resist or as a move suggesting an important development in confessional Reformed theology cannot be decided here. As Bavinck infers that marks of the divine will be found in humanity, it is appropriate to turn there.

III An organic anthropology: The individual, the relation and whole

Bavinck's organic vision of reality recognizes a fundamental difference between humanity as the pinnacle of God's creation and everything else in creation. While he affirms that the cosmos displays the vestiges of God, only humanity is created in the *image* of God. Because this is so, humanity reflects triniformity and the pattern of the organic unity-in-diversity in a higher mode unshared by the rest of creation. Bavinck summarizes his thought in an eloquent statement:

> The visible world is as much a beautiful and lush revelation of God as the spiritual. He displays his virtues as much in the former as in the latter. All creatures are the embodiments of divine thoughts, and all of them display the footsteps or vestiges of God. But all these vestiges, distributed side by side in the spiritual as well as the material world, are recapitulated in man and so organically connected and highly enhanced that they clearly constitute the image and likeness of God. ... Thus man forms a unity of the material and the spiritual world, a mirror of the universe, a connecting link, compendium, the epitome of all of nature, a microcosm and, precisely on that account, also the image and likeness of God, his son and heir, a micro-divine-being.[71]

These claims imply several things in Bavinck's theological anthropology on the level of the individual, on the relationship between male and female and with regard to humanity as a whole. As one shall see, Bavinck characterizes each of these levels with organic descriptions of unity and diversity that are polemically set over against what Bavinck thinks are 'mechanical' views of the *Imago Dei*. Here, Bavinck's polemic highlights the eclecticism typical of his thought. While it was noted in the previous section of this chapter that Bavinck happily receives the classical accounts of theology proper as provided by the ancient and medieval traditions, he distances himself from aspects of that tradition in theological anthropology for its purportedly inorganic

---

[71] Bavinck, *RD*, 2: p. 562.

character. Just as Bavinck appropriates particular doctrines and ideas from a variety of different thinkers, he also freely critiques them, whether classical or modern, where he sees fit without adopting the line of reasoning of those figures wholesale.

First, then, it is significant that Bavinck's articulation of the human individual is self-consciously set in contrast to the 'mechanical view' he finds in Roman Catholic anthropology.[72] In Bavinck's view, Rome makes an infused and extrinsic grace of God a prerequisite for the attaining of humanity's final destiny. This superadded gift did not modify human nature but rather consecrated it so that the capacity to please God in obedience is attained.[73] This doctrine, in different forms, found its home in Thomas and the scholastics and was maintained against the Reformers. As such, in Bavinck's description, 'Roman Catholic theology has a dual conception of humanity: humankind in the purely natural sense, without supernatural grace, is indeed sinless but only possesses natural religion and virtue and has his destiny on earth; humankind endowed with the superadded gift of the image of God has a supernatural religion and virtue and a destiny in heaven.'[74] Accordingly theologians who accept this conception are prone to debate which properties of human beings belonged to their natural constitution and which belonged to that which they receive by grace. The fall did not distort or ruin the image of God in humanity; human nature remains wholly intact. The only thing lost by humanity in the post-lapsarian situation was the superadded gift required to attain a meritorious obedience before God. In Bavinck's reading of the Roman Catholic understanding of justification, human beings receive again this supernatural gift, which enables them to begin the process of performing good works that merit *ex condigno* eternal life.[75]

Rome's emphasis on the loss of an external original righteousness leads directly to a definition of sin that accents the negative loss of that righteousness rather than a reconfiguring of human nature such that it positively desires evil. The natural person's concupiscence is, in Bavinck's assessment, increasingly treated not as a reflection of sin by Rome but as a 'naked' feature natural to humanity. Post-Tridentine Roman Catholic theology, therefore, 'appeal[ed] to Aquinas, Bonaventure, Duns Scotus, and others' to establish a definition of original sin as 'only the loss of original righteousness'.[76] This is

---

[72] Bavinck also often sets the organic, Trinitarian, worldview as a distinct option between mechanistic worldviews, often represented by the two poles of deism and pantheism, and other 'less consistent' forms of Christian theism. See Mattson, *Restored to Our Destiny*, pp. 54–60 and Bavinck, *Beginselen der psychologie*, pp. 27–33.

[73] Bavinck, *RD*, 2: p. 540. Abraham Kuyper shares this assessment. See especially his *Common Grace: God's Gifts for a Fallen World*, Jordan J. Ballor and Stephen Grabill (eds), Nelson D. Kloosterman and Ed M. van der Maas (trans.) (Bellington: Lexham Press, 2016), pp. 156–8.

[74] Bavinck, *RD*, 2: p. 541.

[75] Bavinck, *RD*, 2: p. 543. For Bavinck, any reward that comes from God is only possible by virtue of divine condescension: 'Every creaturely right is a given benefit, a gift of grace, undeserved and nonobligatory. All reward from the side of God originates in grace; no merit, either of condignity or of congruity, is possible.' Bavinck, *RD*, 2: p. 570. The covenant, then, is crucial in Bavinck's theology to maintain the gratuity of the promised Adamic reward. Bavinck, as Mattson observes, affirms creaturely rights only *ex pacto*. See Mattson, *Restored to Our Destiny*, p. 72.

[76] Bavinck, *RD*, 3: p. 97. Also, Crisp: 'Roman Catholics argue that original sin is essentially a privative state, wherein fallen human beings lack the original justice and righteousness with which our first parents were created.' Oliver D. Crisp, 'On Original Sin', *International Journal of Systematic Theology* 17 (2015): p. 256. Crisp cites the *Catechism of the Catholic Church*, Part 1, §2. ch. 1. par. 7.

that which the Reformers counter in their emphasis that 'original sin is not just a loss of something but simultaneously a total corruption of human nature.'[77]

An organic anthropology implies something different; 'if a human being is an organic unity' then he or she is fundamentally either good or evil.[78] Here Bavinck stresses a strong disagreement with Jonathan Edwards, who described one's inability to do good as a mere moral inability. For Bavinck depravity is not merely a moral but also a natural impotence.[79] Likewise, the dual view of Rome tears asunder the organic unity of human nature, and its mechanistic anthropology is vitally connected to a mechanistic hamartiology:

> To divide persons in two – like Rome and in part like the Lutherans – and to say that in the realm of the supernatural and spiritual they are incapable of any good but in the natural realm they can do things that are totally good is contrary to the unity of human nature, to the unity of the moral law, and to the teaching of Scriptures that humans must always be images of God, do everything they do the glory of God, and always everywhere love God with all their heart, mind, and strength.[80]

In contrast, Bavinck argues that the Reformed distinction between broad and narrow aspects of God's image is a more appropriate articulation of the human individual as made in the image of God in an organic unity.[81] The two aspects make up the image of God, and the narrow aspect is so intimately 'bound up' with the broader sense of the image of God such that with the entrance of sin the former is lost while the latter is 'ruined'.[82] Consequently, grace restores human nature fundamentally, having 'the greatest significance for his or her whole life and labor, also in the family, society, the state, art, science, and so forth'.[83] The natural person is lost, depraved and distorted in sin, and cannot appropriately function without supernatural grace even in so-called natural affairs; sin marks the distortion of humanity's imaging essence and not merely a loss of a supernatural gift from God.[84]

---

[77] Bavinck, *RD*, 3: p. 98.
[78] Bavinck, *RD*, 3: p. 120. Bavinck locates the origin of the organic motif in the time after the rationalism and optimism of the eighteenth century in *RD*, 3: p. 88.
[79] Bavinck, *RD*, 3: p. 122.
[80] Bavinck, *RD*, 3: p. 123.
[81] Bavinck, *RD*, 2: p. 554. These comments may shed light on Bavinck's short remark on Aristotle in another place: 'After all, just like Plato, Aristotle also ascribed more than one soul to human beings, and just like his predecessor, he did not succeed in combining these souls into one organic unit.' Herman Bavinck, 'The Unconscious', in John Bolt (ed.), Harry Boonstra and Gerrit Sheeres (trans.), *Essays on Religion, Science, and Society* (Grand Rapids: Baker Academic, 2008), p. 180. More clearly in his *Beginselen der psychologie*, Bavinck remarks that 'the harmony of the animated life, of head and heart, soul and body, object and subject, perception and thinking, reason, and sensation, the higher and lower "I", were not found in Greek psychology', p. 18. Dutch original: 'De harmonie van het zieleleven, van hoofd en hart, ziel en lichaam, object en subject, waarneming en denken, rede, en zinlijkheid, hooger en lager ik werd in de Grieksche psychologie niet gevonden.'
[82] Bavinck, *RD*, 2: p. 554.
[83] Bavinck, *RD*, 2: p. 554.
[84] In a discussion on the pollution of sin, Bavinck sets the Reformed view over against the mechanistic anthropology he discerns in Roman Catholicism again: 'The image of God is not an external and mechanical appendage to us but integral to our very being, it is our health.' Bavinck, *RD*, 3: p. 174.

The organic unity of the human person is a microcosm of the organism that is the kingdom of God. Just as in the kingdom of God the diverse spheres of life are united by a common idea and telos antithetical to the fragmentation that sin brings about, the human personality in its diverse faculties is to be united as a coherent whole in obedience to God. Restoration as a member of God's kingdom involves the full redemption and uniting of the human personality – a personality that internalizes the commands of God. 'The righteousness of the Kingdom of God consists in this, that a person may be fully a person, such that everything within a person may be subject to the person's spiritual, eternal essence.'[85] Sin tears what was once united such that the members of a person in this stage of redemptive-history work in disharmony: 'Understanding and heart, consciousness and will, inclination and power, feeling and imagination, flesh and spirit, these are all opposed to each other at the moment, and they compete with each other for primacy.'[86] Consistent with Bavinck's motif of grace restoring and perfecting nature, then, restoration involves the reunification of the individual's faculties under the kingdom of God such that obedience is done not as a burden but as an act of freedom. The kingdom of God comprises free personalities with their respective individualities working under the unity of God's lordship as a single organism.[87]

The parallel between the kingdom of God and the individual as organisms runs closely to the cosmos itself: Bavinck's organic motif characterizes his view of every layer of God's created order, and just as the cosmos is a unity in diversity, so the human being and its faculties comprise a superlative yet creaturely unity in diversity.[88] In this respect, Bavinck's equal emphasis on the whole of humanity as an organism does not eclipse his prior emphasis on the dignity of every individual and their respective eternal destinies. 'Every human being, while a member of the body of humanity as a whole, is at the same time a unique idea of God, with a significance and destiny that is eternal!'[89]

The second aspect of the *Imago Dei* goes beyond the organic character of each individual, and consists in the relationship that obtains between male and female.[90] This is not surprising, since for Bavinck humanity images not merely one aspect or

---

[85] Herman Bavinck, 'The Kingdom of God the Highest Good', Nelson Kloosterman (trans.), *The Bavinck Review* 2 (2011): p. 142. So, Bavinck in *RD*, 1: 362: 'Such a Christianity was not externally imposed ... but was inwardly assumed in one's conscience by a free personality.' I discuss the kingdom of God as an organism and its relation to Bavinck's epistemology in the next chapter.

[86] Bavinck, 'The Kingdom of God', p. 143.

[87] 'Precisely by means of the single shared life of the organism, the individual members of the organism are maintained and preserved in their differentiation and uniqueness.' Bavinck, 'The Kingdom of God', p. 144.

[88] Bavinck, *RD*, 2: p. 555. On the ontological hierarchical connotations of this discussion in Bavinck in conjunction with his rejection of neo-Platonism, see Mattson, *Restored to Our Destiny*, pp. 131–45. For a full discussion of Bavinck on the faculties of man as aspects of the *Imago Dei* see Bavinck, *RD*, 2: p. 587; *RD*, 3: pp. 103–13.

[89] Bavinck, *RD*, 2: p. 587. Indeed, embedded within humanity's creation as God's image in protology is an implicit but organically connected eschatology – an eschatology to be gained by obedience to the covenant stipulations voluntarily granted by God.

[90] Mattson mentions the woman as an image of God, but then does not consider more fully the relationship between male and female as a constitutive part of the image in *Restored to Our Destiny*, p. 145.

person within the Godhead but the whole triune God. In short, for Bavinck, 'the triune being, God, is the archetype of man'.[91]

This aspect comes to a greater clarity in Bavinck's short treatise on the Christian family.[92] Bavinck suggests that it is insufficient merely to affirm that the female is made in the divine image equally with Adam.[93] Appealing to Gen. 1.27, Bavinck insists that 'both together' are created in God's image, entailing that 'both, and not the one separate from the other, but man and woman together, *in mutual relation*, each created in his or her own manner and each in a special dimension created in God's image and *together* displaying God's likeness'.[94] This is why, Bavinck argues, Scripture includes both feminine and masculine relational traits as analogies to God's character. The relationship that maintains both unity and difference, exhibited by the two genders working together in obedience unto God, is that which displays an organic unity-in-diversity. 'Together in mutual fellowship they bear the divine image. God himself is the creator of duality-in-unity'.[95] This understanding goes even further as Bavinck provocatively argues that the bearing of a child brings forth a 'three-in-oneness', such that 'Father, mother and child are one soul and one flesh, expanding and unfolding the one image of God, united within threefold diversity and diverse within harmonic unity'.[96] Families are organic unities and are the foundational building blocks of society.

Absent in Bavinck's account, it should be noted, is the ascription of multiple wills to the Godhead or an eternal relation of authority and submission that correspond respectively to the Father and the Son. Bavinck is also not appealing to the Trinity for a thorough-going social programme – his dogmatic sketch here is much more modest, finding patterns of unity and diversity based on the faint analogies that humanity and creation reflect. He does, however, seek to maintain a balance between the uniqueness of the Trinity and the implied inappropriateness of seeking univocal applications from His being to creation, on the one hand, and the Christian impulse to see the triune God in the back of reality, on the other.[97] Again this is well expressed in Eglinton's claim that the Trinity is not like anything else and yet all else is like the triune God.[98]

A point of intersection between Bavinck's understanding of male and female and of humanity as a whole emerges as he considers the *physical* and *ethical* unity between

---

[91] Bavinck, *RD*, 2: pp. 554–5.
[92] Herman Bavinck, *The Christian Family*, Nelson Kloosterman (trans.) (Grand Rapids: Christian's Library Press, 2012). Dutch original: *Het Christelijke Huisgezin* (Kampen: Kok, 1912).
[93] Bavinck writes: 'The woman herself, seen as a human being, bears the image and likeness of God fully as much as the man does.' *The Christian Family*, p. 3.
[94] Bavinck, *The Christian Family*, p. 3. Emphasis mine. This is especially stimulating when one considers Karl Barth's doctrine of the *Imago Dei*, in which the language of relation is central. See Karl Barth, *Church Dogmatics*, 4 vols. in 13 pts., G. W. Bromiley, T. F. Torrance, et al. (ed. and trans.) (Edinburgh: T&T Clark, 1958), III/1: pp. 191–206. Also, on Karl Barth's positive use of Bavinck's *Dogmatics*, see John Visser, 'Karl Barth's Appreciative Use of Herman Bavinck's Reformed Dogmatics', *Calvin Theological Journal* 45 (2010): pp. 79–86. A close comparison of the two on the *Imago Dei* is thus warranted.
[95] Bavinck, *The Christian Family*, p. 5.
[96] Bavinck, *The Christian Family*, p. 8.
[97] Cf. Bavinck, *RD*, 2: p. 330.
[98] Eglinton, *Trinity and Organism*, p. 89.

them.[99] God uses the same earthly material to form the woman out of the man, and 'the manner in which the woman received her existence served to place her in the kind of relationship to the man such that she is inseparably bound to him, and thereby the unity of the human race is completely preserved'.[100] There is unity by virtue of natural solidarity. Not only so:

> the woman was created not to be self-sufficient, nor to be independent of the man, nor apart from his mediation; she is not a unique principal and head of the human race, but she herself was formed out of the man, out of his flesh and blood. The human race is one entity, a body with one head, a building with one cornerstone.[101]

This brings us to the third aspect: unlike the individualism Bavinck finds within Pelagianism and modern philosophy, humanity as a whole is one organism in unity-and-diversity. Due to the teleology embedded within the creation of the human race, Bavinck argues that the *Imago Dei* is too rich to be confined by the individual or by the family.

> [The *Imago Dei*] can only be somewhat unfolded in its depth and riches in a humanity counting billions of members. Just as the traces of God (*vestigia Dei*) are spread over many, many works, in both space and time, so also the image of God can only be displayed in all its dimensions and characteristic features in a humanity whose members exist both successively ... and contemporaneously side by side.[102]

Again, in the context of defending creationism with respect to theological anthropology, Bavinck writes of the unity of the human race in terms of both physical and ethical solidarity: 'Creationism preserves the organic – both physical and moral [*beide physische en moreele*] – unity of humanity and at the same time it respects the mystery of the individual personality.'[103] This holistic unity of the entire human race is

---

[99] This emphasis on the ethical unity of humanity in religion recalls Bavinck's appreciation and subversion of Ritschl's theology. In Bavinck's mind, 'It must gratefully be acknowledged that Ritschl has so clearly and lucidly described the ethical character of Christianity. ... [For Ritschl] the human race is destined to become an ethical unity, the Kingdom of God, which the whole of physical nature serves and to which it is subject.' Herman Bavinck, 'The Theology of Albert Ritschl', John Bolt (trans.), *The Bavinck Review* 3 (2012): p. 156.
[100] Bavinck, *The Christian Family*, p. 4.
[101] Bavinck, *The Christian Family*, p. 4. Bavinck wrestles with this organic view of the family in relation to the issue of political and ecclesial women's suffrage within his anti-revolutionary party. He developed a rather 'progressive' view later in his life, much to Kuyper's discomfort, affirming universal suffrage – a controversial stance within his party because of the connotations that linked general suffrage with the ideals of the French Revolution. Bavinck's rationale can be found in his *De Vrouw in de Hedendaagsche Maatschappij* (Kampen: Kok, 1918). See also Niels van Driel, 'The Status of Women in Contemporary Society: Principles and Practice in Herman Bavinck's Socio-Political Thought', in John Bolt (ed.), *Five Studies in the Thought of Herman Bavinck, a Creator of Modern Dutch Theology* (Lewiston: Edwin Mellen Press, 2011), pp. 153–95; James Eglinton, 'Democracy and Ecclesiology: An Aristocratic Church for a Democratic Age?' in John Bowlin (ed.), *The Kuyper Center Review*, vol. 4: *Calvinism and Democracy* (Grand Rapids: Eerdmans, 2014), pp. 134–46.
[102] Bavinck, *RD*, 2: p. 577.
[103] Bavinck, *RD*, 2: p. 587; *GD*, 2: p. 634.

what distinguishes humanity from angels, in which an ethical unity does not obtain. Here, then, the concept of a federal covenant comes to the fore as essential in Bavinck's account of humanity as an organism.

> Only humanity in its entirety – as one complete organism, summed up under a single head, spread out over the whole earth, as prophet proclaiming the truth of God, as priest dedicating itself to God, as ruler controlling the earth and the whole of creation – only it is the fully finished image, the most telling and striking likeness of God.[104]

Hence, the assertion of the organic in Bavinck's anthropology means that a single head is required: 'Humanity cannot be conceived as a completed organism unless it is united and epitomized in one head. In the covenant of grace Christ has that position, and he is the head of the church; in the covenant of works that position is occupied by Adam.'[105] Emphatically this preserves the natural and ethical bond that binds all of humanity:

> The covenant of works and the covenant of grace stand and fall together. The same law applies to both. On the basis of a common physical descent an ethical unity [*ethische eenheid*] has been built that causes humanity – in keeping with its nature – to manifest itself as one organism and to unite its members in the closest possible way, not only by ties of blood but also by common participation in blessing and curse, sin and righteousness, death and life.[106]

In sum, for Bavinck, an absolute unity-in-diversity in the triune God implies a superlative organic unity-in-diversity in the bearers of his image, in the human being and in the entire human race.[107] The archetypal unity-in-diversity obtains by perichoretic union and God's simple essence, while the ectype finds its unity by means of ethical and natural solidarity. Here, the covenant and its federal head's ethical union with the human race are conceived not merely as a voluntaristic special ordinance of God (though they include that). It is a special ordinance of God which preserves and respects the ontologically triune features of humanity.

Clearly, then, the organic motif is not merely an organizing device that Bavinck deploys without significant theological motivations, and in this regard Bavinck is certainly to be located as a world view theologian characteristic of the neo-Calvinist tradition.[108] By virtue of Bavinck's Trinitarian doctrine of God, he shapes his doctrines of creation and anthropology in resistance to both uniformity and atomistic diversity with vigorous rigour, all the while deploying various thinkers in an eclectic manner.

---

[104] Bavinck, *RD*, 2: p. 576.
[105] Bavinck, *RD*, 2: pp. 577–8.
[106] Bavinck, *RD*, 2: p. 579; *GD*, 2: p. 624.
[107] All of this has interesting implications for Bavinck's account of original sin. On this, see Nathaniel Gray Sutanto, 'Herman Bavinck on the Image of God and Original Sin', *International Journal of Systematic Theology* 18 (2016): especially pp. 184–90. Parts of this section of this chapter can also be found in a modified form in this article.
[108] Cf. 'Conclusion: Bavinck as "Worldview" Theologian', in James Eglinton, *Trinity and Organism: Toward a New Reading of Herman Bavinck's Organic Motif* (London: T&T Clark, 2012), pp. 128–9.

Before moving on to the next chapter, however, a sketch of Bavinck's organicism in relation to his doctrine of revelation remains necessary.

IV Revelation as organic

Though work has been done on the organic character of Bavinck's understanding of general and special revelation respectively, less is written on the organic manner in which the two modes of revelation link together.[109] General revelation is organic as both creation and providence teleologically project the glory of the triune God, impressing that glory to the heart and psyche of every human creature. Special revelation is that verbal divine self-disclosure intrinsically communicated by the human personalities utilized by the divine will. Those human agents, in turn, are themselves created and organically located within their historical particularities. This section, therefore, observes that the two modes together constitute an organic unity for Bavinck, such that there is an organic centre of the content of both modes of revelation, forming a unity-in-diversity. This section thus serves well as a pathway to the discussion in the next chapter on Bavinck's understanding of *wetenschap* and knowledge as organic.

What emerges in the previous sections is that Bavinck rigorously attends to the various dualisms that arise within the history of Christian doctrine. There is a uniformity that functions as the authoritarian tyrant that flattens out created diversities, on the one hand, and a diversity that reduces all particularities into atomistic singulars that have no relation to the created wholes of which they were a part, on the other. In conveying his beliefs on revelation, Bavinck takes no exception to the general mode of reasoning in Reformed theology which distinguishes between two modes of divine self-disclosure as general and special revelation. As the closing of the first chapter of the Stone lectures on the *Philosophy of Revelation* indicates, Bavinck was committed to the bond that ties both modes of revelation: 'General revelation leads to special revelation, and special revelation points back to general revelation. The one calls for the other, and without it remains imperfect and unintelligible. Together they proclaim the manifold wisdom which God has displayed in creation and redemption.'[110] General and special revelation are harmonious and non-contradictory as they express the unity of God's thoughts as a single organism: 'God's thoughts cannot be opposed to one another and thus necessarily form an organic unity.'[111]

Bavinck's *Certainty of Faith* summarizes it thusly: 'Revelation is an organism with a life of its own', such that 'as history in general is no mere sum of incidents but an organic unity of interrelated incidents but an organic unity of interrelated events tied by a single idea, so the words and facts that belong to the sphere of special revelation comprise a system ruled by one thought, one plan one goal.'[112]

---

[109] Cf. Eglinton, *Trinity and Organism*, pp. 131–81.
[110] Herman Bavinck, *Philosophy of Revelation: A New Annotated Edition*, Cory Brock and Nathaniel Gray Sutanto (eds) (Peabody: Hendrickson, 1908), p. 25.
[111] Bavinck, *RD*, 1: p. 44.
[112] Bavinck, *The Certainty of Faith*, p. 61.

Bavinck's chapter on general revelation in the *Dogmatics* begins with a survey of the doctrine as articulated in Augustine, medieval and Reformed theology, and within his account he particularly emphasizes historical examples of the union and severing of the two modes of revelation. The severance of that bond became somewhat explicit in medieval Catholic scholasticism and was restored by the Reformational emphases on the noetic effects of sin and its concomitant commitment to the necessity of Scripture to interpret revelation aright. If 'scholasticism' made the 'distinction between natural and supernatural theology [as a result of natural revelation]' into an 'absolute contrast', Bavinck argued, the Reformation redefined that distinction by claiming that sin has so darkened the mind that natural revelation would inevitably be distorted in its reception apart from regeneration and Scripture.[113] The value in general revelation is not that it 'has furnished us a natural theology or religion. ... Such a natural religion cannot be found anywhere, nor can it exist', but rather that it provides Christians with a point of contact with non-believers while signalling special revelation's 'connectedness with the whole cosmic existence and life'.[114]

Regeneration and special revelation correspond to both subjective and objective sides to the epistemological situation that attends the human knower: 'Objectively needed by human beings to understand the general revelation of God in nature was the special revelation of God in Holy Scripture, which, accordingly, was compared by Calvin to glasses. Subjectively needed by human beings was the eye of faith to see God also in the work of his hands.'[115] This principle that was rigorously upheld by the Reformation did not always survive the challenges that followed the centuries after it; the bond was 'broken' in important progressions throughout the history of theology such that in pivotal instances 'reason again achieved some measure of authority alongside of faith'.[116] This manifested itself in several ways: in the writings of independent treatises on natural theology, in the conviction that reason alone was sufficient to prove some central tenets of the Christian faith or even in the opposite cases where reason is so disregarded that it mutes entirely the connection that special revelation has with the structures of the created world and mind.[117]

Bavinck assesses this historical development by arguing that Scripture makes no distinction between natural and supernatural modes of revelation, considering them both instead under the same terms such that 'all revelation, also that in nature is supernatural'.[118] The whole of redemptive history testifies to the religious character of

---

[113] Bavinck, *RD*, 1: pp. 303–4. Eglinton rightly commented that '[Bavinck] then critiques this movement [in distinguishing natural and supernatural modes of revelation] as becoming inherently dualistic, particularly in the development of medieval Roman Catholic theology.' *Trinity and Organism*, p. 140.

[114] Bavinck, *RD*, 1: p. 322.

[115] Bavinck, *RD*, 1: p. 304. On page 348, Bavinck associates regeneration with an internal mode of revelation: 'Just as in the sciences the subject must correspond to the object, and in religion subjective religion must answer to objective religion, so external and objective revelation demands an internal revelation in the subject.' The theological category and neo-Calvinistic emphasis on common grace are also significant to understand Bavinck here, as Chapter 4 will explore.

[116] Bavinck, *RD*, 1: pp. 305–6.

[117] Bavinck, *RD*, 1: pp. 305–6.

[118] Bavinck, *RD*, 1: p. 307. Later, Bavinck writes that though this distinction has some validity if defined rightly, this 'contrast first surfaces in the work of the church fathers'. Bavinck, *RD*, 1: p. 355.

creation, the natural human longing for the divine, the all-encompassing character of divine providence and non-verbal revelation. Divine condescension in self-disclosure is not simply on account of the necessities that arise from the introduction of human sin into the created order – God speaks even in the pre-lapsarian order; his intentions have never been otherwise:

> Hence, in the state of integrity, according to the teaching of Scripture, natural and supernatural revelation go together. They are not opposite but complementary. Both are mediate and bound to certain forms. Both are based on the idea that God in his grace condescends to human beings and conforms himself to them. And the modes of both are that God makes his presence felt, his voice heart, and his works seen. From the beginning, by theophanies, word, and deed, God made himself known to people.[119]

Contrary to a strict division between natural and supernatural revelation, therefore, Bavinck argues that all modes of revelation are supernatural in their *sources* while in some cases entirely natural in some *aspect* of the manner by which they are conveyed. This is by virtue of the identical divine agent who remains the subject of both modes of revelation.[120] The content and goal of revelation, therefore, are identical for both modes. Though the Trinitarian God is revealed climactically in special revelation, Christians can return to general revelation and see marks of the Trinity and the centrality of Christ in a clearer fashion – seeing increasingly the patterns of unities-in-diversities that exhibit creation's organic character. Provocatively, Bavinck likens this process as one of assimilation:

> The whole of revelation, summed up in Scripture, is a special revelation that comes to us in Christ. Christ is the center and content of that whole special revelation. … Now special revelation has recognized and valued general revelation, has taken it over and, as it were, assimilated it. And this is also what the Christian does, as do the theologians. They position themselves in the Christian faith, in special revelation, and from there look out upon nature and history.[121]

A disjunction between natural and supernatural revelation leads to the incapability of special revelation to connect with nature and history, leading it to function only in a mechanical and 'superadded' fashion. 'When this distinction [between natural and supernatural revelation] was understood as a separation – which could easily happen – special revelation came altogether to stand by itself, without any connection with nature and history. In that case, its historical and organic character was denied.'[122] Bavinck

---

[119] Bavinck, *RD*, 1: p. 310.
[120] Cf. Bavinck, *RD*, 1: pp. 367–76.
[121] Bavinck, *RD*, 1: p. 321. On the same page, Bavinck adds a nuance by distinguishing between the subjective epistemological (and redemptive) necessity of Scripture as the lens by which one reads nature correctly, and the objective reality that nature precedes Scripture.
[122] Bavinck, *RD*, 1: p. 358. Hence, a paragraph later Bavinck writes: 'In Roman Catholicism this supernaturalistic and dualistic system has been consistently worked out.'

performs this conviction as he mutes the organic motif when general revelation is discussed apart from special revelation.[123] Indeed, other than passing references to the connectedness of creation, its organic character is not explicitly discussed by Bavinck until the union of the two is explicitly invoked. Eglinton suggests the organic motif would make 'a sharp disappearance' precisely because of Bavinck's belief that creation's triniformity is only enjoyed by those armed with Scripture and regeneration.[124] It is in those instances that the language of organic connectedness and that of unity-and-diversity emerge consistently.

The goal of redemptive revelation is the teleological promise of redemption – a redemption not merely of individual souls but of the whole of humanity and the cosmos as organisms. Here, Bavinck's view on revelation systematically coheres with his organic anthropology: 'It is none other than to redeem human beings in their totality of body and soul ... to redeem not only individual, isolated human beings but humanity as an organic whole'; it is nothing less than to redeem 'the whole world in its organic connectedness, from the power of sin. ... Sin has spoiled and destroyed everything: the intellect and the will, the ethical and the physical world.'[125] Inherent in this goal is the reunification of one's knowledge and person such that humanity can think God's thoughts after him, to see Christ as the centre of all things, and to see creation for what it is. In short, it is a total organic correspondence between objective reality and subjective appropriation that sees creation, redemption and history as unities-in-diversities with God's glory as the unifying goal and Christ as the unifying centre: 'Objective revelation passes into subjective appropriation. In Christ, in the middle of history, God created an organic center; from this center, in an ever widening sphere, God drew the circles within which the light of revelation shines.'[126] Bavinck's summary of the Christian world view in the *Dogmatics* communicates the culmination of these insights:

> The worldview of Scripture and all of Christian theology is a very different [worldview from monism or naturalism]. Its name is theism, not monism; its orientation is supernatural, not naturalistic. According to this theistic worldview, there is a multiplicity of substances, forces, materials, and laws. It does not strive to erase the distinctions between God and the world, between spirit (mind) and matter, between psychological and physical, ethical and religious phenomena. It seeks rather to discover the harmony that holds all things together and unites them and that is the consequence of the creative thought of God. Not identity or uniformity but unity and diversity is what it aims at.[127]

Bavinck's emphases are clear: general and special revelation communicate the organic unity of God's thoughts, and the two are assimilated into the human consciousness

---

[123] Eglinton, *Trinity and Organism*, pp. 149–51.
[124] Eglinton, *Trinity and Organism*, p. 150.
[125] Bavinck, *RD*, 1: p. 346.
[126] Bavinck, *RD*, 1: p. 383. In this light, it is significant that the only mention of the 'organic' in Bavinck's section of scientific principles occurs after he introduces Scripture into the discussion in his concluding remarks, in *RD*, 1: p. 231.
[127] Bavinck, *RD*, 1: p. 368.

through regeneration in a manner that counters the dissecting and atomizing powers of sin. Only when the two modes of revelation are taken together by the epistemic agent that reality's organic character comes to the fore, forming a worldview that sees a harmonious whole in the midst of the diversities encountered in creation.

It has been observed elsewhere that Bavinck was critical of pre-modern accounts of Scripture and its inspiration precisely because they understood these theological loci too mechanically.[128] By this, Bavinck meant that pre-modern theologians often conceived of inspiration in a manner that did not sufficiently appreciate the historical and psychological conditions that mediate the process of Scriptural inspiration – a link that would tie God's inspiration with the fullness of human authorship and meticulous divine providence.[129] Though Bavinck redefines the organic language he inherited from his nineteenth- to twentieth-century philosophical counterparts, and uses it for his own purposes, it remains significant that Bavinck describes the organic developments made by the Romantics in his introductory section on the doctrine of revelation in a manner that closely resembles his own descriptions:

> By contrast [to rationalism], Hamann, Claudius, Lavataer, Herder, Jacobi, and others placed more stress on the kinship between religion and art and thus associated revelation with the inspiration of genius. They expanded the concept of revelation to such an extent that almost everything seemed to originate from revelation: religion, poetry, philosophy, history, and language are all seen as expressions of the one and same original life. ... And the person of Christ came to stand in the center of all those revelations: everything pointed to him, and everything revolved around him.[130]

The developments by the mediating theologies that followed them, then, resulted in a more 'organic' account of revelation:

> When we compare this newer concept of revelation with what was generally accepted before that time, we find that it is distinguished by the following features: (1) Special revelation, which is the basis of Christianity, is more organically conceived and more intimately connected in heart and conscience with general revelation in nature and history; (2) scholars adhering to the new concept attempt to understand special revelation itself as a historical process, not only in word but also in deed, both in prophecy and miracle, which then culminate in the person of Christ; (3) they view its content as existing exclusively or predominantly in religious-ethical truth, which aims primarily, not at teaching, but at moral

---

[128] Bavinck, *RD*, 1: p. 415; Eglinton, *Trinity and Organism*, p. 165.
[129] 'The old theology construed revelation, after a quite eternal and mechanical fashion, and too readily identified it with Scripture. Our eyes are nowadays being more and more opened to the fact that revelation in many ways is historically and psychologically "mediated" (*vermittelt*).' *Philosophy of Revelation*, p. 21. This does not imply, however, that Bavinck considers there to be authentic errors in Scripture precisely because he considers it to be an organism. See the discussions in Eglinton, *Trinity and Organism*, pp. 155–82, and Richard B. Gaffin, *God's Word in Servant Form: Abraham Kuyper and Herman Bavinck on the Doctrine of Scripture* (Greenville: Reformed Academic Press, 2008).
[130] Bavinck, *RD*, 1: pp. 289–90.

amelioration, redemption from sin; and (4) they make a sharp distinction between the revelation that gradually took place in history and its documentation or description in Holy Scripture; the latter is not itself the revelation but only more or less accurate record of it.[131]

Significant differences remain between Bavinck's organicism and the modern accounts he outlines in these two texts. Bavinck made no disjunction between revelation and Scripture – though revelation is not reducible to Scripture, Scripture is nonetheless the revealed word of God and the only means through which Christ, the triune God's will and the history of redemption are known. To create a dichotomy between religious and Christological truths that affect moral renovation and its supposedly non-essential, disposable (and potentially erroneous) historical claims is ironically to recapitulate the very mechanistic tendency that the mediating theologians wanted to reject in the first place.[132] Scripture's historic, theological and metaphysical claims have to be taken seriously as a single organic whole that possesses no contradictions with the truths revealed in the general studies of nature and history.

Nonetheless, the affinities are also clear. The holism with which Bavinck describes the Romantics marks his own thoughts – Christ is the centre of revelation towards which all things point and from which all things flow. Revelation incorporates the historical process of inspiration and the mediation of the personalities from which that revelation was penned. There is a connectedness that persists between revelation as an undergirding and pervasive ground that inspires the other fields of study – revelation is not merely the foundation for religious truth claims. Comparing Bavinck's description of the Romantics above to his rationale concerning the necessity that one explore a philosophy of revelation in his Stone lectures is instructive:

> The world itself rests on revelation; revelation is the presupposition, the foundation (*grondslag*), the secret (*geheim*) of all that exists in all its forms. The deeper science pushes its investigations, the more clearly will it discover that revelation underlies all created being. In every moment of time beats the pulse of eternity; every point in space is filled with the omnipresence of God; the finite is supported by the infinite, all becoming is rooted in being. Together with all created beings, that special revelation which comes to us in the Person of Christ is built on these presuppositions. The foundations of creation and redemption are the same.[133]

Hence, the task of a philosophy of revelation is not simply the exploration of the idea of revelation in the abstract, general sense. It is rather to correlate, trace and explore the connections that revelation has with the diverse fields of human knowing: 'A *philosophy of revelation* … will trace the idea of revelation, both in its form and content, and correlate it with the rest of our knowledge and life.'[134] As such, lest its task devolve into 'idle' speculation, it follows every other field of knowledge by being regulated by

---

[131] Bavinck, *RD*, 1: pp. 291–2.
[132] See the discussion in Bavinck, *RD*, 1: pp. 415–48.
[133] Bavinck, *Philosophy of Revelation*, p. 24.
[134] Bavinck, *Philosophy of Revelation*, p. 22. Emphasis in original.

revelation itself. 'The philosophy of revelation – just like that of history, art, and the rest – must take its start from its object, from revelation.'[135] It is these convictions that form the backbone for Bavinck's constructive labours in the Stone lectures.

These observations anticipate the argument of the next chapter: if organicism characterizes Bavinck's descriptions of creation in light of God, anthropology and revelation, what are the implications for Bavinck's account of knowledge? If revelation is an organism, does Bavinck consider human knowing, and the character of science itself, as organisms? It will be made clear that Bavinck answers these in the affirmative.

---

[135] Bavinck, *Philosophy of Revelation*, p. 23.

3

Organism and *Wetenschap* – the structure of Bavinck's epistemology

The whole was before the parts, and out of the whole, the members of the organism of science have slowly grown and entered into maturity. And still this process of 'differentiation' continues. ... So that this unity is never forgotten, the division of science into a multitude of subjects is seen as a healthy and normal phenomenon.[1]

Christianity has made us first understand that the world, that humanity, that science is one.[2]

The previous chapter displayed Bavinck's organic worldview with respect to three key theological loci: the doctrines of God, anthropology and revelation. The theme of unity-in-diversity was traced through them: the doctrine of God as Trinity means that creation is characterized as an organism containing various levels of unities-in-diversities; unity-in-diversity shapes Bavinck's account of the individual, the individual in relation with others and the whole of human race; general and special revelation form a single organism as Christ is the uniting centre in nature, history and Scripture. These objective organic realities are then suggestively connected to their absorption into the human subjective consciousness. The question that can be asked, then, is this: How, and in what way, did Bavinck also deploy the organic motif in reference to the structure of human knowledge and the sciences (*wetenschappen*)?

Answering this question might also illuminate two different emphases that arise in the secondary literature on Bavinck's epistemology – emphases that might, initially, be read to contain an implicit tension. One set of readings emphasizes that Bavinck advocates a strong distinction between the methods and grounds for the sciences, while another places a premium on those texts in Bavinck where he articulates that

---

[1] Dutch original: 'Het geheel was er vóór de deelen, en uit het geheel zijn de leden van het organisme der wetenschap langzamerhand uitgegroeid en tot wasdom gekomen. En nog altijd zet dit proces der "Differenzirung" zich voort ... Mits deze eenheid nooit vergeten wordt, is echter splitsing der wetenschap in eene veelheid van vakken als een gezond, normaal verschijnsel te beschouwen'. Bavinck, *Christelijke wetenschap*, p. 59.

[2] Bavinck, 'Christendom en Natuurwetenschap', p. 197. Dutch original: 'het Christendom heeft het ons't eerst doen verstaan, dat de wereld, dat de menschheid, dat de wetenschap ééne is.'

theology and its principles ought to play an influential, even transformative, role in characterizing the other sciences.

The former set of readings argue that Bavinck straightforwardly follows Aquinas, holding a firm distinction between theology and the other sciences, such that the priorities, methodology and *principia* of the theological sciences ought not be confused with the other disciplines. Christians, therefore, can claim no 'privileged knowledge' with respect to natural affairs.[3] While this set of readings do not deny that Scripture is the norm for human thought, the emphasis is placed on the diversity of the sciences rather than an underlying unity precisely in order to highlight theology's independence from the sciences.

The latter set of readings emphasize the unity of the sciences in such a way that all of the sciences ought to be considered theological and that this unity outweighs whatever boundaries one might draw between them. Wolter Huttinga, for example, argues that Bavinck understands theology to be the *telos* of the sciences and that it transcends its own boundaries into other domains. 'Science, realizing itself in the deepest and fulfilled sense, becomes theology.'[4] Theology is privileged not merely because it deals with divine matters but also because 'it intensifies and concentrates the movement of knowing in which all the sciences share.'[5] Thus, it follows that 'Bavinck's understanding of "theology" *crosses the borders* of theology as an academic discipline and becomes something more encompassing'.[6]

Likewise, James Eglinton and Michael Bräutigam further claim that Bavinck and Adolf Schlatter imbue theology with a unique unifying capacity: theology ought to be in the university because, without it, the sciences become disconnected and atomistic. *Wetenschap* cannot do without theology:

> In addition to their rejection of a dualistic separation of theology and science, both of these theologians claimed that theology was necessary within the academy precisely to prevent the fragmentation of its various faculties and departments. Their common assertion is that theology alone is able to serve as an integrative force among the academic disciplines, as only theology provides a coherent framework that enables them to function properly and collaborate in harmony. They foresaw the university as becoming a cacophony of arbitrarily associated faculties when deprived of theology.[7]

---

[3] Bolt, 'Herman Bavinck on Natural Law and Two Kingdoms', p. 93. Emphasis in original. See also Laurence O'Donnell, '"Bavinck's Bug" or "Van Tillian" Hypochondria?: An Analysis of Prof. Oliphint's Assertion That Cognitive Realism and Reformed Theology are Incompatible', in Peter Escalante and W. Bradford Littlejohn (eds), *For the Healing of the Nations: Essays on Creation, Redemption and Neo-Calvinism* (Landrum: Davenant Trust: 2014), pp. 153–4.

[4] Wolter Huttinga, '"Marie Antoinette" or Mystical Depth? Herman Bavinck on Theology as Queen of the Sciences', in James Eglinton and George Harinck (eds), *Neo-Calvinism and the French Revolution* (London: Bloomsbury, 2014), p. 145. Emphasis mine.

[5] Wolter Huttinga, '"Marie Antoinette" or Mystical Depth?', p. 154. See also Philip J. Fisk, 'The Unaccommodated Bavinck and Hodge: Prolegomena with Natural Certainty', *Trinity Journal* 30 (2009): pp. 109, 125; S. P. van der Walt's Afrikaans study of Bavinck's philosophy echoes this interpretation, considering Bavinck's structure of the sciences as a 'unity and diversity [*eenheid en verskeidenheid*], *Die Wysbegeerte van Dr. Herman Bavinck* (Potchefstroom: Pro Rege, 1953), pp. 125–7.

[6] Huttinga, '"Marie Antoinette" or Mystical Depth?' p. 154. Emphasis mine.

[7] Eglinton and Bräutigam, 'Scientific Theology?' p. 30.

The organic motif has played little to no role in the above discussions. The underlying argument in this chapter, then, is that reading Bavinck's account of knowing and science in light of the organic motif accommodates both emphases while significantly nuancing them. That is, there is no need to choose between an emphasis on the diversity of the sciences and their principles and the theological unity that undergirds them. As a single organism, science and the structure of human knowing, too, contain a unity-in-diversity. The readings that emphasize the diversity of the sciences, then, are correct insofar as they observe that Bavinck is careful to ensure that theology does not merely dictate the other sciences, as if the material content of the sciences can be exclusively deduced from theology's *principia*. However, they are one-sided insofar as they mute Bavinck's organic concerns in characterizing the theological character of the sciences because of the inherent unity within the organism of knowledge. Interpreters of Bavinck that emphasize how he prescribed that theology 'crosses the borders' of its principles and boundaries to the other sciences, too, might become one-sided when they neglect to attend to the diversities that reside within that organism.

The organic motif nuances and reinterprets both sets of readings, cutting across them while securely situating Bavinck as standing on the classical orthodox tradition with his own neo-Calvinistic stamp. The structure of knowledge and *wetenschap* forms a single organism in unity and diversity.

This chapter proceeds as follows. First, through a close investigation of Bavinck's *Reformed Dogmatics, Christelijke wetenschap, Christelijke wereldbeschouwing* and other key texts, I will show that Bavinck himself characterizes knowledge as an organism. This involves three interconnected and cumulative claims: (a) there is a unified Christian worldview according to which theology provides the resources to develop a philosophy and understanding of knowledge, (b) theology is the queen of the sciences because all of science is theological and (c) though methodological distinctions have to be made because of human finitude when one pursues the sciences, all of science is ultimately a singular whole with multiple operative foundations. Finally, I close by considering the relation between Bavinck's organic account of knowing and his understanding of the kingdom of God and sphere sovereignty while raising a few questions that arise from Bavinck's construction in relation to his post at the Free University of Amsterdam.

I Organic knowing

For Bavinck, human knowledge bears a distinctly organic shape precisely because revelation and the cosmos are interconnected and organic wholes as well. The organic character of existence and revelation forms the basis on which human knowledge takes place and flourishes. This is a constant note throughout Bavinck's *oeuvre*. Early in his career, Bavinck delivered a lecture on the topic of whether a 'systematic' theology is desirable, in 'The Pros and Cons of a Dogmatic System [*Het voor en tegen van een Dogmatische System*]'.[8] As he considers an affirmative answer to this question, he

---

[8] Herman Bavinck, 'The Pros and Cons of a Dogmatic System', Nelson D. Kloosterman (trans.), *The Bavinck Review* 5 (2014): pp. 90–103.

grounds his claims on a prior conviction that all of knowledge itself is a systematic unity because of the organic character of the cosmos:

> After all, everything that exists is systematic. The entire cosmos was created and arranged according to a fixed plan. It is not an aggregate of materials and forces that were accidentally merged. If it were, it would not constitute a cosmos, a unity. But all things are oriented toward each other, exist together in an unbreakable connection, together constitute a system, an organism.[9]

One sees patterns of the organic unity of all things within the differing levels of organic life – from plants to animals to human beings. In each case, what makes an organism distinct is the observation that it is a whole that unifies the sum of its parts in a systematic manner:

> Within organisms, each small part is governed, formed, and predisposed by the whole. Thus the whole precedes the parts, and supplies each part with its own function within the whole. Within the organic for the first time we encounter a whole in terms of its parts, unity in diversity, principle within the system.[10]

This naturally follows from the theses of the previous chapter. Knowledge relates parts to wholes because of the Christian conviction that God himself exists as the Trinity – the archetype of all organic existence. Here, he explicitly follows Kuyper in affirming that the intelligible areas of life rest upon this confession:

> He, the Triune One, shows us in himself the entirely perfect system: origin, type, model, and image of all other systems. For this reason, it is an altogether remarkable and glorious idea with which Dr. Kuyper concludes his explanation of the Antirevolutionary Program, namely, that life in theological, moral, juridicial, social, and political arenas will never be plumbed as long as the investigation does not come to rest in God himself, that is, in the confession of his Sacred Trinity.[11]

These observations resist the idea that the pursuit of systems may cultivate narrowness of mind. For Bavinck, seeing all things through the triune archetype is the grounds on which one can establish an encompassing and scientific knowledge of all things. A 'scientific system', he writes, 'attempts to discern order and connection' within the 'endless series of phenomena' that encounters the human knower.[12] The flourishing of the natural sciences and human knowledge depends on the affirmation that systematic knowledge is attainable:

> If everything were chaos, a motley mass, that activity would be impossible; science would then not be able to exist. But the person who pursues knowledge proceeds on the

---

[9] Bavinck, 'The Pros and Cons', p. 90.
[10] Bavinck, 'The Pros and Cons', p. 91.
[11] Bavinck, 'The Pros and Cons', p. 92.
[12] Bavinck, 'The Pros and Cons', p. 92.

basis of the assumption that systems exist everywhere, that what exists can be known, that an idea, a word, lies at the foundation of everything. Without that presupposition, science would destroy itself; and the suicide of science may not be demanded, either. Without Reason existing outside of us, Reason within us is a purposeless enigma. To practice science is to seek for the Word that has made all things.[13]

A systematic knowledge is supposed to reflect the systematic character of that which is external to one – it fulfils the desire that has been implanted by God himself:

> Thus, a scientific system may be nothing other than a reproduction in words, a translation into language, a description, a reflection in our consciousness, of the system present in things themselves. Science does not have to create and to fantasize, but only to describe what exists. We contemplate what God has thought eternally beforehand and has given embodied form in the creation.
>
> So then, no one can speak evil of seeking a system. To describe all things systematically, to search for the system of things, is rather a calling and a duty and a yearning placed in the human heart by God himself.[14]

These claims are especially stimulating when one recalls Bavinck's belief that revelation in both general and special modes manifests the organic unity of the thoughts of God. For Bavinck, God's knowledge can be reflected by the knowledge that human beings possess in some analogical fashion as they internally appropriate God's revelation. Behind Bavinck's construal here is the Reformed orthodox distinction between archetypal and ectypal knowledge – the divine archetype desires to produce in his image bearers an 'ectypal knowledge' of the contents of his mind, not by way of ontological fusion but by 'displaying them to the human mind in the works of his hands'.[15]

Just as in any organism, human knowledge bears the shape of a unity-in-diversity precisely because it conforms to its source. God's revelation has its 'centre' in the Son as the Logos, and hence he himself 'is the first principle of cognition, in a general sense of all knowledge, in a special sense, as the Logos incarnate, of all knowledge of God, of religion, and theology (Matt. 11:27)'.[16] Science is the processed reception of revelation: 'All science [*wetenschap*] is the rendering of the thoughts [of God] laid down by God in his works.'[17] It follows that reflection on the God who reveals is of fundamental significance for the pursuit of science. Science cannot impose itself on theology, neither can theology merely dictate to science its course, but if science, 'driven by free

---

[13] Bavinck, 'The Pros and Cons', p. 93. This bears similarities with Kuyper's understanding of the purpose of scholarship as grounded in the *Logos*. See especially his *Scholarship: Two Convocation Addresses on University Life*, Harry van Dyke (trans.) (Grand Rapids: Christian's Library Press, 2014).
[14] Bavinck, 'The Pros and Cons', p. 93.
[15] Bavinck, *RD*, 1: p. 233.
[16] Bavinck, *RD*, 1: p. 402.
[17] Bavinck, *Christelijke wetenschap*, p. 58. Dutch original: 'Want alle wetenschap is vertolking der gedachten, die door God in zijne werken neergelegd zijn.'

convictions, of course, and not by coercion – allies itself with the Christian faith [it] will be able to do more and labor more energetically for the spiritual and intellectual unity of humankind. Such unity is guaranteed in the unity of God and is the hope of all religion.'[18] The consistent tone is that the obtaining of intellectual unity depends upon recognizing the resources that the Christian faith possesses for academic pursuit.

Organic knowing, thus, depends upon theology and revelation:

> The justification of theology is grounded in the essence of the Christian religion. Revelation addresses itself to human beings in their totality and has the whole world as its object. In all areas of life it joins the battle against deception. It offers material for the profoundest thought processes and in the field of science plants the knowledge of God alongside of and in organic connection with that of humanity and the whole.[19]

It is here that Bavinck's short treatise on worldview is relevant. Bavinck writes that, in the past century, the individual felt a 'disharmony between our thinking and feeling, between our wants and acts'.[20] A discord exists between religion and culture, science and life, such that a unified 'world-and-life view' is felt to be missing.[21] Modernity, despite this, continues to resist the Christian faith as an obsolete position. Bavinck seeks to vindicate the view that such a renunciation is mistaken, for the Christian worldview provides significant answers to the enduring questions of the human spirit, the relationship of thinking and being, of being and becoming, of becoming and act, and the character of who one is, the world, and one's task in the world.[22] Christianity's explanatory power resides precisely in its capacity to provide harmony. 'Autonomous thinking', Bavinck writes,

> cannot find a satisfactory answer to these questions; it oscillates between materialism and spiritualism, between atomism and dynamism, between nomism and antinomism. But Christendom maintains a balance and reveals to us a wisdom which reconciles man with God, but because of that also with himself, with the world, and with life.[23]

---

[18] Bavinck, *RD*, 1: pp. 299–300.
[19] Bavinck, *RD*, 1: p. 607. Bavinck echoes Kuyper, who advises university students not just to 'work through the books on [one's] shelf, but proceed as demanded by your ability to absorb, in keeping with the organic interconnectedness of knowledge'. *Scholarship*, p. 18.
[20] Bavinck, *Christelijke wereldbeschouwing*, p. 8. Dutch original: 'Er is eene disharmonie tusschen ons denken en gevoelen. Tusschen ons willen en handelen.'
[21] Bavinck, *Christelijke wereldeschouwing*, p. 8. 'Er ontbreekt eene "einheitliche" wereld-en-levenbeschouwing, en daarom is dit woord de leuze van den dag en het zoeken daarnaar de arbeid, waaraan allen deelnemen, die belangstellend meeleven met hun tijd.' Bavinck cites James Orr's *The Christian View of God and the World* as a source concerning the significance of the term 'worldview'. Bavinck's comments on Orr are expanded in his 'Eene belangrijke apologie van de Christelijke Wereldbeschouwing', *Theologische Studiën* (1894): pp. 142–52. On Orr's influence on Kuyper, see Peter S. Heslam, *Creating a Christian Worldview: Abraham Kuyper's Lectures on Calvinism* (Grand Rapids: Eerdmans, 1998), pp. 92–5.
[22] Bavinck, *Christelijke wereldbeschouwing*, p. 14.
[23] Bavinck, *Christelijke wereldbeschouwing*, p. 14. Dutch original: 'Het autonome denken vindt op die vragen geen bevredigend antwoord; het oscilleert tusschen materialisme en spiritualisme, tusschen

The content of the Christian faith thus provides the conceptual and metaphysical resources to unify the disparate phenomena that one encounters, preventing an unstable oscillation between poles in tension. It provides a real alternative – an organic explanation of reality quite antithetical to the mechanical interpretations of the modern age that reduce reality into purely material terms.[24] One turns now to the first of three interconnected claims that come from these convictions – the validity of the search for a unified world view. The confession that the world is an 'organism' is the basis 'alone' on which 'philosophy and worldview have a right and ground of existence'.[25]

a. A 'unified worldview' – the organic and the mechanical

If the cosmos is indeed an organism, and if knowledge bears an organic shape that appropriates the organic revelation of God, then Bavinck contends that a unified and distinctly Christian worldview is attainable. Beneath the distinctions and particularities of each field of knowledge is a harmonious view of the whole. The world reveals God's wisdom, and it is 'the same divine wisdom that binds the world into an organic whole that plants in us an urge for a unified [*einheitliche*] worldview'.[26] The use of the German adjective with a Dutch noun, *einheitliche wereldbeschouwing* (or, the fully German *einheitliche Weltanschauung*), appears in some key places in Bavinck, as one shall see, as he was keen to maintain and establish the unity that undergirds all knowing.[27]

A consideration of Bavinck's statements concerning the achievability of a unified world view requires some attention to Bavinck's description of the holistic concerns behind both philosophy and theology. In his 1883 inaugural address at the theological school in Kampen, Bavinck utilizes a German phrase in affirming that theology is a 'universal science' [*Universalwissenschaft*]. Much like philosophy, theology assumes a central position and covers every area of life – the difference is that philosophy looks at all things from the 'standpoint of man' while theology is theocentric. Both disciplines seek to explain all the phenomena of life but with different tools, methods and questions of inquiry. Both, therefore, must go together – but in order to do that, a 'reconciliation' between the two must take place. How is reconciliation achieved? 'The reconciliation of both is given in Christ. Once [this is so] they fall perfectly together. The view of God is also that of the true man.'[28]

---

atomisme en dynamisme, tusschen nomisme en antinomisme. Maar het Christendom bewaart het evenwicht en openbaart ons eene wijsheid, welke den mensch met God, maar daarin ook met zichzelven, met de wereld en met het leven verzoent.'

[24] Bavinck, *Christelijke wereldbeschouwing*, p. 39.
[25] Bavinck, *Christelijke wereldbeschouwing*, p. 32. Dutch original: 'Indien deze mogelijk is, dank kan dit alleen daaruit verklaard worden, dat de wereld een organisme is en dus eerst als zoodanig is gedacht. Dan alleen heeft philosophie en wereldbeschouwing recht en grond van bestaan, also ook op dit hoogtepunt der kennis subject en object samenstemmen, als de rede in ons beantwoordt aan de principa van alle zijn en kennen.'
[26] Bavinck, *Christelijke wereldbeschouwing*, p. 32.
[27] One other early commentator has observed the same significance in Bavinck's use of the term: Cornelius Jaarsma, *The Educational Philosophy of Herman Bavinck: A Textbook in Education* (Grand Rapids: Eerdmans, 1935), pp. 41–7.
[28] Bavinck, *De wetenschap der H. Godgeleerdheid*, pp. 35–6. Dutch original and full text: 'Eene "Universalwissenschaft" is dus de Theologie. 'Zij komt daarin met nog ééne wetenschap overeen,

What does that reconciliation by Christ look like? Further clarity may be achieved by observing Bavinck's 1902 lecture on theology and religious studies, written as a reflection on the modern demand that religious studies ought to be a confessionally neutral discipline in distinction from the pietistic character of theology. Religion, Bavinck argues consistently, cannot be divorced from a holistic picture of all things. Just like any other science, the person's pre-commitments are always involved when one engages in scholarship; the divisions within the university thus cannot pretend to veil the interconnectedness between the disciplines or the scholar's personhood. Philosophy, especially, 'has always strived for a unified worldview [*einheitliche Weltanschauung*], a systematic world-and-life view. In its own way, every philosophical system has been an attempt to understand the universe.'[29] It is superficial, therefore, to say that the Christian viewpoint or the gospel cannot touch the subjects that are under philosophy or the literary sciences (like religious studies). Instead, it should 'naturally' be the case:

> Naturally, the obligation rests on the Christian to practice and teach the history of religions and the philosophy of religion (and all scholarship) from a Christian point of view. The fact that these disciplines actually belong to the literary department makes no difference. After all, the gospel of Christ is a joyous message not just for some people in certain circumstances, but for *every* person and for the *whole* person, for the learned as the simple, and no more for the theologian than for the literary scholar, the historian, the philosopher. I therefore fail to see why a Christian treatment of these disciplines is not permitted or not possible.[30]

Philosophy, therefore, must exist in close relation to theology precisely because its subject matter is unlimited and because theology is the means by which philosophy finds its ultimate satisfaction and foundations. Bavinck makes this connection explicitly in another place. 'Because philosophy does not limit itself to the finite', he writes, it comes into contact with God 'who is the final cause of all things'.[31] Further, 'If religion contains a worldview in seed-form, and philosophy, searching for the final ground for all things, always seeks for God, then it follows naturally that they ... must search

---

met de Wijsbegeerte. Ook deze neemt een centraal standpunt in en omvat alle gebied des levens en des wetens. Toch is tusschen beide het onderscheid groot. De Philosophie is anthropocentrisch; zij beziet alle dingen van het standpunt des menschen uit, bij zijn licht; zij is de beschouwing des menschen, met hem tot middelpunt en maatstaf. Maar de Theologie is theocentrisch; zij beziet alles van boven, van God uit, bij Diens licht; zij is de beschouwing Gods over de dingen, met Hem tot centrum en maatstaf. Beide gaan nu naast elkaar, dikwerf strijdend, maar toch veel meer dan elk van beide erkennen wil, de eene aan de andere tot dankbaarheid verplicht. De verzoening van beide is in Christus gegeven. Eens vallen zij volkomen samen. De beschouwing Gods is tevens die van den waren mensch.'

[29] Herman Bavinck, 'Theology and Religious Studies', in John Bolt (ed.), Harry Boonstra and Gerrit Sheeres (trans.), *Essays on Religion, Science and Society* (Grand Rapids: Baker Academic, 2008), p. 58.

[30] Bavinck, 'Theology and Religious Studies', p. 59, emphasis in original.

[31] Bavinck, *Christelijke wereldbeschouwing*, p. 34. Dutch original: 'Want de philosophie beperkt zich niet tot het eindige en komt dus ook met God als laatste oorzaak aller dingen in aanraking'.

together inwardly into the essence of the matter and not compete with one another.'[32] The unification of religion and philosophy, Bavinck writes succinctly, requires the Christian worldview: 'The Christian worldview alone meets this requirement.'[33] In effect Bavinck's argument is that what philosophy demands is actually 'guaranteed and explained by the testimony of God in his word'.[34]

To be clear, Bavinck here is not only claiming that Christian theism provides the answers to philosophy's questions, or that it is the product of a truly consistent philosophical undertaking. Rather, on the next page, he is clear that Christian theism is the grounds on which philosophy depends. The Christian religion, for Bavinck, 'makes known to us through her revelation the same theism that upon unprejudiced investigation appears to be the foundation [*grondslag*] of all science and philosophy'.[35] The message, by now, is clear – a unified worldview is available because of the organic connectedness of knowledge, and thus the Christian, too, must 'strive toward a unified worldview [*Hij moet streven naar eene einheitliche wereldbeschouwing*]'.[36]

Bavinck's firm statements concerning the necessity and desirability of a cohesive worldview, however, do not display an over-occupation with the intellect to the neglect of feeling or the heart. To the contrary, as already implied, his convictions originate in the prior belief that human beings are organic wholes and must be treated as such – it is axiomatic that the heart and head ought to be seen as a single unity. 'There is not another God for the child and the elderly, for the simple and the learned, for the heart and the head.'[37]

The organic unity of the affections and reason will receive a fuller treatment in Chapter 7. Bavinck's polemical concern here is the dualism that he perceived within the nineteenth- to twentieth-century academy, which makes a strict distinction between faith and knowledge, between theology and science and thus between the mind and heart.[38] The postulation that persons can leave all religious and philosophical

---

[32] Bavinck, *Christelijke wereldbeschouwing*', p. 35. Dutch original: 'Indien religie in kiem eene wereldbeschouwing bevat, en philosophie, zoekend naar den laatsten grond aller dingen, altijd naar God zoekt, dan volgt daaruit vanzelf, dat zij … innerlijk in het wezen der zaak moeten samenstemmen en niet met elkander strijden kunnen.'
[33] Bavinck, *Christelijke wereldbeschouwing*', p. 35. Dutch original: 'Aan dezen eisch voldoet alleen de Christelijke wereldbeschouwing.'
[34] Bavinck, *Christelijke wereldbeschouwing*, p. 33. Dutch original: 'En wat de wijsbegeerte alzoo naar haar wezen eischt, dat wordt ons gewaarborgd en verklaard door het getuigenis Gods in zijn woord.'
[35] Bavinck, *Christelijke wereldbeschouwing*, p. 36. Dutch original: 'En de Christelijke religie maakt ons door hare revelatie met datzelfde theisme bekend, dat bij onbevooroordeeld onderzoek de grondslag van alle wetenschap en wijsbegeerte blijk te zijn.'
[36] Bavinck, *Christelijke wetenschap*, p. 80. One hears echoes of Trendelenburg; as Frederick Beiser summarizes: 'The special sciences, vis., physics, chemistry or biology, each deal with some part or aspect of the universe; but this does not satisfy philosophy, which wants to know the universe as a whole.' *Late German Idealism*, pp. 29–30.
[37] Bavinck, *Christelijke wereldbeschouwing*, p. 35. Dutch original: 'Er is niet een andere God voor het kind en den grijsaard, voor den eenvoudige en den geleerde, voor het hart en het hoofd.'
[38] Eglinton and Bräutigam note that Bavinck also discerns that this dualism is maintained in a different mode by his denomination's decision to preserve the division between the 'scientific' character of the Free University and the pastoral purpose of the theological school at Kampen. By keeping the two institutions separate, Bavinck argued, the Reformed churches were reinforcing the dualism of the 1876 Higher Education Act: '[Bavinck] alleged that the Act, in annexing the heart to the pietists and the head to the modernists, had rendered theological education a shambolic experience for both sides. … Evidently, Bavinck's insistence on the place of theology in the university was counter-cultural even within his own church.' 'Scientific Theology?' p. 42.

convictions aside when they engage in the sciences already assumes a disunity in the human person that cannot be held consistently. At every point, the scholar remains a whole human person, and thus no fact simply speaks for itself:

> For it is impossible, just to mention an example, to base the sciences in general … on facts that are accepted as certain by all without distinction. It is precisely the facts about which there is immediately a difference of opinion; everyone observes them through his own eyes and his own pair of lenses. To the degree that the sciences lie closer to the center and cease to be merely formal, the subjectivity and personality of the scientific investigator play a larger role. It is totally futile to silence this subjectivity, to deny to faith, religious and moral convictions, to metaphysics and philosophy their influence on scientific study. One may attempt it but will never succeed because *the scholar can never be separated from the human being*. And therefore it is much better to see to it that the scientific investigator can be as much as possible a normal human being, that he not bring false presuppositions into his work but be a man of God completely equipped for every good work. To that end the knowledge that God has revealed of himself in his Word is serviceable; it does not hinder but rather advances scientific study and research.[39]

Here, then, the claim is that the involvement of the human person as a single unit must be sufficiently appreciated when one considers the character of the sciences. To posit that convictions can be separated from the task of scholarship in some 'presuppositionless' way only veils one's inevitable subjectivity.[40] This is further reinforced, Bavinck considers later on, by the theological belief that sin has darkened the mind, which prohibits the belief that a 'neutral' approach would produce a basic unity in every scholar's scientific findings. 'No science, however "presuppositionless," is or will ever be able to undo this division [created by the noetic effects of sin] and bring about, in the life of all nations and people, unity in the most basic convictions of the human heart.'[41] Disunity in religion prevents true intellectual unity from becoming a reality. Rather, intellectual unity becomes possible if those engaged in scholarship would openly discuss their convictions about theology beforehand and

---

[39] Bavinck, *RD*, 1: p. 43. Emphasis mine. See also p. 51.

[40] The claim that a scientific conception of theology ought to be 'presuppositionless' was, of course, first clearly advocated by D. F. Strauss's *Life of Jesus*, who developed the neo-rationalistic strand of thinking present within his teacher, F. C. Baur. The juxtaposition of the practical and thus spiritual character of the church's confession and the 'objective' and scientific study of theology that was discussed and debated within the German Academy was clearly felt by Bavinck, as one can see from his discussions of the likes of Franz Overbeck, Paul Largarde, Julius Kaftan and Albrecht Ritschl. See, for example, Bavinck, *RD*, 1: pp. 37–46, 49–51, 69–70, 170–4, 421–2, 541–5; 'The Theology of Albrecht Ritschl', John Bolt (trans.), *The Bavinck Review* 3 (2012): pp. 123–63. Cf. Zachhuber, *Theology as Science*.

[41] Bavinck, *RD*, 1: p. 298. Oliver O'Donovan communicates similar ideas: 'In speaking of man's fallenness, we point not only to his persistent rejection of the created order, but also to an inescapable confusion in his perceptions of it. This does not permit us to follow the Stoic recipe for "life in accord with nature" without a measure of epistemological guardedness.' *Resurrection and the Moral Order: An Outline for Evangelical Ethics* (Grand Rapids: Eerdmans, 1994), p. 19.

become persuaded that it is the unity of God that can provide a coherent picture of reality.[42] Thus, by the same token, Bavinck encourages the Christian to bring into her scholarship the things that she knows by revelation.

The mechanistic interpretation of the world is the antithesis of Bavinck's prescriptions. The modern world, in Bavinck's view, offers a mechanical vision that cannot do justice to the human personality or the personal character of creation and the God who stands behind it. It reduces all phenomena into matter, offering no unifying thread that binds the diversities one encounters. As such, when the mechanical worldview seeps into society, it undermines 'all notions of religion, morality, and justice'.[43] Scholarship under a mechanistic worldview would be fundamentally misguided, and this is a product of its divorce from Christianity: 'In a certain sense it is therefore possible to separate Christianity and culture. But to the degree by which it detaches and withdraws itself as a culture from Christianity, and natural science withdraws from the theistic confession, it ceases to be culture in the real sense of the word or true scholarship and thus it loses its beneficial influence.'[44]

The picture that Bavinck is drawing so far is as follows. Without the Christian confession of the organic connectedness of all things, one is hard-pressed to unify the disparate phenomena encountered in life. The relationship between spirit and matter, between the things that stem from anthropology, on the one hand, and the empirical hard sciences, on the other, becomes inchoate. The temptation is to reduce one to the other, perhaps, or to refuse to provide an account that can connect one field to another. 'Sin dissolves; sin "moves from forged unity into diversity"; sin propagates atomism and individualism to the extreme. Sin is a disorganizing power possessing no reason for existence and thus no purpose in itself.'[45] It becomes difficult to account for the diverse faculties of the human person: What is the relationship between the intellect and the will, and how does one study reality in a manner that accounts for one's inevitable subjectivity without dissolving that study into an act of introspective projection? For Bavinck, Christian revelation discloses a reality that is interconnected, behind which a triune God exists. On revelational grounds, genuine diversity can be affirmed without reducing one phenomenon to the other. One's self is an organic unity that is not arbitrarily located in this universe – at every point the person is connected to the world, such that a natural impulse within human persons spurs them to grasp the unity that underlies the whole of reality. There is a natural 'fit' – an organic link – between the organic wisdom that the world embodies and the mind's longing for a unified worldview. This is what Christianity offers.

Bavinck fleshes this out in greater detail, as we shall consider in the next two sections the way in which Bavinck unifies faith, theology and the sciences. 'The one who believes in religion and thus the existence, revelation, and knowability of God,

---

[42] Bavinck, *RD*, 1: p. 299. In these kinds of statements, Eglinton and Bräutigam sense the influence of Kuyper behind Bavinck's thought. See 'Scientific Theology?' pp. 43–4.
[43] Bavinck, 'Christianity and Natural Science', p. 102. Bavinck makes the same observation in *Modernisme en Orthodoxie*, p. 11.
[44] Bavinck, 'Christianity and Natural Science', p. 102.
[45] Bavinck, 'The Kingdom of God', p. 141.

must demand that mind and heart, faith and science, will be able to live in piece with one another. He must strive for one "unified" [einheitliche] worldview.'[46]

b. Theology as the queen of the sciences and the theological character of the sciences

Theology is the appropriation of the revelation of God, and theology thus codifies the revelation that stands behind all of knowledge. The Trinity, an organic cosmology and theological anthropology are pillars on which science flourishes.

Bavinck conceives of the relationship between theology and the other sciences under the classical language of *regina scientarum* – theology is the queen of the sciences. It is important here to discern the grounds on which Bavinck can make such a claim and the manner in which theology governs in this role.

There are at least two reasons that ground Bavinck's belief that theology is the queen of the sciences: (1) theology is the queen by virtue of the direct object of its study – God himself and (2) theology is queen because all of the sciences themselves are theological.

First, then, theology is the queen of the sciences because it has a unique subject matter – it transcends all of the other sciences because God in his self-disclosure is the object of theology's study. 'She is *the* science', Bavinck describes, and 'high it stands above the all sciences'.[47] All of the other sciences have their place and aim studying the various objects of the cosmos, but theology fixes the eye on the Creator himself. Bavinck's emphasis on the unity of the sciences thus cannot compromise the distinctive character of theology's starting point and end; each science has its own principles, and in the same way theology 'has its own clearly identifiable object, which, since it is none other than God, the creator and sustainer of all things, gives theology the right to the place of honor among the circle of the sciences'.[48] This is the case, Bavinck goes on, irrespective of the contemporary attitude towards theology as a discipline – she remains entitled to the position not out of pity but out of just desert.

In the *Dogmatics*, Bavinck first affirms that theology has characteristics in common with all of the other sciences. All of science has an inherent value apart from utility – knowledge cannot be a function of pragmatic benefits, but rather a matter of understanding the content of God's own revelation, existing for his glory. Yet, this is true of theology in a particular manner – in a 'special sense', Bavinck notes, theology is 'from God and by God, and hence for God as well. ... Amidst all the [other] sciences it maintains its own character and nature.'[49] Such a knowledge does not only result in

---

[46] Bavinck, *Christelijke wetenschap*, p. 80. Dutch original: 'Wie aan de religie en dus aan het bestaan, de openbaring en de kenbaarheid Gods gelooft, moet eischen, dat verstand en hart, dat geloof en wetenschap met elkander in vrede zullen kunnen leven. Hij moet streven naar eene "einheitliche" wereldbeschouwing.'
[47] Bavinck, *De Wetenschap der H. Godgeleerdeheid*, pp. 33–4.
[48] Bavinck, *De Wetenschap der H. Godgeleerdeheid*, p. 34. Dutch original: 'Evenals ze naast andere wetenschappen een eigen beginsel had, zoo heeft zij ook een eigen, duidelijk aanwijsbaar object, dat, daar het niets anders is dan God zelf, de Schepper en Onderhouder aller dingen, der Theologie aanspraak geeft op de eereplaats in den kring der wetenschappen.'
[49] Bavinck, *RD*, 1: p. 53.

blessedness but is in itself the definition of 'blessedness and eternal life'.[50] Dogmatics thus strives for the reflection and recording of the knowledge of God 'in the human consciousness'.[51] Its scientific character depends on God's own initiative, and the high order of its goal demands, therefore, that it belongs not 'in a church seminary, but in the university of the sciences (*universitas scientiarum*)'.[52] Again, 'In the circle of the sciences, theology is entitled to the place of honor, not because of the persons who pursue this science, but in virtue of the object it pursues; it is and remains – provided this expression is correctly understood – the queen of the sciences'.[53] The proper study of theology thus requires that one take advantage of 'philosophical, historical and linguistic' studies in order to be adequately prepared.[54] In these ways Bavinck's affirmations are clearly consistent with the classical and Thomistic view of theology's exalted subject matter as a science.[55]

Bavinck tilts this conception with a neo-Calvinistic tinge. The directly divine object of study in theology actually directs the scholar *to* the other sciences rather than *away* from them – and here is the second ground on which Bavinck can assert theology's primacy over the other fields of study: all of the other sciences are theological. Bavinck makes this point in his Kampen inaugural address right after he describes the transcendently distinct character of theology. Theology, he warns, 'stands in the closest relation to all other sciences, but that relationship must not be sought ... first and exclusively in the anthropological character of theology, but in the *theological character* of the other sciences'.[56] Precisely because the triune God is the source of all revelation, every science must come into contact with him. Indeed, the theological shape of each science will come to the fore as one studies each closely, for the 'deeper all these particular sciences penetrate into the depths of created life, the more directly and as face to face they come to stand across of him, who creates all the fullness of that life and still sustains [it], and [who] is the object of Theology'.[57] He would later repeat

[50] Bavinck, *RD*, 1: p. 53.
[51] Bavinck, *RD*, 1: p. 54.
[52] Bavinck, *RD*, 1: p. 54.
[53] Bavinck, *RD*, 1: p. 54. So, Eglinton and Bräutigam: 'For Bavinck ... [theology's] unique object means that its methodology will differ somewhat from the natural sciences. This is so as unlike the natural sciences, where one must go and investigate (with knowledge as the goal of the scientific process), theology's object speaks for himself: God practices self-disclosure.' 'Scientific Theology?' pp. 44–5.
[54] Bavinck, *RD*, 1: p. 617. Bavinck takes these prescriptions seriously. A look at his notes from his studentship at Leiden University reveals that he wrestled with subjects like logic, philosophy, Dutch and church history, the history of religions, literature and Arabic. These notes can be found in the Bavinck archives in the Free University of Amsterdam, inventory numbers 19-37, each of which is peppered with notations especially in Dutch, Latin, German and Greek.
[55] Bavinck makes this explicit connection in *Christelijke wetenschap*, p. 100, n. 67.
[56] Bavinck, *De Wetenschap der H. Godgeleerdheid*, p. 35. Emphasis mine. Dutch original: 'Toch staat zij weer met alle andere wetenschappen in het nauwste verband. Maar dat verband moet niet allereerst en uitsluitend met de la Saussaye gezocht worden in het anthropologisch karakter der Theologie, maar in het theologisch karakter der andere wetenschappen.'
[57] Bavinck, *De Wetenschap der H. Godgeleerdheid*, p. 35. Dutch original: 'Hoe dieper alle die bijzondere wetenschappen indringen in de diepte des geschapenen levens, te meer rechtstreeks en als van aangezicht tot aangezicht zij komen te staan tegenover Hem, die al de volheid van dat leven schiep en nog steeds onderhoudt, en het object is der Theologie.' Wolter Huttinga's description is thus apt: 'When Bavinck praises the discipline of theology he does not do so within a framework that praises faith as opposed to knowledge. On the contrary, the fact that theology "seeks God in everything" does not render it unworldly, but ultimately, "worldly".' '"Marie Antoinette" or Mystical Depth?' p. 146.

this point in his *Philosophy of Revelation*, where he writes that it is a mistake to practice theology 'as if all the other sciences, particularly the natural sciences, have nothing whatever to do with God … such a dualism is impossible'.[58]

Towards the end of the Kampen inaugural address, Bavinck assigns a prophetic role to theology's task. It envisions an end in which the secular and the sacred are visibly brought together in the sphere of knowledge – theology anticipates the eschatological hope that the sciences will manifest itself as a coherent unit. The queen and 'prophetess' directs the sciences into its theological end as every person orients oneself towards the knowledge of God. Just as the distinctions between sacred and profane communities will be no more, so there will be 'no separated, no sacred or profane sciences. There is then only one holy, glorious science, which is theology: to know all things in God and God in all things.'[59] These concluding comments may harken the reader back to the opening statements of Bavinck's address. He began by invoking Rauwenhoff, a modern professor at Leiden, who proposed in a theological magazine that theology's ongoing vitality within the contemporary age depends on the degree to which she adjusts to secularism. Succinctly, the rally call was that theology 'must become secularized'.[60] Bavinck's response to such a proposal is clear – theology must maintain its transcendent and spiritual character, and contrary to it adjusting itself to the secular demands of the day, one must instead reinterpret the sciences in a sacred manner. Theology must not become secularized, but the sciences must once again be sanctified.

Bavinck also recognizes the complications of theology's role within the academy in his own contemporary context and the present age within salvation history. Despite its exalted character within the sphere of the sciences, there remains a distinction between the present age in which sin continues to exert an atomizing power and the final day in which all of knowledge achieves theological unification. In the present dispensation, sacred and profane individuals live alongside one another as the kingdom of God remains a spiritual and not yet visible reality. It is appropriate, therefore, that Bavinck concludes his pamphlet on common grace with a reflection on the manner in which theology ought to govern in this day. Theology, Bavinck contends, continues to depend on the gifts produced by common grace, and thus it 'accords to the other sciences their full due'.[61] As a result, her rule is exercised in the form of service rather than by some domineering force. In Bavinck's words,

> Theology's honor is not that she sits enthroned above them as *Regina scientarium* [queen of the sciences] and waves her scepter over them but she is permitted to serve them all with her gifts. Theology also can rule only by serving. She is strong when she is weak; she is greatest when she seeks to be least. She can be glorious when she seeks to know nothing save Christ and him crucified. … In the middle of the human woe that life reveals all about us, and also in science, theology raises

---

[58] Herman Bavinck, *Philosophy of Revelation: A New Annotated Edition*, Cory Brock and Nathaniel Gray Sutanto (eds) (Peabody: Hendrickson, 20), p. 70.
[59] Bavinck, *De Wetenschap der H. Godgeleerdheid*, pp. 48–9.
[60] Bavinck, *De Wetenschap der H. Godgeleerdheid*, p. 5.
[61] Herman Bavinck, 'Common Grace', Raymond C. Van Leeuwen (trans.), *Calvin Theological Journal* 24 (1989): p. 65.

its doxology of the love of God shown forth in Jesus Christ our Lord. And she prophesies a glorious future in which all oppositions, including those between nature and grace, shall be reconciled, and all things, whether on earth or in heaven, shall again in Christ be one.[62]

One cannot interpret here that Bavinck is retracting his statements on theology's role as the queen of the sciences. Already in the *Dogmatics*, we have seen, Bavinck was careful that his reader obtains a proper understanding of what the title entails.[63] Rather, in this train of thought one discerns most clearly the manner in which Bavinck understands theology's governance. Theology continues to learn from the other sciences in humble reciprocation. She serves them with her gifts – she can unify them and give them their proper context, and she can show how they are closely interconnected. But she directs the sciences in a doxological manner as an act of service and prophetic witness.[64]

In sum, theology retains a place of honour within the university and the sciences because of its divine object of study. It also has a special place because all of the sciences are decidedly theological and thus find their meaningful shape by theology's governance. Christian scholarship, therefore, witnesses to the final day where all of science is unified under Christ. We now turn to consider the implications of Bavinck's thoughts so far on how he conceives of the *principia* of the different sciences.

c. An 'organism of science': *Principia* and unity-and-diversity

It is apparent by now that theology and the sciences are interwoven. Theology is transcendent in the same way that the Christian religion is transcendent. 'Certainly, Christianity is in the first place a religion, but not merely a religion. It is an entirely new life that can penetrate and enliven every life sphere and life form. Thus Christianity is not coextensive with the church. It is far too rich to allow itself to be expressed within its walls.'[65] As a result, 'We speak of a Christian society, of a Christian school. There is nothing human that cannot be called Christian. Everything within and outside the church that is enlivened and governed by Christ who exercises sovereignty over all things, constitutes and belongs to the Kingdom of God.'[66] In Christ, recall, Bavinck envisions all things being united, and it is the *telos* to which Christian scholarship points, especially in the way that scholarship relates theology with the other sciences.

Indeed, all of the above emphases – that knowing is organic, that theology is the servant-queen of the sciences, that a unified worldview is achievable – illumine Bavinck's summative claims in his 1902 inaugural address as a professor of theology at

---

[62] Bavinck, 'Common Grace', p. 65.
[63] Bavinck, *RD*, 1: p. 54. See also Huttinga, '"Marie Antoinette" or Mystical Depth?' pp. 152–3.
[64] In a politically charged address that argued for the union of the theological school of Kampen and the Free University, however, Bavinck rhetorically claimed that theology's service to the other sciences is not on a par with Scripture: '*Scripture* is the lamp for the feet of the other sciences, but not theology [*De* Schrift *is de lamp voor den voet der overige wetenschappen, maar niet de Theologie*]', in *Het Recht der Kerken en de Vrijheid der Wetenschap* (Kampen: Zalman, 1899), p. 19. Emphasis his.
[65] Bavinck, 'The Kingdom of God', p. 157.
[66] Bavinck, 'The Kingdom of God', p. 158.

the Free University of Amsterdam. Attending his basic thesis that theology is scientific, Bavinck went on to argue that Christianity has laid foundations for the flourishing of the sciences. Features that were 'peculiar to Christianity' created 'the notion of a singular, all-encompassing science'.[67] The natural sciences 'owe their existence' to Christianity, and the historical discipline is 'a fruit of the Christian faith': Bavinck located these sciences as part and parcel of that single 'all-encompassing science' located 'in the university': 'the greatest creation of the Christian faith'.[68] The Son from the Father is the light, and thus an '"*einheitliche*" worldview came into being'.[69]

This unity of the sciences, to hit a familiar note, is not a bare uniformity, but rather a unity-in-diversity:

> Certainly, science is one, but this unity is no uniformity; it does not exclude diversity, just as all manner of diversity exists in the cosmos, of matter and spirit, things visible and invisible, so too the one science subdivides into various particular sciences, which all proceed from a particular presupposition in accordance with their special objects, practice a unique research methodological, and possess a variable degree of certainty.[70]

These claims from his Free University Address are not surprising precisely because of the central organizing principle of Bavinck's thought: the organic motif. This section will further clarify the organic shape of the sciences by paying attention to the way in which Bavinck describes the epistemological *principia* of the various fields of science and the rather flexible way in which he uses the term. In short, Bavinck respects the integrity of the independence of the sciences, and yet unites them all by the principles of Christian theism – *wetenschap* conforms to an organic shape of unity-in-diversity such that the *principia* of theology (Scriptural revelation and the doctrinal content of faith) remain the *principia* of the other sciences in *addition* to their own individual *principia*.[71] The goal here is not to be exhaustive in describing the differing *principia* of each individual science but rather to show the manner in which Bavinck feels the freedom to place theology's *principia* underneath the other sciences. These claims are intelligible, as one shall see, only when read through the organic motif.

This section thus elaborates upon two types of claims that appear to reoccur throughout Bavinck's corpus, each emphasizing the unity or diversity of the sciences, respectively. All of the sciences have the same principle of knowledge – the Son himself 'is the first principle of cognition, in a general sense of all knowledge'.[72] He would write that "the incarnation of the Word, the all-dominating fact and fundamental principle

---

[67] Bavinck, 'Religion and Theology', p. 114.
[68] Bavinck, 'Religion and Theology', p. 115.
[69] Bavinck, 'Religion and Theology', p. 115.
[70] Bavinck, 'Religion and Theology', p. 121.
[71] Marinus de Jong also makes this observation as he says that, for Bavinck, the development of the sciences resembles 'an organism that continues to grow'. 'The Heart of the Academy: Herman Bavinck in Debate with Modernity on the Academy, Theology and the Church', in *The Kuyper Center Review*, vol. 5: *Church and Academy* (Grand Rapids: Eerdmans: 2015), p. 70.
[72] Bavinck, *RD*, 1: p. 402.

of all science, is also the source and continuing principle of the kingdom of God',[73] and yet, in other places, he emphasizes a strong distinction between the principles of theology and those of science:

> The principles out of which the other sciences are built rests in the nature of man, lying as innate ideas in his reason or conscience, in his intellect or feeling. But this is not so with our science [of theology]. Her *principium* lies not in our nature, and cannot be developed in us through effort or exercise; rather it fights with the whole of our nature. That principle ... is first implanted in us in the faith that was the fruit of the working of the Holy Ghost.[74]

These statements are best read through the lens of the organic. Bavinck says as much in his treatment on Christian scholarship. Science began with the entire world as its object but continued to expand, dividing itself into specialized parts. 'The whole was before the parts', and as the 'organism of science' gradually evolved the process of 'differentiation' continues.[75] The language of 'organism' is once again applied to maintain that science and knowledge form a single unity with diverse parts that continues to develop towards a teleological end. The act of specialization may compromise the prior and underlying unity behind the sciences, but if 'this unity is never forgotten, the division of science into a multitude of subjects is seen as a healthy and normal phenomenon'.[76] It is inevitable that some 'division of labor' [*arbeidsverdeeling*] would obtain, given the broad demands of scientific pursuit.[77] The language of 'division of labour' will prove to be significant later, but for now one follows Bavinck into this significant train of thought. Consider the following:

> The world is one whole and yet endlessly varied. Matter and spirit, nature and history, man and animal, soul and body, church and state, family and society, trade and industry; they are interconnected together, and stand with each other in all sorts of connections. But they are also mutually distinguished, each has its own character and nature, life and law. This diversity in unity also has in view the special sciences.

---

[73] Bavinck, 'The Kingdom of God', p. 147.
[74] Bavinck, *De Wetenschap der H. Godgeleerdheid*, pp. 19–20. Dutch original: 'Want de beginselen, waaruit de andere wetenschappen worden opgebouwd, rusten in de natuur des menschen, liggen als "ideae innatae" in zijn rede of geweten, in zijn verstand of gevoel. Maar alzoo is het met deze onze wetenschap niet. Haar principium ligt van nature niet in ons, en kan ook door geen inspanning of oefening in ons gekweekt worden; veeleer strijdt het met heel onze natuur. Dat beginsel wordt door ons eerst erkend en in ons gelegd met het nieuwe leven der wedergeboorte, wordt ons eerst ingeplant in dat geloof, dat vrucht is van de werking des H. Geeste.'
[75] Bavinck, *Christelijke wetenschap*, p. 59. Dutch original: 'Het geheel was er vóór de deelen, en uit het geheel zijn de leden van het organisme der wetenschap langzamerhand uitgegroeid en tot wasdom gekomen. En nog altijd zet dit proces der "Differenzirung" zich voort.'
[76] Bavinck, *Christelijke wetenschap*, p. 59. Dutch original: 'Mits deze eenheid nooit vergeten wordt, is echter splitsing der wetenschap in eene veelheid van vakken als een gezond, normaal verschijnsel te beschouwen.' Van der Walt observes the same point as he argues that for Bavinck 'science [wetenskap] produces more parts as an 'organism [organisme]' that slowly grows in *Die Wysbegeerte van Dr. Herman Bavinck*, p. 127.
[77] Bavinck, *Christelijke wetenschap*, p. 59. It's an open question at this point whether this development of divisions is positive in its effects for theology's influence within the academy.

In the university, both the unity of science [as a whole] along with the independence and particularity of all the special sciences must be given their rightful place.[78]

The unity of the sciences does not diminish the distinctions that exist between the objects of knowledge and the methods appropriate to their study. Thus, Bavinck appreciates the differences between scientific foundations and religious foundations,[79] with the former having its *principium cognoscendi externum* in the created world, and the work of the Logos and the light of reason form the *principium cognoscendi internum* of science.[80] In this way, Bavinck follows the long tradition of Reformed orthodoxy in its implementation of Thomistic motifs; Bavinck's claim is that in one's study of the world, there should be a liberal use of the 'general concepts' and 'common notions' that are implanted by the Logos in humanity.[81] Further, Bavinck argues, following Bacon and Schopenhauer, that 'the starting point of all human knowledge is sense perception. ... Truth must not be drawn from books but from the real world. Observation is the source of all real science.'[82] Scholasticism's allegiance with Aristotle leads it, in Bavinck's judgement, to appreciate the priority of the senses more satisfactorily than Plato.[83]

This appreciation for the different methods and grounds of epistemological justification of the different fields of science is heightened in places where Bavinck seeks to ensure that theology's norms are not constricted by the other sciences. Theology is not like the other sciences, where rational or empirical certainty are often demanded. Rather, theology finds its certainty in faith. So, after observing that Aristotle establishes the existence of different kinds of certainties and grounds, Bavinck writes:

> We all feel certain about the things we can perceive with the senses. Nor do we doubt the most basic, self-evident, undemonstrable principles of the various sciences, such as the axioms on which mathematics is based. Similarly, we are also completely certain about the truths that in science are inferred through logical deduction from an established premise which are therefore based on sufficient proof.[84]

Moreover, now favourably upholding a principle from Fichte, he went on:

> We do not obtain and maintain our deepest convictions, our world and life view, by way of scientific demonstration. These are not a product of understanding or

---

[78] Bavinck, *Christelijke wetenschap*, p. 59. Dutch original: 'De wereld is één geheel en toch eindeloos verscheiden. Stof en geest, natuur en geschiedenis, mensch en dier, ziel en lichaam, kerk en staat, gezin en maatschappij, handel en nijverheid; zij hangen onderling saam, en staan met elkaar in allerlei verband. Maar zij zijn onderling ook onderscheiden, hebben elk een eigen aard en natuur, een eigen leven en wet. Deze verscheidenheid in de eenheid behooren ook de bijzondere wetenschappen in het oog te houden. In de universiteit moet zoowel de eenheid der wetenschap als ook de zelfstandigheid en de eigenaardigheid van alle bijzondere wetenschappen tot haar recht komen.'
[79] Bavinck, *RD*, 1: pp. 207–79.
[80] Bavinck, *RD*, 1: p. 233.
[81] Bavinck, *RD*, 1: pp. 225, 232.
[82] Bavinck, *RD*, 1: p. 226.
[83] Bavinck, *RD*, 1: p. 229.
[84] Bavinck, *The Certainty of Faith*, p. 21. Original: Herman Bavinck, *De Zekerheid des Geloof* (Kampen: Kok, 1901).

of the will. These beliefs are located deeper, in the depths of the soul, in the heart. They are part of man himself; they are, as it were, part of his essence; they *are* him, as he was born, raised, and molded in a particular environment. J. G. Fichte (1762-1815) said that the philosophy a man chooses determines what kind of man he will be. The shape of one's thought is often nothing more than the history of his heart.[85]

It would be a mistake, Bavinck thought, to try to show that theology can satisfy the norms and grounds of the other sciences, for doing so would lead to theology's loss, betraying a misunderstanding of its character. The testimony of the Spirit in regeneration and the particularly revelatory source of its object means the necessity of preserving this methodological independence. It is in these contexts that Bavinck can characterize the other sciences as 'non-theological' [*niet-theologische*].[86] There exists, Bavinck argues, 'a unique religious certainty, it should be made plain both in its distinction from and its connection with other kinds of certainty. ... Even within the circle of the non-theological sciences, there are varying kinds and degrees of certainty.'[87] Rational justification cannot be demanded of theological convictions in the same way it may be demanded of the other sciences precisely because divine authority 'is the foundation of religion and therefore the source and basis of theology as well'.[88] Likewise, Bavinck is resisting Schleiermacher's move in submitting theology under the norms of ethics, conceived as a non-theological science.[89]

A cursory reading of the above claims can easily lead one to conclude that Bavinck demarcates the sciences in such a way that, though theology remains the queen of the sciences, those sciences are divided into neat distinctions such that the norms, methods and goals of each cannot transgress its assigned jurisdictions. Here, however, one must remember Bavinck's own reminders above that 'the organism of science' has a unity that cannot be 'forgotten'.[90] Instead of entertaining the temptation to charge Bavinck with inconsistency in his earlier claim that all of the sciences are theological,[91] an application of the organic motif preserves Bavinck's emphasis on the real diversity of the sciences along with its underlying unity. This diversity is in large part due to the necessity imposed upon the academy by the division of labour that attends the fact of human finitude:

> All science is one. ... Because of the limits of our view and of our understanding, however, the scientific enterprise is divided up into many kinds of science, each of which chooses its own group of phenomena as the object of investigation. ... They attempt, as it were, to uncover the basic idea, the life force of those phenomena,

[85] Bavinck, *Certainty of Faith*, p. 23, emphasis in original. This line, taken from Fichte, is a repetition of what Bavinck says earlier in 1897's *Beginselen der psychologie*, p. 77: 'Fichte properly said ... one's philosophy is often nothing other than the history of his heart'. Dutch original: 'zeide Fichte terecht ... iemands philosophie is dikwerf niet anders dan de geschiedenis van zijn hart.' Bavinck expresses the same ideas in relation to speech and language in *De Welsprekenheid: Eene lezing voor de studenten der Theol. School te Kampen, 29 November 1889* (Kampen: Zalsman, 1901), pp. 8–9.
[86] Bavinck, RD, 1: pp. 77, 260; GD, pp. 60, 267.
[87] Bavinck, *RD*, 1: pp. 76–7.
[88] Bavinck, *RD*, 1: p. 77.
[89] Bavinck, *RD*, 1: p. 260.
[90] Bavinck, *Christelijke wetenschap*, p. 59.
[91] See the above discussion, especially, on Bavinck's *De Wetenschap der H. Godgeleerdheid*, pp. 35, 48–9.

in order from that point of view to describe and illuminate everything belong to a particular field, in order to know each thing not only in itself but also – and this too is required for genuine science – in the light of, and in connection with, and from the standpoint of, the whole.[92]

A holistic picture continues to emerge in our analysis of Bavinck on this subject: the whole must be known in order to understand the parts of the unity of science. Bavinck reminds us of this again in his 1887 article on Christianity and natural science.[93] Consistent with his claims in the 1904 *Christelijke wetenschap*, his words, betraying a Kuyperian persuasion, are worth quoting in full:

> Depending on the object, [science] divides itself into many particular sciences in accordance with each object, principle, and method of investigation; theology should not dictate to and impose its method upon natural science. Each particular science is 'sovereign in its own sphere'. But as the objects of the different sciences are not separated side by side, all parts of creation, on the contrary, closely cohere; even God and the world are not deistically separated or pantheistically identified but in their duality are once again one, so are all the sciences closely related; *each fills the other, each is an integral part of the whole. Science is one, and therefore animated by a single highest principle.* (emphasis mine)
>
> And what principle can or may that be other than the Christian one? On the ground there is but a choice between two principles, the theistic and the pantheistic. On the standpoint of polytheism, deism etc., there is no unity of science, no encyclopaedia of all sciences, no 'scientific teaching' possible. *Christianity, Christian-theism has first laid the foundation and paved the way for the organic unity of science.* (emphasis mine)
>
> Such a science is thus our ideal, which, coming forth from Christian principles, saves us from philosophical wanderings and preserves the unity of the various sciences; which was given by the light of the revelation that investigates all things, thereby properly [raising us] to [undertake] a more serious and deeper study; [an ideal] independent of the church and state, her own mistress, is with all other things subject to him who is king also of the courtyard of the sciences.[94]

---

[92] Bavinck, 'Pros and Cons', p. 94.
[93] Bavinck, 'Christendom en Natuurwetenschap', pp. 184–202.
[94] Bavinck, 'Christendom en Natuurwetenschap', pp. 201–2. Dutch original: 'Naar gelang van de objecten, verdeelt zij zich in vele bijzondere wetenschappen en heeft in overeenstemming met haar voorwerp dan telkens een ander beginsel en eene andere methode van onderzoek; de theologie mag haar methode niet voorschrijven en opdringen aan de natuurwetenschap, maar ook evenmin de laatste aan de eerste, gelijk thans geschiedt. Elke bijzondere wetenschap is weer "souverein in eigen kring". Maar gelijk de objecten der verschillende wetenschappen niet los naast elkander staan, alle deelen der schepping integendeel ten nauwste samenhangen, God zelfs en wereld niet deistisch gescheiden noch pantheistisch identisch zijn, maar in hun tweeheid weer één, – zoo zijn ook alle wetenschappen ten nauwste verbonden; *de eene vult de andere aan; elke is een integreerend deel van het geheel. De wetenschap is ééne, en daarom door één hoogste beginsel bezield.*
En welk beginsel kan of mag dat anders zijn dan het Christelijke? In den grond is er maar keuze tusschen een tweetal, beginselen, het pantheistische en het theistische. Op het standpunt van het polytheisme, van het deisme enz. is er geen eenheid der wetenschap, geen encyclopaedie aller wetenschappen, geen "Wissenschaftslehre" mogelijk. *Het Christendom, het Christelijk Theisme heeft*

Theology thus cannot dictate her methods to the other sciences, yet it is Christian theism that supplies the sciences with their foundations. Understood in this way, Bavinck's distinction within the *Dogmatics* between scientific and religious foundations cannot mean to imply that the two are simply disconnected. Rather, each 'fills' the other, as Bavinck claims here. The theology of Christian theism as a third option between the 'pantheism' that leads to the uniformity of the sciences and the 'deism' that segregates the sciences into a cacophony, Bavinck argues, is one of the claims that undergird how the sciences must be understood. It is in this sense that Bavinck's lament on the frequent failure of Christianity to perform a truly 'organic reformation' of the cosmos in relation to the sciences comes to light; Christianity often rejects the 'unbelieving results of science', but there remains 'no inner reformation of the sciences on the basis of a different principle'.[95]

Finally, in Bavinck's desire to unify all of the various sciences, one must consider Bavinck's claim that the *principia* of all of the sciences are found in Scripture and its dogmatic content. Bavinck makes this claim in three key places: in the *Dogmatics*, in *Christendom en natuurwetenschap* and in *Christelijke wereldbeschouwing*. In especially the first two, one finds a measured understanding of the manner in which he understands this proposition.

In a discussion concerning the relationship between Scripture and other sciences, Bavinck warns that the admonishment that one cannot infer the mundane facts of life from Scripture has been unfortunately abused in order to distance scholars from any use of Scripture in scholarly study. Hence, Bavinck writes this:

> Much misuse has been made of Baronius' saying: 'Scripture does not tell us how the heavens move but how we move to heaven.' Precisely as the book of the knowledge of God, Scripture has *much to say also to the other sciences*. It is a light on our path and a lamp for our feet, also with respect to *science and art*. It claims authority in *all areas of life*. Christ has [been given] all power in heaven and on earth. Objectively, the restriction of inspiration to the religious-ethical part of Scripture is untenable; subjectively the separation between the religious life and rest of human life cannot be maintained. Inspiration extends to all parts of Scripture, and religion is a matter of the whole person. A great deal of what is related in Scripture is of *fundamental significance* also for the other sciences. At every moment science and art come into

---

eerst den grond gelegd en den weg gebaand voor deze organische eenheid der wetenschap. Wat men ook van materialistische zijde smale op Kerk en Christendom het zal toch wel mede aan den Christ. godsdienst dank zijn te weten, dat de Christelijke volken geweest zijn en nog zijn de dragers der cultuur, dat de lijn der wereldgeschiedenis heenloopt door de gedoopte natiën.
Zulk eene wetenschap zij dus ons ideaal, welke, van Christelijke beginselen uitgaande, ons voor allerlei wijsgeerige afdwalingen behoedt en de eenheid der verschillende wetenschappen bewaart; die bij het licht door de openbaring geschonken alle dingen onderzoekt en daardoor juist tot des te ernstiger en dieper navorsching opgewekt wordt; die onafhankelijk van Staat en Kerk, haar eigen meesteresse, alleen met alle andere dingen onderworpen is aan, Hem, die ook Koning op het erf der wetenschappen is.' Emphases mine.
95 Herman Bavinck, 'The Catholicity of Christianity and the Church', John Bolt (trans.), *Calvin Theological Journal* 27 (1992): p. 246. Bavinck was aware that his claims could be taken into a triumphalist direction, and distances himself from those trajectories. See, for example, *Het Recht der Kerken*, pp. 17–18.

contact with Scripture; *the primary principles for all of life are given in Scripture.* This truth may in no way be discounted.⁹⁶

The English translation here veils the force of Bavinck's language in the original Dutch text. Instead of using the Dutch wording to convey Scripture's status as the first principle for all areas of life, Bavinck uses the more technical Latin word, *principia*. So it reads: 'At every moment science and art come into contact with Scripture; the *principia* for all of life are given in Scripture.'⁹⁷

This reasoning is basically identical to the one in *Christendom en natuurwetenschap*. There, Bavinck first warns that Scripture is not a textbook out of which one can infer the contents of the other sciences – revealed theology assumes natural revelation, and then moves on to consider nevertheless Scripture's essential role in relation to science, specifically with regard to its unity. He writes:

> Scripture ... frequently touches all the other mundane sciences. It is not dualistic: she distinguishes between the natural and the spiritual but she does not separate them. The one is connected to the other. ... Christianity has made us first understand that the world, that the humanity, that science is one. Therefore, revelation is not strictly limited to religious and ethical being, but also lets the midpoint of its light shed over the whole of natural life, heaven and earth, plant and animal, angel and man, over all of creation. And therefore the object of theology is not the bare knowledge of God, but also that of the creature insofar as it stands in relation to him and reveals him.⁹⁸

Bavinck continues to wrestle with this question: if it is true that Scripture provides the scholar of science with revealed knowledge, would this not impinge upon his research? Would one now simply deny that the earth revolves around the sun because it appears

---

⁹⁶ Bavinck, *RD*, 1: p. 445. Emphases mine. It is worth noting that the abused statement of Baronius to which Bavinck refers is identical with the reasons O'Donnell gives in order to say that philosophy does not have its cognitive principle in Scripture, in '"Bavinck's Bug"or "Van Tilian Hypochondria?"' p. 156. On page 465, Bavinck affirms that the authority of Scripture extends over all the limited authorities of the sciences.

⁹⁷ Bavinck, *GD*, 1: p. 472. Dutch original: 'Ieder oogenblik komen wetenschap en kunst met de Schrift in aanraking, de *principia* voor heel het leven zijn gegeven in de Schrift.' My emphasis. He is repeating here what he regards as the difference between Calvin and Luther: 'Not only the church but also home, school, society and state are placed under the dominion of the principle of Christianity. ... The Bible is, for Luther, only a source for salvation truth, whereas for Calvin it is the norm for all of life'. 'The Catholicity of Christianity and the Church', p. 238.

⁹⁸ Bavinck, 'Christendom en Natuurwetenschap', p. 197. Dutch original: 'Maar nu is het ter anderer zijde evenzeer waar, dat de Schrift, juist om ons eene zuivere "geestelijke" kennis te geven, dikwerf met al die andere mundane wetenschappen in aanraking komt. Dualistisch is zij niet; zij onderscheidt wel het natuurlijke en het geestelijke maar zij scheidt het niet; het eene staat met het andere in verband; ethos en physis liggen niet gescheiden naast, maar grijpen telkens in elkaar; het Christendom heeft het ons 't eerst doen verstaan, dat de wereld, dat de menschheid, dat de wetenschap ééne is. Daarom kan de openbaring niet strikt tot het religieus-ethische beperkt wezen, maar laat van dit middelpunt uit haar licht ook vallen over heel het natuurlijke leven, over aarde en hemel, plant en dier, engel en mensch, over al het geschapene. En daarom is object der Theologie niet bloot de kennis Gods, maar ook die der creatuur inzoover zij tot God in relatie staat en Hem openbaart.'

that Scripture teaches this assertion, as in previous centuries?[99] Not so, Bavinck thinks, but neither is the solution to separate between natural and spiritual truths. Rather, Bavinck voices a familiar note: the scholar engaged in research remains a personality with an inevitable subjectivity. If all of this can be granted, Bavinck thinks, so must one admit that the Christian cannot deny the influences one receives from revelation: 'For the Christian, this question was answered in principle: [one's influences] can only be derived from revelation.'[100]

These notes are repeated often in Bavinck's *Dogmatics*. The Christian person cannot 'reject the greater light given him and must then look at all of nature and history, as well as the religions of non-Christian nations and people, by that light'.[101] It is, after all, revelation that makes the difference between the Christian and non-Christian worldview. 'The knowledge of believers is unique in that they view the whole of life religiously, theologically, and see everything in God's light, from the perspective of eternity (*sub specie aeternitatis*). That is the difference between their worldview and a philosophical or scientific worldview.'[102] With these things considered, one, it seems, must significantly nuance Bolt's claim that in Bavinck's view Christians have no privileged knowledge over natural affairs, since Christians are uniquely equipped to see the world in an organic fashion.[103]

Lastly, Bavinck writes in *Christelijke wereldbeschouwing* concerning the foundational status of revelation with a particularly Trinitarian and Johannine tinge. The wisdom from the 'Divine Word' lays upon one the 'confession' of God as the 'Father, almighty, creator of heaven and earth', a confession, Bavinck argues, that forms 'not merely the first article of the Christian faith but also the principle and foundation of all knowledge and science'.[104] Indeed, the deeper one goes the deeper one will understand that truth rests on the divine wisdom, who is the 'Word' that was 'in the beginning with God and was God'.[105] In a manner that harkens one back to his statements concerning the necessity of the Trinity for the pursuit of the sciences in his 'Pros and Cons' lecture, Bavinck reasserts that whoever 'denies this Wisdom undermines the foundation of all science'.[106] The sense of Bavinck's reasoning here is not merely ontological but epistemological, and having to do not with a principle of deduction – as if all information can be deduced from theological propositions – but with epistemological

---

[99] Bavinck, 'Christendom en Natuurwetenschap', p. 198.
[100] Bavinck, 'Christendom en Natuurwetenschap', p. 201. Dutch original: 'Voor den Christen is die vraag in beginsel beantwoord; slechts aan de openbaring kunnen zij worden ontleend.'
[101] Bavinck, *RD*, 1: p. 78. In context, that revelation includes the person of Christ, along with the prophets and apostles in Scripture.
[102] Bavinck, *RD*, 1: p. 110.
[103] Cf. James K. A. Smith, *Awaiting the King: Reforming Public Theology* (Grand Rapids: Baker Academic, 2017), pp. 157–8.
[104] Bavinck, *Christelijke wereldbeschouwing*, p. 21. Dutch original: 'En tot verklaring zal zij alleen in staat zijn, als zij zich voorlichten laat door de wijsheid van het Goddelijk Woord, die ons de belijdenis op de lippen legt van God den Vader, den Almachtige, Schepper des hemels en der aarde. Deze belijdenis is niet alleen het eerste artikel van ons Christlijk geloof, maar ook de grondslag en hoeksteen van alle kennis en wetenschap.'
[105] Bavinck, *Christelijke wereldbeschouwing*, p. 29. Dutch original: 'En dieper doorgedacht, is alle waarheid begrepen in de Wijsheid, in het Woord, dat in beginner bij God en zelf God was.'
[106] Bavinck, *Christelijke wereldbeschouwing*, p. 29. Dutch original: 'Wie deze Wijsheid loochent, ondermijn het fundamentum van alle wetenschap.'

justification.[107] Ontologically, divine wisdom continues to sustain science whether one accepts him or not. One *undermines* one's justification for believing in the pursuit of science, however, when one denies this wisdom.

If the confession of divine wisdom provides us with an epistemological justification for the pursuit of science, the fullness of truth is also opened up by attending to Scripture's content. Scripture is the 'first [*eerst*]' source out of which one understands 'the full truth [*volle waarheid*]' concerning the nature of reality as an organic unity and diversity that overcomes the one-sidedness of past philosophy, whether Plato or Aristotle.[108]

II The kingdom of God and sphere sovereignty

With the preceding analysis in view, it is profitable to step back and relate Bavinck's understanding of knowledge as an organism to his account of the kingdom of God. One finds an interesting structural parallel between the two. Bavinck conceives of the kingdom of God as that which is eternal and spiritual, the highest good towards which humanity is oriented that envisions all things under the rule of God. In Bavinck's words, 'The Kingdom of God as the highest good consists in the unity, the inclusion, the totality of all moral goods, of earthly and heavenly, spiritual and physical, eternal and temporal goods.'[109] The distinctions that obtain within the created order are not in opposition, as if the pursuit of the eternal meant the resistance of the temporal. Rather, sin is the force that obfuscates the underlying unity, often reducing diversity into autonomous atomism. The good, by contrast, 'constitutes a unity' that 'automatically organizes'.[110]

This kingdom is the unity that precedes the diversity of the life spheres found in creation – it provides them with their shape, purpose and direction without reducing one to the other and without elevating them above their appropriate function. This language is familiar by now, as it befits Bavinck's understanding of the kingdom, too, as a single organism. 'It is an organism whose totality not only precedes and transcends the individual parts but also simultaneously forms the basis, the condition, and the constitutive power of the parts.'[111] Precisely because the kingdom is an organism can Bavinck then insist that the diversity of the parts is maintained in their fullness – it respects the expression of the individual personality and places each sphere in its proper location and function.

Each sphere thus has its own unique expression within the kingdom – this is, of course, no less than the Kuyperian understanding of sphere sovereignty.[112] Bavinck reflects primarily on the spheres of the church, family, state and culture and asserts that

---

[107] For a further elaboration of this, see 'Holism and Three Implications' in Chapter 6.
[108] Bavinck, *Christelijke wereldbeschouwing*, p. 45.
[109] Bavinck, 'The Kingdom of God', p. 141.
[110] Bavinck, 'The Kingdom of God', p. 141.
[111] Bavinck, 'The Kingdom of God', p. 144.
[112] Bavinck, 'The Kingdom of God', p. 159. Bavinck expresses the same ideas in 'Souvereiniteit der wetenschap', in *De Bazuin* (Zalsman: Kampen, 11 April 1902).

the Reformation restores the independence and freedom proper to them. 'Before the Reformation [the spheres] existed in service to the church.'[113] Bavinck locates science under the sphere of culture, thereby including its practice within the cultural mandate that God assigns to humanity in the genesis account. Hence,

> Culture exists because God bestowed on us the power to exercise rule over the earth. It is the communal calling of the human race to make the world its own and to shape it as the property and instrument of personality. Humanity was given power to transform the entire treasury of created life forms, whether spiritual, moral, as well as natural, into a pure organism and to rule over it. That occurs in two ways: science and art.[114]

Science and art find their reason and existence in the kingdom of God, no less than the other spheres of life in their unique expressions. Again, one must coordinate Bavinck's organic understanding of the spheres with his sober realization that sin continues to persist in the present order – in Bavinck one finds no totalitarian or triumphalist account according to which each sphere is expected to embrace Christianity or God's rule over all things in a harmonious and unified agreement. 'Here on earth', Bavinck writes, 'all those goods are not yet one; here holiness and redemption, virtue and happiness, spiritual and physical good do not yet coincide. More often here on earth the righteousness of the Kingdom of God is bound with the cross, and through many tribulations we must enter the Kingdom of Heaven (Acts 14.22).'[115] Sin has created real oppositions, and in this life our expectations must be curbed, in the hope of the future eschatological realization of the kingdom. One can certainly relate to Bavinck's claims here from the perspective of the twenty-first century. Here, one finds that scholarship and the empirical sciences are often presented as incompatible with the confessional seminary or the church; the family's ideals are often in conflict with those of the state, and the expression of religion lie uncomfortably with the ideals of philosophy and culture. Technological advancement is heralded to be identical with the claims of progress, whereas the belief in some absolute God is associated by many with the backward norms of the past – a belief that can only be held in either ignorance or nostalgic wishful thinking.

Nonetheless, the goal remains: 'The ideal is that the oppositions appearing everywhere – with the individual, the family, the state, the church, culture, and so forth, and whereby each of these repeatedly interferes with the others – that all those oppositions gradually disappear and find their resolution in the kingdom of God.'[116] Moreover,

> To the extent that each of these various life spheres answers more and more to its essential idea, it loses its sharpness and isolation from the others and prepares the way all the more the coming of the Kingdom of God. For that kingdom, since

---

[113] Bavinck, 'The Kingdom of God', p. 161.
[114] Bavinck, 'The Kingdom of God', p. 161.
[115] Bavinck, 'The Kingdom of God', p. 141.
[116] Bavinck, 'The Kingdom of God', p. 163.

it is the highest good, destroys nothing but consecrates everything. It includes every good, a kingdom wherein all the moral good that is now spread throughout the various spheres and comes into being in each sphere according to its nature and in its appropriate manner, is incorporated as purified and perfected. It is a kingdom wherein the human personality obtains its richest and most multiform manifestation, a community life of the highest order wherein all oppositions are reconciled and individual and community, state and church, cultus and culture are integrated in perfect harmony. ... In the Kingdom of God, full sovereignty is handed over to the Messiah, a sovereignty that has descended from him in the various life spheres and returns completely once more to God, who will be all in all. ... So, in spite of so much that seems to contradict it, do not deprive me of the idea that this Kingdom of God is the essential content, the core, and the purpose of all of world history.[117]

The future realization of this kingdom is one that God achieves by a unilateral act of divine intervention, to be sure, yet those who find themselves in line with the Reformation have that prophetic task to witness to this vision of the future. Its task is to set the trajectory of that future unification wherein the antithesis is fully realized and sin is no longer an atomizing power in God's creation. Christians continue to stand on the kingdom that is already present yet invisible, harkening them back to Scripture – the unifying revelation from God which explains all human living precisely because it is the book of the core underneath the spheres of life, namely, the book of God's kingdom:

> Scripture is the Book of the Kingdom of God, not a book for this or that people, for the individual only, but for all nations, and for all of humanity. It is not a book for one age, but for all times. It is a Kingdom book. Just as the Kingdom of God develops not alongside and above history, but in and through world history, so too Scripture must not be abstracted, nor viewed by itself, nor isolated from everything. Rather, Scripture must be brought into relationship with all our living, with the living of the entire human race. And Scripture must be employed to explain all of human living.[118]

The structural parallel seems clear by now. The organism of the kingdom of God as a unity in diversity, the consciousness of the distinction between the fallen age and the *eschaton* and thus the prophetic task of Christianity to witness to a future where the unity is no longer veiled in obscurity by sin is a macro-organism in which the organism of science (*wetenschap*) finds its location. Just like the kingdom, science and knowledge form a single organism, according to which an underlying unity undergirds the development of the process of differentiation of the distinct spheres of knowledge. Sin causes that unity to be often forgotten, but it is the Christian view of knowledge that again harkens back to the unified purpose, character and foundation

---

[117] Bavinck, 'The Kingdom of God', p. 163.
[118] Bavinck, 'The Kingdom of God', p. 163.

of the spheres. Scripture is the book of the kingdom, just as Scripture is the book that underlies all of science, and theology is the queen of the sciences, not merely because of its transcendent subject matter but because it permeates all of the spheres of human life and knowing and thereby rallying one to see all things under the kingdom of God.

III Summary

It seems that the overwhelming evidence produced above implies that the following propositions ought to condition interpretations of Bavinck's epistemology henceforth:

(1) *Wetenschap* is a single organism containing a unity-in-diversity.
(2) From the perspective of diversity, each science is methodologically distinct and directed at different objects due to the need for a division of labour.
(3) From the perspective of unity, each science depends upon Trinitarian and scriptural Christian principles for them to be seen organically.
(4) Theology is the queen of the sciences because,

   a. its subject matter is higher than the other sciences and thus one cannot impose the methods of the other sciences upon theology or vice versa; and,
   b. its subject matter touches and shapes the other sciences, providing them with their principles because of the theological character of the other sciences.

In the next chapter, I shall observe Bavinck's account of dualistic or mechanical knowing, which he often associates with the epistemology of medieval Roman Catholicism, and consider some implications of his epistemology.

Before moving on, however, it is worth noting a few implications that flow from Bavinck's epistemology, especially as it relates to the role of theology within the university. Bavinck himself notes that the principles that shape his understanding of Christian science are embodied in a Christian university.[119] However, what is initially attractive may become quite problematic in concrete application. Even with Bavinck's insistence that theology's influential and central role in the organism is one of prophetic witness and service, questions in relation to practical specificity and the contemporary standard of academic freedom naturally arise. When one looks closely at the early history of the Free University of Amsterdam, where the visions of Kuyper and Bavinck are supposed to take place as an institution of higher education that bases its independence on the intention 'to pursue Christian science', one finds complications immediately.[120] Kuyper's criteria for the employment of faculty members involve not merely that the candidate is intellectually capable but that the candidate must be dedicated to investigating a science that is 'Christian according to

---

[119] Bavinck, *Christelijke wetenschap*, p. 108.
[120] van Deursen, *The Distinctive Character of the Free University*, p. 21.

its principle, method, and result', which necessarily involves that, like theology, his science 'must seek its light by [the] Word', wrestling with the questions of what it is that makes Christian scholarship distinct from non-Christian ones.[121] From its inception and at least to the generation of Valentine Hepp, Bavinck's successor as a lecturer of dogmatics at the university, the commitment to the principle that 'all sciences are subject to the Scriptures, the Scriptures are opened up by exegesis, exegesis proceeds from dogmatics' is rigorously maintained.[122] All of this seems to suggest that theology plays less of a role of service and more as the queen that dictates to her subjects how each ought to operate; though the faculty in its early years never ceased to contemplate on how the sciences may inform theology, the direction at times seems more unilateral than reciprocal.

Bavinck's role and person in all of this, however, is somewhat ambiguous. In the first place, it was clear that Bavinck stood with Kuyper on the character of the sciences. Van Deursen writes that, for Bavinck, intellectual capability or expertise in research are secondary to a professorial candidate's commitment to Reformed principles of scholarship: 'Science always requires more precise definition. ... It can be reformed or roman catholic [sic] or naturalistic but never neutral. Bavinck accordingly proceeded on the assumption that in the matters of appointments, devotion to the principle must weigh more heavily than scientific quality.'[123] The faculty members further thought that this conviction ought to apply not solely to the process of hiring lecturers but also to their students. It was difficult to graduate from the Free University if a student betrayed a lack of commitment to these Kuyperian ideals. In 1911 the issue came to a head when a student named A. Winckel was denied a doctorate in theology precisely because he was judged to have failed to stand on Reformed principles. In this case, Bavinck's voice was among those who denied Winckel his doctorate. Van Deursen recounts the case as follows:

> One ought for all examinations to investigate whether the examinee accepted the principles and stand of the Free University. The Senate adopted by a vote of seven to give with one abstention the position of Fabius and Woltjer. At Bavinck's request the nays were recorded: Bavinck, Geesink, H.H. Kuyper, Rutgers and Sillevis Smitt. To the yeas belonged Anema, Fabius, Grosheide, and J. Woltjer. Of the remaining four – Boueman, Diepenhorst, Van Gelderen, and R.H. Woltjer – one must have abstained. The Senate, however, could only advise. The curators lined up behind the minority. One who would not practice science on the basis of *gereformeerde* principles could attain a doctorate anywhere, but not at the Free University.[124]

---

[121] Van Deursen, *The Distinctive Character of the Free University*, pp. 54–5.
[122] Van Deursen, *The Distinctive Character of the Free University*, p. 92.
[123] Van Deursen, *The Distinctive Character of the Free University*, p. 88. Abraham Flipse also notes Bavinck's allegiance to Kuyper's 'strong emphasis on an underlying worldview' in the former's rejection of macro-evolutionary accounts of human origins in 'The Origins of Creationism in the Netherlands: The Evolution Debate among Twentieth-Century Dutch Neo-Calvinists', *Church History* 81 (2012): pp. 112–16 (116).
[124] Van Deursen, *The Distinctive Character of the Free University*, p. 89.

Despite this episode, Bavinck's characteristically irenic and curious mind also made himself the subject of controversy. Outside of publication, Bavinck would propel the argument that the older exegesis of the biblical creation account was in need of revision because of the new scientific consensus that resulted from current historical and scientific research.[125] This caused the other faculty members to have reservations (even suspicions) on Bavinck's orthodoxy, no less because in writing and in his teaching Bavinck seemed reticent to arrive at traditionally Reformed answers and was exceedingly sanguine about the contemporary theological and scientific scenes. 'Bavinck was not averse to consulting ethicalist theology and garnering there whatever suited him. ... [He] had always had an aversion to that word [conservative], at times that must have made his life as a Reformed theologian difficult.'[126] All of these observations suggest that Bavinck was open to the idea that the organism of knowledge would continue to develop in surprising ways, even taking on a distinct shape by virtue of new findings in the sciences – even those that he takes to be less central in the organism. If science is indeed one, then this, at least, could follow: the unity of the whole could be reformulated by a new change in one of its parts. In principle, it seems that Bavinck would be open to this idea.

In any case, the second-generation neo-Calvinist scientists between 1920 and 1930 read Bavinck in precisely this way to ground their argument that the university should be more open to the results of modern science. Abraham Flipse notes that these scientists were encouraged 'by some ideas of the late Bavinck, who had shown more openness to modern culture, they stressed that the contemporary situation was different from the nineteenth century ... and mainstream science could not be considered suspect just because it was based on non-Calvinist principles'.[127]

How these characteristics of Bavinck hang together with his rather convicted commitment to Reformed principles, however, is where the tension lies.

---

[125] Van Deursen, *The Distinctive Character of the Free University*, p. 94; Bavinck would say so as much, on 2 February 1917, particularly with regard to the 'duration and order [*duur en orde*]' of the creation account, as cited in George Harinck, Cornelis van der Kooi and J. Vree (eds), 'Als Bavinck nu maar eens kleur bekende': Aantekeningen van H. Bavinck over de zaak-Netelenbos, het schriftgezag en de situatie van de gereformeerde kerken, November 1919 (Amsterdam: VU Uitgeverij, 1994), p. 77.

[126] Van Deursen, *The Distinctive Character of the Free University*, p. 96. This conforms well with the well-known existential crises that Bavinck dealt with throughout his life and career, of which Willem J. De Wit provides a brief outline in *On the Way to the Living God: A Cathartic Reading of Herman Bavinck and An Invitation to Overcome the Plausibility Crisis of Christianity* (Amsterdam: VU University Press, 2011), pp. 16–51.

[127] Flipse, 'The Origins of Creationism in the Netherlands', p. 118.

4

Between Aquinas and Kuyper

To say that there is not a consensus view on Aquinas's understanding of natural law is to understate drastically the depth and scope of controversy on the matter.[1]

The preceding chapter argues that Bavinck understands science to be a single organism. There are distinct fields of science because the process of differentiation is a natural one as the organism of science grows and as the reality of human finitude necessitates some division of labour with regard to the scientific task. The theology of Christian theism facilitates the unity of the distinct sciences. To grasp further Bavinck's concerns in this construction, one ought to consider the way in which Bavinck characterizes the epistemology of Roman Catholicism as mechanistic, dualistic and non-organic, as represented by his criticisms of Thomas Aquinas in numerous places.[2] These criticisms do not entail that there are no Thomistic motifs in Bavinck – as demonstrated before – and Chapters 6 and 7 will elucidate precisely how Bavinck retrieves Thomas's account of perception and reasoning.

Hence, the way Bavinck uses and critiques Thomas, just as he uses and critiques many aspects of idealism or Aristotelianism for his own purposes, highlights the eclecticism that characterizes his writing. The previous chapter has already suggested that there may exist significant differences between the two theologians, no less because Bavinck operates with a broader notion of science (*wetenschap*) from the medieval notion of *scientia*, though he was certainly aware and appreciative of the latter. Recall this claim by Thomas, for example: 'It is impossible and ridiculous to hold that the principles of one science are the same as those of another science', for, if that were the case, it would erroneously 'follow from this that all things in the sciences were the same and, consequently, that all the sciences were one science'.[3] Bavinck agrees

---

[1] Nicholas Wolterstorff, *Justice: Rights and Wrongs* (Princeton: Princeton University Press, 2008), p. 39.
[2] Recent commentators also record aspects of Bavinck's critique of Thomas. This includes Bavinck's critique of Thomas on mystery and natural theology (in Eglinton, *Trinity and Organism*, pp. 97–9), on the function of proofs and ontology (in Mattson, *Restored to our Destiny*, pp. 14–15, 45, 132) and on the relationship between nature and grace and epistemology (in Brian Mattson, 'A Soft Spot for Paganism?: Herman Bavinck and "Insider Movements"', *The Bavinck Review* 4 (2013): pp. 36, 40–2).
[3] Thomas Aquinas, *Commentary on Aristotle's Posterior Analytics*, Richard Berquist (trans.) (Notre Dame: Dumb Ox Books, 2007), I. 43 c. For Aquinas, science is different from the sense of *wetenschap* with which Bavinck worked. In Aquinas the sciences are based on first principles that are either self-evident or from the principles traceable to a higher science. This necessitates that there are multiple sciences, precisely because there are multiple first principles that correspond to the differing sciences (though a

with Thomas that the diversity of sciences does mean that each science proceeds with differing principles, methods and aims. However, though Thomas does not deny that all of the sciences do ultimately cohere together, Bavinck's emphasis lies also on the *porousness* of the boundaries between the sciences. 'All Science is one,'[4] he affirms, and thus, 'each [science] fills the other, each is an integral part of the whole. Science is one, and therefore animated by a single highest principle. ... Christian-theism has first laid the foundation and paved the way for the organic unity of science,'[5] such that at 'every moment science and art come into contact with Scripture; the *principia* for all of life are given in Scripture.'[6]

That Bavinck uses the organic motif to shape his theological epistemology suggests, therefore, that past descriptions of Bavinck's epistemology as mere reproductions of Thomism should be modified. However, observing Bavinck's self-conscious criticisms of the purportedly inorganic epistemology of Thomas and Rome remain significant to understand Bavinck's organic concerns. Bavinck appreciates Thomas but self-consciously develops and modifies Thomas's thought in important respects. When the reference in the previous chapter concerning Bavinck's positive answer to the question of whether a distinctly Christian expression of every sphere of life is achievable is reproduced in full, Bavinck juxtaposes his account to a Roman Catholic one:

> [Because Christianity is not merely a religion, but a new life that penetrates every sphere], we speak of a Christian society, of a Christian school. There is nothing human that cannot be called Christian. Everything within and outside the church that is enlivened and governed by Christ who exercises sovereignty over all things, constitutes and belongs to the Kingdom of God. For Rome, the church and the Kingdom of God are one. Thus Rome's church views everything that does not flow from it and is not consecrated by it to be unholy and profane. But the Reformation recognizes the life spheres outside the church in their independence. No Protestant church may denigrate the territory of human living outside the church as unclean or profane. ... The Kingdom of God was present already among Israel. It progresses secretly like leaven and does not – unlike the church – constitute a separate community over against the state and culture.[7]

As it will be clear, Bavinck's comments here find their parallel in his critique of Thomas's account of knowledge. The second section of this chapter, then, formulates a preliminary defence of Bavinck's critique of Thomas in light of some recent criticisms of Bavinck. More specifically, the defence addresses the criticism that

---

few paragraphs later he notes that 'first axioms' like the law of identity is a common principle for all of the sciences). However, Bavinck seems to be aware of this as he considered the differing first principles that are operative when a particular division of labour is being considered, and in his claim that the first principles of all of life are also found in Scripture. Both claims, as seen in the previous chapter, are reconciled if one reads Bavinck's view of *wetenschap* in light of the organic motif of unity-in-diversity..

[4] Bavinck, 'The Pros and Cons', p. 94.
[5] Bavinck, 'Christendom en Natuurwetenschap', pp. 201–2.
[6] Bavinck, *GD*, 1: p. 472. Dutch original: 'Ieder oogenblik komen wetenschap en kunst met de Schrift in aanraking, de *principia* voor heel het leven zijn gegeven in de Schrift.'
[7] Bavinck, 'The Kingdom of God', p. 158.

Bavinck's interpretation of Thomas as a nature/grace dualist depended upon a neo-Thomistic nineteenth- to twentieth-century interpretation that has been dissolved by contemporary reconsiderations of Thomas. Such a defence is relevant to the present thesis because the criticisms of Bavinck on this very issue serve to fortify the interpretation that Bavinck, though often unwittingly, was actually repristinating Thomas in his epistemology. These criticisms of Bavinck are mistaken insofar as they suggest that Bavinck's interpretation of Thomas is outdated and no longer repeated in the current literature. Bavinck's interpretation is still echoed by a stream of literature coming from many contemporary Roman Catholic Thomists. Thus, Bavinck's critique of Thomas cannot be dismissed and ought to be situated within the current and in-house Thomist debates. Indeed, the primary objective here is not to argue that Bavinck's interpretation of Aquinas is wholly correct, nor is the purpose here to pit Bavinck against Thomas. Rather, I suggest that a failure to attend to Bavinck's critique of Thomas seems to eclipse the organic structure of Bavinck's epistemology and the *eclecticism* that characterizes Bavinck's use of sources.

I then consider two implications stemming from the preceding analysis and the organic shape of Bavinck's epistemology. The first involves re-articulating the difference between Kuyper and Bavinck on the connection (or lack thereof) between regeneration and science. The central claim here is that the difference between Bavinck and Kuyper hinges upon the former's idea that there are two understandings of science, rather than two different sciences. Addressing the affinities and differences that exist between the two neo-Calvinists also serves to clarify Bavinck's organic epistemology in important ways. The second implication I draw towards the end of this chapter involves elucidating the distinction that Isaiah Berlin draws between mechanical and organic knowing in a Bavinckian fashion by way of a few analogies and thought experiments, connecting it also to what Charles Taylor and Hubert Dreyfus call *Gestalt Holism*.

I Bavinck's Thomas and Roman Catholic epistemology

Bavinck recognized that Aristotle was perhaps the first thinker to conceive of reality as an organism and a developing whole with a *telos*: '[Aristotle] derived his theory of becoming from the facts of organic life, seeing in it a self-actualizing of the essential being in the phenomena, of the form in the matter.'[8] The notion that reality develops as a single whole, though reconceived by some into a materialistic doctrine of evolution, Bavinck notes, is reinterpreted by and developed from Aristotle throughout philosophical and theological history up until modern and Romantic thought:

> This idea of [organic] development aroused no objection whatever in Christian theology and philosophy. On the contrary, it received *extension and enrichment*

---

[8] Herman Bavinck, *Philosophy of Revelation: A New Annotated Edition*, Cory Brock and Nathaniel Gray Sutanto (eds) (Peabody: Hendrickson, 2018), p. 10. See also Bernard Mulcahy, *Aquinas's Notion of Pure Nature and the Christian Integralism of Henri de Lubac: Not Everything is Grace* (New York: Peter Lang, 2011), p. 98 on Aristotle's organic account of science. Cf. Bavinck *Christelijke wereldbeschouwing*, p. 55.

by being linked with the principle of theism. For the essence of it, it appears also in modern philosophy, in Lessing, Herder and Goethe, Schelling and Hegel, and in many historians of distinction. Some of these, it is true, have severed the idea of development from the theistic basis on which it rest in Christianity, and by so doing have reverted to the ancient pre-Christian naturalism. ... Whatever terms Goethe and Herder, Schelling and Hegel might employ to designate the core and essence of things, they never regarded nature as a *dead mechanism*, but as an eternally formative power, a creative artist.[9]

Despite this recognition, however, Bavinck characterized Roman Catholic epistemology as a whole as inorganic, in contrast to the organicist character of the romantic era and the movements within the Reformation. Here, I shall detail those criticisms, particularly in the *Reformed Dogmatics*, before I then turn to the recent criticisms of Bavinck's interpretation, considering whether it is as outdated as some claim.

Bavinck's take on Thomas should be situated in his claim that Christianity is a vital reality that ought to leaven the rest of society – an aim not fully realized unless the principles of the Reformation are rigorously followed:

In [both Pietism and Methodism] there is a failure to appreciate the activity of the Holy Spirit, the preparation of grace, and the connection between creation and re-creation. That is also the reason why in neither of them does the conversion lead to a truly developed Christian life. Whether in Pietistic fashion it withdraws from the world or in Methodist style acts aggressively in the world, it is always something separate, something that stands dualistically alongside the natural life, and therefore does not have an organic impact on the family, society, and the state, on science and art. ... The Reformation antithesis between sin and grace has more or less made way for the Catholic antithesis between the natural and the supernatural.[10]

Bavinck regards the lack of an organic understanding between creation and re-creation, between faith and reason with regard to *wetenschap* as one of the 'defects' that cling to past endeavours towards developing Christian scholarship. He writes:

The first [defect] were faith and reason, although [they] were initially closely united and harmoniously connected, [they] were soon after once again torn apart and loosely placed side by side. Each of the two brought its own set of truths. So, there were supernatural truths, which were accepted on account of authority; and beside

---

[9] Bavinck, *Philosophy of Revelation*, p. 10. Emphases mine. For Hegel's development of Aristotle, especially in his *Phenomenology of Spirit*, see Nicholas Adams, *Eclipse of Grace: Divine and Human Action in Hegel* (Oxford: Wiley-Blackwell, 2013), pp. 17–117 and Allegra de Laurentis, 'Absolute Knowing', in Kenneth Westphal (ed.), *The Blackwell Guide to Hegel's Phenomenology of Spirit* (Oxford: Wiley-Blackwell, 2009), pp. 246–64. On Hegel's use of Aristotle outside of the *Phenomenology*, see Alfredo Ferrarin, *Hegel and Aristotle* (Cambridge: Cambridge University Press, 2001). Bavinck's observation and the current scholarship thus further suggest that a claim of opposition between Aristotelian realism and modern absolute idealism must be articulated with great nuance and care.

[10] Bavinck, *RD*, 3: p. 568.

it stood also natural truths which could be found by reason. *There* exclusively and only faith alone was possible, *here* pure and accurate knowledge was accessible. The result was that these two truths were separated and stood side by side and finally some were even led to the opinion that truth itself was not one, but that which was true in philosophy could in essence be false in theology, and vice versa.[11]

Another clearer statement, perhaps, is found in Bavinck's address on the catholicity of the church, as seen in these two statements:

> It is not difficult from this to see how it became necessary for Rome to set itself over against culture, the state, society, science, and art. According to Rome, Christianity is exclusively church. Everything depends on this. Outside the church is the sphere of the unholy.[12]

> Rome thus maintains the catholicity of the Christian faith in the sense that it seeks to bring the entire world under the submission of the church. But it denies catholicity in the sense that the Christian faith itself must be a leavening agent in everything. In this way an eternal dualism remains, Christianity does not become an immanent, reformed reality. This dualism is not an antinomy in which one of the realities annuls the other. Rome does not abolish the natural order in Manicheaen fashion but suppresses it. It leaves marriage, family, possessions, earthly vocations, the state, science, and art intact and even permits them, in their own place, a greater space and freedom than Protestantism tends to do. Nonetheless it downgrades the natural by stamping it as profane and unhallowed.[13]

It is thus important to be clear that Bavinck is not denying that Rome sees revelation as the authority over human thought or that theology is the queen of the sciences. Rather, the critique here, it seems, is that Rome fails to endorse that the Christian faith and conversion ought *also* to have a leavening influence in all spheres of life.[14] Rome

---

[11] Bavinck, *Christelijke wetenschap*, p. 17. Dutch original: 'Ten eerste werden geloof en rede, ofschoon aanvankelijk ten nauwste vereenigd en harmonisch verbonden, spoedig weder uit elkaar gerukt en los naast elkander geplaatst. Ieder van beide bracht zijn eigen stel waarheden mede. Er waren dus bovennatuurlijke waarheden, die op gezag werden aangenomen; en daarnaast bestonden er ook natuurlijke waarheden, die door de rede gevonden konden worden. *Daar* was enkel en alleen geloof mogelijk, *hier* was zuiver en nauwkeurig weten bereikbaar. Het gevolg daarvan was, dat deze beide waarheden gescheiden naast elkander stonden en ten slotte bij sommigen zelfs leidden tot de meening, dat de waarheid zelve niet één was, maar dat hetgeen waar was in de philosophie, valsch kon wezen in de theologie en omgekeerd.' Sameer Yadav recently registers the same concerns when he writes that 'most attempts to articulate a principled way of distinguishing theological inquiry from philosophical inquiry strikes [him] as wrongheaded.' Further, 'Thomists in particular are often inclined to marking out which issues "properly" belong to theologians and which to philosophers.' *The Problem of Perception and the Experience of God: Toward a Theological Empiricism* (Minnesota: Fortress Press, 2015), p. 75 and 75, n. 13, respectively.
[12] Bavinck, 'The Catholicity of Christianity and the Church', p. 230.
[13] Bavinck, 'The Catholicity of Christianity and the Church', p. 231.
[14] One may see a contrast in Alister McGrath, who argued that theology is not to be considered as the 'queen of the sciences' but rather as the 'base, not the apex, of the sciences'. *A Scientific Theology*, vol. 2: *Reality* (London: T&T Clark, 2007), p. 229. For Bavinck, theology is *both* the apex and the base; in his judgement (with McGrath), Roman Catholicism sees theology merely as the apex.

has a solely vertical direction, whereas the Reformation has a distinctly horizontal dimension that Rome lacks. This is the difference, per Bavinck, between an organic account of nature and grace and a Roman Catholic account. In this sense, Eglinton's distinction between the non-antithetical dualism of Rome and the antithetical dualism of Bavinck is accurate.[15] The former fails to confront the individual in such a way that a false dichotomy emerges: either a complacency content with the natural life ensues or it is avoided altogether in pursuit of the supernatural.

Bavinck's criticisms of Thomas Aquinas should be understood in this context – that of Thomas as a frequent dialogue partner in relation to Bavinck's articulation of an organic worldview and Christianity's leavening character. Bavinck understands Thomas to hold a vertical epistemological dualism, where there are natural, rational truths at the bottom with relative independence from the theological truths in the second level. The theological level may confirm or clarify some aspects of the truths of reason, but this bottom level enjoys a high degree of epistemological self-sufficiency, despite it being soteriologically insufficient.[16]

Bavinck criticizes Thomas in many ways, but at least three interconnected criticisms from his *Prolegomena* alone are relevant for our present purpose. The objections involve (1) an inadequate appreciation of common grace, (2) a strong distinction between nature and supernature and (3) an insufficient use of Scripture.

First, in Thomas there is an insufficient account of the necessity of common grace in natural affairs. In the *Reformed Dogmatics*, Bavinck observes, 'In the Middle Ages Thomas not only asserted that as rational human beings can – without supernatural grace – know natural truths', which leads to the later perceived sufficiency of natural theology.[17] He also argues that the Reformation countered this by their implementation of common grace: 'By it they were protected, on the one hand, from the Pelagian error, which taught the sufficiency of natural theology ... but could, on the other hand, recognize all the truth beauty, and goodness that is present also in the pagan world.'[18] As such, while Roman Catholicism can commend the existence of science and art on the basis of nature alone, Bavinck insists that 'science, art, moral, domestic, and social life, etc., were derived from that common grace and acknowledged and commended with gratitude'.[19] The Reformation restored these convictions 'in opposition to the Roman view that the *naturalia integra supernaturalia amissa* ("natural gifts have remained and only the supernatural lost")'.[20]

Bavinck reiterates this in his discussion of apologetics. After observing with appreciation the historical character of the apologetics found in the biblical period,

---

[15] Eglinton, *Trinity and Organism*, pp. 40–1, 96. This is rather different from Sytsma's interpretation that Bavinck follows the dictum of grace perfecting nature, in 'Thomistic Epistemology', p. 8, n. 22. Bavinck uses the dictum, as Sytsma notes, in *RD*, 1: p. 322. However, in context Bavinck is admitting only a *sense* in which the dictum is right, namely that grace finds its context in nature and takes it to its end.

[16] On Bavinck's agreement with Thomas that general revelation is soteriologically insufficient, see *RD*, 1: p. 312–14.

[17] Bavinck, *RD*, 1: p. 319.

[18] Bavinck, *RD*, 1: p. 319.

[19] Bavinck, *RD*, 1: p. 319. Bavinck cites Calvin, Witsius and Turretin, among others.

[20] Bavinck, *Philosophy of Revelation*, p. 164. See also pp. 40, 42–3.

Bavinck argues that 'these arguments were later taken over in Christian theology but in the process frequently changed in position and character.'[21] This change, though based on faith, evolved into a two-tiered epistemology:

> Scholasticism ... in its attempt to turn the truth of faith into the content of reason, in time created a division between natural and supernatural truths, a division that had a detrimental effect on both. For the former could be established by reason, but the latter could only be accepted on authority. In the former, therefore, *real science was possible*; in the latter there was room only for faith.[22]

It was this division that led to the development of rationalistic apologetics, whereby the truths of special revelation became dependent upon a justificatory preamble of natural theology. Bavinck's admission that there is a sense in which the truths of nature comprise a preamble is therefore rather different from Rome's in important respects, at least in his perspective.[23] For Bavinck, it means simply that the truths of special revelation connect with the truths of general revelation, whereas for Rome the latter erects the foundations and motivations for belief in the former.[24] Again, Bavinck emphasizes that on this natural level 'science is even possible'.[25]

Second, Bavinck critiques Thomas's supernaturalism, according to which theological matters are set above natural matters. This is apparent in the practice of natural theology so advocated by medieval scholastic thought, where some truths of God could be known by natural reason, while other supernatural, mysterious truths are known by authority alone, accepted in meritorious faith.[26] As a result, in this 'Catholic theology knowing and believing, reason and authority, natural and supernatural revelation, occur dualistically side by side.'[27] The Reformation encountered this structure directly in their insistence that illumination and special revelation are necessary to read general revelation aright.[28] The Catholic division is detrimental because it fails to uphold the bond between general and special revelation, causing reason gradually

---

[21] Bavinck, *RD*, 1: p. 510.
[22] Bavinck, *RD*, 1: p. 510. Emphasis mine. Bavinck cites Thomas as one representative of this scholastic position. Alvin Plantinga registers the same criticism in 'Augustinian Christian Philosophy', *The Monist* 75 (1992): pp. 316–20. So, Diller: '[In the *locus classicus* of *Summa Theoloiae* I. q. 12] we find that faith's advantages over reason have to do with the limitations of reason. Knowledge by faith, however, is without intellectual vision and therefore lacks real understanding. Knowledge of God's essence is not available in this mortal life but awaits the beatific vision that surpasses faith because it is a direct seeing'. *Theology's Epistemological Dilemma; How Karl Barth and Alvin Plantinga Provide a Unified Response* (Downers Grove: IVP Academic, 2014), p. 200, n. 90.
[23] See Bavinck, *RD*, 1: p. 322.
[24] Bavinck, *RD*, 1: p. 512. Norman Kretzmann seems to express the sort of interpretation of Thomas that Bavinck has in mind, according to which natural theology 'offers the best route by which philosophers can, as philosophers, approach theological propositions'. *The Metaphysics of Theism: Aquinas's Natural Theology in Summa Contra Gentiles* (Oxford: Clarendon Press, 1997), p. 22.
[25] Bavinck, *RD*, 1: p. 512.
[26] Bavinck, *RD*, 1: pp. 304, 571–2, 620–1.
[27] Bavinck, *RD*, 1: p. 304. Cf. Matthew Levering, *Proofs of God: Classical Arguments from Tertullian to Barth* (Grand Rapids: Baker Academic, 2016), p. 60.
[28] Bavinck, *RD*, 1: p. 304. To make sense of Bavinck's claim here, one could remember the distinction between *God's* revelation, which renders all men inexcusable, and the unregenerate individual's reception and expression of that revelation, which in Reformed theology always produces false

to gain autonomy. When this bond is severed, even the Reformed were vulnerable to its negative consequences: 'In civil matters, then in science, soon also in philosophy, [within the Reformed] reason elevated itself to a position alongside of and over against faith.'[29] This elevation of reason due to a dualistic understanding of natural and supernatural spheres is the same root problem behind what Bavinck considered to be common in medieval and historical–rationalist apologetics, something that, in Bavinck's judgement, even Calvin failed completely to avoid.[30] The scholastic model likewise depended so much on Aristotle that their dogmatic system slowly became a system of philosophy.[31]

Bavinck detects this dualism in Thomas's classification of the virtues as well. For Thomas, theological virtues are set apart because their object is directed towards God: 'The intellectual and moral virtues are according to human nature, the theological virtues are above nature.'[32] Intellectual virtues include wisdom, knowledge and understanding, while religious disposition falls under moral virtue. Bavinck argues that this distinction cannot be maintained because of its dualistic character, for the 'moral virtues and also the religious disposition must be renewed and reborn to be truly good.'[33] The Reformation therefore rightly remedies this dualism when it incorporates theological virtues 'into religion itself as the primary acts of internal religion'.[34]

Finally, Thomas omits a discussion on the doctrine of Scripture in the beginning of his dogmatic structure. Because of this, Bavinck judges Thomas's organization as 'inferior' to Bonaventure's, who by contrast included a doctrine of Scripture in the prologue to his *Breviloquium*.[35] Instead, Thomas treated the essence of theology first, which led to the doctrine of the preambles of faith in scholasticism. Characteristically, Bavinck commends the Reformed for countering this in their insistence that theological foundations are necessary for dogmatics, as represented by Calvin's *Institutes*. 'The starting point of the *Institutes* is theological, but Calvin does not proceed from an abstract concept of God but from God as he is known by humanity and nature and Scripture.'[36] Later Protestant Scholasticism, however, reverted back to the old order and thus further severed the connection of dogmatics with the 'life of faith'.[37] This observation is significant because in Bavinck's insistence that a doctrine of Scripture be placed first in the organization of dogmatics, he resists the dualistic structure he thinks is characteristic of both Thomistic epistemology in general and dogmatics in particular.[38]

---

theology. Willem J. Van Asselt, 'The Fundamental Meaning of Theology: Archetypal and Ectypal Theology in Seventeenth-Century Reformed Thought', *WTJ* 64 (2002): pp. 323, 325.

[29] Bavinck, *RD*, 1: p. 306.
[30] Bavinck, *RD*, 1: pp. 512–13.
[31] Bavinck, *RD*, 1: pp. 145–6.
[32] Bavinck, *RD*, 1: p. 240. Thomas's discussion of the virtues is, for Bavinck, not yet a mature acknowledgement of the subjective side of religion, which Bavinck traces from the Reformation unto modern thought.
[33] Bavinck, *RD*, 1: p. 240.
[34] Bavinck, *RD*, 1: p. 240.
[35] Bavinck, *RD*, 1: pp. 98–9.
[36] Bavinck, *RD*, 1: p. 101.
[37] Bavinck, *RD*, 1: p. 102.
[38] For a fruitful recent Reformed account that utilizes Aquinas on the relationship between Scripture and natural knowledge, see Steven Duby, 'Scripture as Cognitive Principle of Christian Dogmatics', *Neue Zeitschrift für Systematische Theologie und Religionsphilosophie* 61 (2019): pp. 223–40.

II 'Bavinck's mistake': Re-situating Bavinck's account of Thomas within the current internal Thomist debates

It would be beyond the scope of the present study to enter into the debates of current scholarship on Thomas Aquinas regarding the accuracy of Bavinck's critiques of Thomas. However, given the existence of recent and rather harsh criticisms of Bavinck regarding his interpretation of Thomas, it is appropriate to draw some implications from the interpretation of Bavinck offered here that might be relevant to those critiques. What I attempt, therefore, is not an assessment of Bavinck's interpretation of Thomas but rather a preliminary assessment of the critiques launched against Bavinck, generated by his interpretation of Thomas. Fortunately for the present purposes, whether Bavinck's interpretation of Thomas is correct need not be adjudicated here because it would require a close investigation of the primary texts and the in-house Thomist debates. Situating Bavinck's criticisms within the current stream of debates internal to the scholarship on Thomas is sufficient not to discredit Bavinck's account and to better appreciate Bavinck's organic concerns.

The criticisms against Bavinck's reading of Thomas revolve centrally around the claim that Bavinck's reading is dependent upon an outdated nineteenth-century interpretation of Thomas. Following Echeverria and Arvin Vos, John Bolt argues that Bavinck's interpretation depends on Cajetan and neo-scholastic readings of Thomas.[39] Bolt claims that this interpretation has been decisively 'discredited' in recent decades by proponents of the *nouvelle theologie*, 'who insisted that human reason always operates within a teleology of belief and unbelief'.[40] Catholic theology and Aquinas in particular do not hold a '*duplex ordo* of natural knowledge and supernatural knowledge', nor does Rome operate 'in a two-tiered epistemological universe'.[41] Bavinck was merely a 'child of his time' who fell into the 'trap' of reading Thomas through the lens of the 'sixteenth-, seventeenth-, and especially nineteenth-century neo-scholastic' interpreters.[42] Furthermore, the noetic effects of sin in Aquinas, argues Bolt, lead to the view that human natural knowledge of God does not purchase true divine cognition.[43]

---

[39] Bolt, 'An Adventure in Ecumenicity', pp. 76–89. Arvin Vos, *Aquinas, Calvin, and Contemporary Protestant Thought: A Critique of Protestant Views on the Thought of Thomas Aquinas* (Grand Rapids: Eerdmans, 1985). In another place, Bolt argued that 'Bavinck himself contributed to the problem [of anti-Thomism] with his general assessment of Roman Catholic thought but also provided the basis for an antidote [by rejecting von Harnack's "hellenization thesis"]', 'Doubting Reformational Anti-Thomism', in Manfred Svensson and David VanDrunen (eds), *Aquinas Among the Protestants* (Oxford: Wiley-Blackwell, 2017), p. 131.

[40] Bolt, 'An Adventure in Ecumenicity', p. 80.

[41] Bolt, 'An Adventure in Ecumenicity', p. 78.

[42] Bolt, 'An Adventure in Ecumenicity', p. 80.

[43] Bolt, 'An Adventure in Ecumenicity', p. 80. Bolt cites Eugene F. Rogers, Jr, 'The Narrative of Natural Law in Aquinas' Commentary on Romans 1', *Theological Studies* 59 (1998): pp. 254–76. Chapter 7 returns to this topic. Bolt, insofar as he is missing that revelation might be *felt* rather than accessed by reason, might still be missing Bavinck's central concerns.

Paul Helm also launches an identical critique of Bavinck. Neo-Calvinism, in Helm's view, has as a whole misunderstood the natural law position and Thomas:

> This misunderstanding has taken the form of frequent warnings against the nature-grace 'dichotomy' or 'dualism', according to which 'pure nature' is the intact human state unaffected by the Fall, except for the loss of the *donum superadditum*. This view is in fact the brainchild of various Roman Catholic Counter-Reformation theologians. In rejecting it, and condemning it as Pelagian in contrast to the Augustinianism of the Reformation, the Reformed theologians who did so also mistakenly turned their backs on the entire mediaeval tradition. For the retention of 'pure nature' was most certainly not Thomas Aquinas's estimate of the effect of the Fall on human nature, for example, yet it came to be regarded by Reformed thinkers such as Kuyper and Herman Bavinck as the standard, unchanging Roman view.[44]

In another place, Helm identifies Bavinck's neo-Calvinistic interpretation of Calvin and negative evaluation of Thomas's alleged 'pure nature' theology as simply 'Bavinck's mistake'.[45] Again, Helm argues that Bavinck's criticisms of Thomas were dependent on Counter-Reformational theologians like Cajetan and Bellarmine – readings that have been challenged by Henri de Lubac and Arvin Vos.[46]

It must be acknowledged, first, that the theology propounded by the thinkers stemming from the *nouvelle theologie* marks a significant strand in contemporary Roman Catholic thought, distinct from the theology espoused by neo-scholasticism, and often congenial with Bavinck and Kuyper's neo-Calvinistic emphasis on the intrinsic relationship between nature and grace. It must also be emphasized that Thomas's thinking is complex, perhaps suggesting that Bavinck's interpretation of him merits more critical attention by a closer reading of both primary texts, coupled with a fair attention to internal debates concerning Thomas's views. Indeed, great thinkers often generate such discussions and disagreements concerning how best to interpret their writings.[47]

However, I suggest two brief assessments of these charges. First, I argue that discrediting Bavinck's interpretation of Thomas as an advocate of a two-tiered epistemology, with a concomitant commitment to a 'pure nature' theology, would be too quick. There are still many Catholic theologians and interpreters of Thomas who interpret him in precisely this way, as Echeverria admits.[48] After observing this intra-

---

[44] Helm, 'Religion and Reason from a Reformed Perspective', p. 69.

[45] Paul Helm, *Calvin at the Centre* (Oxford: Oxford University Press, 2010), pp. 328–32. James Eglinton includes Helm's critique within a recent 'back-lash' against neo-Calvinism. For this observation and a preliminary response, see James Eglinton, 'To Transcend and to Transform: The Neo-Calvinist Relationship of Church and Cultural Transformation', in John Bowlin (ed.), *The Kuyper Center Review*, vol. 3: *Calvinism and Culture* (Grand Rapids: Eerdmans, 2013), pp. 163–97.

[46] Helm, *Calvin at the Centre*, p. 312.

[47] The debates around how to interpret Hegel or Barth, for examples, also come to mind.

[48] 'I do not mean to deny that there have been and still are Catholic rationalists of this sort, but such rationalism is a corruption of Aquinas' thought and by implication the teaching of Vatican 1.' Eduardo Echeverria, 'The Reformed Objection to Natural Theology: A Catholic Response to Herman Bavinck', *Calvin Theological Journal* 45 (2010): p. 99. However, this assertion seems to beg the question. The Catholic theologians that Echeverria has in mind do not believe they are corrupting Aquinas's thought.

Roman Catholic debate from both a general and particularized perspective, I shall build upon the arguments of some recent work by Vanhoozer, Smith and Webster, and suggest that Bavinck's organic epistemology and interpretation of Thomas are critiqued because substantive disagreements exist between his critics and Bavinck himself.

First, then, this section makes some general observations regarding the ongoing character of this debate, and then it situates Bavinck's interpretation within a recent resurgence of the 'pure nature' interpretation of Thomas in the last decade.[49]

Linda Zagzebski, for example, says that the extent and powers of natural human reason still form the question that distinguishes Protestant and Catholic accounts of knowledge:

> Although both traditions agree that natural human faculties have suffered damage as a result of original sin, Catholic theology has commonly maintained that the will suffered more than the intellect, and that our powers of reasoning can still hope to achieve much that points the way to Christian belief. Catholic philosophy also has a long tradition of natural law, which implies that our reason is a potent source of knowledge about moral matters. The extension to matters metaphysical is relatively easy. The idea is that both moral and metaphysical knowledge have important underpinnings in the knowledge of human nature, and the knowledge of human nature is within the reach of ordinary human reason.[50]

Likewise, in a dialogue with Gavin D'Costa, Oliver Crisp argues,

> The Reformed traditionally have denied the adage, beloved of some Thomists, that grace perfects nature. They have replied, instead, that grace regenerates nature, redirecting it back to God by repairing what has been damaged, or almost effaced (Calvin says both things at different times in his works). That which has been damaged or almost effaced, is of course, the divine image and its concomitant in Reformed theology, the sense of the divine. So it is not merely that grace must perfect that which is imperfect, but functional. It is more that grace must repair what is severely damaged.[51]

---

[49] Though the following debate is not recognized by the current critics of Bavinck, Kevin Vanhoozer offers a significant interaction with it in *Biblical Authority after Babel: Retrieving the Solas in The Spirit of Mere Protestant Christianity* (Grand Rapids: Brazos, 2016), pp. 44–50.

[50] Linda Zagzebski, introduction to *Rational Faith: Catholic Responses to Reformed Epistemology*, Linda Zagzebski (ed.), Library of Religious Philosophy 10 (Notre Dame: University of Notre Dame Press, 1993), pp. 3–4. James Turner likewise remarks that for Rome 'faith gives no *epistemological edge*'. In Mark A. Noll and James Turner, *The Future of Christian Learning: An Evangelical and Catholic Dialogue*, Thomas A. Howard (ed.) (Grand Rapids: Brazos, 2008), p. 106. One may add Diller's observation as well concerning Plantinga: 'Plantinga rejects [the] Thomist characterization of faith and knowledge, and recommends an Augustinian view. On this view knowing something by way of testimony is not necessarily inferior to knowing something by way of deductive argument.' *Theology's Epistemological Dilemma*, p. 200.

[51] Oliver D. Crisp, 'On Being a Reformed Theologian', *Theology* 115 (2012): p. 21. If one believes that the sense of the divine refers to the content of the knowledge of God produced by the Logos, perhaps it is more accurate to say that the sense of the divine is suppressed, rather than damaged.

In response, D'Costa does not deny Crisp's observation, except to admit that not all Thomists affirm the adage that 'grace perfects nature'.[52] Indeed, this provokes the suggestion that there is no single interpretation of Thomas that is established to the point that other interpretations could be so easily discredited. Michael Rota argues that Thomas was no evidentialist,[53] while others contend for the opposite.[54] Furthermore, Bavinck's observation in the previous section regarding Bonaventure's superior sensitivity over Aquinas concerning the grounding of philosophy in Scriptural revelation is also still echoed quite recently by Larry Siedentop:

> No doubt [Bonaventure, Albert the Great, and Thomas Aquinas] claimed to reject 'pagan' philosophy when it conflicted with Christian revelation. Yet Bonaventure remained within the Augustinian tradition – concerned, above all, with relating the individual will to God's will – while adapting some arguments from Aristotle. Albert the Great and Thomas Aquinas, on the other hand, sought to integrate far more of Aristotle … with Christianity.[55]

Provocatively, Rik van Nieuwenhove suggests that integralist interpreters of Thomas may be (wrongly) motivated by the post-Barthian anxiety to deny that philosophical reason can be used as a preamble to dogmatic construction, leading them mistakenly to mute the demonstrative character of Thomas's use of philosophy.[56] Fergus Kerr argues that current interpretations of Thomas are incommensurably conflicting,[57] while Matthew Levering also affirms that later interpreters of Thomas read him in a dualist manner 'not due to ill-will or rationalism, but because of the divergence in what he says at various places'.[58]

---

[52] Personal correspondence between Crisp and D'Costa, cited in Crisp, 'On Being a Reformed Theologian', p. 25, n. 13.

[53] Michael Rota, 'What Aristotelian and Thomistic Philosophy Can Contribute to Christian Theology', in Oliver D. Crisp, Gavin D'Costa, Mervyn Davies and Peter Hampson (eds), *Theology and Philosophy* (London: T&T Clark, 2012), p. 112. He gives a nice and short summary on the various 'Thomist' views on page 113, n. 1.

[54] See Hugo Meynell, 'Faith, Foundationalism, and Nicholas Wolterstorff', in Linda Zagzebski (ed.), *Rational Faith: Catholic Responses to Reformed Epistemology*, Library of Religious Philosophy 10 (Notre Dame: University of Notre Dame Press, 1993), pp. 79–109; Ralph MacInerny, *Praembula Fidei: Thomism and the God of the Philosophers* (Indiana: Catholic University of America Press, 2006).

[55] Larry Siedentop, *Inventing the Individual: The Origins of Western Liberalism* (United Kingdom: Penguin Books, 2014), p. 298. For an account of the debate regarding whether Aquinas falls within the Augustinian tradition, and an argument for the conclusion that he is indeed within that tradition in his account of the image of God, knowledge and illumination, see Lydia Schumacher, *Divine Illumination: The History and Future of Augustine's Theory of Knowledge* (Oxford: Wiley & Blackwell, 2011), pp. 155–80.

[56] Rik van Nieuwenhove, *An Introduction to Medieval Theology* (Cambridge: Cambridge University Press, 2012), pp. 171–210. Elsewhere Van Nieuwenhove writes that the 'readings of those scholars who deny that Aquinas allows for a demonstration of the existence of God by the natural light, seem therefore rather problematic', 'Catholic Theology in the Thirteenth Century and the Origins of Secularism', *Irish Theological Quarterly* 75 (2010): p. 341.

[57] Fergus Kerr, *After Aquinas: Versions of Thomism* (Malden: Blackwell, 2002), pp. 15–16.

[58] Personal correspondence with Peter Leithart, cited in Peter Leithart, *Athanasius*, Foundations of Theological Exegesis and Christian Spirituality, Hans Boersma and Matthew Levering (eds) (Grand Rapids: Baker Academic, 2011), p. 188, n. 49.

Levering's illuminating comment sheds light on a recent resurgence of Catholic scholarship reacting against de Lubac's interpretation of Thomas. Indeed, some theologians in the last decade have argued that Cajetan's reading of Thomas is actually in keeping with Thomas's thinking and that de Lubac has misread Cajetan as well – accounts not sufficiently acknowledged by Bolt, Echeverria or Helm. Steven Long's work *Pura Natura* is one representative work. In it he calls for a return to the Thomistic doctrine of pure nature, which he thinks was expressed in Vatican I and *Aeterni Patris*.[59] Nature and natural reason ought to have its own relative autonomy and intelligibility apart from grace in order that the supernatural character of grace can be sufficiently appreciated.[60]

Bernard Mulcahy argues against the integralist account of nature and grace found in de Lubac and Radical Orthodoxy, particularly regarding natural law and Thomas's epistemology of the sciences:

> Thomas contends that the natural, God-given light of the human intellect is what makes the Gentiles (and, for that matter, all humans) 'a law to themselves'. Without revelation and even in our fallen state, human intelligence is able to frame general principles of right action.[61]

> There are, Aquinas observes, two kinds of sciences: those which use axioms recognized in the natural light of human understanding (such axioms as, for example, the principles of non-contradiction, identity, consistency, etc.) and those which use axioms recognized in the light of a yet higher science (as, for example, when mathematics or biology draws on logic). *Sacra doctrina* is a science of a second type. The superior science from which it derives its principles is, Thomas boldly declares, nothing less than the *scientia divina* itself, God's very own understanding, which is communicated to the angels and saints in the beatific version.[62]

Furthermore, following the observation that Thomas organizes the sciences by way of sub-alternation in which theology takes the highest supernatural level that builds on the lower natural sciences, he writes that theology and philosophy are ordered vertically in this way:

> [Thomas] compares the two ways of knowing, the natural (philosophical) and the supernatural (Christian and theological), and tells us that each has its own method. ... Against all psychological theories of supernatural illumination, Thomas insists that the natural human intellect is itself the means by which God creatively and providentially endows us with understanding. Our nature, he insists, is sufficient for its own intellectual activity: *no further intervention or illumination is needed for our natural knowing.*[63]

---

[59] Steven A. Long, *Natura Pura: On the Recovery of Nature in the Doctrine of Grace* (New York: Fordham University Press, 2011), p. 211.
[60] Long, *Natura Pura*, pp. 93–7, 155.
[61] Mulcahy, *Not Everything is Grace*, p. 88.
[62] Mulcahy, *Not Everything is Grace*, p. 103.
[63] Mulcahy, *Not Everything is Grace*, pp. 106–7. Emphasis mine. Mulcahy's account is especially relevant when one considers Wolter Huttinga's recent work in connecting Bavinck strongly with the theology of Millbank's *Radical Orthodoxy*. See Huttinga, *Participation and Communicability*.

Laurence Feingold, also arguing that the pure nature tradition finds its home within Thomism maintains that, contrary to de Lubac, the beatific vision is not constitutive of humanity's natural end. Rather, he draws from Thomas in his consideration that limbo is the purely natural end for the human soul, while the beatific vision is a supernatural end.[64] Although it never obtains concrete existence, pure nature can nonetheless be intelligible on its own as abstracted from its actual existential conditions. Thomas's metaphysical realism seems to imply that God is obligated to bestow the beatific vision universally if this were truly the natural eschatological end of humanity. This scenario serves to argue that integralist accounts of nature and grace undermine the gratuity of grace, rendering God wrongly vulnerable to charges of injustice.[65] These authors appeal to this kind of text from Thomas to establish the distinct ends and virtues of the natural from the supernatural:

> If man were ordained to no other end than that which is proportionate to his natural faculty, there would be no need for man to have any further direction the part of his reason, beside the natural law and human law which is derived from it. But since man is ordained to an end of eternal happiness which is disproportionate to man's natural faculty … it was necessary … that man should be directed to his end by a law given by God.[66]

Andrew Swafford gives a succinct summary of the pure nature tradition as represented by the Counter-Reformational readings of Thomas and the contemporary defenders of that tradition:

> For the pure nature tradition, human nature is self-contained and integral in its own right, and for that reason it has no strict exigency for anything beyond what is contained within the definition of nature. In this light, it cannot be said that grace is necessary for the functioning of human nature, for such a statement would negate the gratuity of grace.[67]

Hence, the above authors argue that Henri de Lubac is overconfident about his interpretation of Aquinas and that he simultaneously misrepresents the pure nature tradition. In effect, they argue that de Lubac often holds views in contradistinction to Thomas because of his conviction that a distinctly Christian expression of humanism is achievable.[68] As these texts convey, the pure nature Thomists are trying to preserve

---

[64] Laurence Feingold, *The Natural Desire to See God according to St. Thomas Aquinas and His Interpreters*, 2nd edn (Naples: Sapientia, 2010), pp. 235, 250.

[65] On this point de Lubac appeals to Ockham's dictum that God owes nothing to any creature, in direct opposition to Thomas. See Andrew Swafford's concise discussion of the *Debitum Naturae* in *Nature and Grace: A New Approach to Thomistic Ressourcement* (Cambridge: James Clark & Co, 2015), p. 82.

[66] Aquinas, *ST*, I-Iae, q. 91, a. 4. Quoted in Swafford, *Nature and Grace*, p. 134. Cf. *ST*, III, q. 9, a. 2; Steven A. Long, 'On the Possibility of a Purely Natural End for Man', *The Thomist* 64 (2000): pp. 211–37; see also the discussion in Steven A. Long, 'Obediential Potency, Human Knowledge, and the Natural Desire for God', *International Philosophical Quarterly* 37 (1997): pp. 49–51.

[67] Swafford, *Nature and Grace*, p. 47.

[68] Swafford, following Feingold and Long, argues that (1) de Lubac misses the distinction between specific/generic obediential potency in Cajetan and Thomas, (2) de Lubac wrongly rejects the

the important theological insight that grace does not merely bring nature to perfection but truly brings something new and gratuitous – something 'disproportionate' – to it.

The polemical tone of this debate between extrinsicist 'pure nature' Thomism and de Lubac's intrinsicist account has subsided, leading to Steven Long's admission that in Thomas there exists 'two sets of texts': one which lends itself to de Lubac's interpretation and the other to the pure nature tradition.[69] Swafford, who argues that the pure nature tradition (which he defends) is 'organically' developed from principles readily found in Thomas,[70] nevertheless concedes that Thomas is ambiguous:

> Let us state upfront that the exegetical questions [regarding whether Thomas Aquinas was a nature/grace dualist] is largely insoluble, since it all depends on which texts are interpretively privileged over others. One set of texts lends support to the legitimacy of the pure-nature tradition, while others clearly favor de Lubac.[71]

Nonetheless, the existence of current nuanced defences and advancements within the pure nature Thomistic tradition must be taken into account when considering Bavinck's criticisms. Failure to attend to the complexity of the debates internal to the current scholarship on Thomas may lead to facile dismissals of Bavinck's interpretation of Thomas. David Grumett likens this recent string of scholarship to a 'firing line' against de Lubac's retrieval of Thomas.[72] As a result, Grumett provides a reminder that de Lubac's project is a distinctly Augustinian one. He in turn argues that de Lubac himself acknowledged the existence of significant differences between Thomas and Augustine, such that the question of whether an appeal to Thomas is necessary at all to follow de Lubac's integralism arises. In Grumett's words,

> In this article it has been clearly shown, however, that the primary theological inspiration for de Lubac's theology of grace and nature was neither Thomism nor secularism, but Augustinianism. De Lubac necessarily engaged Thomas in order to develop an alternative to contemporary neo-Thomist readings of him. In so doing, de Lubac elucidated Thomas's Augustinian heritage and showed how Thomas consciously used Augustine rather than read him neutrally. De Lubac thereby proved that real theological choices needed to be made between Augustine and Thomas, and that the notion that their theologies could be melded into an overarching 'orthodoxy' was untenable.[73]

---

debitum naturae because he has a more voluntaristic account of what God owes to natural man, whereas the proponents of the pure nature tradition are more consistent realists and (3) de Lubac also misses that Thomas considers it possible to abstract 'pure nature' apart from its existential concrete instantiations, such that a natural end is distinguished from a final end. On this third point, Keith Johnson also provides a brief outline on the internal Thomist debate on the matter in *Karl Barth and the Analogia Entis*, pp. 76–7.

[69] Long, *Natura Pura*, pp. 12–13.
[70] Swafford, *Nature and Grace*, 37.
[71] Swafford, *Nature and Grace*, p. 37. Swafford finally argues that Matthias J. Scheeben's theology provides a middle way that preserves the virtues of both interpretations. See *Nature and Grace*, pp. 143–94.
[72] David Grumett, 'De Lubac, Grace, and the Pure Nature Debate', *Modern Theology* 31 (2015): p. 124.
[73] Grumett, 'De Lubac, Grace, and the Pure Nature Debate', p. 138.

Given the lively character of the debates between thinkers representing various streams of theology on Thomas, a charitable reading of Bavinck would perhaps suggest that he is not simply 'trapped' as a passive recipient of the intellectual climate of his day. Bavinck's critique of Thomas is quite in line with the 'pure nature' Thomism still propelled today. Further, the extensive manner in which Bavinck engages with Thomas directly (along with other Catholic theologians contemporary to his time) points to the conclusion that Bavinck was not merely dependent on secondary readings of Aquinas. It is thus better to suggest that Bavinck offers a reading of Thomas consistent with one voice within ongoing discussion, namely, with the 'pure nature' interpretation still asserted in the present day.

Secondly, Peter Leithart has argued that the retrieval efforts of Thomas by Henri de Lubac and the *nouvelle theologie* do not escape the dualism between nature and grace they found problematic within neo-scholasticism. Leithart argues that de Lubac still reasons, at times, as if nature and supernature were in opposition in his attempt to preserve the gratuity of the supernatural.[74] Despite making significant improvements, the debates between Rahner and de Lubac and the pure nature Thomists show that they often spoke as if nature and supernature were opposed rather than connected while neglecting sufficiently to acknowledge the fallenness of creatures. Because of this, Leithart suggests that the terminology of nature/supernature should be reconsidered, pointing to Athanasius's biblicization of metaphysics instead as a way forward in order to recapture a metaphysical vision in which ontology is fundamentally found within an economy of divine grace. Kevin Vanhoozer expresses similar frustrations to the in-house debates on interpreting Thomas and summarizes the issues by following Leithart's judgement:

> Peter Leithart speaks for many Protestants when, observing this intra-Catholic debate, he comments that the problem is that both neoscholastics and their *nouvelle* detractors appear to chalk up humanity's distance from God to their createdness, not fallenness. On the contrary: the problem is not that God (or the supernatural) is 'external' to creation but rather that the whole realm of creation has become alienated from God through sin ... not because human nature has by grace been 'elevated' but because human sinners (persons) have by grace been forgiven.[75]

Significant to the present purpose, Vanhoozer connects these claims explicitly to Herman Bavinck's 'observation that grace is not opposed to nature but to sin'[76] precisely because created existence already participates in 'grace': 'The gospel of Jesus Christ presupposes an ontology of grace, consists in an economy of grace, and continues in a teleology of grace.'[77] These points link well with Bavinck's emphasis on the necessity of common grace and his ambivalence towards making a distinction between natural and

---

[74] Leithart, *Athanasius*, p. 37.
[75] Vanhoozer, *Biblical Authority after Babel*, p. 49.
[76] Vanhoozer, *Biblical Authority after Babel*, p. 50.
[77] Vanhoozer, *Biblical Authority after Babel*, p. 49. On the same page Vanhoozer connects this to the idea that, for the Reformation, 'grace does not simply perfect or complete but restores and transforms nature.'

supernatural revelation, preferring instead to emphasize the organic unity of general and special revelation and the all-encompassing supernatural character of revelation.[78] In James K. A. Smith's recent iteration, because 'creation is reaffirmed in Christ's resurrection, and because "nature" is only known "in Christ", any Christian account of even our "this-worldly" life has to be unapologetically *evangelical*, rooted in what we know in – and because of – the gospel.'[79]

Building upon Vanhoozer, Leithart and Smith here, I suggest that Bolt's (and Helm's) critiques of Herman Bavinck are materially motivated by the rather tenuous relationship between their epistemologies and Bavinck's, as evidenced by their explicit critiques of Bavinck's epistemology.

Bolt's alternative, hinted at above, is to argue that the Bible (or, special revelation) could not be used to construct a biblical philosophy; rather, it is best to say that 'a particular philosophy or view of the human person' is appropriately '*consistent with* or *at odds with* biblical teaching about the image of God'.[80] Indeed, Bolt argues that Bavinck started a misguided trajectory of Biblicism, which led to the birth of Dooyeweerd's Reformational philosophy, and an unending regress of mistaken attempts at 'purifying' one's worldview.[81] Despite critiquing the Hellenization thesis of Adolf von Harnack, Bolt maintains that 'Bavinck himself contributed to the problem with his general assessment of Roman Catholic thought.'[82] Thus, though the Bible may inform our philosophical endeavours, it is misguided to seek a 'biblical' or truly Christian philosophy because this is not what the Bible is for. Here, in Bolt's direct critique of Bavinck, the differences between the two thinkers emerge. For Bavinck, as previously noted, a truly 'Christian treatment' of philosophy can be developed.[83]

Human beings are not mechanical creatures that can siphon off one 'set' of propositions from another. Indeed, image bearers of God who are embodied as psychosomatic wholes come to topics with all that they know.[84] The relationship between nature and grace and the truths of general and special revelation do not pose two parallel lines or two hermetically sealed silos that do not interact with one another. They are all known organically in the consciousness of creatures. As such, Bavinck rejects a methodological atomism that prioritizes the acquisition of knowledge by way of quantitative addition and a structure that implies a two-tiered epistemology.[85]

---

[78] Leithart, *Athanasius*, pp. 89–116; Bavinck, *RD*, 1: pp. 307–12.

[79] Smith, *Awaiting the King*, p. 156. Emphasis in original. Cf. Craig G. Bartholomew, *Contours of the Kuyperian Tradition* (Downers Grove: IVP Academic, 2017), pp. 45–75.

[80] Bolt, 'An Adventure in Ecumenicity', p. 88, emphases in original.

[81] Bolt, 'An Adventure in Ecumenicity', pp. 86–8. In Bolt's view, this regress is a negative one. But this is not necessarily so – perhaps, in the eyes of someone engaged in Reformational philosophy this work is not regress but simply a development of scholarship.

[82] Bolt, 'Doubting Reformational Anti-Thomism', p. 131.

[83] See the above discussion on Bavinck, 'Theology and Religious Studies', p. 59.

[84] For a model of human knowing congenial to Bavinck's, see Hubert Dreyfus and Charles Taylor, *Retrieving Realism* (Cambridge: Harvard University Press, 2015). For more information on this, see below on gestalt holism.

[85] Bavinck implies that the method of 'quantitative addition' is connected with an inorganic epistemology when he rejects the notion of a 'hierarchy of truths' with regard to the articles of faith: 'Faith on the side of the Reformation, however, is special (*fides specialis*) with a particular central object: the grace of God in Christ. Here an arithmetic addition of articles, the knowledge of which and the assent to which is necessary for salvation, was no longer an option. Faith is a

As noted earlier, the observation that Scripture is not a manual for philosophy for Bavinck is not reason enough to deny the fundamental significance that the Bible bears for other fields of knowledge: 'A great deal of what is related in Scripture is of *fundamental significance* also for the other sciences. At every moment science and art come into contact with Scripture; *the primary principles* [principia] *for all of life are given in Scripture*. This truth may in no way be discounted.'[86] Statements like these do not seem readily amenable to Paul Helm's view, according to which he denies that Scripture speaks of an epistemology.[87] Rather, for Helm reason bears a judicial role with regard to natural affairs.[88] What Bavinck is after, it seems, is not a purified Biblicism but rather an exploration of how the content of Scripture can play a leavening role on the other sciences; this leavening can already be discerned by the way in which Bavinck organizes the sciences into an organic whole – an organic motif he derives by a reflection on the Trinity's being.

Indeed, Bavinck's claims here should be taken as consistent with John Webster's retrieval of Bonaventure's account of Scripture's illuminating powers:

> But it is also clear that the light of Scripture is superior because it is not simply one of the set of other illuminations of the arts of the mind, but that which affords comprehensive illumination of technical, intellectual, and moral culture in its entirety. The illumination given by Scripture pervades and interpenetrates the whole of creaturely knowing; it is its surrounding atmosphere, not simply another set of materials on which to work.[89]

Hence, to affirm that the *principia* for every science are from Scripture is not identical with saying that Scripture is a manual for every science – neither does it necessarily conflict with Bavinck's affirmation that illumined reason is a *principium cognoscendi* with respect to science. Rather, it is merely to affirm the holism entailed by Bavinck's organic view: each form of revelation, general and special, is unintelligible without the other. The organic motif and the holism it implies allow for a modified and more flexible view that multiple *principia* are always operative in the different fields of inquiry, despite some degree of methodological priority granted to one or another. Each part demands the perspective of the whole, and the unity behind the diversity resulted from the developing differentiations out of the growing 'organism of science' cannot be forgotten.

As such, it is Bavinck's conviction that Christian theology can 'fashion for herself' a philosophy while using the tools found in any pre-existing philosophies freely. This might include, for example, Aristotelianism or Berlin Romanticism.[90] There is no singular

---

personal relationship to Christ; it is organic and has put aside quantitative addition.' Bavinck, *RD*, 1: p. 614. See also James Eglinton's discussion in, '*Vox Theologiae*: Boldness and Humility in Public Theological Speech', *International Journal of Public Theology* 9 (2015): pp. 17–25.

[86] Bavinck, *RD*, 1: p. 445. Emphases mine.
[87] Helm, *Faith, Form and Fashion*, pp. 64–5.
[88] Helm, *Faith, Form and Fashion*, pp. 57–9.
[89] John Webster, '*Regina atrium*: Theology and the Humanities', in *The Domain of the Word: Scripture and Theological Reason* (London: T&T Clark, 2012), p. 176.
[90] Bavinck, 'The Theology of Albrecht Ritschl', p. 123.

philosophical handmaiden to Christianity, and thus all philosophies can be re-assimilated with Christian principles. The conviction that a distinctly Christian expression can be achieved in every field of inquiry is indeed a part of what makes neo-Calvinism distinctive among the various Reformed streams of thought.[91] Significantly, Helm's charge that the neo-Calvinists dissolve the 'exclusively spiritual character of the Church' because they emphasize the achievability of a Christian expression of every sphere of life seems identical to the objections lodged by pure nature Thomists against de Lubac.[92] As one commentator observes, de Lubac is often critiqued for risking a conflation between 'the natural and supernatural' because of his emphasis on theology's capacity to display 'its inner intelligibility and beauty of Christian doctrine and its ability to interpret all of reality'.[93] Here, Helm and the pure nature Thomists display similar patterns of reasoning in their objections against neo-Calvinism and de Lubacian integralism – which again indicates the differences between Bavinck's epistemology and Helm's.

III On organisms and machines

a. Re-articulating the difference between Bavinck and Kuyper

Bavinck's organic epistemology and account of the sciences differ considerably, at least in his view, with the account provided by Roman Catholic thinking. A distinctly Christian expression of each science is achievable, and Bavinck's neo-Calvinistic impetus for a Christian university is thereby established. Naturally, these observations call to mind the relationship between Bavinck and Kuyper, as the evidence above shows a close affinity between the two archetypical neo-Calvinists. Theology and the Christian faith play an important role, as Eglinton and Bräutigam observe, in unifying the diverse sciences and in providing the resources properly to understand their character: 'Bavinck's views on the place of theology in the university were strongly Kuyperian.'[94] Also, in Bolt's brief summary of Bavinck's worldview as essentially organic, Bolt admits that 'the content of Bavinck's and Kuyper's worldview is virtually identical'.[95]

---

[91] Helm comments and laments that Kuyper's thought 'came to supplant the two-kingdoms idea and has transformed the idea of natural law into that of a number of cultural spheres, from mathematics to art, each retaining their own integrity in a kind of hierarchy, and each capable of distinctive Christian expression'. Helm, 'Religion and Reason from a Reformed Perspective', p. 69.

[92] Helm, 'Religion and Reason from a Reformed Perspective', p. 69.

[93] Joseph A. Komonchak, 'Theology and Culture at Mid-Century: The Example of Henry de Lubac', *Theological Studies* 51 (1990): pp. 582–3.

[94] Eglinton and Bräutigam, 'Scientific Theology?' p. 48. Bavinck explicitly connects his understanding of how the Christian faith ought to benefit and influence the sciences within the context of a university with Kuyper in *Christelijke wetenschap*, p. 108. This claim could be further nuanced, however, as Bavinck's view on theology's place seemed to have matured over time.

[95] John Bolt, *Bavinck on the Christian Life: Following Jesus in Faithful Service* (Wheaton: Crossway, 2015), p. 141. In an appreciative review, Cory Brock states that Bolt's treatment nonetheless does not give the organic the 'expansive treatment' it deserves in 'Review' of John Bolt, *Herman Bavinck on the Christian Life* in *Calvin Theological Journal* (forthcoming), p. 2 (page reference refers to a pre-print manuscript). See also Abraham Flipse on the agreement of Kuyper and Bavinck in their 'worldview' approach to the question of empirical science in 'The Origins of Creationism in the Netherlands', pp. 112–16.

Yet, the report by R. H. Bremmer concerning the differences between Bavinck and Kuyper should be kept in mind, lest the results of the above exposition be misunderstood. This is necessary in order to properly locate the epistemological affinities (and divergences) between the two Dutch thinkers. With Bavinck's organic account of the sciences and the way in which that account is polemically situated against Roman Catholic epistemology already firmly in view, it seems appropriate to revisit the discussions concerning the material similarities between Bavinck and Kuyper.

A set of student notes records the critiques that Bavinck apparently lodged against Kuyper's understanding of 'two kinds of science', according to which the antithesis produced by regeneration entails an antithesis in the scholarship of believers and unbelievers.[96] In these notes, students record that Bavinck made three salient criticisms of Kuyper.[97]

First, Bavinck claimed that Kuyper was too 'speculative' in his account of science.[98] Kuyper too comfortably relies on deductions from principles and fails to take sufficient account of the empirical phenomena itself in the objects of study. Bavinck emphasized the daily experience that scholars, whether regenerate or unregenerate, continue to labour together in the same scientific enterprise.

Second, Bavinck argued that Kuyper mixes two distinct categories: regeneration is a personal category and not one of principle. As such, to make a correspondence between regenerate and unregenerate humanity with 'principles' is unduly to conflate two distinct 'terrains'.[99] On this point, John Bolt provides a concise summary:

> To conflate the scientific distinction between truth and falsehood with the personal one of regenerate and unregenerate people is to commit a logical fallacy technically known as *metabasis eis allos genos* (crossing over into a different genus). To mix a metaphor, it is to substitute an orange for an apple in an argument. In this instance, according to Bavinck, to identify the scientific work of the regenerate with truth and that of the unregenerate with the lie is categorically false. Not only is there much that is true in the scientific work of unregenerate people, but Christian faith in itself gives no one a corner on scientific truth.[100]

The third criticism, then, is connected to the second. Bavinck argued that regeneration is not the source from which true science is produced. According to the notes, again, Bavinck capitalized on Kuyper's admission that 'the unregenerate and regenerate both

---

[96] Kuyper's claims on the two sciences are found in *Encylopedia of Sacred Theology: Its Principles* (Norwood: Charles Scribner's Sons, 1898), pp. 150–75. Hereafter, *EST*.
[97] The account is detailed in R. H. Bremmer, *Bavinck als Dogmaticus* (Kampen: Kok, 1961), pp. 39–45.
[98] Bremmer, *Bavinck als Dogmaticus*, p. 39. Dutch original: 'Bavinck opperde verder als kritiek, dat Kuyper het begrip der wetenschap niet empirisch, maar speculatief ontwikkelde.'
[99] Bremmer, *Bavinck als Dogmaticus*, p. 40. Dutch original: 'De fout is hier "Dat hij van 't terrain der beginselen overgaat tot het terrain der personen."' On Kuyper's understanding of the relationship between regeneration and science, see *EST*, pp. 219–28.
[100] Bolt, *Bavinck on the Christian Life*, p. 134. Bolt reiterates Bremmer's observations concerning Bavinck's objections against Kuyper in 'Doubting Reformational Anti-Thomism', p. 135.

perform formal scientific work. ... Regeneration has no influence on many parts of science. ... Whether one is regenerate or not, one can then come to knowledge.'[101]

Two caveats should be noted before these notes are taken into account. First, these notes were written between 1896 and January 1897.[102] This is significant because these lectures, therefore, were recorded before (1) the completion of the first edition of the *Dogmatics* as a whole and (2) the writing of the most thorough works by Bavinck on science and worldview, namely, *Christelijke wetenschap* (1904), *Christelijke wereldbeschouwing* (1904) and *Philosophy of Revelation* (1908). Second, Bavinck himself did not write these lecture notes: they are unpublished notes taken by one of his students.[103] So, though I shall argue that my analyses are consistent with Bremmer and these notes, one should take these factors into account and give due hermeneutical weight on the published works in which Bavinck most clearly deals with the structure of *wetenschap*.[104]

It is clear that Bavinck unlinks regeneration with the practice or attainment of science. Believers and unbelievers alike can engage in higher inquiry precisely because common grace is a theological reality. Bavinck argues in no uncertain terms that common grace and not nature qua nature is the principle from which non-believers can do science:

> The arts and the sciences have their *principium* not in the special grace of regeneration and conversion but in the natural gifts and talents that God in his common grace has also given to nonbelievers. Therefore Christian theologians of all times have profited from pagan art and have insisted upon a classical education for every man of learning, including the theologian.[105]

Though Bavinck differs from Kuyper in that the latter emphasizes the noetic effects of sin more heavily than Bavinck, Bavinck would still admit that fallen reason requires divine aid in natural affairs:

> God did not leave sin alone to do its destructive work. He had and, after the fall, continued to have a purpose for his creation; he interposed common grace between sin and the creation – a grace that, while it does not inwardly renew, nevertheless restrains and compels. All that is good and true has its origin in this

---

[101] Bremmer, *Bavinck als Dogmaticus*, p. 40. Dutch original: "'de onwedergeborenen en wedergeborenen verrichten beiden formeel wetenschappelijke arbeid ... De wedergeboorte heft op vele deelen van de wetenschap geen invloed ... Of men wedergeboren is of niet, men kan dan wel tot kennis komen.'" On the next page, Bremmer also notes that Bavinck, unlike Kuyper, makes a strong distinction between the certainty of confessional faith and the certainty of scientific faith.

[102] Bremmer, *Bavinck als Dogmaticus*, p. 39, n. 75.

[103] The notes were handwritten by A. Terpstra, as Bremmer notes in *Bavinck als Dogmaticus* p. 39, n. 75. It is unfortunate that Bolt attributes the words from Bremmer's citations to Bavinck himself (*Bavinck on the Christian Life*, p. 134), when a student was the writer of the notes.

[104] It is also worth noting that Bremmer's account of Bavinck involves the thesis that Bavinck was greatly influenced by neo-Thomism (see *Bavinck als Dogmaticus*, pp. 328–9). Cory Brock recently challenges this thesis in his 'Herman Bavinck and Neo-Thomism: Toward a Nuanced Rendering'. M.Th. Thesis, University of Edinburgh, 2014.

[105] Bavinck, 'Common Grace', p. 64.

grace, including the good we see in fallen man. ... *Consequently*, traces of the image of God continued in mankind. Understanding and reason remain, and he possesses all sorts of natural gifts.[106]

Consistent with the observations made in the previous chapter, Bavinck argues that religious disunity is the root of scientific disunity precisely because a denial of Christian revelation prevents practitioners of *wetenschap* from attaining an organic worldview. Christianity offers a greater light that provides insight on the grounds and telos that properly account for the presence of good works in non-believers. Bavinck's *Christelijke wetenschap* repeats this same point. Though there are not two kinds of science produced by two kinds of people, there is a Christian understanding of science in contrast to a non-believing one: 'Belief and unbelief, Christian and positivist conceptions of science stand diametrically against each other. Compromise is here not possible, but an obligation to choose definitively.'[107] Accordingly, 'faith and science stand in a relationship of conception and birth, as tree and fruit, as work and wage; the knowledge is the fruit and the wage of faith.'[108]

For Bavinck the connection between faith and science thus does not consist in the claim that the unregenerate will fail to do science, but that they are lacking the resources to understand its proper character and place. They have a kind of atomistic knowledge. True science, in Bavinck's judgement, continues to flourish in his day only because it 'in fact still rests in part on Christian foundations. But to the same extent it seeks to undermine this, [science] labors also to her own destruction.'[109] Indeed, the 'newer practice of nature and history, in her noblest form, consciously or unconsciously presupposes the thoughts of Christianity.'[110] Eglinton's and Bräutigam's comments concerning Bavinck's discussion of this are appropriate: 'Having claimed that the universe cannot be coherently viewed without metaphysics, Bavinck turns the reader toward the revelation of the Triune God.'[111] It seems fitting that Bavinck concludes his treatment on Christian science with a reflection on how revelation informs the believer of the true character of things, which makes their knowledge quite alien to unbelief:

> Because there is in science, just as in everywhere else, much falsehood and counterfeiting, God gives to us in his revelation a guide and a signpost, which

---

[106] Bavinck, 'Common Grace', p. 51. Emphasis mine.
[107] Bavinck, *Christelijke wetenschap*, p. 9. Dutch original: 'Geloovige en ongeloovige, Christelijke en positivistische opvatting van de wetenschap staan lijnrecht tegenover elkander. Vergelijk is hier niet mogelijk, maar besliste keuze plicht.'
   Bolt also rightly notes that Bavinck affirms the conflict between Christian and non-Christian science in *Bavinck and the Christain Life*, p. 140.
[108] Bavinck, *Christelijke wetenschap*, p. 16. Dutch original: 'Geloof en wetenschap staan dus tot elkander in verhouding als ontvangenis en geboorte, als boom en vrucht, als werk en loon; het weten is de vrucht en het loon des geloofs.'
[109] Bavinck, *Christelijke wetenschap*, p. 97. Dutch original: 'Wel is waar staat de wetenschap heden ten dage op eene aanzienlijke hoogte; zij rust feitelijk voor een deel nog op Christelijke grondslagen. Maar in dezelfde mate als zij deze ondermijnt, arbeidt zij ook aan haar eigen verderf.'
[110] Bavinck, *Christelijke wetenschap*, pp. 104–5. Dutch original: 'Meer nadruk behoort nog hierop te vallen, dat de nieuwere beoefening van natuur en geschiedenis, in haar edelsten vorm bewust of onbewust de gedachten van het christendom onderstelt.'
[111] Eglinton and Bräutigam, 'Scientific Theology', p. 46.

directs our steps in the practice of science and protects us from straying. Christian science is a science that examines all things in the light of his revelation, seeing, therefore, things as they truly are in their essence. In the eyes of the world this may be foolishness, but the foolishness of God is wiser than men, and the weakness of God is stronger than men. For we can do nothing against, but for, the truth.[112]

These statements do not give Christians automatic superiority over the practice of science, but it certainly does give them an advantage in the knowing enterprise, at least in Bavinck's view – revelation provides the knowledge of things as they truly are, which makes them quite strange to the world.

The difference between Bavinck and Kuyper is thus summarized accordingly: Bavinck is more modest in his claims concerning the principles of unbelieving and believing science; he refuses to transfer the principle of regeneration unto the practice of science itself. Bavinck makes a distinction not between two sciences (in some ontological sense that flow out of two kinds of persons) but in two *conceptions* of science. Thus, Bavinck can more readily affirm that non-believers are often more capable, more learned and more skilled in the sciences than Christians. Bavinck is also more comfortable with embracing the proper functionality of the unbeliever's noetic capacities even after the fall, due to common grace.

However, their affinities, it seems to me, are still maintained in that both have an organic understanding of science and of human knowledge such that the whole precedes the parts. Both hold that knowledge of the whole is the context in which each part is properly understood. Indeed, Bavinck makes a distinction between atomistic knowing and organic knowing; unbelievers have knowledge, but Christians have a knowledge, a science, which forms a coherent organism. Bavinck 'foresaw the university as becoming a cacophony of arbitrarily associated faculties when deprived of theology'.[113] The distinction is not between not knowing and knowing but between atomistic (mechanical) knowing and organic knowing.

b. Bodies and propositions

In both the previous and current chapters, something of Bavinck's Romantic spirit is evident. Consider, here, Isaiah Berlin's summary of the organic vision of Romanticism: 'The world can be conceived organically – like a tree, in which every part lives for every other part, and through every other part – or mechanistically ... in which the parts are external to one another. ... These are very different conceptions of life,

---

[112] Bavinck, *Christelijke wetenschap*, p. 130. Dutch original: 'Maar omdat er in de wetenschap, evenals overal elders, zooveel schijn en namaak is, schonk God ons in zijne openbaring een gids en een wegwijzer, die bij de beoefening der wetenschap onze schreden richt en ons voor afdwaling behoedt. Christelijke wetenschap is dus zulk eene wetenschap, die bij het licht dier openbaring alle dingen onderzoekt en ze daarom ziet, gelijk zij waarlijk, in hun wezen zijn. In het oog der wereld moge dit dwaasheid zijn, maar het dwaze Gods is wijzer dan de menschen en het zwakke Gods is sterker dan de menschen. Want wij vermogen niets tegen, maar voor de waarheid.'
[113] Eglinton and Bräutigam, 'Scientific Theology', p. 30.

and they do belong to different climates of opinion, and are influenced by different considerations.'[114]

What is the upshot of all of this? If Bavinck considers knowledge and *wetenschap* to be single organisms, what are the implications? In this section preliminary inferences are drawn that clarify and develop ideas from Bavinck and Isaiah Berlin's influential account. The construal of this relationship will further implicate the way the nature and structure of human knowledge is understood. These two ways can be communicated in terms of some analogies or thought experiments.

The first is the *mechanical* view. A highly advanced machine, such as an automobile, is composed of individual parts that go together in a specific way mapped out by a design. The individual components of the automobile may be extricated: there are wheels, steel bars, screws, springs and so on. Once extricated, the disconnected components seem to have little or no relation to the others. Comprehending the steel bar, for example, does not require a prior understanding of the wheels and vice versa: each component can be considered entirely on its own without reference to the others, and the assembling of the parts together to form an automobile is merely one contingent way that the parts may be assembled. The steel bar can serve different purposes, and the wheel, too, can be used otherwise.[115]

The analogy is this: just as the steel bar and wheels could be considered in isolation but also be compounded together into a greater whole, so can the truths of nature (or general revelation) and the truths of special revelation be considered in relative isolation. 'There is a tree in front of me' and 'the triune God exists' are two propositions that have no direct relevance to one another. Logical inferences can be drawn to connect the two propositions, like an inference concerning the decision of the Trinity to create and sustain all of creation. However, knowledge of the tree can be gained without knowledge of the Trinity with no significant loss. General and special revelation each provides a set of propositions that may be compounded together to form a larger aggregate of propositions.

Another analogy will render the point more precise. Perhaps Andreas has before him some dough, tomatoes, zucchinis and cheese. Further, Andreas has no knowledge of Italian food and thus no comprehension of the idea of a vegetarian lasagna. Nothing else but a stroke of genius would enable Andreas to take the ingredients before him to make the classical dish. There is no direct or obvious inference to be made that forms a knowledge of vegetarian lasagnas simply by examining the ingredients before him. However, upon receiving a recipe for vegetarian lasagnas from a distant Italian friend, Andreas suddenly re-investigates the ingredients and sees them anew. He does not merely see individual kinds of food that bear no relation to each other but the requisite ingredients to bake an authentic Italian lasagna. The reception of the recipe now causes Andreas to think of lasagnas when he encounters tomatoes, zucchinis and the like.

In the same way, here knowledge of special revelation causes the knower to see the *vestiges* of God in all of creation, but not the other way around. General revelation

---

[114] Isaiah Berlin, *The Roots of Romanticism* (Princeton: Princeton University Press, 2001), p. 5.
[115] I owe this 'mechanical' analogy to Oliver D. Crisp, 'Analytic Theology', in Oliver Crisp and Michael Rea (eds), *Analytic Theology: New Essays in the Philosophy of Theology* (Oxford: Oxford University Press, 2009), p. 36.

bears the marks of triniformity precisely because the knowledge of the triune God was disclosed to the Christian in the verbal revelation of Scripture, just as the primal ingredients of lasagna can only be seen as such when a prior knowledge of lasagnas is obtained. This analogy does not deny that the ingredients can be known individually as isolated kinds of food but knowledge of them as *ingredients for a lasagna* can be known only in an a posteriori manner. Though this analogy is not too different from the automobile analogy discussed earlier, it highlights specifically the priority of special revelation as the lens that interprets general revelation.

The food analogy is a midway point between the mechanical view and the *organic* view. In the latter way of construing the relationship, a rather vivid thought experiment may help. Consider Sera Phim, who is a non-corporeal angelic being, who, as such, has never encountered anything like a human body and who has no knowledge of what makes a human body. One day Sera glides around and by accident finds a dead human heart on her path. She comes closer and is perplexed by what she encounters. She goes further along and finds a sticky, red and wet net of string-like objects – the interconnected web of arteries found in a human body – and is further confused: What is this red object that looks like a set of small tubes? By the end of the day she has encountered all the individual main components that make up the human body, but, presumably, she would not be able to know this. All she thinks is that she has found some odd, soggy pieces of corporeal objects – she will not know how each works, or what they are supposed to do, nor would she know that they are all supposed to go together. At least, not until she finds a working human body and learns how it works. But even when she does find one, she will not have a proper understanding of the heart without considering the whole cardiovascular system. She will not have a proper understanding of the brain apart from the skeletal structures that make up the body. Articulated differently, knowledge of the parts requires a knowledge of the whole, no individual part can be properly understood without a prior knowledge of other parts and so on. Each thing requires another to be fully intelligible.

Here, knowledge of the body is necessary to know how the parts can form the body just as special revelation is necessary to understand general revelation. Further, on this picture of things, general and special revelation work together as one organism. Knowledge of the whole is a requisite properly to know the parts, and each part calls for knowledge of another, for each to be rightly construed. The tree is not organically known without being regarded as something created, creation cannot be understood apart from the character or plan of the creator and so on. Here, too, the analogy works in emphasizing how the knowledge of the whole is greater than a knowledge of the sum of its parts – seeing how the whole of the human body functions is greater than knowing the heart *as* a heart in a greater system. An epistemic account for the parts of general revelation is inaccessible prior to the light disclosed in special revelation and vice versa. Though neither analogy is meant to be totalizing or wholly accurate precisely because human beings live in a revelational and (common) graced universe such that a primordial and divinely initiated contact already obtains between their consciousness and the world, both the lasagna and bodily analogies seem to be consistent with Bavinck's thought: 'General revelation leads to special revelation, special revelation points back to general revelation. The one calls for the other, and without it remains imperfect and unintelligible. Together they proclaim the manifold wisdom which God has displayed in creation and redemption.'[116]

In this sense, these observations connect well with the previous chapters by supplying the proviso that working towards a knowledge of the whole through the careful investigation of the parts is due not to the nature of the objects known but to the necessity of human finitude. Knowledge is a single organism, but a mastery of the whole is impossible for a single human knower and requires the attentiveness of humanity as a whole – a task actualized in and corresponds with the citizens of the eschatological kingdom of God.

Along these lines, Bavinck's organic account seems to be consonant with what Hubert Dreyfus and Charles Taylor call *Gestalt Holism*:

> The point has often been made about gestalts that they can't be seen as simply composed of their parts. Or to put it another way, the meaningful elements they contain cannot be identified on their own, but only in relation to the whole. This high note is the climax of a long rising passage in this song. But its nature as climax doesn't reside in the note itself. The same note in another song has a quite different valence. This kind of holism undercuts completely the atomism of input. These elements are what they are only in relation to the whole and to each other. It is not that, independently identified, they have to be combined in a certain way in order to yield truth. It is independent identification as such which is impossible.[117]

A more appropriate term that denotes Bavinck's position might simply be *Organic Holism* – a holism of a distinctly Reformed variety. 'The whole cannot be explained in an atomistic manner by a combination of its parts, but on the contrary the parts must be conceived in an organic way by unfolding the totality.'[118]

Intuitions cannot settle in this case which account of knowledge, the mechanical or the organic, provides a more accurate picture of human knowing. It seems that the plausibility of Bavinck's account rests on whether his understanding of the organic character of reality is first accepted. Indeed, Bavinck's organic epistemology must be correlated with his organic ontology, such that the Trinity *ad intra* implies an organic cosmology and epistemology *ad extra*. Further, the organic motif is Bavinck's preferred means of articulating the relationship between general and special revelation and the scientific enterprise in ways that nuance his affinities with Kuyper and make him critical of the purportedly mechanical epistemology of Roman Catholicism.

This chapter has not yet discussed the significance of the organic motif in Bavinck's account of the connection between subject and object. It is to this subject that the next two chapters turn.

---

[116] Bavinck, *Philosophy of Revelation*, p. 25. The next chapters further elaborate on Bavinck's view of this primordial contact between consciousness and reality.
[117] Dreyfus and Taylor, *Retrieving Realism*, pp. 43–4.
[118] Bavinck, *Philosophy of Revelation*, p. 173.

5

Bavinck, Thomas Reid, the 'gap' and the question of subjects and objects

This study has so far unfolded Bavinck's use of the organic motif in his theological epistemology, with a particular reference to the structure of human knowledge and the relationship of theology to the other sciences. In so doing, the differences and similarities that Bavinck saw between himself and other thinkers, such as Thomas Aquinas and Abraham Kuyper, were broached in order to further elucidate his epistemological concerns. This also sheds light on the secondary literature and why various interpreters have focused on the real distinctions of the sciences, on the one hand, and the unity of the sciences, on the other. The result is that although Bavinck does make a distinction between the diverse fields of knowledge, the basis of that diversity also orchestrates it as a single organism, with Scripture and Christian principles constituting that unity. These considerations show that Bavinck deploys the organic motif for positive and constructive purposes, relating it to the distinctive neo-Calvinistic doctrines of sphere sovereignty and the transformative (leavening) effects of Christianity upon knowing and culture.

In Bavinck's thought, however, a Christian recasting of the world as an organism does not merely vindicate the possibility of a unified worldview. Indeed, in his account, understanding the world as a created organism produces another epistemological fruit – and this has to do with the correspondence that obtains between subjects and objects, mind and world. In a paradigmatic summary (which will receive greater attention in Chapter 6), Bavinck wrote the following: 'If [a unified worldview] is possible, it can only be explained from the fact that the world is an organism and thus should first be thought in such a manner. Only then does philosophy and worldview have a right and ground of existence.' Further, it is only 'on this pinnacle of knowledge that subject and object harmonize'.[1] Therefore, to penetrate more deeply into Bavinck's use of the organic motif in epistemology, one should also turn to the manner in which the subject–object problem is treated by him through the application of organic language. Considering this issue will reveal that Bavinck's deployment of that motif is not merely ad hoc or pragmatic. Rather, the organic motif fills in and answers acute

---

[1] Bavinck, *Christelijke wereldbeschouwing*, pp. 32–3. Dutch original: 'Indien deze mogelijk is, dan kan dit alleen daaruit verklaard worden, dat de wereld een organisme is en dus eerst als zoodanig is gedacht. Dan alleen heeft philosophie en wereldbeschouwing recht en grond van bestaan, als ook op dit hoogtepunt der kennis subject en object samenstemmen'.

epistemological problems with precise specificity. To ascertain the epistemological yields and the significance of Bavinck's moves, however, will require this chapter and the next, as clarity needs to be advanced concerning Bavinck's conception of the relationship – and gap – between subjects and objects.

This chapter has three sections. First, I review an argument from a stream of secondary literature briefly surveyed in the introduction, mostly represented by Cornelis van der Kooi and Henk van den Belt. Their argument suggests Bavinck's indebtedness to post-Kantian epistemologies that made a strong distinction between subjects and objects and the constructive powers of the mind in forming the objects of knowledge. This observation, however, must be tempered by a potential defeater in the appropriation of Bavinck as a proto-Reformed epistemologist, as found in the works of Alvin Plantinga and Nicholas Wolterstorff. If Plantinga and Wolterstorff are right, then Bavinck has to be seen as offering a strict alternative to those epistemologies that question whether beliefs directed at external reality can be unmediated or properly basic. Wolterstorff, more specifically, has argued that there are strongly Reidian connotations in Bavinck's thought. As such, Bavinck is seen by some as indebted to post-Kantian epistemologies (which make knowledge of objects susceptible to the mind's subjective functions) and to a Reidian common-sense realism (which grants an unmediated access to reality). As these readings seem mutually exclusive, one ought to ask this: Are they accurate?

The second section hints at an answer by offering an analysis of Bavinck and Reid on perception. At first glance, it strengthens the Reformed epistemologist reading by observing that Bavinck diagnoses the modern epistemological conundrums in much the same way as Reid. Both consider the malaise of modern epistemology to be the creation of an inflexible gap between subjects and objects, making it difficult to ascertain how it is that objects can be known at all. The third section, however, demonstrates that, despite Bavinck's objections to the subject–object dichotomizing tendencies of modern epistemology, he maintains that there is, indeed, a fundamental difference between mental representations and the objects that they represent – there is no access to reality to which the constructive effects of the mind do not apply. This further showcases that assertion of a clear conceptual continuity between the epistemologies of Bavinck and Reid cannot be sustained.

The conclusion of this chapter hints at the solution to this apparent conundrum in interpreting Bavinck by pointing to his use and appreciation of the German idealist and empirical realist Eduard von Hartmann.[2] The next chapter, in turn, will substantiate the claim that what is at first glance a similarity between Bavinck and Reid is actually reflective of a prior accidental similarity between Reid and von Hartmann. That is, to understand the epistemological moves made by Bavinck between subjects and objects, and the relevance of the organic motif to this aspect of his thought, his critical appropriation of von Hartmann must be appreciated. Eduard von Hartmann (1842–1906) was an absolute idealist from Berlin. Although he is relatively unknown today, his philosophical work on the nature of the unconscious in 1869 was considered

---

[2] As it will become clear in this chapter and the next, due to the variety of ways in which realism and idealism can be defined, the two, as Bavinck recognized, are not mutually exclusive.

to be the 'pinnacle' of studies on this issue, meriting the critical attention of major figures like Friedrich Nietzsche, and triggered the writing of encyclopaedia articles dedicated to his view.[3] His *Philosophy of the Unconscious*, regarded as his magnum opus, ran eleven editions during his lifetime; von Hartmann was certainly noteworthy enough to merit Bavinck's attention.

Bavinck's critical appropriation of von Hartmann, in turn, will then illuminate why it is that both claims – that Bavinck was a proto-Reformed epistemologist and, at the same time, indebted to post-Kantian idealism and subjectivism – are partly right.

I Bavinck and world-directed beliefs: Two interpretations – reformed epistemology and post-Kantian trajectories

It is difficult to deny the truth in Henk van den Belt's claim that Bavinck's epistemology is 'dominated' by the distinction and correspondence between subject and object.[4] Indeed, Bavinck defines the nature of truth, science and knowledge in precisely those terms. He says this in numerous places. First, in the *Dogmatics*: 'Science always consists in a logical relation between subject and object. Our view of science depends on the way we relate the two.'[5] Secondly, in the *Certainty of Faith*: 'Truth is agreement between thought and reality and thus expresses a relation between the contents of our consciousness and the object of our knowledge.'[6] Finally, in *Christelijke wereldbeschouwing*: 'Knowledge is indeed always and can never be other than a relation between subject and object. Once one or both falls away, there is no more knowledge.'[7] On the opening page of his *Beginselen der psychologie* (Foundations of Psychology), he considers a demarcation between the phenomena in the internal consciousness and the realities outside to be axiomatic: 'But consciousness gradually awakens to the distinction between what is perceived and perception; between the object, which caused the pain, and the pain itself; between the concern which is desired and the desiring self, that is, between object and subject, matter and spirit, the not-I and the I.'[8] In his treatise on the Christian worldview, Bavinck argues that the rupturing of 'the harmony of subject and object [and of] knowing and being' is the result of the

---

[3] Angus Nichollas and Martin Liebscher, 'Introduction: Thinking the Unconscious', in Angus Nicholls and Martin Liebscher (eds), *Thinking the Unconscious: Nineteenth-Century German Thought* (Cambridge: Cambridge University Press, 2006), pp. 1–2.
[4] van den Belt, *The Authority of Scripture*, p. 294.
[5] Bavinck, *RD*, 1: p. 214.
[6] Bavinck, *The Certainty of Faith*, p. 19.
[7] Bavinck, *Christelijke wereldbeschouwing*, pp. 18–19. Dutch original: 'Want weten is juist altijd en kan nooit anders zijn dan eene relatie tusschen subject en object. Zoodra een van beide wegvalent, is er geen weten meer'.
[8] Bavinck, *Beginselen der psychologie*, p. 1. Dutch original: 'Maar langzamerhand ontwaakt het bewustzijn en leert hij onderscheiden tusschen het waargenomene en de waarneming; tusschen het voorwerp, dat de pijn veroorzaakte en de pijn zelve; tusschen de zaak, die begeerd wordt en die begeerte zelve, d.i. tusschen object en subject, stof en geest, niet-ik en ik'. Crucially, he later notes that it is the Logos that connects these same, disparate, phenomena: *Beginselen der psychologie*, p. 76.

oscillation between rationalism and empiricism in modern epistemology – a problem which he then tries to address throughout the chapter.[9]

It is exactly here that van den Belt makes the further claim that Bavinck is most influenced by the philosophy contemporary to his time.[10] Bavinck, he argues, introduces a subjective element into theology and the epistemological process by emphasizing the constructive influences of the mind in his prolegomena. More clearly, he elaborates that Bavinck is located between 'naïve realism and the transcendental idealism of Kant'.[11] While noting Bavinck's affinities with von Hartmann, van den Belt wonders whether Bavinck's emphases on the subject tend him towards epistemological subjectivism. Indeed, in interpreting the way in which subjects and objects correspond in Bavinck, Cornelis van der Kooi expresses the same reserved worries with respect to Bavinck's position and questions whether Bavinck ultimately succeeds in evading subjectivism:

> [Bavinck's] expression betrays, in a high degree, a post-Kantian situation, and could never really have been uttered by someone like Calvin. Bavinck's expression can nourish the thought that the existence of things can be acknowledged only as they appear to the mind's eye. That would be a modern Cartesian point of departure. One can naturally not accuse Bavinck of such a position. There are too many elements in his theology that would prevent that. It is true, however, that his focus is strongly directed to the religious subject to whose mind's eye the things of revelation must appear if he or she wants to find them worthy or true. One can ask whether, to the extent that the focus is on the knowing subject, this naturally leads in detaching the subject a-historically from the community on which this subject is dependent for his knowledge.[12]

This set of readings locates Bavinck well within the post-Kantian tradition of modern epistemology that assumes the subjective influences of the human mind in forming the objects of knowledge.

At this point, however, it is necessary to consider a potential tension raised by the invocation of Bavinck as a precursor to the project of the Reformed epistemology of Plantinga and Wolterstorff.[13] The tension is raised because this project is formed

---

[9] Bavinck, *Christelijke wereldbeschouwing*, p. 16. Dutch original: 'In beide gevallen [empiricism and rationalism] en naar beide richtingen wordt de harmonie van subject en object van kennen en zijn verbroken.'

[10] Van den Belt, *The Authority of Scripture*, pp. 266–7.

[11] Van den Belt, *The Authority of Scripture*, p. 267. Here, I presuppose the new dimensions of complexity reintroduced by the so-called 'third-wave' of Kantian scholarship, in which Henry Allison's *Kant's Transcendental Idealism: An Interpretation and Defense* (Yale: Yale University Press, 2004) remains central. In this wave, the debate between (transcendental) idealism and realism hinges not on ontology so much as on whether there exist certain epistemic conditions in one's knowledge of objects. Thus, the distinction between phenomena and the things-in-themselves rests on two modes of talking about the same object, rather than two numerically distinct entities. As we shall see, there are hints that Bavinck is not unaware of these complexities.

[12] van der Kooi, 'The Appeal to the Inner Testimony of the Spirit', p. 108. Van der Kooi is commenting specifically on Bavinck's *RD*, 1: p. 586 – a passage to which I will return in this chapter.

[13] In what follows, I am not suggesting that Plantinga and Wolterstorff offer an epistemology that eschews an affirmation that human knowers are bound by their situatedness and finitude in the

precisely as an alternative to the modern trajectory that nurtures a kind of evidentialist scepticism with respect to beliefs about the external world. To appreciate how Bavinck is being invoked by the Reformed epistemologists, though, first requires paying attention to the contours of the project as a whole.

The project advanced by Plantinga and Wolterstorff consists in the rejection of the classical foundationalist assumption that justification in the form of sufficient evidence is necessary for knowledge. In more formal terms, Plantinga defines the epistemological thesis of classical foundationalism this way:

> A belief is acceptable for a person if (and only if) it is either properly basic (i.e., self-evident, incorrigible, or evident to the senses for that person), or believed on the evidential basis of propositions that are acceptable and that support it deductively, inductively, or abductively.[14]

A belief is properly basic if it is formed immediately, and not mediately by an inference from another belief. A belief is properly basic because these immediate beliefs enjoy the status of being justified. Reformed epistemology takes issue not with the positing of properly basic beliefs as the foundations of one's noetic structure but in the classical foundationalist criteria that beliefs can only be properly basic if they are self-evident, incorrigible or evident to the senses. There is a strong *evidentialist* bent behind this, applied not merely to everyday beliefs but also to beliefs about God. If it is the case that a belief is justified only if it is incorrigible, evident to the senses or self-evident, or inferred from beliefs that are incorrigible, evident to the senses or self-evident, and so on, then beliefs about God, too, must be justified in the same way. Evidence is required for belief in God, and no 'immediately formed belief about God possesses the merit in question'.[15]

Classical foundationalism thus includes two more basic commitments: first there is the deontological commitment which claims that rational agents have an obligation to hold their beliefs with sufficient evidence, and are guilty – failing to live up to their epistemic obligations – when they do not provide said evidence. In Plantinga's words, 'More precisely, your assent to p is justified only if the degree of your assent to p is proportional to the degree to which p is probable with respect to what is certain for you. If you believe in some other way, then you are going contrary to your epistemic obligations; you are guilty; you are flouting epistemic duty.'[16]

---

epistemic process. Indeed, Plantinga and Wolterstorff are well attuned to the lack of a neutral 'view from nowhere', and instead emphasize an epistemology that takes into account the dependent ways in which knowers are related to their environment and contexts. Hence, Kevin Diller is correct in characterizing Plantinga and Bavinck as critical realists insofar as the modest definition he offers is kept in mind: 'Plantinga's response ... is aligned with Plantinga's Dutch ascendents Bavinck and Kuyper. Human knowers occupy a stance of epistemic dependence. There simply is no privileged, neutral point of view.' Diller, *Theology's Epistemological Dilemma*, p. 108. On Wolterstorff's theory of situated rationality, see Nathan D. Shannon, *Shalom and the Ethics of Belief: Nicholas Wolterstorff's Theory of Situated Rationality* (Eugene: Pickwick, 2014).

[14] Alvin Plantinga, *Warranted Christian Belief* (Oxford: Oxford University Press, 2000), pp. 84–5.
[15] Nicholas Wolterstorff, 'Herman Bavinck – Proto Reformed Epistemologist', *Calvin Theological Journal* 45 (2010): p. 136.
[16] Plantinga, *Warranted Christian Belief*, p. 87.

The second commitment is that of internalism: the view of epistemic justification according to which knowers require cognitive access to the grounds or properties they need in order for their beliefs to be justified (or warranted).[17] 'The basic thrust of internalism ... is that the properties that confer warrant upon a belief are properties to which the believer has some sort of special epistemic access.'[18] The polemical side of Reformed epistemology is not to meet this challenge but to challenge its validity in the first place.

In response, Plantinga and Wolterstorff argue that the criteria provided for what counts as proper basicality is much too restrictive. Many of our common beliefs are held in good epistemic order even if they are not self-evident, incorrigible or evident to the senses to us. Perceptual beliefs, as prime examples, are immediately formed beliefs, and common rational agents are well within their epistemic rights in holding them as reliable in a properly basic way, though these beliefs are not self-evident, incorrigible or maximally evident to the senses. Wolterstorff argues for it in this way:

> [The Reformed epistemologist] answer was that not only is classical foundationalism not a tenable thesis for beliefs about God, it is not a tenable thesis for very many beliefs at all. Perceptual beliefs are formed and held immediately rather than by inference; surely many of these we are entitled to hold. Yet, none of them satisfies the classical foundationalist's criteria for certitude: The propositional contents of the beliefs are not necessarily true nor are they reports of states of consciousness. This is also true for memory beliefs, for inductive beliefs, for testimony beliefs, and for other kinds of beliefs. Classical foundationalism is just false as a general theory of entitlement.[19]

In another place, Plantinga appeals to the reasoning of Thomas Reid to elaborate upon this particular objection to the classical foundationalist thesis, in this way:

> But how much of this can be seen to be probable with respect to what is certain for us? How much meets the classical conditions for being properly basic? Not much, if any. I believe that I had cornflakes for breakfast, that my wife was amused at some little stupidity of mine, that there really are such 'external objects' as trees and squirrels, and that the world was not created ten minutes ago with all its dusty books, apparent memories, crumbling mountains, and deeply carved canyons. These things, according to classical foundationalism, are not properly basic; they

---

[17] Plantinga prefers the term 'warrant' to 'justified' for his definition of knowledge in response to Gettier. Warrant is 'a normative, possibly complex quantity that comes in degrees, enough of which is what distinguishes knowledge from mere true belief'. Alvin Plantinga, *Warrant: The Current Debate* (Oxford: Oxford University Press, 1993), p. 4.

[18] Plantinga, *Warrant: The Current Debate*, p. 6. Hence, Michael Bergmann: 'According to internalists, for a belief to be justified it is not enough that it *has* certain virtues (such as being reliably formed or supported by the evidence), the person holding it must be *aware* that he has those virtues.' *Justification Without Awareness: A Defense of Epistemic Externalism* (Oxford: Oxford University Press, 2006), p. 3. Emphasis in original. Kevin Diller notes that this internalist emphasis on justification and the believer's responsibility to gain cognitive access to the evidences that justify his beliefs is a kind of 'epistemic-works righteousness' (*Theology's Epistemological Dilemma*, p. 114).

[19] Wolterstorff, 'Herman Bavinck', p. 137.

must be believed on the evidential basis of propositions that are self-evident or evident to the senses (in Locke's restricted sense) or incorrigible for me.[20]

The upshot is that if classical foundationalism is accepted, then many of the beliefs that we ordinarily take for granted must be rendered suspect. It is epistemically impossible to justify our beliefs in the way that classical foundationalism says we must, and the inevitable result is a vicious kind of scepticism with respect to our everyday beliefs. More seriously, Plantinga further argues that the classical foundationalist thesis *itself* cannot meet its own criteria. In other words, the classical foundationalist claim [that a belief is justified if, and only if, it is properly basic (i.e. incorrigible, self-evident or evident to the senses), or mediately formed on the basis of properly basic beliefs] is itself not a properly basic belief (on classical foundationalist criteria), nor inferred from properly basic beliefs. The classical foundationalist picture, then, is not only much too restrictive but also self-referentially incoherent.[21]

The alternative picture that Plantinga and Wolterstorff offer, then, is that perceptual beliefs, memory beliefs and inductive beliefs are all formed immediately, and are so formed in a properly basic way. Following Reid, they agree with the principle of credulity, to the effect that rational agents are entitled to the epistemic credentials of their ordinary beliefs unless they have good reasons to doubt them (i.e. in the form of defeaters). Whereas classical foundationalism raises *positive* criteria – that rational agents must provide positive evidence before their beliefs can be justified – Reformed epistemologists, following Reid, advocate a *negative* thesis: rational agents are warranted in holding their beliefs in the *absence* of good reasons to doubt them. Moreover, they hold that *beliefs about God* can be warranted in much the same way as their perceptual, memorial or inductive beliefs. In Wolterstorff's judgement, there is no 'relevant difference among perceptual beliefs, memorial beliefs, and the like, on one hand, and beliefs about God, on the other hand'.[22] If this is so, then beliefs about God can be warranted in the absence of evidence, much like perceptual, memorial and inductive beliefs.

It is here that Wolterstorff's and Plantinga's appeals to Herman Bavinck are relevant and intelligible. Consider this particular passage on the proofs for God's existence from Bavinck, cited to good effect by an earlier essay by Plantinga, and Wolterstorff's article:

> Now it appears as if belief in the existence of God is based on these proofs and has no foundation apart from them. ... The contrary, rather, is the case. There is not a single thing whose existence is certain to us only on the basis of proofs. We are fully convinced – prior to any argumentation – of our own existence, the existence of the world around us, the laws of logic and morality. ... We accept that

---

[20] Plantinga, *Warranted Christian Belief*, p. 98.
[21] Plantinga, *Warranted Christian Belief*, pp. 93–7.
[22] Wolterstorff, 'Herman Bavinck', p. 137. Diller summarizes this accurately with respect to Plantinga: 'In his constructive model for how Christian belief might have warrant, the means by which we *receive* the knowledge of God are treated as analogous processes that deliver properly basic warranted belief independent of argument or evidence. The counter examples of memory, introspection and others indicate that knowledge formed in this way is not necessarily deficient.' *Theology's Epistemological Dilemma*, p. 123.

existence – without constraint or coercion – spontaneously and instinctively. And the same is true of God's existence.[23]

The Reformed epistemological tinge to Bavinck's reasoning in such passages seems clear: 'Bavinck points out that belief in God relevantly resembles belief in the existence of the self and of the external world – and, we might add, belief in other minds and the past. In none of these areas do we typically *have* proof or arguments, or *need* proofs or arguments.'[24] As such, Wolterstorff observes that Bavinck was an 'anti-evidentialist' concerning beliefs about God precisely because he takes 'an "innocent until proven guilty" approach to entitlement'.[25] Human beings are hard-wired to believe in the deliverances of their perception, memory and induction with respect to external reality. 'Rather than trying to assemble propositional evidence for most of what we believe, our only option is to be watchful for the emergency of reasons for giving up one or another of our beliefs.'[26] It is for specifically these reasons that Wolterstorff concludes that Bavinck's analysis of the way beliefs are formed and how one is entitled to their ordinary beliefs align him closely with Thomas Reid.[27]

An important and implicit result here is that, on Bavinckian grounds, much like Reid's, an unproblematic access to the external world is granted, and, by parity of reasoning, an unproblematic access to the apprehension of God. Ordinarily, human beings can take for granted that their beliefs about the world are reliably held because they are created in such a way that they have a direct access to the world. Reid, Wolterstorff reasons, thus provides an alternative to the modern sceptical stance towards whether we can have knowledge of external reality and, concomitantly, of divine reality. Indeed, Wolterstorff argues that Kant erected an epistemological boundary between mental representations and external reality that precipitates an anxiety in modern theologians about whether one can properly refer to God.[28] Implied in Wolterstorff's and Plantinga's reading of Bavinck, then, is that Bavinck and Reid provide a rather unified response to the internalist 'guilty until proven innocent' approach of much contemporary epistemology that renders dubitable whether our beliefs are actually directed to the external world.

When the readings of Wolterstorff and Plantinga are coupled with those of van der Kooi and van den Belt, a curious picture emerges. On the one side, Bavinck is

---

[23] Bavinck, *RD*, 2: p. 90. See: Alvin Plantinga, 'Reason and Belief in God', in Alvin Plantinga and Nicholas Wolterstorff (eds), *Faith and Rationality: Reason and Belief in God* (Notre Dame: University of Notre Dame Press, 1983), pp. 64–5; Wolterstorff, 'Herman Bavinck', p. 141. Due to its publication date, Plantinga was using an earlier translation of a portion of Bavinck's *God and Creation*: Herman Bavinck, *The Doctrine of God*, William Hendricksen (trans.) (Grand Rapids: Eerdmans, 1951), p. 78.

[24] Plantinga, 'Reason and Belief in God', p. 65, emphases in original.

[25] Wolterstorff, 'Herman Bavinck', p. 143.

[26] Wolterstorff, 'Herman Bavinck', p. 143.

[27] 'Furthermore, though I have not had time to explore the matter in this article, an important influence on Reformed epistemology has been the eighteenth century Scots philosopher and Presbyterian clergyman, Thomas Reid, and there are astoundingly Reidian-sounding passages in Bavinck's *Reformed Dogmatics* (e.g. 1. 223–4)'. Wolterstorff, 'Herman Bavinck', p. 146.

[28] Nicholas Wolterstorff, 'Is it Possible and Desirable for Theologians to Recover From Kant?' *Modern Theology* 14 (1998): pp. 1–18. See also his 'How Philosophical Theology Became Possible within the Analytic Tradition of Philosophy', in *Analytic Theology: New Essays in the Philosophy of Theology* (Oxford: Oxford University Press, 2009), pp. 156–68.

regarded as providing a clear and reliable access to objective reality, to the extent that those beliefs about reality can be warranted without evidence or argumentation. They are properly basic beliefs. On the other side, Bavinck is interpreted as offering an epistemology in which the subjective starting point so influences one's perception of the world that a worry is raised about whether he provides sufficient reasons to guard against epistemological subjectivism. Can Bavinck's writing so lend itself towards both conclusions?

To address this tension, I argue in the rest of this chapter that although Bavinck's views may have some Reidian connotations, he offers an account of perception and correspondence between subjects and objects that resists identification with Reid's, which sheds light on why van der Kooi and van den Belt might read him the way they do.[29] Further, as the next chapter will also show, Bavinck thinks that Christians specifically have an obligation to offer material and theological reasons for why it is that humans can reliably trust their perceptual and ordinary beliefs about external reality. These analyses, in turn, would display how Bavinck's organic motif plays a significant role in addressing the epistemological problems he encounters in modern philosophy. It is precisely the neglect of taking into account the organic motif that has caused the aforementioned interpretations to become somewhat one-sided.

II Herman Bavinck and Thomas Reid on perception and the problem of the 'gap'

To these ends, the rest of this chapter proceeds in three steps. First, I exposit the modern problem as interpreted by Bavinck and Reid – namely, that modern epistemology, with a few exceptions, posits a seemingly unbridgeable gap between the mental image as perceived by the human mind and the external object (an object that is thought to have first caused a mental image of that object to become present in the mind). Second, I exposit Reid's response to this problem while following closely Wolterstorff's interpretation and appropriation of Reid. Once Reid's response is in place, I present the response of Herman Bavinck. In short, I argue that Bavinck affirms the gap between the external object and the mental image of that object which the mind perceives but seeks to establish a link between the gap by an appeal to divine revelation and an organic ontology. Reid, however, sought to eliminate the gap by denying that knowledge is mediated by mental images – for Reid, the mind is aware not of a mental representation but of the external object itself. Finally, I close with some comments on the way in which Bavinck's and Reid's respective responses affect their understandings of the knowledge of God.

Before I begin my analysis, the contextual differences between the two thinkers must be acknowledged. Thomas Reid's birth (1710–96) predates Bavinck's death by almost two centuries. Furthermore, as a philosopher, Reid addressed primarily philosophical

---

[29] As will become clear, because Bavinck was not working within the methods of analytic epistemology, he cannot be clearly located as an advocate either of internalism or externalism. A key passage here is *Christelijke wereldbeschouwing*, p. 15.

issues. The answers he offered and the problems he sought to resolve were distinctly philosophical and rarely, if ever, did he engage in explicitly theological discourse. Further, Bavinck was not an analytic theologian – he wrote prior to the rise of analytic philosophy and did not think or write in terms of the logic set out by contemporary analytic methodology. Nicholas Wolterstorff's retrieval, refinement and application of Reid's epistemology, by contrast, stand squarely in the analytic tradition. This makes an analysis among the thinkers somewhat tricky. However, given the explicit use of both Bavinck and Reid in Wolterstorff and the overlap of concerns between Bavinck and Reid, an analysis in order to anticipate Bavinck's employment of the organic motif to bridge the gap between subjects and objects is still both possible and desirable, given that these caveats are acknowledged.

a. A 'problem' in modern epistemology

For Reid, since Descartes, philosophers have wrongly created a dual-object view of the thing known. The philosophers were commendable insofar as they sought to give an account of the belief that common persons take for granted, namely, 'that the object which they distinctly perceive certainly exists'.[30] The analysis that the philosophers offer, however, goes wrong when they assume principles that are ungrounded.

Two of these principles include the belief (1) that a thing cannot produce a cause where it is not present and (2) that an immediate cause of apprehension must be identical with the immediate object apprehended; these principles lead to the deduction that the immediate object perceived in the external world is not a physical object but a mental idea immediately in one's mind. This mental image, in turn, is that which mediates indirectly the external object that first caused that image to be perceived in the mind. This creates a gap between the object that the mind perceives and the thing outside of the mind. More precisely, Wolterstorff specifies that it is the 'belief that physical objects are too distinct for us to have an immediate apprehension of them; our knowledge of them has to be mediated by mental representations'.[31]

As a result, Reid observes that philosophers have 'split objects into two, where others [the unlearned and the common person] can only find one'.[32] The separation between mental ideas and external objects seems to imply either scepticism at best or solipsism at worst, especially when it may involve claims according to which the external world is only accessible by an inference from or an examination of mental ideas.[33] The advocates of the theory of mediation may argue that ideas provide a

---

[30] Thomas Reid, 'Essays on the Intellectual Powers of Man', in *The Works of Thomas Reid, D.D.: Now Fully Collected, With Selections from His Unpublished Letters* (Edinburgh: Maclachlan, Stewart and Co., 1846), p. 369. The narrative that follows here is a familiar one; Charles Taylor and Hubert Dreyfus have recently presented another rendition of this narrative in their *Retrieving Realism*, pp. 1–26.

[31] Nicholas Wolterstoff, *Thomas Reid and the Story of Epistemology* (Cambridge: Cambridge University Press, 2001), p. 44. Wolterstorff uses the 1858 edition of Hamilton's collected works of Thomas Reid. Ryan Nichols's *Thomas Reid's Theory of Perception* (Oxford: Clarendon Press, 2007) also offers an account of Reid's epistemology largely consistent with Wolterstorff's, but a focus of this chapter is Wolterstorff's retrieval of Reid.

[32] Reid, 'Intellectual Powers of Man', p. 369.

[33] Reid, 'Intellectual Powers of Man', p. 299.

window to reality, but their arguments fail to command Reid's agreement.[34] Reid is convinced that the denial of immediate access to reality entails the veracity of the conclusions of Hume and Berkeley, effectively rendering the existence of the external world as a philosophical hypothesis rather than a 'dictate of our perceptive powers'.[35]

In Wolterstorff's judgement, Kant's epistemological construction would have been equally vulnerable to Reid's critiques because it still falls into the same species of Locke's phenomenalism.[36] The only difference between them is that, in Locke, there is an 'ontological duality of types of entities (subjective states vs. external objects and qualities)', while in Kant, there is a 'duality of ways in which the intuitional given is conceptualized as, and presented to, a person (as subjective states of self vs. as objective entities)'.[37] Both espouse an account of knowledge whereby the external world (or Kant's thing-in-itself) is only knowable by some mediated subjective state, whether it be an idea (Locke) or the product of an intuition processed by the categories of the ego (Kant). In Wolterstorff's analysis, both epistemologies call the accessibility of the external world into question.

This move created the 'boundary' between the phenomenal and the noumenal – a boundary that produces significant implications for thinkers since Kant, among which is an anxiety in modern theologians about whether one can meaningfully speak about God. Experience limits knowledge, and the intuitions given in experience must be processed by the active receptivity of the categories in the mind. As such, 'Knowledge of the transcendent, Kant has been saying, is unavailable to us, since the bounds of the intuitional employment of the categories define the bounds of human knowledge, and those bounds coincide with the bounds of time.'[38] Claims to the effect that one can attain knowledge of things-in-themselves and of the divine, then, are to be regarded with suspicion at best.

Herman Bavinck's articulation of the perceived problem is almost identical with Reid's. In the *Reformed Dogmatics*, Bavinck expresses his dissatisfaction in Plato, Descartes, Leibniz and Rosmini, because by an affirmation of innate ideas they raise an 'untenable dualism between subject and object'.[39] He traces a distinction between a mental representation of a thing and the thing itself to the medieval scholastics but argues that modern philosophy perpetuates 'an ever-growing gap between a thing and its representation'.[40] He pinpoints the problem in this way: 'The error underlying this theory seems to be that the actual object of our perception is said to be, not the thing outside of us, but some impression or neural vibration within us.'[41] In limiting objects

[34] Reid, 'Intellectual Powers of Man', p. 300.
[35] Reid, 'Intellectual Powers of Man', p. 299.
[36] Wolterstorff, *Thomas Reid*, p. 103. What Wolterstorff labels 'the way of ideas' is described in this thesis as 'the theory of mediation'. Reid, of course, had not yet read Kant, as Kant was his contemporary.
[37] Wolterstorff, *Thomas Reid*, p. 90.
[38] Wolterstorff, 'Is it Possible and Desirable for Theologians to Recover From Kant?' p. 12.
[39] Bavinck, *RD*, 1: p. 224. Bavinck follows Voetius and the Reformed scholastics in their objections against modern epistemology here.
[40] Bavinck, *RD*, 1: pp. 227–8.
[41] Bavinck, *RD*, 1: p. 228. See also pp. 216–20. Hegel and Schleiermacher, who rose above the epistemology prevalent in their day, are the ones who finally reconnected 'subject and object', in Bavinck's judgement, in *RD*, 1: p. 521.

of knowledge to the representations internal to the mind, modern epistemology cannot seem to evade the charge that their main theses introduce a vicious scepticism concerning the external world.

In the Stone lectures, Bavinck extends these objections to Kant in much the same way as Wolterstorff. Though Kant cannot deny that 'the existence of on objective world' is a belief presupposed by every common person and that perception is a starting point of knowledge, Kant nevertheless misidentifies the products of sense perception.[42] Instead of beginning with the claim that sense perception reliably transmits knowledge of external reality, Kant thought that sense perception 'discovers nothing but an orderless mass of phenomena'.[43] 'Scientific knowledge', in turn, 'is possible and attainable only when the human mind introduces order into the chaos and subjects it to its own law'.[44] Kant's emphasis on the necessary constructive activities of the mind on the chaotic representations received in perception nurtures the later idealist axiom that knowledge of reality is wholly the product of the mind. Although Bavinck admits that this is an unintended consequence of Kant, it remains undeniable to him that Kant continues the trajectory towards the worst forms of subjective idealism that create two distinct worlds: an inner 'world of perception' that is 'in part or in whole a product of the perceiving subject', on the one hand, and an outer world, to which one has no real access, on the other.[45]

In Bavinck's judgement, this epistemological trajectory towards subjective idealism that limits knowledge to the internal representations of the mind also leads to reductionist forms of theology. It was Albrecht Ritschl, in Bavinck's judgement, who was the theologian that incorporated Kant's epistemology into a whole theological system.[46] At the root of Ritschl's theology is the epistemological distinction between 'things as they are in themselves, outside of any relation to our observation, from things as they are for us'.[47] Bavinck considered this error to be the engine driving Ritschl's constructive efforts leading to the affirmation that theology is merely a set of value judgements. Concomitant to this commitment is the claim by Ritschl that theologians cannot gain knowledge of God as he is in himself, but only as he is for us. 'Not only is revelation here robbed of its specific character and in Christianity restricted to Jesus, but Ritschl's epistemology also pushes him to reduce its content.'[48]

It is clear, then, that for Bavinck and Reid (and Wolterstorff), modern epistemology and the influence of Kant had led to serious and negative consequences for one's confidence in the basic faculties of perception and whether knowledge of external reality can be taken for granted. Their responses to this challenge, then, required them to figure out a way in which those two theses could be preserved. While their

---

[42] Bavinck, *Philosophy of Revelation*, p. 58.
[43] Bavinck, *Philosophy of Revelation*, p. 58.
[44] Bavinck, *Philosophy of Revelation*, p. 58.
[45] Bavinck, *Philosophy of Revelation*, p. 58. In Bavinck's view, 'Kantianism' is also untenable because it presupposes that God does not reveal himself in history. See, here, Bavinck, *RD*, 1: 340. Bavinck's historical analysis is consistent with James Brown, *Subject and Object in Modern Theology: The Croall Lectures Given in the University of Edinburgh 1953* (London: SCM Press, 1953), pp. 19–20, 168.
[46] Bavinck, 'Albrecht Ritschl', pp. 123–63.
[47] Bavinck, 'Albrecht Ritschl', p. 128.
[48] Bavinck, 'Albrecht Ritschl', p. 158.

diagnoses of the problem is nearly identical, however, it is here that their differences begin to emerge.[49]

b. Reid's proposal

Reid's response to the above epistemological conundrum is multifaceted, but for our purposes can be boiled down to two major moves.[50] The first is to deny that perception involves external reality causally acting upon something in the knower. For Reid, causation is tied to volition; nature, having no volition, lacks causal powers. This polemic is set against Locke's view, according to which perception involves the causation of ideas in the knower by external objects.[51] So, Reid reads his contemporary philosophers as thinking 'that the object perceived acts upon the mind in some way similar to that in which one body acts upon another, by making an impression upon it'.[52] This, however, 'contradicts the commonsense of mankind'.[53] Reid wants to account for perception differently; rather than arguing that in perception the mind is passive, Reid affirms that perception is essentially an act of the subject, an exercise of some original faculty of the make-up of humanity. In perceiving objects, we apprehend what they are by an act of the intellect.

This act of perception produces a different picture altogether. In Reid's account, perceiving an object is not accomplished by way of a mediate idea or mental image that was caused by the object. Rather, one perceives *the object itself* – an immediate and *direct* perception. In perception, one apprehends the object and attains an 'irresistible conviction' that it exists.[54] For Reid, the claim that a direct perception of the object is what commands our knowledge of and response to the external world is merely a recognition of what the learned and the unlearned alike already take for granted. This claim may not be susceptible to further philosophical dissection, but it is the only claim that does justice to the common sense of humanity. In the final analysis, Reid appeals to the creative design of God who 'intended that we should have such knowledge of the material objects that surround us, as is necessary in order to our supplying the wants of nature ... and he has admirably fitted our powers of perception to this purpose'.[55]

Reid's account is, of course, more nuanced than the brief sketch that I have presented here. He believes that, in perception, objects are processed through the natural pathways of one's biological constitution. He also leaves open whether perception should be conceived in terms of presentation or conceptual apprehension. What *is* clear is that

[49] I further explore the consequences of modern epistemology to whether knowledge of God can be attained, and Bavinck's and Reid's respective responses, in Nathaniel Gray Sutanto, 'Herman Bavinck and Thomas Reid on Perception and Knowing God', *Harvard Theological Review* 111 (2018): pp. 115–34. Parts of this section can also be found in a modified form in that article.
[50] Among them, of course, is Reid's contention that the results of adopting the theory of mediated knowledge runs against the cherished deliverances of 'common sense'.
[51] For an elaborate analysis of Reid on this, see Wolterstorff, *Thomas Reid*, pp. 61–74. What is in view here is objectual apprehension, but Reid, it seems, would also affirm direct propositional apprehension.
[52] Reid, 'Intellectual Powers of Man', p. 254.
[53] Reid, 'Intellectual Powers of Man', p. 254.
[54] Reid, 'Intellectual Powers of Man', pp. 258–9.
[55] Reid, 'Intellectual Powers of Man', p. 260.

in Reid's account perception involves '*direct, immediate* apprehension'.[56] Instead of trying to establish the existence of the external world (or, as for Wolterstorff, whether theological predication bears referential success) by working around the theory that knowledge is mediated by mental representations, Reid gets rid of mediation altogether, and that is the key insight that Reid offers as a solution to the problem of the gap. This is not to say that the apprehension of the external world does not make use of concepts. Concepts are necessary to apprehend reality but are not mere mental impositions on raw data; rather they are instantiated by the external object.

Wolterstorff puts Reid's insight to good use as a response to Kant's boundary.

> If we understand perception of an object as awareness of the object – *rather than as awareness of mental representation caused by the object* – then it will not make sense to follow Kant in the further step he takes of thinking of concepts as rules for structuring the objects of our awareness. *For now the objects of our awareness are not mental states but eagles and dogs.* And eagles and dogs are already structured; they don't await structuring by us.[57]

From here, this follows:

> How do concepts work on this alternative picture? To perceive an eagle under the concept of eagle is to perceive it to be what it is. Concepts are not barriers between mind and reality but links. … If that is so then properties are at one and the same time entities that we grasp and entities that external objects possess. They are the links.[58]

Hence, first, instead of seeking to bridge the gap erected between subject and object, Reid (and Wolterstorff) erased the gap altogether by way of direct apprehension. There is no 'space', or boundary, 'between being acquainted with something under some concept and having a belief about that entity; to be acquainted with something under some concept just is for one's acquaintance to evoke a *de re* / predicative belief about that entity'.[59] Second, in Reid's account an appeal to divine activity is ultimately necessary for an initial creational make-up of the human being as one is equipped with the necessary apparatus for reliable perception. If this is the case, then the scepticism nurtured by modern epistemology evaporates precisely because there is no good reason to believe that the objects of perception are merely internal to the mind. In normal conditions, rational agents are quite well within their rights to hold that their powers of perception are reliable and that the world of perception is identical with the outside world. Unless there are good reasons to doubt that what is perceived truly is reality (such as, say, if there are good reasons to believe that one is suffering a hallucination or that the agent has consumed too much alcohol), then it is rational to continue to assume that the perceptual beliefs obtained are, indeed, reliable. In other words, perceptual beliefs enjoy the epistemic status of being properly basic.

[56] Wolterstorff, *Thomas Reid*, p. 98. Emphasis in original.
[57] Wolterstorff, 'Is it Possible and Desirable for Theologians to Recover From Kant?' p. 17. Emphases mine.
[58] Wolterstorff, 'Is it Possible and Desirable for Theologians to Recover From Kant?' p. 17.
[59] Wolterstorff, *Thomas Reid*, p. 159. This is a straightforward account of direct realism.

c. Bavinck's proposal

At first glance, Bavinck's proposed solution seems identical to Reid's. Recall that Bavinck thinks the root problem is the disconnect between a mental representation and the thing external to the knower. Bavinck argues that, in perception, one gets a 'faithful' interpretation of the external world.[60] Even more strongly, Bavinck faults Ritschl for limiting knowledge to perception without including the external world, for in Bavinck's view Ritschl should have seen that 'the predicate brings us to the subject; perceptions draw us to essences'.[61] Essences of things are given in perception, and thus Bavinck could claim that 'the object of perception *is not any phenomenon within myself but the thing outside myself*'.[62] In perception, one is immediately convinced of the existence and objectivity of the external world.

Upon closer inspection, however, Bavinck arrives at this conclusion in a quite non-Reidian way. In Bavinck's desire to reject a boundary provided by the epistemological gap, Bavinck admits, first of all, that some gap must be acknowledged. Bavinck accepts a truth in epistemological realism, according to which the mind can know the mind-independent things external to the knower – but how, exactly, does the mind access external reality? Bavinck says this: 'Realism ... holds fast to the existence of the world because that world is, in an *ideal* sense, *given* in the *representation* itself.'[63] It is clear here what he is *not* denying: 'It does not deny *the distinction* that exists between the representation and the thing but at the same time maintains the inseparable connection between the two because it takes the representation as it presents itself.'[64] There is a distinction between the ideal representation and the thing in itself, but there is communication of the thing in the representation.[65] Again, this time acknowledging Thomas and the medieval scholastics,

> So on the one hand there is an essential difference between the thing and its representation, because the thing exists outside of us, has real existence there, while the second exists in us and *merely has ideal existence*. On the other hand, there is complete correspondence: the representation is an image, a faithful ideal reproduction of the object outside of us.[66]

---

[60] Bavinck, *RD*, 1: p. 229.
[61] Bavinck, 'Albrecht Ritschl', p. 131.
[62] Bavinck, *RD*, 1: p. 228. Emphasis mine.
[63] Bavinck, *RD*, 1: pp. 223–4. Emphases mine.
[64] Bavinck, *RD*, 1: p. 224. Emphasis mine.
[65] In this way Bavinck's analysis of knowledge differs from one articulation of Hegel's, in which one 'cannot begin from the assumption that the determinations or categories of thought and reality are conceivably distinct from one another, or that they might conceivably "correspond" to one another. It cannot begin with any conceivable distinction between thought and being at all.' Stephen Houlgate, *An Introduction to Hegel: Freedom, Truth and History*, 2nd edn (Oxford: Blackwell, 2005), p. 45. However, it is congenial with another articulation, in which Hegel regards subject and object as distinct but as a pair in relation. For this view, see Adams, *The Eclipse of Grace*. Despite some of the overlapping epistemological concerns, Bavinck self-consciously distanced himself from Hegel's ontology. On this, see Eglinton, 'To Be or to Become – That is the Question: Locating the Actualistic in Bavinck's Ontology', pp. 104–24.
[66] Bavinck, *RD*, 1: p. 227. Cf. Sytsma, 'Herman Bavinck's Thomistic Epistemology', p. 29, emphasis mine.

Bavinck accepts the existence of a gap, but it is a fixed gap. It is here that Bavinck criticizes modern philosophy for creating an 'ever growing gap' between the image and the external object.[67] Why, exactly, does Bavinck affirm the existence of this gap?

A few pages before the above statements, Bavinck's rejection of empiricism provides some clues. The problem with empiricism, Bavinck thinks, is that it conceives of the mind as passive as a mere recipient of impressions caused by external objects. This cannot be the case, however, as it 'is firmly established, first of all, that in its intellectual activity the human mind is never totally passive or even receptive but also always more or less active'.[68] Reid would agree, as he conceives of perception as an act of the intellect by which minds apprehend reality. But Bavinck's sense is rather different. For Bavinck, the mind not only judges, connects or compares perceptions – it adds to it. Here, Bavinck explicitly agrees with Kant, who 'rightly says' that experience can give us what is but not what it could not be: one cannot experience universal and necessary truths.[69] For Bavinck: 'After all, we possess not only particular and incidental truths but also universal and necessary truths ... which empiricists have tried in vain to deduce from experience.'[70] These universal truths are *a priori* starting points for all argumentation – presupposed as the basis for understanding.

It is especially significant that the word translated as 'representations' above is the Dutch word *voorstellingen*. A closer investigation of how Bavinck uses this word in *Christelijke wereldbeschouwing* shows the post-Kantian connotations of Bavinck's use, further signified to the use of the German *Vorstellung* in the German edition of the book.[71] Bavinck investigates epistemology in the first chapter of this booklet, in which he critiques idealism for failing to produce a proper process of reasoning: it seeks to establish the existence of the outside world by way of an inference from the circle of one's representations (*voorstellingen*): 'Out of one representation [the idealist] can merely infer another, but [he] can never by reasoning bridge the distance between thinking and being.'[72] Though idealism is right in arguing that the object can only be known by

---

[67] Bavinck, *RD*, 1: p. 227. Again, compare this with one interpretation of Hegel's attempt to connect subject and object: 'Hegel's objection is not primarily to Kant's ontology – in ontology in which there are phenomena and noumena, or appearances and things in themselves. ... Hegel's primary objection is to the logic which guides the account – a logic in which phenomena and noumena are opposed, where appearances and things in themselves are utterly separate.' Adams, *The Eclipse of Grace*, pp. 22–3. There is, of course, an important difference of emphasis. Hegel responds to Kant by offering an alternate account of logic – a logic of distinctions in inseparable relation (thereby vindicating the connection and essential difference between two poles) – whereas Bavinck appeals to a triune ontology to connect the two poles, as one shall see.

[68] Bavinck, *RD*, 1: p. 220.

[69] Bavinck, *RD*, 1: p. 220.

[70] Bavinck, *RD*, 1: p. 220. For Reid one does not need to account for how the belief in causality or necessary truths originate. One merely finds oneself believing these truths (presumably because of how human beings are hard-wired), and one is perfectly justified in believing so. Kevin Hector summarizes Kant (and Hegel) in a manner consistent with Bavinck: 'Apart from the mind's application of such universals, sensible appearances break up into a series of disconnected This-Here-Nows.' *The Theological Project of Modernism: Faith and the Conditions of Mineness* (Oxford: Oxford University Press, 2015), p. 142.

[71] Herman Bavinck, *Christliche Weltanschauung*, Hermann Cuntz (trans.) (Heidelberg: Carl Winter, 1907), pp. 9, 20. See footnote 32 in the next chapter for a further discussion on this *Vorstellung*.

[72] Bavinck, *Christelijke wereldbeschouwing*, p. 18. Dutch original: 'uit de eene voorstelling kan hij slechts tot een andere besluiten, maar nooit overbrugt eene redeneering de klove tusschen het denken en het zijn.'

representations, the existence of the outside world is not meant to be inferred from them. Rather, it is to be axiomatic that in 'sensations and representations a trustworthy knowledge of the objective reality' is given.[73] In 'sensation and representation' lie the maxims of truth and science.[74] The external world is not established by an inference from representations, but representations are those through which we know the external world.

In the *Philosophy of Revelation*, Bavinck reiterates this point. Before elaborating on some salient criticisms against subjective forms of idealism, Bavinck concedes that idealism contains undeniable features of truth:

> The truth of idealism lies in this, that the mind of man, in other words, sensation and representation [*voorstelling*], is the basis and *principium* of all knowledge. If there be an objective reality, a world of matter and force, existing in the forms of space and time, then it follows from the nature of the case that the knowledge of it can reach me through my consciousness only. In this sense it is quite proper to affirm that the object exists for the subject alone, and that the world is our representation. Apart from consciousness I know nothing, whether of myself or of any province of reality. In the defense of this truth, idealism holds strong ground over against that naïve naturalism which thinks it possesses ... a directly given reality, and which loses sight of the influence exerted by the subject in every perception of an object.[75]

In sum, there is an essentially *constructive* activity by the mind on the thing it perceives – the mind does not merely apprehend objects. Nor does Bavinck appeal to the wiring of humanity simply to believe in universal and necessary truths, as Reid does. Bavinck elaborates on this further as he discusses the role of faith for theological construction. There, he argues that the subjective starting point is necessary, no less because all knowledge begins there: 'Certainly the subjective starting point is not peculiar to theology. All that is objective can be approached only from the vantage point of the subject: the "thing in itself" is unknowable and does not exist for us. ... All life and all knowledge is based on a kind of agreement between subject and object.'[76] The subjective consciousness is the window through which the world is seen:

---

[73] Bavinck, *Christelijke wereldbeschouwing*, p. 20. Dutch original: 'dat wij in de gewaarwordingen en voorstellingen eene betrouwbare kennis van de objectieve werkelijkheid bezitten.'

[74] Bavinck, *Christelijke wereldbeschouwing*, p. 20. Dutch original: 'Dit nu is het feit, dat aan alle gewaarwording en voorstelling ten grondslag ligt. Wie het ontkent, ondermijnt alle waarheid en wetenschap.'

[75] Bavinck, *Philosophy of Revelation*, pp. 48–9; *Wijsbegeerte der Openbaring*, p. 46. It is significant that Bavinck considered these lectures as a further elaboration upon the themes found in *Christelijke wereldbeschouwing*. See *Philosophy of Revelation*, p. 23, n. 61. The *Philosophy of Revelation* is Bavinck's way of tracing out how it is that the philosophies that are produced independently of special revelation (in response solely to general revelation) in some ways anticipate the Christian worldview. They 'trace' revelation and 'correlate' it with the rest of our 'knowledge and life' (p. 24).

[76] Bavinck, *RD*, 1: p. 586. This definition of knowledge as agreement of subject and object and how to account for that agreement is the focus of modern epistemology. Cf. Brown, *Subject and Object in Modern Theology*, pp. 20–4.

'All that is objective exists for us only by means of subjective consciousness; without consciousness the whole world is dead for us.'[77]

It is tempting to take a wooden interpretation of what Bavinck says here and infer that the world's existence is dependent upon the consciousness of human beings. That would render Bavinck as a subjective idealist of a higher order, making epistemology *and* ontology contingent upon the subject's activity. Rather, he explicitly links the claim that the thing in itself 'does not exist for us' with the epistemic claim that it is 'unknowable'. What he says is *not* that the things in themselves do not exist but that *knowledge* of things in themselves does not exist. Despite the provocative choice of words, the sense of Bavinck's claim is epistemological rather than metaphysical. His sense is that the subject has no epistemological access to the thing in itself, no access to reality that is not affected in some way by the subjective consciousness. There is no direct access and thus knowledge should not be conceived as though external objects could be known 'in themselves' – to do so would be to succumb to what Bavinck calls a 'naive naturalism' that fails to take into account the activity of the subject in the knowing event.[78]

An affirmation of this gap leads Bavinck to wonder how a correspondence may be established between the subject and object – a problem that Bavinck takes seriously. A reflection on the way the brain produces a mental image distinct from the neural activity that communicates the world posits for one an 'insoluble riddle'.[79] A few pages later, Bavinck makes this riddle even more perplexing when he brings into consideration that the objects of science are not particulars but universals. The mind abstracts universals from individual particulars, but 'the universality we express in a concept does not exist as such, as a universal, apart from us. ... It has its basis in things and is abstracted from it and expressed in a concept by the activity of the intellect.'[80] The universal in the mind is not in the particular; again, how does the concept in the mind actually help us 'approximate' reality? Bavinck admits that it is 'strange, even amazing, that converting mental representations into concepts and processing these again in accordance with the laws of thought, we should obtain results that correspond to reality'.[81] When one couples this Aristotelian mode of thinking with Bavinck's affirmations concerning the mediating role of representations, the gap between subject and object is even clearer.

One wonders if Bavinck would have been vulnerable to the critiques lodged by Reid and Wolterstorff against Locke had he left matters there, as he is clearly indebted to certain modern epistemological categories that distinguish internal representations and external reality. He has offered an account of perception incompatible with that which Reid constructed. However, as we have seen before, Bavinck admits of a correspondence between the two sides of the gap. How exactly did he do this?

---

[77] Bavinck, *RD*, 1: p. 564.
[78] In this and the preceding analysis I am in agreement with Cornelis van der Kooi, 'Internal Testimony', p. 108. Chapter 7 will elaborate on the implications of this claim: because there remains a gap between representations and external objects, Bavinck argues that knowledge of things can be non-conceptual, leading to a rather Romantic picture of the unity of self, knowledge and external reality.
[79] Bavinck, *RD*, 1: p. 228.
[80] Bavinck, *RD*, 1: p. 231.
[81] Bavinck, *RD*, 1: p. 231.

III Towards Bavinck's use of Eduard von Hartmann

Although Bavinck and Reid offer similar diagnoses on the modern problem of the seemingly unbridgeable gap between subjective representations and objective reality, their responses to the problem are rather different. While Reid eliminates the gap altogether by offering an account which pictures intellects as picking out external objects, Bavinck maintains that the existence of the gap is undeniable. The question then arises: What accounts for the apparent ease with which Bavinck can say that rational agents can continue to enjoy their ordinary beliefs about the world with epistemic warrant? What, in other words, accounts for his apparent similarity with Thomas Reid in their mutual objection of the 'gap' between subjects and objects, such that knowledge of external things can be taken for granted – a reading that does lend itself to the project of Reformed epistemology? I suggest, in the next chapter, that Bavinck's critical appropriation of Eduard von Hartmann explains these phenomena. Eduard von Hartmann offered an epistemological and metaphysical account between naive realism and subjective idealism, to the effect that internal representations reliably communicates external reality precisely because both take part in an absolute Unconscious whole. In other words, subjects and objects participate in a larger unity and as such must be held in equipoise. This, then, explains why the ordinary person can take their perceptual beliefs for granted while providing the logical grounds needed by philosophers, who peer more deeply into this subject, to explain why those perceptual beliefs are indeed reliable.[82] Using the conceptual resources provided by a Christian and theological interpretation of the organic, Bavinck, as the next chapter shows, reinterprets von Hartmann's unconscious absolute in a stimulating manner. In this way, the potential worries raised by van der Kooi and van den Belt at the beginning of this chapter will also be addressed.

Bavinck should thus be located as a theologian who wrestled with the nineteenth- to twentieth-century trends in philosophical discourse that put a premium on the life of the unconscious, representational thinking and the spontaneous/instinctive life. Indeed, the common-sense connotations felt by Wolterstorff and Plantinga in Bavinck are reflective of the broader trend in that century that focuses on what lies underneath active consciousness. In his 1915 study on the unconscious, Bavinck regarded consciousness as a 'wondrous phenomena', considering it to be 'one of the seven mysteries of the world'.[83] Related to the intuitive life and practical reason, consciousness provides an immediate contact with 'psychic phenomena. ... It is a direct and concomitant consciousness.'[84] It is what distinguishes the sensations perceived as a self's own, rather than another's: 'Sensations, observations, memories, thoughts, judgments, and so forth do not exist by themselves or float in the air. They are what they are first because they are my or your or his or her sensations, and so on.'[85]

---

[82] This seems to imply that Eduard von Hartmann, precisely because he does not work within the methods of analytic philosophy, does not operate neatly within externalist/internalist parameters of justification or warrant.
[83] Bavinck, 'The Unconscious', p. 175.
[84] Bavinck, 'The Unconscious', p. 176.
[85] Bavinck, 'The Unconscious', p. 176.

Bavinck relates these insights on the psychic faculties and the immediate awareness of consciousness, whether in relation to the contents of the inner life or of external objects, to the Scriptural notion of the 'soul'.[86] He is not an anomaly in this regard. In 1908, Abraham Kuyper would also publish a politically driven study on the place of the instinctive life in the individual and social consciousness.[87] In that study, Kuyper relativizes the importance of rational deliberation and places a focus on the instincts that drive art, religion and the genius, the paradigms of romantic exemplars.[88] He envisions a kind of knowing that is no longer discursive but intuitive, and a collective consciousness that works in harmony before God in a manner that 'drew off the contemporary fascination with instinct and social psychology'.[89] In a striking passage, he distinguishes between proper and improper accounts of 'common sense':

> What is frequently dismissed as 'common sense' is something very different from what the French call *sens commun*. *Sens* is above all the expression of the instinctive life and the word *commun* calls for an organic society. *Sens commun* is the sensibility that the interested parties have in in common.[90]

The instinctive and intuitive lives of the individual and collective consciousness are predicated on an organic anthropology: the singular and the whole, and the phenomena 'not subject to the reflection of the thinking intellect':[91] 'All such phenomena are the natural effect of our organic unity. Anything organized by that very fact comes under the "psychology of the crowd", and it is almost exclusively the instinctive factors of life that explain the psychology of the "man in the mass"'.[92] Kuyper thus construes common sense not as the ordinary world-directed propositional beliefs that are elicited on a daily level but as an intuitive, pre-reflective, connectedness that binds psychic phenomena and the individual with the society: it is more romantic than it is Reidian.[93] For Bavinck, too, there is a primordial and pre-reflective unconscious life that connects

---

[86] Bavinck, 'The Unconscious', p. 197.

[87] Abraham Kuyper, *Ons Instinctieve Leven* (Amsterdam: W. Kirchner, 1908). English translation: Abraham Kuyper, 'Our Instinctive Life', in James Bratt (ed.), *Abraham Kuyper: A Centennial Reader* (Grand Rapids: Eerdmans, 1998), pp. 255–77.

[88] Kuyper was politically motivated, to be sure. This work emphasizes the pre-rational life of the people in order to emphasize the closeness of his political programme with the common masses, and further to establish himself as a man of the 'little people' (*de kleine luyden*). See especially James Bratt, *Abraham Kuyper: Modern Calvinist, Christian Democrat* (Grand Rapids: Eerdmans, 2013), pp. 350–5.

[89] Bratt, *Abraham Kuyper*, p. 351. In particular, Kuyper's treatment 'appealed to a French authority, Gustav Le Bon, a pioneer in the study of social psychology, Le Bon was most famous for showing how a crowd could become a being in itself with a will of its own that swept up those of its individual members' (Bratt, *Abraham Kuyper*, p. 353).

[90] Kuyper, 'Our Instinctive Life', p. 266. Cf. George Marsden, 'The Collapse of American Evangelical Academia', in Alvin Plantinga and Nicholas Wolterstorff (eds), *Faith and Rationality: Reason and Belief in God* (Notre Dame: University of Notre Dame Press, 1983), p. 250.

[91] Kuyper, 'Our Instinctive Life', p. 265.

[92] Kuyper, 'Our Instinctive Life', p. 265.

[93] This is not to say that Kuyper did not value the life of the rational intellect. Like Bavinck, he would argue that 'a few genuine scholars whose all-absorbing studies' should plunge themselves into 'the depth of things' in order to bring into closer synthesis the rational and practical life. Bratt, *Abraham Kuyper*, p. 352.

representations with objects. These can be explained, further, only if an organic vision of creation is deployed. James Bratt's apt summary of Kuyper's 'Our Instinctive Life' can easily be used to characterize Bavinck's own position: 'Kuyper valorized intuition against rationalization, vital conviction against learned pose, the reasons of the heart against a science that could but weigh and measure.'[94]

In the next two chapters, it shall become clearer that although Bavinck's realism is of the distinctly post-Kantian variety, he is motivated by materially theological claims regarding the Trinity and revelation in his construal of the relationship between subjects and objects. As it will become apparent, for Bavinck idealism and realism are not two wholly distinct options, contrary to popular caricatures, but rather two poles in a spectrum, each defined by an emphasis on the nature of the mode by which the world is accessed. To be sure, Bavinck is clearly (most) critical of *subjective* idealism, but not all forms of idealism are identical.[95] The absolute in Eduard von Hartmann's absolute idealism lends itself towards particularly Christian ways of answering specifically modern epistemological problems with acuteness and precision. In this, absolute idealism does not involve the claim that reality is a projection of finite human minds – the term 'idealism' in absolute idealism denotes, instead, the view that certain *epistemic and ontological conditions* (normally involving the view that the world is encountered by one as pre-conceptualized) always obtain in the knowing process.[96] In this way, Bavinck also showcases that, if related rightly, idealism and realism can be seen as not merely compatible but complementary. A theological-realist account of knowing is grounded in an absolute. It is to Bavinck's use of Eduard von Hartmann, then, that this study now turns.

---

[94] Bratt, *Abraham Kuyper*, p. 252.
[95] Commenting on Hegel, Bavinck wrote: 'In presenting this view idealistic, philosophy is not merely toying with abstract conceptions or idle ratiocinations, but *takes its start from reality – reality, to be sure, as seen by it*. Even Hegel, who certainly of all philosophers has most sinned by *a priori* constructions, had far more knowledge of the facts of nature and history than his opponents have given him credit for.' Bavinck, *Philosophy of Revelation*, p. 47. Emphasis mine.
[96] John McDowell, *Mind and World* (Cambridge: Harvard University Press, 1996), pp. 4–9, 44, 83; Paul Redding, *Analytic Philosophy and the Return of Hegelian Thought* (Cambridge: Cambridge University Press, 2007), p. 8. Even Berkeley's anti-materialistic idealism has been shown to be non-inimical to a realist view of knowledge. On this, see especially Gregory Trickett, 'Idealism and the Nature of Truth', in Steven B. Cowan and James S. Spiegel (eds), *Idealism and Christianity*, vol. 2: *Idealism and Christian Philosophy* (London: Bloomsbury, 2016), pp. 29–50. Andrew Inkpin's short comment is appropriate: 'Idealism [involves the view] that entities are defined by a particular mode of access.' *Disclosing the World: On the Phenomenology of Language* (Cambridge: MIT Press, 2016), p. 238. See also Bavinck's distinction between 'thoroughgoing' and 'half-hearted' idealism; the former denotes subjective idealism, while the latter those who follow Locke in positing secondary qualities to the constructive powers of the mind but not primary qualities, in *Philosophy of Revelation*, p. 60.

6

The Absolute and the organic – Bavinck and Eduard von Hartmann

Chapter 5 elaborates on two further trajectories within the secondary literature on Bavinck's account of perception. The first involves the observations by Cornelis van der Kooi and Henk van den Belt, on the distinctly critical realistic (post-Kantian) and subjectivist connotations in certain key passages in Bavinck's account. The second recounts the way in which Wolterstorff and Plantinga read Bavinck as a precursor to their Reformed epistemology. This reading rests, at least in part, on the presence of purportedly Reidian connotations in Bavinck's epistemology, especially as Bavinck insists that modern epistemology wrongly inserts a wedge between subject and object, and as Bavinck argues that ordinary beliefs about external reality can be held in a properly basic way. An implicit tension between the two set of readings is this: How can Bavinck be indebted to a post-Kantian subjectivist bent, on the one hand, and have Reidian connotations, on the other? This question is particularly acute especially as Reidianism is seen to be an alternative to post-Kantian subjectivist and scepticist tendencies with respect to beliefs about external reality.

In an attempt to untangle and elucidate all of the issues involved, the chapter then explored how Reid rejects 'the way of ideas' in favour of the view that subjects perceive objects immediately without the role of representations. It then went on to argue that Bavinck, quite unlike Reid, posited a strong distinction between representations (through which one knows the external object) and the things in themselves. This suggests that although Bavinck is quite insistent that knowing subjects can access external objects in themselves, there are certain epistemological conditions that always attend the epistemic process, among which is the constructive role of the subject in the act of perception. Knowledge of things, in Bavinck's view, is always through mental representations; the consciousness mediates knowledge of objects and adds to it in some way.[1]

This suggests that the Reidian connotations in Bavinck's epistemology are more accidental than substantial. It seems that unlike Reid, Bavinck affirms the mediation

---

[1] In this regard Cornelius Jaarsma is right to summarize Bavinck's view thusly: 'The world of perception is given in our consciousness, not as a dream or hallucination, but as appearance and idea (voorstelling) which actualizes the existence of the objective world.' *The Educational Philosophy of Herman Bavinck*, pp. 48–9.

of representations in the denial of naive (direct) realism. If that is so, a curious shared affirmation arises: namely, that prior to reasoning man can be (in some way) initially warranted in the belief that external reality is susceptible to the powers of the human faculties. What accounts for this apparent similarity? I suggest that Bavinck's similarities with Reid are not so much a reflection of his dependence on the common sense or direct realistic tradition but more a signal of his use of Eduard von Hartmann. This is so because von Hartmann seeks to construct a mediating position between subjective idealism and naive realism. Hence, the similarities that obtain between Bavinck and Reid are actually a reflection of a prior accidental similarity between von Hartmann and Reid. Stated positively, Bavinck's reconnoitering of the epistemology of Eduard von Hartmann is what accounts for the apparent similarity and differences between Bavinck and Reid. I shall suggest this by observing the way in which Bavinck and von Hartmann reject subjective idealism, their affirmation of how both the subject and object must be treated in equipoise and their appeal to some ontology in which subject and object participate. These moves will thus further broach on an issue left loose in the previous chapter, namely, how Bavinck understands the nature of epistemic justification.

This chapter contributes to the thesis in three ways. First, it clarifies how Bavinck is a principled yet eclectic thinker as it observes that his epistemology draws from von Hartmann, and how Bavinck would deploy the organic motif to accommodate insights from various epistemologies. Second, and more significantly, I will demonstrate that Bavinck's deployment of the organic motif in order to connect subject and object is developed within the context of an engagement with the problems and grammar of nineteenth- to twentieth-century philosophical discourse. In doing so, the significance of the organic motif, in Bavinck's view, in its capacity to resolve some apparent philosophical problems with respect to perception and knowledge will also be clarified. Third, some important themes involved in Bavinck's organic account for subsequent chapters will be considered, including his view that revelation is pre-reflective, that contact with God and reality are primordial facts and that these two claims are accounted for by an appeal to the organic.

The following argument follows Bavinck's use of von Hartmann in the third chapter of the *Philosophy of Revelation* and von Hartmann's own argumentation in his magnum opus, the *Philosophy of the Unconscious*, before culling material from Bavinck's deployment of the organic motif with respect to the subject–object discussions in the rest of Bavinck's corpus.[2] Henk van den Belt, as we have seen, noted Bavinck's use of von Hartmann before, yet it seems necessary to offer further justification for my use of von Hartmann, especially as *Philosophy of the Unconscious* is not explicitly referenced

---

[2] Cf. Eduard von Hartmann, *Philosophy of the Unconscious: Speculative Results According to the Inductive Method of Physical Science*, William Coupland (trans.), 9th edn (London: Routledge, 2000). Where seemingly relevant, I make a reference to Von Hartmann's German text: Eduard von Hartmann, *Philosophie des Unbewussten: Speculatie Resultate nach Inductiv-naturwissenschaftlicher Methode*, 3 vols, 10th edn (Leipzig: Hermann Haacke, 1890). The differences between the ninth edition in the English translation and the tenth edition are merely in pagination and in some added appendices, with the former including all three volumes in a single work and the latter dividing the three volumes into three books.

by Bavinck in the third chapter of his Stone lectures, despite Bavinck's invocation of his name multiple times throughout the chapter.

First, Bavinck was clearly aware of von Hartmann's *Philosophy of the Unconscious*, as seen both in his use of it in his psychological study on the relationship between the unconscious and consciousness[3] and in a handwritten notebook that studies the text's argument at length, noting what Bavinck considers to be the most salient points of each chapter and section.[4] The second reason will be found in the material congeniality observed between Bavinck and von Hartmann and Bavinck's explicit invocation of von Hartmann's name at crucial points within the text; there are also many references to von Hartmann's Unconscious Absolute, as I shall demonstrate in this chapter.

Bavinck's initial descriptions of von Hartmann in his notes immediately reminds the reader, at least prima facie, some of Bavinck's own tendencies. Bavinck notes that in von Hartmann 'the inductive method is preferred.'[5] The philosophy of the unconscious also 'distinguished', Bavinck surmises, between 'perception (representation) and apperception (consciousness)'.[6]

Further, despite Bavinck's clear preference for a realistic epistemology over 'idealism', his desire to be located somewhere between subjective idealism and naive realism can also be discerned in von Hartmann's epistemology. Von Hartmann says as much, as seen most clearly in these two passages. First, he affirms, 'All belief in an *immediate* self-apprehension of the Ego in the act of self-consciousness depends on the same self-delusion as the naïve realistic belief [*Glaube*] in the immediate conscious apprehension of the thing in itself that exists independently of consciousness.'[7]

---

[3] Bavinck, 'The Unconscious', pp. 175–98.
[4] This notebook (*Notitieboekje met aantekeningen betreffende de zesde druk van Die Welt als Wille und Vorstellung geschreven door Arthur Schopenhauer, en Eduard von Hartman, Philosophie des Unbewussten [Berlin 1882]*) is found as item 279 in the Bavinck archives at the Free University of Amsterdam. The notes on Von Hartmann in the notebook, though not explicitly paginated, are thirty-six pages long and are preceded by more notes on Arthur Schopenhauer's *Die Welt als Wille und Vorstellung*. The heading of the notes indicates that Bavinck is working with the ninth edition of the text, which is dated 1882. From here I will refer to the notes as BNVH (Bavinck's notes on Von Hartmann).
[5] Bavinck, BNVH, p. 1. 'De induct. Method heeft de voorkeur'. Cf. Von Hartmann, *Philosophy of the Unconscious*, I: p. 8. That Bavinck prefers the inductive, empirical, method in scholarly study is commonly acknowledged. See, for example, Bavinck, *Modernisme en Orthodoxie*, p. 12. Indeed, Bavinck objects to pragmatism precisely in that it fails to be 'sufficiently' empirical, in his *Philosophy of Revelation*, p. 48. He is not, however, unaware of its drawbacks and lists potential weaknesses of it (including failing to take into account one's inevitable subjectivity) in *Beginselen der psychologie*, pp. 7–8.
[6] Bavinck, BNVH, p. 1. Bavinck specifically switches to the English when he denotes perception and apperception here: 'De philoso … altijd als berust op [Leibniz's discovery of unconscious representations, and] onderscheidde dus perception (voorstelling) en apperception (bewustzijn)'.
[7] Von Hartmann, *Philosophy of the Unconscious*, II: p, 79, emphasis in original; *Philosophie des Unbewussten*, II: p. 29. Recall Bavinck's reasoning in *RD*, 1: p. 586: 'Certainly the subjective starting point is not peculiar to theology. All that is objective can be approached only from the vantage point of the subject: the "thing in itself" is unknowable and does not exist for us.' See also the *Philosophy of Revelation*, p. 49, in which he says that 'naive naturalism' assumes falsely that there is a 'directly given reality' accessible apart from 'the influence exerted by the subject in every perception of an object'.

Second, and even more explicitly, von Hartmann writes the following towards the end of the third volume of the *Philosophy of the Unconscious*, under chapter XV ('The Ultimate Principles'), section five, entitled 'The Possibility of Metaphysical Knowledge':

> [With the assumption of the heterogeneity of thought and thing], only two standpoints are possible: that of naïve Realism and that of Subjective Idealism. The former fails to see that everything that I can express in words and reach with my thoughts can always only be my own thoughts, but never a reality lying beyond the same; that thought can never denude itself of the character of thought, and erroneously confuses itself or the thinkable (intelligible) with that which lies beyond thought (trans-intelligible). ... The second standpoint [Subjective Idealism] corrects this error ... but it commits the other fault of *denying* that which is placed beyond the limits of thinking, because it is *unattainable* to thinking, and therewith annihilates the possibility of all knowledge, in that thinking is lowered to a dream without object and therewith without truth.[8]

Naturally, von Hartmann posits the Absolute Unconscious as the Subject in which thought and being, subject and object, are reconciled because they are reconceived as two modes of the same monistic existence.[9] In Bavinck's brief summary of this section, he notes that von Hartmann's philosophy navigates into 'naïve realism or idealism [*naief realism of het idealisme*]', as it posits an 'identity-philosophy [*De identiteitsphilos.*]', a 'philosophy of the Unconscious' [*de philos. Onbewuste*] according to which 'thinking and being' [*denken en zijn*] are one.[10] As such, von Hartmann's critical (idealistic) realism is already palpable: he affirms that objects are truly independent of finite minds, yet are accessed by way of the consciousness of the subject, which always contributes something to the knowing process.

As this chapter will further demonstrate, Bavinck critically appropriates von Hartmann. In the following section, Bavinck's critical appropriation of von Hartmann is observed in his rejection of subjective idealism and in his belief in the availability of the external world. The close reading of the primary texts involved will also be sensitive to the interpretations of Wolterstorff and Plantinga, along with the current scholarship that discusses the debate between realism and idealism, showing further that the distinction between the two is mired with more complexity than the common presentation that the two form the choice between solipsism and objectivism. After the following section, I will then turn to Bavinck's strategy to account for how the subject knows objects by his reinterpretation of the Absolute, and the deployment of the organic motif.

---

[8] Von Hartmann, *Philosophy of the Unconscious*, III: p. 198. Emphasis original.
[9] Von Hartmann, *Philosophy of the Unconscious*, III: pp. 201-3. Emphasis original. Sebastian Gardner's comment here is apt: '[Von Hartmann combines] a metaphysics of absolute idealism with a philosophical *methodology* which denies anything more than auxiliary value to a priori reflection, and according to which derivation from *experience* is the proper source of metaphysical cognition: scientifically processed experience is held to be sufficient to support the most robust metaphysical conclusions' (emphasis in original). 'Eduard von Hartmann's *Philosophy of the Unconscious*', in Angus Nicholls and Martin Liebscher (eds), *Thinking the Unconscious: Nineteenth-Century German Thought* (Cambridge: Cambridge University Press, 2006), pp. 174-5.
[10] Bavinck, *BNVH*, p. 36.

I The 'mistake of idealism' and the immediacy of contact with the world: Bavinck's critical appropriation of Eduard von Hartmann

The above section observes that Bavinck accepts the distinction between subject and object, between the mental representations through which rational agents acquire knowledge and the external objects. The mistake of idealism, therefore, lies not so much in the acceptance of the mediating and key role played by mental images or representations in the epistemic process. Indeed, the mistake, in Bavinck's thinking, is in the attempt to purchase the epistemic reliability of the external world by an inference from internal representations, as the last section had already teased. By observing Bavinck's argumentation in the *Philosophy of Revelation*, his affinities with von Hartmann will emerge in greater clarity, and in doing so will further demonstrate how he brings in the organic motif as a solution to the subject–object dichotomy.

Immediately after Bavinck admits that 'idealism' is correct to affirm that the subject[11] always exerts some influence in every act of perception, Bavinck begins an elaboration on what he takes to be the erroneous inferences made from this starting point by idealists. First, Bavinck argues that idealism wrongly infers from the truth that consciousness is a 'medium' for perception to the conclusion that the objects perceived 'must itself be immanent in the mind'.[12] Consciousness is simply the organ by which the subject knows, and it is not to be confused as the 'principle and source of the knowledge of the object'.[13] Bavinck goes on:

> The mistake of idealism lies in confounding the act with its content, the function with the object, the psychological with the logical nature of perception. Perception is an act of the subject, and sensation and representation, as truly as concepts and conclusions, have a purely ideal, immanent existence. But perception as such terminates upon an object, and sensation and representation, logically considered, by their very nature are related to a reality distinct from themselves. Hence psychology and logic differ in character. It is one thing to consider the representations as they lie in consciousness and another thing in and through them to apprehend reality. To ignore the difference means to remain entangled in a sort of psychologism, imprisoned in one's self and doomed never to reach reality.[14]

Bavinck's reasoning rests on the distinction between 'psychology' and 'logic'. Psychology, in Bavinck's pre-Freudian usage, is the study of the processes and faculties involved in the functioning of consciousness and the acts of cognition. It observes

---

[11] Jaarsma provides a brief account of Bavinck's critique of idealism in *The Educational Philosophy of Herman Bavinck*, pp. 52–7, but without paying sufficient attention to (1) the organic and (2) Bavinck's critical appropriation of the Absolute, especially as he considers Bavinck's view to be a theistic 'monism' (p. 65). This point becomes clearer throughout this chapter.
[12] Bavinck, *Philosophy of Revelation*, p. 49.
[13] Bavinck, *Philosophy of Revelation*, p. 49.
[14] Bavinck, *Philosophy of Revelation*, pp. 49.

the phenomena and the workings internal to the human subject. Logic, on the other hand, has to do with deductions, inferences and epistemology – it draws conclusions from premises and is as such a normative discipline meant to distinguish between valid and invalid forms of reasoning. Logic apprehends reality. Idealism, Bavinck charges, conflates the two. While the idealist correctly observes the findings of psychology, it wrongly identifies those workings with an epistemological process – its mistake lies in conflating mental representations with the only immanent object the subject encounters in perception, rather than seeing that those representations lead subjects to an external object – an object independent of finite minds. As a result, the idealist inevitably shuts the mind up 'in the circle of representations', locking it inside a 'self-constructed prison'.[15]

These remarks bear great consistency with Bavinck's objections against idealism found in his *Prolegomena*, specifically that (1) idealism wrongly identifies a representation with the thing it represents and (2) it wrongly places the 'intellect' as the source of knowledge rather than the organ of knowledge. So, 'If the thing and the representation of it are nevertheless equated with each other, idealism must lead to absolute illusionism.'[16] The 'intellect [*het intellect*] is an instrument, not a source. Idealism equates the organ of knowledge with the source of knowledge.'[17] In these ways, idealism is inferior to realism, in Bavinck's judgement, specifically because idealists miss that the 'distinguishing mark' of representations is precisely that they are *about* something else – they point beyond themselves, *representing* 'that reality ideally'. As such, idealism denies the 'representative character' of representations.[18] Realism, by contrast, argues that the world is 'in an ideal sense, given in the representation itself'. Hence, with the 'idealist' he affirms that ideas or representations are constitutively involved in knowing, but with the realist he asserts that the objects are 'given' in representations.[19]

In the *Philosophy of Revelation*, Bavinck does not identify the 'intellect' as the organ of knowledge but rather the 'consciousness' and an agent's 'subjective perception'. He wrote:

> In other words, no one can know reality except through his consciousness [*bewustzijn*], since it is obviously impossible to know without knowing. Perception on the part of the subject renders a double service; it is at once the condition and the instrument of the perception of the object. Nonetheless there is a great

---

[15] Bavinck, *Philosophy of Revelation*, p. 51. This links well with Beiser's comment concerning what unites the various idealist traditions: 'What makes them belong to a single tradition – is their similar approach to some common philosophical problems. Since Kant, philosophers had become preoccupied with two distinct but closely related issues: how to explain the possibility of knowledge and how to account for the reality of the external world. ... To explain the possibility of knowledge requires demonstrating that there is some kind of *identity* between subject and object; for if the subject and object are completely distinct from one another, they will not be able to interact or correspond with one another to produce knowledge.' *German Idealism: The Struggle Against Subjectivism*, p. 13. Emphasis in original.

[16] Bavinck, *RD*, 1: p. 217.

[17] Bavinck, *RD*, 1: p. 217; *GD*, 1: p. 217. On this page Bavinck lists Spinoza, Fichte, Schelling and Hegel, among others, as the interlocutors in mind.

[18] Bavinck, *RD*, 1: p. 223.

[19] Bavinck, *RD*, 1: pp. 223–4.

difference between the view that subjective perception [*subjective waarneming*] is the means and organ, and the other view that it is the principle and source of the knowledge of the object.[20]

This may be due to a development in Bavinck's philosophy concerning the all-encompassing role that consciousness (and self-consciousness) plays in one's being and thinking. But materially, one should note, there is much overlap in Bavinck's critique of idealism on this point between the *Prolegomena* and the *Philosophy of Revelation*. This is further confirmed when the reader revisits Bavinck's discussion of faith and the introduction of the role of consciousness in the later section of the *Prolegomena*: 'All knowledge comes from without. But on the human side all that knowledge is mediated by their consciousness. Not feeling or heart but the mind, consciousness as a whole (perception, awareness, observation, intellect, reason, conscience) is the subjective organ of truth.'[21]

Returning to the argument in the *Philosophy of Revelation*, Bavinck again reasserts the importance of keeping the proper distinction between the psychological and the logical:

> Epistemology ... teaches the very opposite of what idealism asserts. The perceptive and cognitive activity of man is only in a psychological and not in a logical sense a purely immanent act of the mind. Both perception and representation would cease to be what they are if nothing existed that was perceived and represented. On both the character of logical transcendence is indelibly impressed; by their very nature they point to an objective reality, detached from which they would become equivalent to hallucinations and illusions.[22]

Bavinck discerns that this fundamental error is what mitigates idealism from the ability truly to affirm an objective epistemology, and it manifests itself in two concrete ways. The first, in Bavinck's view, is the application of 'the principle of causality' such that representations are considered as 'effects' that are caused by external objects. This idealist move seeks to ascertain the existence of the external world through a causal inference from internal representations.[23] The second move argues that it is by an act of freedom, rather than an act of inference, that external reality can be affirmed. Bavinck rejects both of these moves, and his reasoning is as follows:

> We find that neither of the two methods leads to the goal contemplated. For previously to all reasoning about representation and will, all humans – the unlearned as well as the learned, and even children and indeed animals – are convinced of the reality of an objective world. Not even the thinker, who by scientific reflection has reached the position of idealism, can divest himself of his belief in this reality.[24]

---

[20] Bavinck, *Philosophy of Revelation*, p. 49; *Wijsbegeerte der Openbaring*, p. 47.
[21] Bavinck, *RD*, 1: p. 565.
[22] Bavinck, *Philosophy of Revelation*, pp. 60–1.
[23] Bavinck, *Philosophy of Revelation*, p. 50.
[24] Bavinck, *Philosophy of Revelation*, p. 50.

The objection here, it seems, consists in the observation that objective reality is never a conclusion to an argument or the product of our conscious willing. Idealism neglects to appreciate the constancy and immediacy with which creatures perceive – and indeed, take for granted – the reality of the external world. Seeking to produce an argument or a chain of reasoning to grasp reality is really to assume falsely that such a process was needed. Here, the common-sense connotations are obvious, but instead of invoking Reid, it is Eduard von Hartmann who is invoked. Bavinck argues that von Hartmann concedes,

> That without this belief it is impossible for man to live. 'Without this faith in the reality and continuity of what we perceive', says he, 'we should be unable to live for a moment, and hence this naively realistic faith, coalescing with the perception itself, by way of intuition, into an indivisible act, forms an indispensable, practically inalienable ingredient of our mental equipment.'[25]

Like von Hartmann, Bavinck generally accepts a characteristic of naive realism in placing a premium on the everyday beliefs that rational subjects ordinarily take for granted: 'Practically we all draw a distinction between the waking and dreaming states, between the representation of reality and hallucination.'[26] What is clear here is that though Bavinck and von Hartmann reject that objects can be immediately or directly perceived apart from the mediation of mental representations, both are congenial to the common-sense thesis that ordinary individuals are within their epistemic rights to assume the accessibility and existence of the external world. Philosophical or metaphysical argumentation should protect this belief, rather than render it susceptible to doubt in order to see whether that belief could be held as a conclusion to an argument. In other words, Bavinck and von Hartmann affirm the *temporal* or *logical immediacy* of knowledge of the external world while also maintaining a *mediated access* view of how one perceives the world.

Accordingly, for Bavinck, 'The human mind must by its very nature be under the necessity of connecting its representations with reality, in which case the procedure can neither be unconscious nor consist of an act of syllogistic reasoning.'[27] The idealist cannot ignore that he is as much a human being as the ordinary non-philosopher. Both experience the daily conviction, 'antecedently to all reasoning', that the external world

---

[25] Bavinck, *Philosophy of Revelation*, p. 50. Bavinck is quoting Eduard von Hartmann, *Kristische Wanderungen durch die Philosophie der Gegenwart* (Leipzig: Friedrich, 1890), p. 190. The kind of 'idealism' Bavinck is critiquing, it seems, is subjective idealism (rather than absolute or objective idealism), as Bavinck's idealist seeks to apprehend reality by way of the subject and her ideas as the starting point. This is further confirmed when Fichte's concession is brought into Bavinck's discussion: 'Even Fichte felt compelled, chiefly by moral considerations, not to regard himself as the only existent being. Every man knows that he does not exist alone, that he is not able to do what he pleases, that on every side he is curbed and hedged in and encounters resistance.' *Philosophy of Revelation*, p. 57.

[26] Bavinck, *Philosophy of Revelation*, p. 51. Cf. Eduard von Hartmann, *Philosophy of the Unconscious*, I: pp. 9–12.

[27] Bavinck, *Philosophy of Revelation*, p. 51. This is tethered to Bavinck's understanding that God reveals himself, our selves and the world, immediately in one's consciousness, prior to thinking and reasoning, below.

surrounds them – a conviction 'indispensable for knowledge and activity'.[28] Indeed though there is an 'irremovable distinction, between the representation and the thing of which it is a representation',[29] Bavinck writes, it is nonetheless 'in and through' these representations that one perceives 'the things themselves'.[30]

Though I will make clear that Bavinck's understanding of how representations immediately communicate reality is pre-cognitive below, it seems undeniable that, materially speaking, Bavinck advocates for something like Wolterstorff's retrieval of a Reidian *belief disposition* – human beings are hard-wired to hold beliefs that are triggered by ordinary circumstances. Humans find themselves immediately believing in the external physical world, that their memory beliefs are reliable and that their perceptual states refer to external things quite non-problematically. These beliefs are acquired not by way of conscious reasoning or argumentation but rather by the make-up of the way we are. We can take much of what we believe for granted, and are epistemically no worse for doing so.[31]

One explicit way in which Bavinck is sympathetic to these common-sense theses is his appeal to G. E. Moore's 'Refutation of Idealism' as he argues that 'in consciousness our own being and the being of the world are disclosed to us antecedently to our thought or volition; that is, they are *revealed* to us in the strictest sense of the word.'[32] Though Bavinck does not cite a particular line in Moore's article, passages that resonate clearly with Bavinck's concerns can be easily found. The argument that idealists fail to extricate subjects from the 'circle' of ideas can be found in Moore. 'There is, therefore, no question of how we are to "get outside the circle of our own ideas and sensations"', Moore reasoned, for to perceive sensations is 'already *to be* outside that circle'.[33] Like Moore, then, Bavinck thought that to begin at the level of a purely subjective consciousness in an attempt to erect a bridge towards the outside world, whether by way of a mental inference or a free volitional act, is to inaugurate an unnecessary process. One must treat subject and object in equipoise.

---

[28] Bavinck, *Philosophy of Revelation*, p. 58.
[29] Bavinck, *Philosophy of Revelation*, p. 53.
[30] Bavinck, *Philosophy of Revelation*, p. 52.
[31] Nicholas Wolterstorff, 'Can Belief in God Be Rational if it Has No Foundations?' in Alvin Plantinga and Nicholas Wolterstorff (eds), *Faith and Rationality: Reason and Belief in God* (Notre Dame: University of Notre Dame Press, 1983), p. 149.
[32] Bavinck, *Philosophy of Revelation*, p. 63. Emphasis in original. The reference to Moore is in a note that follows this line, to G. E. Moore, 'The Refutation of Idealism', *Mind* (1903): pp. 433–53. Bavinck's appeal to Moore, it seems, is not uncritical, as Bavinck also notes a response by the idealist, C. A. Strong, against Moore: C. A. Strong, 'Has Mr. Moore Refuted Idealism?' *Mind* (1905): pp. 174–89. An explicit point of tension between Bavinck and Moore is the latter's rejection of the thesis that mental images exist at all, and thus Moore believes that the idea of a correspondence between mental images and external objects dissolves entirely: 'What reason have we for supposing that there are things outside the mind *corresponding* to things inside it? What I wish to point out is (1) that we have no reason for supposing that there are such things as mental images at all – for supposing that blue *is* part of the content of the sensation of blue', and later he rejects that 'Vorstellungen' refer to subjective experience and relations within the mind. 'Refutation of Idealism', pp. 449, 453, respectively. Emphasis in original. On Reid's influence on Moore, see John Greco, 'How to Reid Moore', *The Philosophical Quarterly* 52 (2002): pp. 544–63.
[33] Moore, 'Refutation of Idealism', p. 451. Emphasis in original. Bavinck's argument in pages 74–5 concerning the inseparability between primary and secondary qualities can also be found in Moore's article.

Nonetheless, as one attends to the argumentation of the *Philosophy of Revelation* thus far, Eduard von Hartmann is invoked more explicitly, especially as both Bavinck and von Hartmann – unlike Reid or Wolterstorff – accept the role of representations as mediators through which rational subjects perceive the world. Although Bavinck does not cite a particular reference in von Hartmann concerning the contact of the external world through the mental representations assumed by all human beings ordinarily, many passages in von Hartmann's *Philosophy of the Unconscious* can be reproduced to showcase his view. In this following passage, for example, Bavinck's reasoning concerning the mistaken application of the 'principle of causality' by idealism and his priority on the beliefs of the non-philosopher seems to be a material replication of von Hartmann's reasoning:

> The Unconscious, must lend a helping hand in order to fulfill the purpose of perception, the cognition of the external world. Accordingly, the animal and child instinctively projects its sense-perceptions as objects outside itself; and, accordingly, to this day, every uninstructed human being thinks he perceives the things themselves, because his perceptions, with the determination of externality, *instinctively* becomes objects to him. Thus only is it possible that the world of *objects* stands there ready for any being, without the idea of the *subject* occurring to it, whilst in conscious thought subject and object must necessarily spring simultaneously from the ideational process [*vorstellungsprocesse herausspringen mussen*]. It is, therefore, wrong to posit the concept of causality as mediator for a conscious segregation of the object, for objects are there long before the causal concept has arisen; and even were this not the case, yet, *even then*, the subject must be simultaneously gained with the object.[34]

The objects are present to subjects 'long before' the principle of causality is even considered, and thus both subject and object should be treated 'simultaneously' in the process of representation. Bavinck seems to be applying von Hartmann's critique of idealism directly. Later, von Hartmann again affirms that the subject and object should be treated as a pair and that the philosopher's task as such should not undermine the intuitions of the 'natural man':

> For it lies in the conceptions themselves that subject and object require each other as correlatives; but this correlation is patent only to the consciousness of the philosopher, not to the unreflecting feeling of the natural man, and therefore to the latter in the intuitive apprehension of the concrete object the relation of the concept of the object to the concept of the subject, and especially the latter remains unconscious.[35]

Bavinck's appreciation for von Hartmann should not eclipse the critical differences between the two. Bavinck is highly critical of von Hartmann's engulfment of the

---

[34] Von Hartmann, *Philosophy of the Unconscious*, I: pp. 350–1; *Philosophie des Unbewussten*, I: p. 303. Emphases in original. Cf. Bavinck, BNVH, pp. 11–12.

[35] Von Hartmann, *Philosophy of the Unconscious*, II: p. 79. Cf. Bavinck, BNVH, pp. 15–17.

individual consciousness into the Absolute Unconscious. For von Hartmann, the Unconscious does not merely lend a 'helping hand' to the problem of perception – it is an absolute monistic principle in which all individuals are engulfed. The finite consciousness is but an instantiation of its activity. In his words, 'All unconscious operations spring *from one same* subject, which has only its phenomenal revelation in the several individuals, so that "the Unconscious" signifies this One Absolute subject'.[36] With respect to the problem of perception specifically, von Hartmann wrote,

> The world consists only of a sum of activities or will-acts of the Unconscious, and the ego consists of another sum of activities or will-acts of the Unconscious. Only so far as the former activities intersect the latter does the world become *sensible* to me; only so far as the latter intersect the former do I become sensible to myself.[37]

In his strategy to prove 'the *essential likeness of Mind and Matter*', he conceived of an Absolute Unconscious in which both subject and object participate.[38]

Bavinck appreciates von Hartmann's point that 'there is no other way of doing justice to both subject and object' except that one affirms a rational 'divine wisdom' which undergirds the structural integrity of both.[39] Yet in Bavinck's judgement, von Hartmann erred in subsuming all things under a single Unconscious principle. If the perception of the external world is 'as Von Hartmann actually represents it … accomplished in us by the great Unconscious (*Onbewuste*), in which case it is no conclusion of ours', Bavinck reasoned, then it follows that 'all self-activity of man in thinking and acting (*denken en handelen*) disappears.'[40] Bavinck charges von Hartmann for failing to appreciate the constitutive individuality of the human person and rejects the implicitly pantheistic assumptions in monistic philosophy. To identify the divine being with the world and with human individuals is to reduce diversity into uniformity and to confuse the Creator for the creature. 'What monism seeks in the wrong direction, and cannot attain unto, has been reached, viz., the unity which does not exclude but includes the multiformity of the … ("system") of philosophy.'[41]

---

[36] Von Hartmann, *Philosophy of the Unconscious*, I: p. 5. Emphasis in original
[37] Von Hartmann, *Philosophy of the Unconscious*, II: p. 242. Emphasis in original.
[38] Von Hartmann, *Philosophy of the Unconscious*, II: p. 81. Von Hartmann's strategy finds material resemblance in John McDowell's recent attempt to offer a reading of Kant and Hegel according to which knowledge of reality hinges on the existence of conceptual conditions that characterize both the act of knowing and the *objects* themselves. See, John McDowell, *Having the World in View: Essays on Kant, Hegel, and Sellars* (Cambridge: Harvard University Press, 2013), pp. 69–89.
[39] Bavinck, *Philosophy of Revelation*, p. 80.
[40] Bavinck, *Philosophy of Revelation*, p. 51. Bavinck does not provide a citation here to von Hartmann's *Philosophy of the Unconscious*, but it is certainly the text in view. It is also worth noting that von Hartmann assigns to the (unconscious) will a rather significant role in the acts of cognition: 'Here we must contemplate the origin of the conscious *idea* [*vorstellung*] as brought about by unconscious mental reactions [*Geistesreactionen*]. There the (unconscious) will, directly influencing the molecule, was to be conceived united with unconscious *representation* [*vorstellung*]; here we must suppose, for the sake of coming to pass of the sensation, an unconscious *will* conceived as an essential factor. … A union of unconscious will and unconscious idea [*vorstellung*] always takes place.' *Philosophy of the Unconscious*, II: p. 86; *Philosophie des Unbewussten*, II: p. 36. Emphases original.
[41] Bavinck, *Philosophy of Revelation*, p. 67.

Clearly, then, though Bavinck drew many of the same logical moves and conceptual grammar from von Hartmann, Bavinck rejected the system underlying them. Von Hartmann's monism was seeking the answers to the right questions but in the wrong direction – answers that, in Bavinck's view, are resident in Christian theism. Bavinck says this in no uncertain terms: 'The only possible way of demonstrating this is by briefly inquiring how we approach reality in what way we discover its content. From this it will appear that neither materialism nor humanism, but only theism, that neither emanation nor evolution, but revelation alone, is capable of solving the problem.'[42] Here, then, Bavinck is not satisfied with leaving the connection between subject and object and one's purchase of reality to the workings of common sense. Bavinck reaches underneath it and sees a theological account of why perception and the gap between representations and reality do not pose a philosophical conundrum.[43] An appeal to the behaviour of the common human being in taking the epistemic access to reality for granted does not negate that this is indeed nonetheless a problem to be solved by an appeal to revelation.

The next section considers how Bavinck does this, and in so doing his use of von Hartmann and reinterpretation of certain key modern motifs will be further elucidated.

II Overcoming the gap: The absolute, revelation and the organic

Bavinck's proposed solution is thus to deploy the resources located in the theological particularity of the Christian faith. Christianity includes 'such a harmonious whole of representations, which reconcile subject and object, man and world, nature and revelation'.[44]

This section presents his arguments to overcome the subject–object gap in the *Philosophy of Revelation* by an appeal to a Christian reinterpretation of the Absolute and to the divine decree. Here, I argue that Bavinck's proposal involves appreciating the (von Hartmannian) absolute idealist insight that subject and object come from

---

[42] Bavinck, *Philosophy of Revelation*, p. 48.

[43] In this regard, Bavinck's comments may remind the reader of the inclinations of Kuyper. As George Marsden notes concerning Kuyper's appeal to God and his works in order to account for perception, 'The common-sense starting point in the assumption of a harmonious correspondence between our subjective perceptions and objective reality, however necessary it is for us to rely on it, dies of a thousand such qualifications unless it has some other supposition to support it [namely, God].' Marsden, 'The Collapse of American Evangelical Academia', p. 250. In Kuyper's own words, we 'in our University resist tooth and nail that wanton rejection of certainty and, honour religious belief as a foundation also for science and scholarship, use our common sense and hold fast to man's immediate knowing of the basic elements of all being and all thought'. *Scholarship*, p. 33.

[44] Bavinck, *Philosophy of Revelation*, p. 190. Elsewhere, he makes a similar point: 'The center of Christianity is the incarnation of the Word, and therein, the reconciliation of God and man, of spirit and matter, of content and form, of ideal and reality, of soul and body, of thought and language, and of word and gesture.' *De Welsprekenheid* (Kampen: Zalsman: 1889), p. 33. Dutch original: 'Want middelpunt des Christendoms is de vleeschwording des Woords, en daarin de verzoening van God en mensch, van geest en stof, van inhoud en vorm, van ideaal en werkelijkheid, van ziel en lichaam, van gedachte en taal, van woord en gebaar.'

a single source and participate in the same reality, though unlike absolute idealism, Bavinck conceives of subject and object as participating in a reality distinct from and created by the (true) Absolute, personal, God. The next section explores how Bavinck appeals more explicitly to an organic worldview to connect subject and object, particularly in *Christelijke wereldbeschouwing* and the *Dogmatics*. Specifically, subject and object correspond because they both come from the same divine wisdom, which forms creation as an organism. Thus, there is great material complementarity between Bavinck's argument in the *Philosophy of Revelation* and the organic motif as found in the rest of his *oeuvre*. In this section some motifs important for subsequent chapters also emerges, including that (1) Bavinck conceives revelation as pre-cognitive (as something prior to thinking and reasoning) and (2) Bavinck argues that contact with the world, self and God are primordial facts of our existence.

a. Philosophy of revelation

Recall above Bavinck's argument that in consciousness one's self and world are somehow 'revealed' prior to all reasoning. The use of that verb provokes certain questions: What accounts for this immediate 'revealing' into our consciousness? Who, or what, is the agent that performs the action referred to in the verb? There is thus 'more' behind this phenomenon into which reflective agents may rightly probe in their 'self-consciousness'.[45] For confidence to be maintained in the 'testimony of our self-consciousness', Bavinck wrote, 'a true unity' is required, a unity that 'idealism has felt' in some significant way.[46] Bavinck argued that the idealists were led by this inclination to probe behind what agents take for granted, to account for the unity of experience and to account for the 'possibility of objective knowledge'. Consequently, they were forced to seek 'some way or other in the Absolute the ground for the objectivity and the reality of our knowledge'.[47] After briefly surveying other idealists, from Malebranche to the Marburg school, Bavinck further notes that Eduard von Hartmann was one who thought that some 'absolute substance' is 'the only true being' in which all things participate as accidents.[48]

It was the absolute – conceived of in differing forms – that served to re-establish some connection between thought and being, subject and object. Bavinck agrees with this recovery of an absolute, but does not see it as supplying an adequate answer.[49] He elaborated on the reason why in this way:

> Hence *the absolute cannot be conceived as an unconscious and involuntary force*. No doubt from time to time the deity has been so conceived by a few 'intellectuals', but pantheism has never been the creed of any people, the confession of any church.

---

[45] Bavinck, *Philosophy of Revelation*, p. 63.
[46] Bavinck, *Philosophy of Revelation*, p. 63.
[47] Bavinck, *Philosophy of Revelation*, p. 63.
[48] Bavinck, *Philosophy of Revelation*, p. 64.
[49] 'Although the attempt to recover after this fashion [namely, in seeking unity in the absolute] the lost unity of thought and being deserves appreciation, it is impossible to regard it as the true solution of the problem.' Bavinck, *Philosophy of Revelation*, p. 64.

Men have, it is true, often broken up, along with the unity of the world and the unity of the human race, the unity of God also; but the personality of God has remained firmly established, always and everywhere, among every nation and in every religion. Just as confidently, as man is convinced of his self-consciousness of his own existence and of the reality of the external world, does he believe also in the reality and personality of God.[50]

Several things are worth noting in this passage. First, von Hartmann's 'Unconscious' absolute is certainly a target of Bavinck's polemics here. In von Hartmann's view, the Unconscious is a 'golden mean' between theism and the naturalistic 'renunciation' of final causes.[51] The activity of the unconscious animates all things and is operative in all objects, mental and non-mental alike.[52] Hence, ascribing consciousness to the Absolute is inappropriate for several reasons. First, it renders theists susceptible to the charge that a conscious being independent of the world is the cause of the negative consequences of creatures with free will and 'world-misery'.[53] Second, denying consciousness to the absolute provides a purportedly unproblematic explanation to the misery encountered in the world, for then the Absolute is indifferent to the being or non-being of existence.

As such, von Hartmann's monism not only denies conscious personality to God but also rejects the principle of 'dualism' in theism, according to which the world and God denote two ontologically distinct entities.[54] Denying consciousness to the absolute preserves the virtues resident in theism while eluding the philosophical problems normally charged against it.

Bavinck overturns these two claims by arguing that (1) personality is intrinsic to God and (2) subject and object are part of a single creation reflective of divine wisdom. This is the case because creation is the product of the free, intelligible decree ordained by God, implying that the world and God are two distinct entities and that the former is created freely (and consciously) by the latter.

To argue for (1), Bavinck returns to an earlier point: that in consciousness, our existence is revealed to us in a pre-cognitive, primordial way. His reasoning here is complex, but can be summarized briefly as follows. In consciousness the existence of the self and the world is revealed prior to thinking, cognizing, willing or reasoning. In other words, for Bavinck knowledge of the self and world somehow come prior to the

---

[50] Bavinck, *Philosophy of Revelation*, pp. 64–5. Emphasis mine. For Bavinck, 'consciousness' refers to the phenomenon internal in the psyche of humanity, and *self*-consciousness is the consciousness directed at the self.

[51] Von Hartmann, *Philosophy of the Unconscious*, II: p. 246. On page 271 Von Hartmann declares that the Unconscious is also the mean between '*theistic dogmatism*' and an '*irreligious atheistic naturalism*'; hence his philosophy can rightly be called '*spiritualistic Monism or Pantheism*'. Emphases in original. On a piece of loose paper, Bavinck mapped a taxonomy on different kinds of 'unconscious' [*Het Onbewuste*] philosophies. After describing subliminal and occultist forms of the unconscious, there is the category of the 'Metaphysical Unconscious' [*Het metaphysiche-onbewuste*], under which Bavinck located Von Hartmann's name. This seems accurate. The piece of paper can be found in the Bavinck archives at *Historisch Documentatiecentrum voor het Nederlands Protestantisme (1800-heden)*. The Free University of Amsterdam library, inventory number 413.

[52] Von Hartmann, *Philosophy of the Unconscious*, II: pp. 247, 264.

[53] Von Hartmann, *Philosophy of the Unconscious*, II: p. 273.

[54] Von Hartmann, *Philosophy of the Unconscious*, II: p. 266.

active use of our cognition in acts of inference or the formation of predication. This is a primordial knowledge, something even prior to the formation of representations.[55] He is not satisfied to leave it merely as a bare phenomenon to be accepted. Rather, he ultimately argues that the testimony of consciousness is trustworthy precisely because it manifests the act of God, who, independently of us, reveals to us our selves and the world. In making this move, Bavinck could then argue that we also know God, as a personal Absolute, in self-consciousness primordially. Bavinck characterizes this as a 'reality that is *immediately* [*onmiddelijk*] given us, antecedently to all reasoning and inference'.[56] Von Hartmann, in excising personality and consciousness from God, therefore, fails to take seriously the testimony of one's self-consciousness, in effect shutting himself off from the clarity of God's (general) revelation.

In consciousness the human being feels that the self is a united being in contact with the external world.[57] Kant, argued Bavinck, kept perception and the world rightly distinct but connected, in that the 'world of perception is given to us in our consciousness, not as dream or hallucination but as phenomenon and representation involving, according to universal belief, the existence of an objective world'.[58] This intuitive, pre-cognitive (and thus pre-predicative) certainty that obtains 'before all thinking' and 'reasoning' includes our knowledge that we exist in a specific 'mode',[59] a mode in which we exist as creatures in the world.[60] Likewise this certainty, or feeling, provides that which bridges the gulf between 'the reality and the representation [*werkelijkheid en de voorstelling*]'.[61]

There is thus a correlation between the immediate pre-cognitive certainty with which we know our selves, and with which we know the world, 'for the representation is connected with reality by the same inner tie that binds self-consciousness to the self'.[62] Bavinck then posits that these facts are manifestations of God's revelatory act in and outside of us, independent of our action. In doing so, Bavinck is explicitly reconceiving the traditional category of general revelation under the philosophical grammar of Schleiermacher. The 'same feeling of dependence' that inheres in the mind also 'inheres in all its representations', for, 'independently of our co-operation' the

---

[55] In this section I have chosen words like pre-cognitive or pre-predicative (prior to thinking and reasoning) rather than pre-propositional in order to leave open the issue of whether knowledge is necessarily propositional. The terms I have chosen have the conceptual merit of being closer to Bavinck's own words, and are more modest in character; they simply affirm that for Bavinck knowledge is possible prior to the ability to articulate what one knows, prior to cognizing it.
[56] Bavinck, *Philosophy of Revelation*, p. 53; *Wijsbegeerte der Openbaring*, p. 51. Emphasis mine.
[57] Bavinck, *Philosophy of Revelation*, pp. 56–8. Bavinck's reasoning is a retrieval of the philosophical grammar of Schleiermacher. On this point, see Cory Brock and Nathaniel Gray Sutanto, 'Herman Bavinck's Reformed Eclecticism: On Catholicity, Consciousness, and Theological Epistemology', *Scottish Journal of Theology* 70 (2017): pp. 310–32.
[58] Bavinck, *Philosophy of Revelation*, p. 58.
[59] Bavinck, *Philosophy of Revelation*, p. 57.
[60] Bavinck, *Philosophy of Revelation*, p. 57. The passage marks a development of Bavinck's thinking in *RD*, 2: pp. 72–4. Cf. James K. A. Smith: 'There is a kind of precognitive perception that is to be distinguished from perception proper – that is, from perception as being cognizant of and attentive to an "object" in front of me.' *Imagining the Kingdom: How Worship Works* (Grand Rapids: Baker Academic, 2013), p. 18.
[61] Bavinck, *Philosophy of Revelation*, p. 59; *Wijsbegeerte der Openbaring*, p. 57.
[62] Bavinck, *Philosophy of Revelation*, p. 59.

world and our egos are 'revealed' to us.[63] Indeed, two pages before this, Bavinck asserts that at every point we 'feel [*voelen*] ourselves dependent on everything around us; we are not alone.'[64] In another place, he would ask rhetorically: 'Do we not feel [*voelen*] with the whole of creation? Are we not connected to all things?'[65]

Bavinck's understanding of revelation's locus in that primordial and pre-cognitive certainty[66] characteristic of the phenomena in one's consciousness allows Bavinck to posit that God, as well as his personality, is included within the number of things that are immediately revealed. Elaborating on his point, noted above, concerning the immediacy with which humanity comes to know God in self-consciousness, Bavinck wrote this:

> This belief [in God] is interwoven with his self-consciousness, more particularly with its double testimony to dependence and freedom. ... The sense of dependence is the core of self-consciousness and the essence of religion, but it is not a mere *de facto* dependence, as the unconscious and the irrational creation is dependent on God; in man it is *feeling* of dependence.[67]

Bavinck's description of knowledge of the world and God as 'immediately' revealed in self-consciousness should not be misunderstood to be identical to the claim that creaturely knowledge of God is an unmediated knowledge of God's essence in himself. In the *Dogmatics*, Bavinck is emphatic about the claim that 'supernatural revelation may not, however, be equated with immediate [*onmiddelijke*] revelation'.[68] There is an ambiguity with regard to the word 'immediate' (*onmiddelijk*) here that needs to be disentangled. By using this word, Bavinck is arguing in the Stone lectures that revelation comes *antecedent* to all thinking, reasoning or cognition – it is a revelation from God in consciousness that comes prior to, and becomes the basis of, our reasoning about the

---

[63] Bavinck, *Philosophy of Revelation*, p. 59. Cf. Schleiermacher, *Christian Faith*, §4. 2. In *Beginselen der psychologie*, pp. 53–4, Bavinck summarizes Schleiermacher consistently: 'Schleiermacher ... defined feeling as the immediate self-consciousness, wherein the subject, before all thinking and willing himself, becomes conscious of his own being and thereupon simultaneously his absolute dependence on God.' Dutch original: 'Schleiermacher ... omschreef het gevoel als het onmiddellijke zelfbewustzijn, waarin de mensch vóór alle denken en willen zichzelf, zijn eigen zijn, en daarin tegelijk zijne volstrekte afhankelijkheid van God bewust wordt.' Cf. Schleiermacher, *Christian Faith*, §3. 2.

[64] Bavinck, *Philosophy of Revelation*, p. 57; *Wijsbegeerte der Openbaring*, p. 55. Cf. Matheson Russell, 'Phenomenology and Theology: Situating Heidegger's Philosophy of Religion', *Sophia* 50 (2011): p. 650.

[65] Bavinck, *De Welsprekenheid*, p. 8. Dutch original: 'Voelen wij niet met de gansche schepping mee? Zijn we niet aan alle dingen verwant?' Paul Vissers also notes Schleiermacher's formative influence on Bavinck's missiologist nephew, J. H. Bavinck: 'Introduction', in John Bolt, James Bratt and Paul Vissers (eds), James De Jong (trans.), *The J. H. Bavinck Reader* (Grand Rapids: Eerdmans, 2008), p. 34.

[66] It is hard to capture the specificity of Bavinck's sense here. Other words that may be serviceable include awareness, feeling (not as an emotion but as pre-predicative *contact*) or attunement.

[67] Bavinck, *Philosophy of Revelation*, p. 65. Emphasis in original. Recall the oft-quoted statement in the opening chapter of the *Philosophy of Revelation* I noted earlier in this monograph: 'Revelation is the presupposition, the foundation, the secret of all that exists in all its forms. The deeper science pushes its investigation, the more clearly will it discover that revelation underlies all created being', p. 24.

[68] Bavinck, *RD*, 1: p. 309; *GD*, 1: p. 319.

external world and God.⁶⁹ It is immediate, therefore, in the sense that it is not mediated by the subject's active use of his rational faculties. However, it's still a revelation from God in the locus of consciousness and in this sense always presupposes that principle that revelation comes from an external divine source, located in some creaturely media (consciousness), and the distinction between archetypal and ectypal knowledge. Bavinck affirms that revelation is not mediated by creaturely reasoning on the one hand but that it is still a mediate knowledge of God precisely because 'the distance between the Creator and creature is much too great to perceive God directly'.⁷⁰ The revelation in consciousness is thus unmediated with respect to creaturely reason, but does not entail a direct (and in that sense, immediate) knowledge of God's essence. Bavinck's point here connects with his claim that revelation is organic in character, and as it is located internally in the human consciousness its tethering to God's creation is preserved organically: 'In cases where he revealed himself internally in the human consciousness by his Spirit, this revelation always occurs organically and hence mediately'.⁷¹

Furthermore, this revelation antecedent to all reasoning is not an innate idea as it presupposes the free will of God in revealing himself and as it therefore assumes that revelation comes from the outside.⁷² The testimony of self-consciousness in connecting one, as dependent, to the self, world and God is to be heeded for it is that divine act that precedes our being and continues to work in and around every individual. Here, it is again worth quoting Bavinck at some length as he relates this notion to the category of general revelation:

> And this is due in the last analysis to the fact that God, the creator of all nature, has not left himself without witness, but through all nature, both that of man himself and that of the outside world, speaks to him. Not evolution, but revelation alone

---

⁶⁹ 'To ignore this fact of self-consciousness, this primary fact, this foundation of all knowledge and activity ... [is] not merely a logical but also an ethical sin.' *Philosophy of Revelation*, p. 54. Also recall Bavinck's remark that 'in consciousness our own being, and the being of the world, are disclosed to us antecedently to our thought or volition; that is, they are *revealed* to us in the strictest sense of the word'. *Philosophy of Revelation*, p. 63. Bavinck connects this with general revelation, as will be seen below.

⁷⁰ Bavinck, *RD*, 1: p. 310. That this is Bavinck's point is made even clearer as he considers whether creatures know God directly in the *eschaton* after this passage.

⁷¹ Bavinck, *RD*, 1: p. 309.

⁷² Bavinck rejects the concept of innate ideas because it is aligned with the procedural mistake of idealism, elaborated at length above, which seeks to infer the epistemological accessibility of external reality from a mental idea: 'This does not mean that our knowing follows the same course and has to be identical with the order of being, that we must first of all know God from and through his idea within us and only then come to know the world.' Bavinck, *RD*, 2: p. 69. Rather, Bavinck's claims in the Stone lectures connect with what he says about God's revelation that precedes all of our knowledge: 'God's revelation precedes both [innate knowledge and acquired knowledge], for God does not leave himself without a witness. With his eternal power and deity he exerts revelatory pressure upon humans both from without and from within. ... It is the same complete revelation of God that introduces the knowledge of God into our consciousness. But in the case of the innate knowledge of God, that revelation acts upon the human consciousness, creating impressions and intuitions [*indrukken en beseffen*]. In the case of the acquired knowledge of God, human beings reflect upon that revelation of God.' Bavinck, *RD*, 2: pp. 73–4; *GD*, 2: pp. 51–2. The word *besef*, translated here as 'intuition' can be rendered as awareness, understanding, appreciation, sense, realization or idea. See the next chapter for a further discussion on this. See also my 'Neocalvinism on General Revelation: A Dogmatic Sketch', *International Journal of Systematic Theology* 20 (2018): pp. 494–516.

accounts for this impressive and incontrovertible fact of the worship of God. In self-consciousness God makes known to us man, the world, and himself. ... Hence this revelation is of the utmost importance ... particularly for epistemology. All cognition consists in in a peculiar relation of subject and object and is built on the agreement of these two. The reliability of perception and thought is not assured unless the forms of thought and the forms of being correspond, in virtue of their origin in the same creative wisdom.[73]

Bavinck's appeal to consciousness, therefore, is not to posit that God is knowable by the mere fact that our consciousness is constituted the way it is. Consciousness as such does not reveal God, but it is rather that *God*, as the free and sovereign divine subject, actively reveals himself to creatures in the locus of their consciousness.[74] It is because of this train of reasoning that Bavinck could assert that 'testimony of self-consciousness' enters to protest von Hartmann's view concerning the unconscious character of the absolute.[75] The starting point of revelation provides Bavinck with the resources to affirm the testimony of consciousness concerning the Absolute's character as a personal God, upon whom humanity feels itself absolutely dependent. Thus, though Bavinck agrees that the connection between subject and object could be obtained by an appeal to an absolute, Bavinck's absolute stands above and behind reality precisely because the two are separated by the act of *creation*. Bavinck's appeal to creation and revelation recalls Bavinck's programmatic statement concerning the twofold character of reality – a chasm demarcates the ontological distinction 'between the Infinite and the finite, between eternity and time, between being and becoming, between the All and the nothing'.[76] The subject and object do reflect a greater, and higher, unity into which they are parts, but this higher unity is not the being of God. In short, creation and revelation reflect that higher divine wisdom without being identical to it.

Creation and revelation both embody that wisdom, Bavinck would later affirm, because an intelligible decree is the basis on which both are carried out. This illumines the passage alluded to above as Bavinck invokes von Hartmann:

As even von Hartmann admits, there is no other way of doing justice to both subject and object except by recognizing that it is one and the same Reason [*Rede*] 'which is active in consciousness as a principle introducing order into the sensations, and in the objective world as the principle of synthesis for the things in themselves'. The forms of being, the laws of thought, and – to add this here for

---

[73] Bavinck, *Philosophy of Revelation*, p. 66. In the passage preceding this quotation, Bavinck discusses the naturality with which humanity universally come to believe in God as they mature in their social and historical contexts; I take this to mean that Bavinck grounds how humanity naturally believe in God in their development on that prior act of God's revelation in consciousness.
[74] Hence, Bavinck may have the resources to evade Barth's charges against Erich Pryzwara's appeal to one's consciousness as the means by which creatures know God. See Johnson, *Karl Barth and the Analogia Entis*, pp. 87–121.
[75] Bavinck, *Philosophy of Revelation*, p. 64.
[76] Bavinck, *RD*, 2: p. 30. Recall also Eglinton, 'To Be or to Become – That is the Question: Locating the Actualistic in Bavinck's Ontology', pp. 104–24.

the sake of completeness – the forms of conduct, have their common source in the divine wisdom.[77]

An identical power is ordering the phenomena internal to consciousness and the features of reality such that the latter is susceptible to the understanding powers of the former. Existence has specific forms intelligible to the laws of thought precisely because existence and the laws of thought are ordered by a divine wisdom and are reflective of it. Reality is not 'co-extensive with the phenomena' but contains the marks of the divine, as it is the 'realization of the decree of God'.[78] It is on this theological 'foundation' [*grondslag*] that 'science' [*wetenschap*] progresses, and truth is found.[79] Reality becomes absorbable by consciousness, and truth is in both as much as it transcends them. God reveals himself in nature and Scripture, and in so doing makes both the objects of our consciousness. 'Knowledge of the truth lies the end of its revelation.'[80]

b. The organic motif and the gap

In the previous subsection, Bavinck's strategy in overcoming the gap between subject and object in his *Philosophy of Revelation* was outlined. There Bavinck appeals to the all-encompassing and primordial character of divine revelation and its locus in consciousness, the personal Absolute that stands behind subject and object and creation as the unfolding of the decree of that absolute. These three theological claims ground Bavinck's argument that subject and object are parts in a larger creation reflective of divine wisdom, and accounts for the possibility of the subject's knowledge of the object. In the next section, I shall argue that Bavinck also appeals to the organic motif in a similar fashion and thus that his claims in the *Philosophy of Revelation* complement his deployment of the organic motif to this philosophical question. Revisiting the paradigmatic statement culled from *Christelijke wereldbeschouwing* concerning the key role in which the notion of the organic plays in the connection between subjects and objects, with the analysis of the Stone lectures in hand, would prove to be illuminating, as now the reader sees some obvious threads that tie them together:[81]

> It is the same divine wisdom that created the world organically into a connected whole and plants in us the urge for a unified worldview. If this is possible, it can only be explained from the fact that the world is an organism and thus has first been thought of as such. Only then do philosophy and worldview have a right and ground of existence, as it is also on this high point of knowledge that subject and

---

[77] Bavinck, *Philosophy of Revelation*, p. 67; *Wijsbegeerte der Openbaring*, p. 67. The capitalized *Rede* in the original Dutch signifies that Bavinck is not appealing to some 'reason' in support of a conclusion but rather to an absolute, divine being who embodies reason. In the footnote (69) Bavinck cites C. Willems's citation of von Hartmann: 'Ed. von Hartmann, in C. Willems, *Die Erkenntnislehre des mod. Ideal*, pp. 56-79.'
[78] Bavinck, *Philosophy of Revelation*, p. 68.
[79] Bavinck, *Philosophy of Revelation*, p. 67; *Wijsgebeerte der Openbaring*, p. 67.
[80] Bavinck, *Philosophy of Revelation*, p. 68.
[81] Parts of the following section can be found in a modified form in Brock and Sutanto, 'Herman Bavinck's Reformed Eclecticism'.

object harmonize, as the reason within us corresponds with the *principia* over all being and knowing. And what philosophy has demanded, according to its essence, is then guaranteed and explained for us by the testimony of God in his word. It is the same divine wisdom that gives things existence and our thought objective validity, that bestows intelligibility to things and the power of thinking to our mind, that makes the things *real* and our ideas *true*. The intelligibility of things is the content of our intellect. Both, being and knowing, have their reason [*ratio*] in the Word, through whom God created all things.[82]

It is appropriate now to comment on this passage in light of the preceding analysis. Notice here that Bavinck is subordinating the themes found in the *Philosophy of Revelation* – the creation of subject and object by the Creator, the way in which subject and object take part in a creation reflective of that divine wisdom, the necessity and unity of general and special revelation and thus the possibility of knowledge – under his understanding of ontology as organic. What is implicit in the Stone lectures is thus explicit here: the organic ontology and the unified worldview called for by Bavinck are presupposed and further expressed by the claims he expounded in the lectures. This should not be surprising, as Bavinck himself argues that the lectures are meant to be an elaboration on and thus read along with *Christelijke wereldbeschouwing*.[83]

The organic motif indeed enriches and undergirds the account Bavinck supplies above. Here I explicate a fuller picture of the way in which Bavinck deploys it to connect subject and object as peppered throughout the *Dogmatics*. The three themes already featured above re-emerge: (1) an organic ontology of creation, (2) the work of divine providence and (3) the ongoing revealing activity of the Word as Logos. I shall demonstrate as well that Bavinck's deployment represents a development of a theme found in Thomas and the scholastics and further portray Bavinck as an eclectic and modern thinker.

First then, for Bavinck an organic ontology of creation in which all things are connected and parts of larger wholes account for the consciousness' perception of objects. After a passage in which Bavinck argues that the world does not exist for us apart from consciousness, he says this: 'Human beings are so richly endowed because they are linked with the objective world by a great many extremely diverse connections. They are related to the whole world. Physically, vegetatively, sensorily, intellectually, ethically, and religiously there is correspondence between them and the world; they are

---

[82] Bavinck, *Christelijke wereldbeschouwing*, pp. 32–3. Dutch original: 'Het is dezelfde Goddelijke wijsheid, die de wereld organisch tot één geheel verbindt en in ons den drang naar eene "einheitliche" wereldbeschouwing plant. Indien deze mogelijk is, dan kan dit alleen daaruit verklaard worden, dat de wereld een organisme is en dus eerst als zoodanig is gedacht. Dan alleen heeft philosophie en wereldbeschouwing recht en grond van bestaan, als ook op dit hoogtepunt der kennis subject en object samenstemmen, als de rede in ons beantwoordt aan de principia van alle zijn en kennen. En wat de wijsbegeerte alzoo naar haar wezen eischt, dat wordt ons gewaarborgd en verklaard door het getuigenis Gods in zijn woord. Het is dezelfde Goddelijk wijsheid, die aan de dingen existentie en onze gedachte objectieve geldigheid geeft; die aan de dingen kenbaarheid en aan ons verstand denkkracht schenkt; die de dingen *werkelijk* en onze denkbeelden *waar* doet zijn. Het intelligibele in de dingen is de inhoud van ons intellect. Beide, het zijn en het kennen, hebben hun ratio in het Woord, waardoor God alle dingen schiep.' Emphases in original.

[83] See Bavinck, *Philosophy of Revelation*, p. 23, n. 61.

microcosms'.[84] It is in this sense that Bavinck commended Schleiermacher and Hegel for recovering a reconnection between subject and object earlier in the *Prolegomena*. They overcame the rationalism of the centuries preceding them, and both specified an organ within the subject that corresponds with that which the subject knows.[85] In both of these thinkers, Bavinck argues, 'thinking and being are most intimately related and correspond to each other'.[86] The romantic spirit that recognizes the unity between self and world is congenial to and re-articulated by Bavinck's Reformed redefinition of the organic.

The organic cosmos has implications for epistemology in the same way that it does for morality and physicality. Against what Bavinck perceives to be a Pelagian or rationalistic modern tendency to bifurcate facts from value, or morality from nature, an organic ontology would parry such attempts. Here he specifically locates the emergence of the organic view in the contemporary outlook of his day.

> The world by its very design is one organic whole. The two spheres, nature ... and morality ... are most closely interconnected and interpenetrate each other at all times. The two, though certainly distinct, are never separated. One cannot designate a point in creation where the counsel and governance of God and the independent will and action of human beings begin. Especially *in this century* the historic and organic view of things has at every point driven out and condemned this Pelagian split.[87]

I suggest at this point that these comments situate Bavinck's use of the scholastics in the discussion of realism found in the *Prolegomena*. After making clear that a gap exists between mental representations and the things, Bavinck appeals to ancient Greek philosophy in its acknowledgement that like can only be known by like, and the scholastics' affirmation of the distinction between the thing known by the mode of cognition, and the mode of the thing known.[88] Further, as David Sytsma notes, Thomas Aquinas also addressed similar questions concerning whether the contents of the mind (and the universals abstracted) do correspond with the reality outside of the mind.[89] Thomas, indeed, argues against the notion that 'our cognitive faculties know only what is experienced within them, for instance, that the senses perceive only the impressions made on their organs'.[90] Instead, Thomas asserts that the things we understand 'are the same as the objects of science' and that the absurd consequence of the above bifurcation between impressions and external objects is that we would only know appearances.[91]

---

[84] Bavinck, *RD*, 1: p. 586.
[85] Bavinck, *RD*, 1: pp. 260, 521. Cf. Schleiermacher, *Christian Faith*, §34. 1.
[86] Bavinck, *RD*, 1: p. 521.
[87] Bavinck, *RD*, 2: p. 376. Emphasis mine.
[88] Bavinck, *RD*, 1: p. 227.
[89] Sytsma, 'Herman Bavinck's Thomistic Epistemology', p. 29, n. 83.
[90] Thomas Aquinas, *Summa Theologiae*, Michael Cardinal Browne (trans.) (London: Eyre & Spottiswoode, 1968), I, q. 85, a. 2. Hereafter, *ST*.
[91] Aquinas, *ST*, I, q. 85, a. 2. See also *ST*, 1. Q. 79, 84, which deals specifically with the intellect and knowledge of material objects, respectively. For a nice elucidation of Thomas on the intellect and the soul in the act of perception, in relation to the claim that the human soul exists both subsistently and inherently, see Gyula Kilma, 'Aquinas on the Materiality of the Human Soul and the Immateriality of the Human Intellect', *Philosophical Investigations* 32 (2009): pp. 163–82.

This scholastic dictum's congeniality with the organic ontology Bavinck espouses provides the rationale, I would suggest, for Bavinck's retrieval of it.[92] The principle 'like is known by like' links with the Thomistic claim that human beings know both material and immaterial things because human beings, too, are material and immaterial; the active intellect abstracts universals from the sensations that the material soul receives in perception. The make-up of human beings as image bearers make them uniquely suited to understanding reality; they are the pinnacle of creation without being detached from it, and are fundamentally connected to it.[93]

Furthermore, as in the *Philosophy of Revelation*, Bavinck argues that the sovereign divine counsel further ensures the organic interconnectedness of all things, romantically characterizing creation as a work of divine art. 'Just as in any organism all the parts are interconnected and reciprocally determine each other, so the world as a whole is a masterpiece of divine art, in which all the parts are organically interconnected. And of that world, in all its dimensions, the counsel of God is the eternal design.'[94] The decree of God is the basis of creation's specific shape. If the triune being of God implies a cosmology of organism *ad extra*, the decree is one specific means by which that organic shape comes to expression. This point also harkens readers back to Bavinck's comment in *Christelijke wereldbeschouwing* concerning the Christian doctrine of creation: 'The teaching of the creation of all things through the Word of God is the explanation of all knowing and knowledge, the presupposition of the correspondence between subject and object.'[95]

Further, Bavinck affirms the ongoing work of the Logos in actively sustaining the subject–object relation. The revelatory work of the Logos that organically connects subject and object is indispensable.[96] The Logos works with and through reason, enlightening it and guiding it in its attempts to apprehend the world, and is also the one who independently produces the contents into the creature's mind. In doing so, the

---

[92] Sytsma's analysis in 'Herman Bavinck's Thomistic Epistemology' draws many valid observations, but focuses too one-sidedly, it seems, on Bavinck's scholastic sources. It seems more fruitful to me instead to pay attention to Bavinck's organic worldview *first*, and, taking that into account, then interpreting particular portions of his text – focusing on how he uses his sources more closely. In doing this, the eclectic character of Bavinck's sources finds a better appreciation.

[93] In reading Bavinck's use of Thomas in light of the organic, one again notes that his use of particular thinkers is not a systematic endorsement of them. Rather, Bavinck negotiates and uses thinkers from both classical and modern eras quite eclectically. This does, however, put Bavinck closer to Kuyper, who in Klapwijk's summary, too, adopts themes from von Hartmann while arguing that subjects and objects fit because of the organic character of creation: 'How does one account for this "fit" [between subjective representation and external object]? 'Kuyper's romantically tinted answer is that our world is like a living organism. Everything in it is organically connected with everything else in it'. Jacob Klapwijk, 'Abraham Kuyper on Science, Theology, and University', in Steve Bishop and John H. Kok (eds), *On Kuyper: A Collection of Readings on the Life, Work, and Legacy of Abraham Kuyper* (Sioux Center: Dordt College Press, 2013), p. 228.

[94] Bavinck, *RD*, 2: p. 392.

[95] Bavinck, *Christelijke wereldbeschouwing*, p. 28. Dutch original: 'De leer van de schepping aller dingen door het Woord Gods is de verklaring van alle kennen en weten, de onderstelling van de correspondantie tusschen subject en object.'

[96] Bavinck, *RD*, 1: p. 231. The sense of the possible, here, I take to be both metaphysical and epistemological. Only when one believes (epistemologically) in the work of Logos can one be warranted to believe that science is possible. Also, only *because* the Logos is actively working is science metaphysically possible.

Logos further ensures that the ideal representation in the mind is a faithful rendering of the world outside. This work is constant and dynamic, sustaining the epistemological situation and ensuring its relative stability and reliability.

From the preceding analyses, one conclusion may be drawn with some considerable certainty, and it is that the term 'critical realism' can hardly be adequate to capture the theological and philosophical depth of Bavinck's conception of the epistemic process. If Bavinck's work can be called critical realism, it is so only in the sense that he accepts that (1) the mind plays a constructive role with respect to knowing and (2) reality remains reliably communicated in perception. The term is at once too broad to apply only to Bavinck, and simultaneously too thin to carry the weight of Bavinck's concerns, notwithstanding the equally weighty consideration that Bavinck could just as accurately be called an absolute idealist in the way he weaves the claim that God is an absolute through whom subject and object are reconciled as a pair in relation.[97] With Bavinck's understanding of how an organic ontology and epistemology involve certain claims about revelation, creation, providence and God as a personal Absolute, perhaps new terminology is required. I suggest, therefore, that terms such as 'Reformed-organic-realism' or, simply, an 'organic epistemology', however less familiar, seem preferable.

III Holism and three implications: A (modified) Christian internalism, the question of subjectivism and nineteenth-century philosophical discourse – towards a development

This chapter builds on the previous chapter in articulating how Bavinck specifically applies the organic motif to connect subject and object, a philosophical problem discussed widely in Bavinck's day and an issue at the heart of Bavinck's understanding of knowledge as a relation between thought and reality. The chapter thus explored how Bavinck connects mental representations and the reality they represent, and showed that Bavinck critically appropriated Eduard von Hartmann's epistemology in situating himself between naive realism and subjective idealism, even deploying von Hartmann's arguments against subjective idealism and appealing to an absolute, a common source from which subject and object originate. We then linked those themes with Bavinck's application of the organic motif: subject and object are connected precisely because they partake in a creation comprised of unities and diversities, and as such are in correspondence both by virtue of their constitution and the Logos who sustains the links between them. This created reality is reflective of an eternal decree that is itself grounded in the triune God's wisdom.

Before moving on to the next chapter, I suggest that three implications arise from the preceding analysis.

---

[97] I am indebted to George Harinck for this suggestion in his response to a presentation I delivered at Kampen Theological University on which this present chapter is based, namely that Bavinck is identifiable as an absolute idealist as much as he could be described in critically realistic terms.

First, the fact that Bavinck went further than the simple insistence on the reliability of our cognitive and perceptive faculties in apprehending reality suggests that an externalist account of epistemic justification cannot do full justice to Bavinck's thinking here. Neither, as we saw, was Bavinck satisfied with a thin theological or metaphysical account of how knowledge takes place. Bavinck appeals to an absolute, a decree, divine wisdom and an organic ontology to ground his insistence that seemingly heterogeneous realities like mental representations and physical objects can correspond. This grounding points to a kind of internalism in Bavinck's thought, suggesting that without them, knowledge might be rendered illusory. It seems that Bavinck is arguing that we have to possess cognitive access to these rich theological insights to ground the knowing situation. Bavinck also says this explicitly; at the outset of his first chapter in *Christelijke wereldbeschouwing*, he asks a question that situates that chapter's argument:

> The fact stands fixed, that we all, of ourselves, and without compulsion, accept the existence of a world outside us, that we, through perception and thinking, seek to make it our mental possession, and that we, in thus acting, obtain a clear and reliable knowledge of its meaning. But on what grounds does the belief in a reality of a being that is independent of our consciousness rest? And what guarantee is there that our consciousness, enriching itself by observing and thinking, corresponds to the world of being?[98]

A few comments on this passage seem appropriate. Bavinck again signals his agreement with the naive realistic assumption that our mental faculties without compulsion and prior to all argumentation can understand reality. We can take this as an assumption, both because we already do it in our daily, ordinary living and because the denial of this starting point leads to solipsism or scepticism. But Bavinck does not leave it at that. He asks further, *on what grounds* can we believe that this is the case? *Why* is reality constituted in such a way that human beings can ordinarily take their understanding of the outside world in a basic, primordial fashion? He wants to probe deeper into the rationale underneath these common-sensical phenomena, and it is precisely this probing that leads him to the rich painting of an organic worldview and ontology that we have observed him doing above. Without that ground, without these reasons that are rooted in the organic, the intellectual mind is rightly unsatisfied.

But how do these two claims – that we can ordinarily take for granted the reliability of our reception of reality and that we need to provide some justificatory grounds for precisely that reliability – go together? Reality, Bavinck often reminds us, must come before philosophizing. Must *every* person then appeal to the organic for their belief in the reliability of their cognitive faculties to be epistemologically justified, for them

---

[98] Bavinck, *Christelijke wereldbeschouwing*, p. 15. Dutch original: 'Het feit staat vast, dat wij allen vanzelf en zonder dwang het bestaan van eene wereld buiten ons aannemen, dat wij ze door waarneming en denken tot ons geestelijk eigendom zoeken te maken, en dat wij, alzoo handelende, eene zuivere en betrouwbare kennis van haar meenen te verkrijgen. Maar op welke gronden rust het geloof aan de realiteit van een van ons bewustzijn onafhankelijk zijn, en wat waarborg is er, dat ons bewustzijn, door waarneming en denken zich verrijkende, aan de wereld van het zijn beantwoordt?'

not to flout their epistemic duties? I suggest here that Bavinck's internalism should be read not as a universal imperative but rather as situated within his task as a Christian theologian seeking to work out the particularities of that worldview and the resources that Christianity can provide in answer to philosophical questions. In other words, I am arguing here that Bavinck thinks that *Christians* specifically should provide a thick theological account in answer to philosophical questions, among which the correspondence between thought and reality is paramount. In this way of picturing it, Bavinck's constructive organic outlook and his demand that we account for the reliability of our beliefs reflects primarily not a universal deontological account of justification but of a specifically Christian responsibility. Christians, that is, are not to be satisfied with leaving deeper questions of bases and grounds unexplored. Revelation, after all, is the 'presupposition, the foundation, the secret' of all that exists, and thus the 'deeper' Christians investigate the more clearly they come into an encounter with the God behind all things.[99] In this manner Christians, in Bavinck's view, ought not be afraid to engage in the serious intellectual questions that occupy the modern world, for they have an obligation and a surety that undergirds their intellectual inquiries.

Read in this light, the oft-quoted statement in the second volume of the *Dogmatics* concerning the Christian mind takes on a new significance:

> The thinking mind situates the doctrine of the Trinity squarely amid the full-orbed life of nature and humanity. A Christian's confession is not an island in the ocean but a high mountaintop from which the whole creation can be surveyed. And it is the task of Christian theologians to present clearly the connectedness of God's revelation with, and its significance for, all of life. The Christian mind remains unsatisfied until all of existence is referred back to the triune God, and until the confession of God's Trinity functions at the center of our thought and life.[100]

Consonant with Bavinck's concerns in the *Philosophy of Revelation* and his understanding of the organic structure of the sciences as observed earlier, Bavinck's holism inclines him towards the relating of every area of knowledge to each other. With God and knowledge of God as the centre of Christian thought, the organic motif in Bavinck's epistemology is simply another way of articulating how that is so. Bavinck's desire to ground subject–object correspondence and the ordinary reliability of perception and cognition in the organic is thus an application of this programmatic desire. There is a functional Christian internalism in Bavinck's thinking. It is *internalism* in the sense that Bavinck argues that Christians ought to have cognitive access or awareness of how the Trinity (and the organic worldview it implies) can provide the grounds for philosophical questions. It is *Christian* in the sense that for Bavinck it is not a universal or naturalized imperative that every person must follow in order to be justified in one's beliefs but rather that Christians have as much a *moral and theological* obligation to fulfil this epistemic duty before the God they confess.

---

[99] Bavinck, *Philosophy of Revelation*, p. 24.
[100] Bavinck, *RD*, 2: p. 330.

The second implication revisits some of the claims observed above concerning the premium that Bavinck seems to place on consciousness and the subject. Recall now the questions raised by Henk van den Belt and Cornelis van der Kooi:

> [Bavinck's] epistemology is dominated by the correspondence between object and subject on three levels: the level of science, the level of general revelation, and the level of special revelation. This tension leads to the theological question whether Bavinck was able to avoid subjectivism.[101]

> Bavinck cooperates in the turning toward the subject, and thereby (probably more than he likes) pays tribute to the anthropocentricism of modernity. ... His focus is strongly directed to the religious subject to whose mind's eye the things of revelation must appear if he or she wants to find them worthy or true.[102]

As we have seen, just as the interpretations of Bavinck that put him squarely in line with Aristotelian–Thomistic epistemology bear some truth, there is much in Bavinck's discussions that lends him towards the readings offered by van den Belt and van der Kooi. Bavinck does place a heavy weight on the role that consciousness plays, and the subject is constructively involved in every epistemic act.[103] In comparison to the strong emphasis on the subject by the Romantics and the ethical theologians, Bavinck stresses the importance of the object in conditioning our reception of it. In comparison to classical epistemology, it is also observed, Bavinck affirms the constitutive role of mental representations in forming knowledge of objects.

Rather than seeking to figure out whether Bavinck prioritizes the subject or the object, the organic motif and the preceding analysis have shown that Bavinck treats subject and object in equipoise. The failure of one-sided rationalism or empiricism is precisely in the way in which the former seeks to purchase knowledge *a priori* that neglects sense experience while the latter does not do justice to the concepts and representations that the subject inevitably brings. In both cases the harmony between subject and object is broken.[104] What Christianity provides in this case is a more balanced and equalizing perspective that treats subject and object as equally important, freeing the epistemologist to go back and forth between the two without fear that one or the other would disappear from the picture. The question of whether Bavinck falls into subjectivism thus loses its force because Bavinck has never intended to begin there as a sole starting point. The Christian worldview, as rendered by Bavinck, does not

---

[101] van den Belt, *The Authority of Scripture*, p. 294.

[102] van der Kooi, 'The Appeal to the Inner Testimony of the Spirit', pp. 107–8. It is worth mentioning that while van der Kooi appeals to the Spirit and the Church to remedy Bavinck's purportedly subjectivist tendencies, Henk van den Belt argues that Bavinck may already have a sufficient emphasis on the Church to limit his subjectivism in *The Authority of Scripture*, pp. 297–8.

[103] It should be noted that the discussion in the preceding chapter focused on Bavinck's understanding of general epistemology. That is, we have discussed revelation and the organic in order to relate it to how Bavinck thinks we come to know objects in general. It has not been the purpose of this study to discuss primarily how Bavinck knows God or Scripture to be trustworthy, which would bring us into discussions of prolegomena proper and natural theology.

[104] Bavinck, *Christelijke wereldbeschouwing*, pp. 16–17.

allow this move, and it provides a step towards going beyond picturing the subject and object as a binary.

Third, what emerges in the preceding chapters is a reading of Bavinck that characterizes him firmly as a nineteenth-century theologian who worked with the conceptual and philosophical tools prevalent in his day. He took for granted certain trends, patterns of reasoning and grammars that are particular to the century within which he wrote, even while he sought to speak into that scene through his orthodox Reformed tradition. The organic motif is invoked to answer those specific questions. The next chapter will further probe into the ways in which the organic motif is used by him to relate the various functions within the faculty of knowing.

7

Revelation, the unconscious, reason and feeling

The ego is not an aggregate of parts, not a mass of phenomena of consciousness, afterwards grouped together by man under one name. It is a synthesis, which in every man precedes all scientific reflection, an organic whole possessing members. It is 'complex' but not 'compound'.[1]

This way of taking cognizance is of the highest significance. … It is not less certain than [reasoning and thinking], but exceeds far above them in certainty. But it is indeed less clear and conscious, precisely because it is not a knowledge in concepts, and is not the fruit of deliberate reflection and reasoning.[2]

The previous chapter argued that Bavinck's organic ontology and retrieval of absolute idealism allows him to connect subjects and objects, representation and reality, knowledge of self and God. The mistake of idealism consists in its failure to acknowledge the primordial character of our knowledge of the world, given through representations and immediately granted in self-consciousness. It hems itself into a sphere of representations in the mistaken attempt to infer the epistemic accessibility of the external world from internal representations, only to miss the inherently 'representational' character of those representations. The reason these representations correctly represent and mediate reality to us is because the revelation of the world and God is direct and immediate, taking place in the locus of consciousness and within an organically unified creation.

The organic motif goes further, however, in that it serves to account for Bavinck's emphasis on the role of the unconscious life in human creatures. This chapter probes more deeply into the structures of Bavinck's account of the relationship between revelation and reason (and thinking), and connects what he wrote in the Stone lectures to the discussion of revelation and the knowledge of God in the second volume of his *Dogmatics*. I shall argue that Bavinck's treatment of revelation as *prior to* cognition and

---

[1] Bavinck, *Philosophy of Revelation*, p. 53.
[2] Bavinck, *Beginselen der psychologie*, pp. 57–8. Emphasis mine. Dutch original: 'Deze wijze van kennisneming is van het hoogste belang; zij is onderscheiden van en voorafgaande aan die door redeneering en denken; zij is niet minder zeker dan deze, maar gaat ze in zekerheid ver te boven. Maar ze is wel minder helder en bewust, juist omdat zij geen kennis in begrippen is en geen vrucht van opzettelijk nadenken en redeneeren.'

thinking in the Stone lectures is consistent with his discussion of revelation as prior to and the basis of both innate and acquired knowledge in the *Dogmatics*. The horizontally focused direction of the third chapter of his *Philosophy of Revelation*, which concerns the relationship between revelation and knowledge of external reality, therefore, complements well the vertical and theological direction of Bavinck's discussion in the *Dogmatics*. Organism implies not only that representations connect one with reality but also that the unconscious ways of living and feeling that characterize basic human activity cohere well with reality. Here, I incorporate insights from Bavinck's *Foundations of Psychology* (*Beginselen der psychologie*) to illuminate his conceptual arsenal. Finally, I observe that these points lead to Bavinck's understanding of feeling not as a distinct faculty of the psyche but rather as an act of the knowing faculty. There is an intuitive kind of knowing that is akin to *feeling* – a non-conceptual knowledge. What emerges is a distinctly Reformed, neo-Calvinistic, yet romantic account of the doctrine of general revelation.

After this, the next section moves into an analysis of Bavinck's discussion of key terms and their conceptual location in Bavinck's thought, thereby indicating that his emphases on feeling and the unconscious do not denigrate an equal focus on conscious reflection as a mode of knowing. In that section, I shall argue that Bavinck's use of 'representation' *(voorstelling)* corresponds with that pre-cognitive, pre-predicative and pre-conceptual sense in which revelation takes place in consciousness, whereas terms like 'association' and 'conceptualization', for Bavinck, correspond with his understanding of innate and acquired knowledge of God. Representations always attend the self as he or she exists in the realm of God's revelation, responding to the 'impressions and intuitions' (*indrukken en beseffen*), produced by God's internal revelation. What the creaturely knower does with that revelation in reasoning, cognition and concept formation corresponds to Bavinck's understanding of innate and acquired knowledge of God. Finally, I revisit Bavinck's discussion of general epistemological principles in his *Prolegomena*, situating what he says about reason as the light of the Logos in humans within his broader affirmation of the light of revelation already encountered in the unconscious, pre-predicative life of feeling.

The organic motif enforces two key moves made by Bavinck: he establishes a connectedness between the unconscious life and the world, along with a connectedness between the unconscious psyche and conscious reasoning in the human self as two loci in which revelation takes place.

The final section of this chapter argues that Bavinck's account structurally fuses two motifs in medieval epistemology, represented by Aquinas and Bonaventure, between what Lydia Schumacher calls *influentia*, on the one hand, and *concursus*, on the other. Then, I note that such a move is rather characteristic of the neo-Calvinist tradition of which Bavinck was a part, producing examples from Kuyper, G. C. Berkouwer and Bavinck's missiologist nephew, Johan H. Bavinck. This chapter thus provides an analysis of Bavinck's understanding of revelation and reason in a manner that situates him within the broader discussions in medieval theology, on the one hand, and neo-Calvinism, on the other. This further displays the fruits that are generated by an organic reading of his theological epistemology consistent with the chapters that have come beforehand.

I Revelation causing primordial awareness – innate and acquired knowledge

The previous chapter broached on the key role of revelation in Bavinck's thought and its locus in the human consciousness. It discussed Bavinck's belief that the epistemic accessibility of external reality and revelation itself are obtained prior to all thinking. Representations connect with reality in an immediate and temporally direct way. As Bavinck wrote,

> In self-consciousness, therefore, we have to deal not with a mere phenomenon, but with a noumenon, with a reality that is immediately given to us, antecedently to all reasoning and inference. Self-consciousness is the unity of real and ideal being; the *self* is here consciousness, not scientific knowledge, but experience, conviction, consciousness of self as a reality. In self-consciousness our own being is *revealed* to us, directly, immediately, before all thinking and independently of all willing.[3]

This primordial contact, or illumination, not only with the self but also with the world in the locus of consciousness, he would go on to write, is 'the foundation of all knowledge and activity', the denial of which commits oneself to making 'not merely a logical but also an ethical sin'.[4] Following Augustine, Bavinck argued that it is in the inner life that the 'seeds and germs of all knowledge and science and art' are to be found.[5] To account for this, Bavinck appealed to revelation, which is the reason, the ground, the cause for the primordial contact that human creatures have with reality, precisely because both partake in God's organic creation. Not only so, this revelation, as a divine act, takes place apart from creaturely agency, and is in fact entirely independent from it: 'Not evolution, *but revelation*, is the secret of the mind; in our self-consciousness, *independently of our cooperation and apart from our will*, the reality of our ego and of the world is revealed to us. Whosoever here does not believe shall not be established.'[6]

Bavinck's doctrine of revelation as articulated in the Stone lectures thus takes a decidedly Romantic tinge – a pre-cognitive awareness, a feeling, of one's self as dependent on God and world – something akin to what George Pattison calls 'romantic presence'.[7] 'This dependence is brought to our knowledge. ... We feel ourselves dependent on everything around us; we are not alone.'[8] This knowledge that is *felt*, rather than inferred, obtains 'before all reasoning and action' as creatures 'exist in a definite way, and inseparable from these is a consciousness of our being and of its specific mode'.[9]

---

[3] Bavinck, *Philosophy of Revelation*, pp. 53–4. Emphases in original.
[4] Bavinck, *Philosophy of Revelation*, p. 54.
[5] Bavinck, *Philosophy of Revelation*, p. 55.
[6] Bavinck, *Philosophy of Revelation*, p. 59. Emphases mine.
[7] George Pattison, *God and Being: An Enquiry* (Oxford: Oxford University Press, 2011), pp. 58–79.
[8] Bavinck, *Philosophy of Revelation*, p. 57.
[9] Bavinck, *Philosophy of Revelation*, p. 57. The previous chapter notes Bavinck's use of Schleiermacher: 'If man is not one with the Eternal in the unity of intuition and feeling which is immediate, he remains, in the unity of consciousness which is derived, forever apart.' *On Religion: Speeches to Its Cultured Despisers*, John Oman (trans.) (Louisville: Westminster John Knox, 1994), p. 40. See B. A. Gerrish, *The Christian Faith: Dogmatics in Outline* (Louisville: Westminster John Knox, 2015), pp.

When these observations are viewed against the previous chapter's argument, a certain logical ordering emerges in Bavinck's account. Revelation, which invokes representations in the human consciousness, is the primordial basis of how creatures know and inhabit God's organic creation – and creaturely reasoning in the acts of thinking and knowledge formation are *derivatives* that are contingent on this prior fact of revelation *and* the primordial, pre-cognitive connections that representations have with reality. 'Self-consciousness does not exist apart from the representations, but lives and realizes itself in them.'[10] To reverse this ordering is to make a mistake typical of subjective idealism – that of rendering knowledge of reality contingent upon one's reasoning. Contact with reality, however, obtains independently of creaturely reasoning.

a. Revelation that 'precedes' innate and acquired knowledge

To grasp the concerns that motivate this part of Bavinck's thought, the discussion on innate ideas and innate knowledge in the beginning of his *God and Creation* is worth considering. That Bavinck affirmed a divine revelation that preceded thinking is now clear enough, but this articulation should not be confused with the doctrine of innate ideas, or even a doctrine of innate knowledge that somehow renders knowledge of God wholly derivable on an *a priori* basis.

It is noteworthy that Bavinck couches his treatment of the matter in terms of the subject–object distinction, and begins with the objective side first.[11] Bavinck resolutely affirmed that revelation comes from a source extrinsic to creatures and that this revelation provided an indirect exposure of the God revealed. This reason why, Bavinck observes, Christian theologians have denied the doctrine of innate ideas is their desire to avoid the twin errors of rationalism and mysticism.[12] Rationalism makes human knowers independent of God's revelation in nature and Scripture because the innate ideas are purportedly sufficient for them to know God and reality, whereas mysticism posits that God is known in some direct and unlimited way. So, although Bavinck affirms that 'God is indeed the light of human souls' and that 'the Logos enlightens every person coming into the world', our knowledge of God is never a knowledge that overcomes the intrinsic conditions entailed by the Creator–creature distinction.[13] Again, the immediacy of which Bavinck speaks in his Stone lectures is not an immediacy of reference (by which God is known in his essence in what Bavinck calls a 'pantheistic' manner[14]) – the immediacy of which he speaks there is that revelation takes place in consciousness apart from human cooperation in thinking and willing.

37–43, on Schleiermacher's feeling of dependence as consistent with Calvin's sense of the divine, 'an original revelation of God' (43); see also Kevin Hector, *Theology Without Metaphysics: God, Language, and the Spirit of Recognition* (Cambridge: Cambridge University Press, 2011), pp. 77–86.

[10] Bavinck, *Philosophy of Revelation*, p. 59.
[11] Bavinck, *RD*, 2: p. 70, in which, after treating the objective side of the matter, he writes, 'We have only highlighted one side of the truth. There is another side, one that is no less important. It cannot be denied, after all, that for us to see we need both the light of the sun (objectively) and our eyes (subjectively).'
[12] Bavinck, *RD*, 2: p. 68.
[13] Bavinck, *RD*, 2: p. 69.
[14] Bavinck, *RD*, 2: p. 69.

Bavinck considers the twin errors of rationalism and mysticism to be a confusion between the order of being and the order of knowing. Though God is first in the former, he is not so in the latter – one moves from the world to God, in the order of knowing, dependent on Scripture and nature. Nevertheless, though Bavinck echoes the classical distinction between the orders of being and knowing to describe the objective side of the epistemological coin, he places an equally important emphasis on the subjective side in this order of knowing. On the subjective side, there is the twofold sense that humans have the innate disposition and capacity to receive revelation, and, further, the presence of an *internal* revelation in the human consciousness that is distinguishable from the revelation that comes from the created world.

This capacity with which human beings are equipped to know religious truths includes 'a "seed of religion," a "sense of divinity," a "divine instinct," an "innate knowledge"' that comports with the eternal truths and laws of thought that are instilled in nature.[15] What this means, exactly, involves an inclination to believe in God, such that belief in God comes spontaneously and naturally to human creatures:

> 'Implanted knowledge of God' [*Cognitio Dei insita*] does not mean that all people are immediately endowed by God himself with sufficient knowledge so as to be able to dispense with revelation. ... What it does say is that we possess both the capacity (aptitude, faculty) and the inclination (*habitus*, disposition) to arrive at some firm, certain, and unfailing knowledge of God. Human beings gain this knowledge in the normal course of development and environment in which God gave them the gift of life. It arises spontaneously and without coercion, without scientific argumentation and proof.[16]

Bavinck is observing that by virtue of being in God's world and living as God's image bearers, human creatures have a natural capacity and tendency, a disposition, to believe naturally in God. These beliefs are formed not on the basis of other beliefs or by way of an argument, but are formed immediately.[17] There is more, however, to this implanted knowledge of God than the mere disposition on the part of humans to

---

[15] Bavinck, *RD*, 2: p. 71. The English translation veils Bavinck's usage of Latin in the original text, signalling his appeal to the classical terminology: 'Bij de religie moet men, of men wil of niet, altijd weer tot een semen religionis, een sensus divinitatis, een instinctus divinus, eene cognitio insita.' Bavinck, *GD*, 2: p. 47. Elsewhere, Bavinck demonstrates that he is not uncritical about this notion that all human beings know the same laws of thought and eternal laws or truths in their conscience. As Bavinck wrote, 'The content of conscience ... differs amongst different peoples. And even if the conscience does contain something "common" or universal "by nature". ... It is very difficult to identify which duties are specifically necessary pronouncements of the conscience entailed innately and not received from outside. ... We always know the conscience only concretely, as it is historically formed within the family, state, and society, through religion, art, and science by all the moral authorities of a people.' Herman Bavinck, 'The Conscience', Nelson Kloosterman (trans.), *The Bavinck Review* 6 (2015): p. 122. There is thus a distinction between the existence of these laws of nature and morality, and the epistemic accessibility of those laws, the latter of which is always culturally particularized.

[16] Bavinck, *RD*, 2: p. 71; *GD*, 2: p. 48.

[17] In passages like these, Bavinck is articulating something like properly basic beliefs; 'a disposition whose output is *immediately* formed beliefs about God'. Wolterstoff, 'Herman Bavinck – Proto Reformed Epistemologist', p. 139.

believe in a Supreme being. The implanted knowledge of God involves not merely the faculties of the human psyche, the testimony of nature and history from the outside but also a revelation that has an 'interior impact' on consciousness.[18] There is, in this sense, an 'innate' knowledge of God – a knowledge that is not ready made, so to speak, but acquired through the sheer power and forcefulness of general divine revelation. In this way of expressing things, Bavinck argues that the distinction between innate and acquired knowledge is somewhat artificial and that somehow *revelation* precedes both innate and acquired knowledge: 'Accordingly, the innate knowledge of God is not opposed to the acquired knowledge of God, for, in a broader sense, also the former can be called acquired. In fact, *God's revelation precedes both*, for God does not leave himself without a witness.'[19]

In other words, in this rather provocative claim Bavinck is arguing that revelation obtains prior to the formation of the beliefs about God that arise from the natural dispositions with which creatures are endowed (in both innate and acquired knowledge of God). Revelation that comes within and without the human consciousness is the primordial basis upon which beliefs about God are naturally formed. 'With his eternal power he exerts revelatory pressure upon humans both from outside and from within.'[20] Bavinck then claims that this revelation creates 'impressions' (*indrukken*) and associates revelation as something that occurs prior to, or apart from, active, conscious, cognition on the part of the human knower. Bavinck writes:

> And humans, having been created in the divine image, were gifted with the capacity to receive the impressions [*indrukken*] of this revelation and thereby to acquire some sense and knowledge of the Eternal Being. The innate knowledge of God, *the moment it becomes cognition and hence not only cognitive ability but also cognitive action, never originated apart from the working of God's revelation from within and without, and is to that extent therefore acquired*.[21]

What is suggested here, it seems, is that revelation and the impressions that arise from it occur prior to conscious thinking and 'cognitive action', in a manner that coheres with Bavinck's claims about revelation in his *Philosophy of Revelation*. The divine light is not an innate idea but rather a revelation that precedes active knowing.

---

[18] 'The knowledge of God is called "innate" and talk of an innate potency or faculty was found unsatisfactory ... over against the theory of innate ideas, it expresses that humans are not born fully equipped with a ready-made knowledge of God, but obtain it mediately, by the interior impact of revelation upon their consciousness.' Bavinck, *RD*, 2: p. 72.

[19] Bavinck, *RD*, 2: p. 73. Though Wolterstorff cites this passage in his 'Herman Bavinck – Proto Reformed Epistemologist', p. 139, he makes no notice of this statement and focuses instead only on the immediately formed beliefs of which Bavinck speaks. Insofar as Wolterstorff and Plantinga focus solely on knowledge as involving warranted (or justified) true belief, Bavinck's articulation of feeling as knowledge remains elusive. Indeed, if feeling is an activity of knowing, then Bavinck is open to the possibility that knowledge can be had without there being an explicit proposition to be believed. Romantic presence is irreducible to propositional belief.

[20] Bavinck, *RD*, 2: p. 73.

[21] Bavinck, *RD*, 2: p. 73; *GD*, 2: p. 51. Emphasis mine. Bavinck expresses this same thought consistently in his Stone lectures: 'For revelation always supposes that the human is able to receive impressions or thoughts or inclinations from another than this phenomenal world, and in a way other than that usually employed.' *Philosophy of Revelation*, p. 175.

A paragraph later, Bavinck confirms this reading as he still articulates a modest distinction between the innate and acquired knowledge of God – keeping in mind what he has already said about how *innate* knowledge can be considered as a species of acquired knowledge:

> In both cases it is the same complete revelation of God that introduces the knowledge of God into our consciousness. But in the case of the innate knowledge of God, that revelation acts upon the human consciousness, creating impressions and intuitions [*indrukken en beseffen*]. In the case of the acquired knowledge of God, human beings reflect upon that revelation of God. Their minds go to work, though processes are put in motion, and with clear heads they seek by reasoning and proof to rise from the observation of creatures to [the reality of] God.[22]

In effect, Bavinck claims that revelation occurs prior to conscious thinking. Though innate knowledge can be considered a species of acquired knowledge because it emerges from this prior revelation as much as acquired knowledge, a distinction remains between the two insofar as acquired knowledge per se involves a clearly active and conscious mode of reasoning on the part of the human knower. Innate knowledge corresponds more closely to the *indrukken en beseffen* that revelation creates in the human consciousness. The Dutch *beseffen*, translated in English as intuitions, can also be rendered as 'awareness', and it seems that the sense of Bavinck's usage here is that revelation can be interpreted as a twofold sense of primordial awareness that corresponds to external and internal revelation. The first, corresponding with objective revelation, involves the pervasive impressions that one receives as a dweller in God's world – the thousands of ways in which human beings interact with and respond in an embodied way to the world often without being self-conscious of it.[23] The second refers to the immediate awareness of the insides of one's psyche, of the thoughts, impressions and stimuli that reside in the internal life of the human soul. Bavinck confirms this as he relates the biblical concept of the heart with the inner life of the psyche and Kant's inner sense in his treatment on the unconscious:

> [In consciousness, there is] observing, remembering, judging, knowing; but also feelings, both sensory and spiritual. ... Consciousness is knowledge, and awareness, 'knowing' what goes on inside of me. And second, it is an immediate awareness. It is a knowledge obtained not through external sense organs or through deliberate research and serious study but directly through immediate experience, through an 'inner sense' [*inneren Sinn*], as Kant called it, in imitation of the *sensus interior* of Augustine and the Scholastics. ... This immediate awareness, which is part of

---

[22] Bavinck, *RD*, 2: p. 74; *GD*, 2: p. 52.
[23] See especially Bavinck's 'Onbewuste voorstellingen' ('Unconscious Representations') in *Beginselen der psychologie*, pp. 78–82, in which he writes that the unconscious 'activities of the soul [*werkzaamheid der ziel*]' (p. 81) include the myriad of mundane activities that humans undergo daily, such as sitting on chairs, walking on streets while failing to notice houses, writing and making mistakes and so on.

and is produced by certain psychic phenomena, has an attendant character: it is a direct and concomitant consciousness.[24]

The point is clear: God's revelation is pervasive, within and without the human subject, and often apart from emerging into active cognition, attending the myriad of ways in which creatures engage in God's world without attending to it in conscious reflection.[25] By claiming that it is God who reveals himself, one 'presupposes that it is not humans who, by the natural light of reason, understand and know this revelation of God'.[26] What is important here, however, is this seemingly clean distinction drawn by Bavinck between the impressions and intuitions, on the one hand, and the clear and acquired knowledge produced by an active mental reflection on those impressions, on the other.

b. Organism, the psyche and feeling as unconscious knowing

It turns out that Bavinck's treatment of the knowledge and revelation of God in the *Reformed Dogmatics* corresponds well with his treatment of revelation in his Stone lectures. An important role is placed on the unconscious life and the pre-predicative character of revelation. Both point to the idea that revelation precedes thinking and conscious willing, and both argue that the locus of revelation is in consciousness, in a pervasive awareness of God – as impressions and intuitions in the *Dogmatics*, and as a feeling of dependence upon the world and God, a feeling prior to thinking and willing in the Stone lectures. Before some further concepts are explored, consider Bavinck's claims in his lecture on revelation and religion in his *Philosophy of Revelation*, in which he argues that the unconscious feelings and activities with which humanity has been endowed is precisely the fruit of (1) an organic ontology and epistemology and (2) revelation.

In this lecture, Bavinck writes,

> Coe says truly, 'that though reason is necessary to guide the ship of life, feeling is the stream that propels it'. Beneath consciousness there is a world of instincts and habits, notions and inclinations, abilities and capacities, which continually sets on fire the course of nature. Beneath the head lies the heart, out of which are the gates of life.[27]

The two go together, Bavinck reasons, just as the facts of history, religious feelings and objective revelation in nature and Scripture have to go together. Characteristically,

---

[24] Bavinck, 'The Unconscious', p. 176. The gloss for the original German is included in the translation cited.
[25] Importantly, Bavinck does not pit one against the other, and argues that human knowers should want to think reflectively of this primordial awareness: 'Humans are not content with impressions and intuitions in any area of knowledge. Mere consciousness of a thing is not enough for them. It is not sufficient for them to know: they want to know they know.' Bavinck, *RD*, 2: p. 74.
[26] Bavinck, *RD*, 2: p. 74.
[27] Bavinck, *Philosophy of Revelation*, p. 173.

Bavinck argues that it is the organic worldview that does equal justice to the unconscious life in the depths of human personality and to the objective world that surrounds humanity. Psychology, a reflection on the depths of the human personality, brings us face to face with metaphysical realities and the God who reveals. On this point, Bavinck is worth quoting in full:

> In reality, all these phenomena of consciousness, so far from being isolated, exist only in intimate mutual relations and ever spring out of the depths of personality. The whole cannot be explained in an atomistic manner by a combination of its parts; but on the contrary the parts must be conceived in an organic way by unfolding the totality. Behind the particular lies the general, and whole precedes the parts. If, for example, we had to learn to see, we should be dead before the task was accomplished. But just as the bird knows how to build its nest, so we bring with us from our birth all kinds of abilities and capacities in our nature. It is the intuitive, organic life which in sensations, in thoughts and actions, gives an impulse to us and shows us the way. Instinct and capacity, norm and law, *precede the life of reflection*. Humans are not sent into the world unarmed, but are equipped in body and soul with rich gifts and powers; they receive the talents which one has only to invest and augment them in the acts of his earthly life. ... And thus it becomes manifest that empirical life is rooted in an aprioristic given, which does not come slowly into existence by mechanical development, but is a gift of God's grace, and a fruit and result of his revelation.[28]

The instinctive, organic life of sensations that precedes the life of reflection coheres with the way reality is given to creatures precisely because God graciously upholds all things and continually reveals the world and himself to them. A focus on Bavinck's understanding of reason and the life of the intellect, therefore, should not eclipse his emphasis on the revelationally conditioned fact that much of human life is operative apart from conscious reflection. 'The intellect', he thought, 'is certainly not total consciousness, not even the most important part of it, but only a certain function of cognition.'[29] Cognitive life involves 'sensory perception, memory, imagination, conscience, reason, and then also the intellect', such that it would be a misunderstanding of human life if knowing is identified with the intellect.[30]

Bavinck's understanding of the knowing faculty comes in its clearest expression in his *Beginselen der psychologie*, in which he delineates the basic components that make up the knowing faculty (*kenvermogen*). There, he affirms a proper place for reasoning but relativizes it as merely one aspect of the faculty: 'Understanding and reason [indicate] so little of the essence of man and the whole of the content of the faculty of knowing; rather they are merely particular activities of the knowing faculty that first began their work as the fundamentals of human knowledge that lies broad

---

[28] Bavinck, *Philosophy of Revelation*, pp. 173–4. Emphases mine.
[29] Herman Bavinck, 'Primacy of the Intellect and of the Will', in John Bolt (ed.), Harry Boonstra and Gerrit Sheeres (trans.), *Essays on Religion, Science, and Society* (Grand Rapids: Baker Academic, 2008), p. 201.
[30] Bavinck, 'Primacy of the Intellect and of the Will', p. 201.

and deep in the unconscious.'[31] Reason is not denigrated in this affirmation, although it does provide it with a proper function located within a specific context – bringing order to the unconscious representations that reside in the psyche.

This discussion of reason's place in the knowing faculty, however, comes after a consideration of the place of feeling (*gevoel*). After summarizing the contemporary positions that describe the faculty of feeling (*gevoelvermogen*), Bavinck argues that one of the primary mistakes in the discussion is the location of feeling as a separate, individual, faculty that runs alongside other faculties (of knowing and desiring): 'Feeling ... taken in the subjective sense and as an immediate sensation or consciousness of agreeable or unagreeable states, is not a particular faculty, nor can it be.' Rather, 'As sensation or consciousness [feeling] belongs with all intuitions [*beseffen*], impressions [*indrukken*], perception, concepts, and so on, to the knowing faculty [*kenvermogen*].'[32] Feeling considers the same objects of knowledge as the intellect, but knows them in a different mode – again, a knowledge prior to thinking and willing. Appealing to Schopenhauer, Bavinck makes the significant move in *locating feeling as a function of the knowing faculty*. In his words,

> Through feeling, we indicate, as Schopenhauer rightly said, all immediate and direct *knowing that precedes thinking and reflection, which is in contrast to knowledge in abstract concepts and in the state of reasoning*. Just as when something is told, we feel instinctively whether [that which is said] is true or untrue. From here it is decisive that feeling in this sense is not a special [separated] faculty, but a special activity within the knowing faculty.[33]

This articulation of feeling as an immediate awareness, sensation or perception, however, should not be mistaken to be a cool, detached and reflective contemplation on the veracity of particular propositions. It is more akin to the knowledge about our sense of touch and of the inner states of the soul. In no uncertain terms, Bavinck argues that it is a knowledge grasped apart from active consciousness, and it is here that he specifies that feeling indicates an inner certainty because it is a knowledge without concepts, as quoted in the very beginning of this chapter: 'This way of taking cognizance is of the highest significance. ... It is not less certain than [reasoning and thinking], but

---

[31] Bavinck, *Beginselen der psychologie*, p. 82. Dutch original: 'Zoo weinig zijn verstand en rede het wezen van den mensch en de gansche inhoud van het kenvermogen, dat ze daarvan veeleer slechts bijzondere werkzaamheden zijn, die dan eerst hun arbeid beginnen, als de fundamenten der menschelijke kennis reeds breed en diep, tot in het onbewuste toe, gelegd zijn.'

[32] Bavinck, *Beginselen der psychologie*, p. 55. 'Nu is het al terstond duidelijk, dat het gevoel, in den eersten, subjectieven zin genomen en als onmiddellijke gewaarwording of bewustzijn van aangename of onaangename toestanden omschreven, geen afzonderlijk vermogen is, noch kan zijn. Als gewaarwording of bewustzijn behoort het met alle beseffen, indrukken, waarnemingen, begrippen enz. tot het kenvermogen.'

[33] Bavinck, *Beginselen der psychologie*, p. 57. Emphasis mine. Dutch original: 'Door het gevoel duiden wij, zooals Schopenhauer terecht zeide, al die onmiddellijke, rechtstreeksche, aan alle denken en reflectie voorafgaande kennis aan, welke tegen de kennis in abstracte begrippen en redeneeiingen overstaat. Zoodra ons iets verteld wordt, voelen wij instinctief, dat het waar of onwaar is. Maar daarmede is dan ook beslist, dat het gevoel in dezen zin geen bijzonder vermogen is, maar eene bijzondere werkzaamheid van het kenvermogen.'

exceeds far above them in certainty. But it is indeed less clear and conscious, *precisely because it is not a knowledge in concepts*, and is not the fruit of deliberate reflection and reasoning.'[34]

A few conclusions may be drawn from the above. First, Bavinck's distinction between feeling and knowing is not so much a distinction between irrational emotions and deliberative reasoning but a distinction between two modes of knowing. Feeling, as immediate awareness and pre-cognitive knowing, indicates the main mode in which creatures live. In daily life creatures do not act on the basis of acting on propositions that have been reflected upon beforehand. Human beings live with an embodied knowing – they avoid buildings as they walk on the street without thinking about the buildings avoided, they can articulate what they feel in their inner life though they also know that what they articulate about that life far reduces their experience of it. Second, philosophy, reasoning and conscious reflection are derivative modes of action – reasoning takes place in the context of a prior knowledge without concepts, and in fact presupposes it. As Kuyper argued, 'All principles arise from practical life.'[35] In being derivative, as one shall see, reason is not insignificant. Indeed, reasoning reflects upon the meaning, the *telos*, the reasons, behind human life, and brings order upon the impressions of the unconscious life. Indeed, Bavinck's organic account of the human faculties requires him to hold feeling and reasoning together without denigrating one or the other.

Finally, the coherence of feeling and conscious reasoning as two modes of knowing and its fit with objective reality, as Bavinck claims in the Stone lectures, are due to God's organic creation and his ongoing act of revelation. Before connecting Bavinck's claims to some broader epistemological moves in the classical tradition and neo-Calvinism in general, a treatment of his view of reason, as significant yet operative within this broader account of knowing, remains necessary.

c. Concept formation and reason in the context of a primordial awareness

The role of reason, as indicated briefly above, is to bring order to the unconscious impressions that are already present in the psyche. Attending to the soul as the subject of conscious and unconscious life, Bavinck argues that representations arise from the intuitions and impressions gathered in being in the world.

> Representations are not the first and the primary thing in the conscious life of the soul. There are also sensations, impressions [*indrukken*], awareness [*beseffen*], intuitions, instinct, and so on. A representation is actually only the name for the

---

[34] Bavinck, *Beginselen der psychologie*, pp. 57–8. Emphasis mine. Dutch original: 'Deze wijze van kennisneming is van het hoogste belang; zij is onderscheiden van en voorafgaande aan die door redeneering en denken; zij is niet minder zeker dan deze, maar gaat ze in zekerheid ver te boven. Maar ze is wel minder helder en bewust, juist omdat zij geen kennis in begrippen is en geen vrucht van opzettelijk nadenken en redeneeren.'
[35] Kuyper, 'Our Instinctive Life', p. 263.

product of a sensation or recollection, and cannot include all of the activity of consciousness.[36]

To be sure, he reminds his readers that this activity of consciousness, of the soul, is not to be confused with conscious thinking and willing. Representations are worked on by 'the soul', 'produced or reproduced, connected or distinguished', he writes, 'consciously or unconsciously, with or without her will'.[37]

The sense of Bavinck's thinking here, it seems, is this: in one's awareness of ordinary objects – the doorknob that is noticed by the hand as distinguished from the door that it unlocks, the typewriter and the words that appear on the page as authors articulate their thoughts on paper – the unconscious life is always at work, making distinctions, producing representations, mental images, of the things encountered. The knowing subject can, in a moment of conscious reflection, recollect and connect representations together, but in doing this he or she is already working with the activity of that unconscious life in producing representations. There is also, again, a certain ordering: impressions are the basis on which mental images arise.[38] It is being in the world, encountering self, world, objects in the world, and ultimately, God and his revealing powers, that render this whole process reliable and suitable for ordinary life.

The role of reason, then, is to work with these representations and to bring about concept formation. In short, 'Thinking is the processing of representations into concepts, of judging and determining, of tracing in the world of perception the thoughts on which they rest, of the law according to which they are governed.'[39] This is stated more explicitly in his Stone lectures, where Bavinck demarcates a clear line that distinguishes between the unconscious life of representations, on the one hand, and the conscious acts of thinking which forms concepts, on the other. There, he wrote that 'between perception and intellect, representation and conceptions, association of representations and conceptual thinking, there is a fundamental difference'.[40] Reasoning, therefore, plays a necessary function in the construction of science, and is itself a particularly *human* capacity that distinguishes them from all other creatures. As such, Bavinck could even claim that in a sense it is a 'higher activity [*hoogere werkzaamheid*]' of the soul, in turning representations into concepts.[41] Stated succinctly in an Aristotelian fashion, Bavinck would claim that 'reason is thusly a characteristic of humanity [*De*

---

[36] Bavinck, *Beginselen der psychologie*, p. 39. Dutch original: 'Voorstellingen zijn lang niet 't eerste en het een en al in het bewuste leven der ziel. Er zijn ook gewaarwordingen, indrukken, beseffen, intuïties, instincten enz. Eene voorstelling is eigenlijk alleen de naam voor het product eener waarneming of herinnering, en kan niet alle werkzaamheden van het bewustzijn omvatten.'

[37] Bavinck, *Beginselen der psychologie*, p. 40. Dutch original: 'Het is de ziel, die ze bewust of onbewust, met of zonder haar wil produceert en reproduceert, verbindt of scheidt enz.'

[38] Later on, however, Bavinck makes a finer distinction between sensations [*gewaarwording*] and perception [*waarneming*]: 'Gewaarwordingen geven indrukken, beseffen, maar waarnemingen verschaffen voorstellingen [Sensations give impressions, awareness, but perceptions provide representations] (fantasia, phantasma, species sensibilis, apperception, Vorstellung, Anschauung).' *Beginselen der psychologie*, p. 75.

[39] Bavinck, *Beginselen der psychologie*, p. 104. 'Denken is het verwerken der voorstellingen tot begrippen, oordeelen en besluiten, of het opsporen in de waarnemingswereld van de gedachte, waarop ze rust, van de wet, waardoor ze beheerscht wordt.'

[40] Bavinck, *Philosophy of Revelation*, p. 56.

[41] Bavinck, *Beginselen der psychologie*, p. 98.

rede is daarom een kenmerk van den mensch]'.[42] When claims like these are situated within Bavinck's broader account of revelation and unconscious knowing, however, it is clear that he is not merely repeating a typical medieval account of theological anthropology according to which reason is the sole or main distinguishing mark of humanity. Involved, also, are the instinctive, intuitive and relational connectedness that mark the lives of all human beings.[43]

Bavinck's affirmations concerning reason's role are perhaps most clear towards the end of his discussion of general epistemological principles in the *Prolegomena*. There, before concluding the section on the necessity of the Logos to uphold the correspondence between subject and object, Bavinck aligns himself closely with Aquinas in affirming that reason is the light of the divine in humanity. His words clearly indicate that a robust affirmation of reason's proper place is not eradicated by either his emphasis on the prior divine light or the knowledge attained by feeling:

> God is the light of reason in which, by which, and through which all things that shine so as to be intelligible, shine. Thomas repeatedly speaks in the same way and uses the same metaphor. Only he points out that this should not be understood pantheistically as Averroes, under neoplatonic influence, taught his students to do and was later followed in this by Malebranche and the ontologistic school. Says Thomas: just as we look into the natural world, not by being in the sun ourselves, but by the light of the sun that shines on us, so neither do we see things in the divine being but by the light that, originating in God, shines in our own intellect. *Reason in us is that divine light*; it is not itself the divine logos, but it participates in it. To be (*esse*), to live (*vivere*), and to understand (*intelligere*) is the prerogative of God in respect of his being (*per essentiam*), ours in respect of participation (*per participationem*).[44]

To draw this section to a close, a few final comments are appropriate. Bavinck affirms that feeling, as an activity of knowing, is a necessary component of human life – it provides a knowledge no less clear or significant than the knowledge gained by a proper use of reason. Revelation, then, is used by Bavinck in a twofold sense that corresponds with his use of both romantic and Thomistic sources. On the one hand, Bavinck argues that revelation is a primordial unveiling of reality, an immediate contact that always obtains prior to thinking and willing that takes shape as a feeling of absolute dependence on God, and thus the context in which all reasoning occurs. The light of the Logos precedes all active reasoning and thus all acquired knowledge. Yet, Bavinck *also* affirms that reason is the light of God in us. Reason participates in revelation as

---

[42] Bavinck, *Beginselen der psychologie*, p. 100.
[43] Bavinck, again, is consistent with Kuyper on this point: 'Still, we may never conclude that the instinctive life alone has value to us, as though reflection could safely be neglected if not eliminated. We have always had a different view of the matter, as is evident from the founding of the Free University. We have consistently stressed that a higher and more certain development of our conscious life calls for reflection and that a political-social-religious group that neglects to arm itself with learning runs the risk of degenerating into a merely emotional undertaking.' Kuyper, 'Our Instinctive Life', p. 266.
[44] Bavinck, *RD*, 1: p. 231. Emphasis mine.

much as there is a romantic presence of God felt by humanity prior to any conscious rational deliberation.

The organic worldview that Bavinck develops posits a further twofold account of organic connectedness: between the unconscious life of feeling and the world, on the one hand, and between the unconscious psyche with conscious reasoning, on the other. He sees no reason to pit one against the other, though historically a binary between them may have been erected. In a manner that again betrays his eclecticism, Bavinck uses both romantic and classical sources. Interpretations of Bavinck's thinking that absolutize one or the other would seem inevitably to eclipse his own creative moves.

II Between *concursus* and *influentia*

To substantiate the point above, this section will suggest that Bavinck's moves potentially blend together what Lydia Schumacher calls the distinction between *concursus* and *influentia* models of illumination (and the work of the Logos). Each of these terms correspond to the epistemological affirmations of Bonaventure and Aquinas, respectively. That Bavinck wrestles with both thinkers, and does so using and critiquing Thomistic tools, has already been shown. My argument, though, is not that Bavinck blended Aquinas and Bonaventure self-consciously in this way. Rather, the manner in which he meshes their thoughts can be discerned conceptually, especially as the romantic overtones of his thinking are noted.[45] In short, for Bonaventure divine illumination involves a divine light that is implanted by God in the minds of all creatures; the divine light attends the being and acts of creaturely intelligence that cannot be shaken away even by the entrance of sin. On this view of things, the deliverances of reason can be in *conformity to* or *inconsistent with* the divine light that is always known and recognized in one's mind. Reason and illumination are thus two distinct things, though the latter is always the context in and from which reason operates. Hence reason's activities are always in *concurrence* with the presence of the divine light (whether accurately or inaccurately). In Aquinas, however, the light in us *just is* the gift of natural reason in God's creatures – and divine illumination obtains when creaturely reason is used in an appropriate way.

These concepts will become clearer as one considers Schumacher's words at length. She says this about Bonaventure:

> It is [Christ's] light that supplements or concurs with the human cognitive light so that it can truly illumine reality. On account of the inner light of Christ, the mind can be directly illumined with the knowledge of God in three main ways, namely through an exterior light (*lumen exterius*); through an interior light (*lumen interius*); and through the superior light (*lumen superius*).
>
> Because the mind presupposes the divine Light in all its efforts to perceive reality by the light, Bonaventure concludes that 'nothing can be understood at all

---

[45] Bavinck defends Bonaventure from the charge that he advocated a theory of innate ideas while suggesting that, as previously noted, Bonaventure's explicit treatment of Scripture as a starting point to the *Breviloquium* is worthy of emulation. Bavinck, *RD*, 2: p. 65, 1: pp. 98–9, respectively.

unless God immediately illumines the subject of knowledge by means of the eternal divine truth'. Despite the fact that God Himself is beyond reach, Bonaventure indicates that He is 'closer to the mind even than the mind is to itself'. Whenever the mind reflects on its powers, it cannot help but reflect on God, for His Light shines forth in the mind 'in a manner that cannot be stopped'. In shining forth by the way of the transcendental concepts, that light renders the human subject the adequate foundation for all knowledge of realities outside, inside, and above itself.[46]

The emphasis in Bonaventure's account is one's radical epistemological dependence on Christ's light, without which scientific inquiry and the pursuit of wisdom are vain, and knowledge of reality cannot obtain. On Aquinas's *influentia* model, things are quite different. For Aquinas, 'An awareness of God as constant as the awareness of the world is not always maintained, but was lost at the fall and must therefore be regained'.[47] Moreover, explicitly contrasting Aquinas from Bonaventure, Schumacher writes:

> Since Thomas holds that sensible rather than transcendental objects are the mind's first objects, he denies that illumination affords *a priori* concepts. For Aquinas ... the divine light is simply the source from which the innate cognitive capacity 'flows in' to human persons. What comes from above, in other words, is not the mind's ideas themselves *but the ability to form ideas on the basis of things below*. Put differently, the divine light is an intrinsic as opposed to extrinsic force. ... Thomas' tendency to *conflate* illumination with the gift of the (Aristotelian) agent intellect has been regarded as a fundamentally anti-Augustinian one.[48]

On the page before this, she says:

> One of the first points Aquinas makes about divine illumination in this part is that it is the source of the 'natural light' of reason, that is, the ability to engage in abstraction or to shed light on the significance of the phantasms that are stored in the memory by forming ideas about them.[49]

---

[46] Schumacher, *Divine Illumination*, p. 142. Schumacher's comments are on Bonaventure's *De reduction atrium ad theologiam* (Florence: Quaracchi, 1938). As one shall see, it is not that the light makes the human subject an adequate foundation for knowledge but that the subject's conformity to the light, which comes from the outside as a true foundation of knowing, is how one obtains (or ceases to suppress) knowledge. On this, Bavinck's comment on Bonaventure is apt: 'Hence, though Bonaventure also assumes that there are truths we do not obtain by sense perception but by interior contemplation and communion with God, even he does not believe in innate ideas in the strict sense of the term.' Bavinck, *RD*, 2: p. 65.
[47] Schumacher, *Divine Illumination*, p. 168.
[48] Schumacher, *Divine Illumination*, p. 176. Emphases mine. The burden of Schumacher's rather controversial thesis, of course, is that Aquinas's *influentia* model follows Augustine, whereas Bonaventure's marks a departure from the Augustinian tradition.
[49] Schumacher, *Divine Illumination*, p. 175.

To narrow the discussion to matters pertinent to the subject at hand, one may consider the exegetical differences between Bonaventure and Aquinas on the enlightenment of the Logos in Jn 1.9. In the *Itinerarium*, Bonaventure argues that the text teaches this:

> Since our mind itself is changeable, it can see such a truth shining forth unchangingly only by means of some light which shines in an absolutely unchangeable way; and it is impossible for this light to be a changeable creature. Therefore our intellect knows in that Light *which enlightens every man coming into this world*, which is the true *Light* and the *Word* who *was in the beginning with God* (Jn 1.9, 1).[50]

Here, one sees the strong distinction Bonaventure draws between the light of the *logos* and the intellectual faculties of the mind – a distinction between a changeable entity and an ever-present unchangeable illumination that is always within the mind. The mind can work in conformity with it or against it. This builds on Bonaventure's comments in the first chapter concerning the necessity of grace for the penetration of reason. 'Since grace is the foundation of the rectitude of will and of the penetrating light of reason, we must first pray, then live holy lives and thirdly concentrate our attention upon reflections of truth.'[51] The changeable nature of reason and the corrupting powers of sin make its conformity to the ever-present light quite difficult. However, notice here that an obtaining of knowledge does not resemble a shift from ignorance to enlightenment but rather a retrieval of what God has always been revealing. For Bonaventure, God does not merely create creatures with the capacity to know. God supplies a divine light that *always* enlightens the mind, despite the mind's frequent inability to acknowledge it.

To clarify, Bonaventure's emphasis on the divine light as a pre-condition for reason's proper operation is not meant to bypass use of one's natural cognitive faculties. Rather, the divine light undergirds cognition as a pre-condition and empowers it for fruitful use. As Webster comments, '[Bonaventure has] an uncluttered sense that created intelligence is *flooded by divine light*, and by the simple fact that it never occurs to him to think that the arts of the mind may be secular. ... The mind's powers are encompassed and *accompanied by* a gift and light which are not of the mind's invention.'[52] Webster, in other words, notices that for Bonaventure there is a distinction between the divine light and creaturely reason and that they are related by way of concurrence: 'Creatures illuminate the world only insofar as their acts are themselves illuminated. Only as acts of knowing are bathed in light can they be the means of seeing our way around the world or of giving ourselves a truthful picture of it.'[53]

This primordial character of illumination informs the shape of Bonaventure's account of the arts. As divine illumination is the font out of which all human

---

[50] Bonaventure, 'The Soul's Journey into God', in Ewert Cousins (trans.), *Bonaventure: The Soul's Journey into God, The Tree of Life, the Life of St. Francis* (Mahwah: Paulist Press, 1978), p. 82, emphases in original. Bonaventure argues that the content of divine illumination includes knowledge of absolute and eternal being – the standard against which one measures all finite beings.
[51] Bonaventure, 'The Soul's Journey into God', p. 63.
[52] Webster, '*Regina atrium*', p. 174, emphasis mine.
[53] Webster, '*Regina atrium*', p. 176, emphasis mine.

knowledge comes to be, all of the arts can be traced back to its divine origins, as God's being and the human's unification with God encircles creation's beginning and end. The title of Bonaventure's 'companion piece to the *Itinerarium*',[54] *On the Reduction of the Arts*, signals these moves: the arts can be reduced in the sense that they inescapably reveal vestiges of God's self to the contemplative mind.[55] Bonaventure is keen on emphasizing, however, that the arts are reduced back to God precisely because divine illumination attends every act of human knowing and is primordially present in the human mind.[56] As such, 'To lead the arts back to theology means, for Bonaventure, to show the organic connection between all the arts and the central concern of the Scriptures or theology. None of the arts, including philosophy, ought to be allowed to stand as an independent and self-sufficient discipline.'[57] The movement of reduction is a 'movement of knowledge' which raises our awareness of reality to a more explicit, 'conscious, cognitive level'.[58] Failure to trace all things back to God would be a fundamental failure to understand the objects under study, as every object of human knowledge is patterned after divine ideas that pre-exist them in God.

The *Reduction* opens with Jas 1.17, which Bonaventure takes to refer to 'all illumination'.[59] A single 'fontal' light produces many lights, and even 'though every illumination of knowledge is internal,' Bonaventure continues to make a distinction between the exterior, inferior, interior and superior lights.[60] The exterior lights refer to the mechanical arts, which have to do with the domestic life: weaving, agriculture, hunting and so on. The inferior light refers to sense perception, while the interior refers to philosophical knowledge. The superior light is the light of grace and holy Scripture.

Bonaventure repeats the same point in various ways: divine wisdom 'lies hidden in sense knowledge',[61] 'the illumination of the mechanical arts is a path to the illumination of sacred Scripture',[62] 'all natural philosophy ... presupposes the Word of God as begotten and incarnate',[63] such that 'the wisdom of God lies hidden in natural philosophy'.[64] If for Bavinck revelation is the 'secret of the mind', so in Bonaventure illumination is what

---

[54] Christopher Cullen, *Bonaventure* (Oxford: Oxford University Press), p. 30. Cullen provides a succinct summary of the *Reduction* and the scholarly impact of the work on pages 30–5. See also Webster's elegant close reading in his '*Regina Atrium*', pp. 174–82.
[55] 'Bonaventure speaks of the philosophical disciplines and states that there is nothing in these disciplines which does not imply a vestige of the Trinity.' Zachary Hayes, 'Introduction', in Bonaventure, *On the Reduction of the Arts to Theology*, Zachary Hayes (trans.) (New York: The Franciscan Institute, 1996), p. 3.
[56] 'Bonaventure seeks an ultimate ground for all human knowledge and action. All human knowledge and art is grounded in the exemplary ideas of the word of God. ... Specifically, he thinks that all knowledge is a form of enlightenment and that all light flows from the fontal source of light.' Cullen, *Bonaventure*, p. 30.
[57] Hayes, 'Introduction', p. 2.
[58] Hayes, 'Introduction', p. 8.
[59] Bonaventure, *On the Reduction of the Arts*, §1.
[60] Bonaventure, *On the Reduction of the Arts*, §1.
[61] Bonaventure, *On the Reduction of the Arts*, §10.
[62] Bonaventure, *On the Reduction of the Arts*, §14.
[63] Bonaventure, *On the Reduction of the Arts*, §20
[64] Bonaventure, *On the Reduction of the Arts*, §23. Behind this is Bonaventure's logos-centric understanding of the Word as the divine exemplar of all things. See, for example, *Breviloquium*, 1. 6. 1-5, 1. 8. 2, 2. 1. 4; Schumacher, *Divine Illumination*, pp. 122, 126; Cullen, *Bonaventure*, pp. 71–7.

lies beneath the arts.⁶⁵ The Scripture manifests in a greater light what humans had already known by illumination: 'It is evident that the *manifold wisdom of God*, which is clearly revealed in sacred Scripture, *lies hidden in all knowledge and in all nature*.'⁶⁶ Cullen's summary here is apt: 'All knowledge must be "reduced" to the one truth of Christ. Indeed, there can be no truth apart from Christ, the Metaphysical Center.'⁶⁷ As a result, 'all knowledge and art reflect the font of intelligibility.'⁶⁸

When Aquinas comments on the Johannine passage, however, one sees the 'conflation' that Schumacher notices between the intellect and illumination. This is seen in the reply to the third objection in *Summa Theologiae* I, q. 12, a. 11:

> All things are said to be seen in God and all things are judged in Him, because by the participation of His light, we know and judge all things; for the light of natural reason itself is a participation of the divine light; as likewise we are said to see and judge of sensible things in the sun, i.e., by the sun's light.⁶⁹

More explicitly in I, q. 88, a. 3, and commenting on the meaning of Jn 1.9, Thomas objects explicitly to a Bonaventurian line of reasoning concerning whether God is ever present in the mind:

> Objection 2: Further, whatever causes a thing to be such is more so. But God is the cause of all our knowledge; for He is 'the true light which enlighteneth every man that cometh into this world' (Jn 1.9). Therefore God is our first and most known object. ... Response to Objection 2: The axiom, 'Whatever causes a thing to be such is more so', must be understood of things belonging to one and the same order, as explained above (81, 2, ad 3). Other things than God are known because of God; not as if He were the first known object, but because He is the first cause of our faculty of knowledge.⁷⁰

As such, though Aquinas clearly affirms the noetic effects of sin, divine illumination is accessed by the gift of the light of natural reason, and one participates in the divine light

---

⁶⁵ Bavinck, *Philosophy of Revelation*, p. 59.
⁶⁶ Bonaventure, *On the Reduction of the Arts*, §26. Latter emphasis mine. Etienne Gilson's comment here is relevant: 'Thus, for him [Bonaventure], the philosophy of St. Albert and St. Thomas was of necessity in error because, while it situated Christ in the center of theology, it did not situate Him in the center of philosophy.' *The Philosophy of St. Bonaventure*, Dom Illtyd Trethowman and Frank J. Sheed (trans.) (Paterson: St. Anthony Guild Press, 1965), p. 28.
⁶⁷ Cullen, *Bonaventure*, p. 32.
⁶⁸ Cullen, *Bonaventure*, p. 90.
⁶⁹ Aquinas, *ST* I, q. 12, a. 11.
⁷⁰ Aquinas, *ST* I, q. 88, a. 3. Thomas's understanding that God's existence 'in a general and confused way is implanted in us by nature, in as much as God is man's beatitude' does not mean that humanity knows 'absolutely that God exists'. Cf. *ST* I, q. 2, a. 1. Thomas's comment on Jn 1.9, interpreting God's enlightening as the gift of natural reason, is consistent with his commentary on the Gospel of John: 'For when the Evangelist says, he *enlightens every man*, this seems to be false, because there are still many in darkness in the world. However, if we bear in mind these distinctions and take "world" from the standpoint of its creation, and "enlighten" as referring to the light of natural reason, the statement of the Evangelist is beyond reproach.' Thomas Aquinas, *Commentary on the Gospel of John*, James A. Weisheipl and Fabian R. Larcher (trans.) (Albany: Magi, 1980), 1: p. 129.

to the degree that one uses reason rightly. Further, it is not the case for Thomas that the knowledge of God 'is closer to the mind' than the mind is to itself (contra Bonaventure). Knowledge of God does not attend every act of the creaturely intelligence; it is not self-evident.[71] Rather, things are known because of God only in the sense that he causes one to have faculties of knowing. For Thomas, God is the cause of knowledge only in the sense that he is one's *principium essendi* – he causes because he creates us with rational faculties. One also sees the conflation between what Reformed theologians call general revelation with reason in Aquinas's interpretation of Rom. 1.19. On the *Sed Contra* of *Summa Theologiae* I, q. 12, a. 12, he writes: 'It is written (Rom. 1.19), "That which is known of God," namely, what can be known of God by natural reason, "is manifest in them".'[72] In this regard, Matthew Levering's comments concerning the difference between Anselm and Aquinas are apt:

> Unlike Anselm, then, Aquinas does not think that the fool is actually, in the strict sense, a fool; the fool's statement is not, as Anselm thinks it to be, logically nonsensical. Rather, the fool, due ultimately to the effects of original sin, lacks the speculative *habitus* that would enable him to reason to God from contingent things.[73]

The natural light of reason, of course, is in need of the supernatural revelation for humanity to attain salvation – Thomas was not a rationalist with respect to the knowledge of God – but this natural light of reason remains the primary mode by which creatures know in the natural realm precisely because God's light in us just is natural reason itself.[74]

In sum, for Bonaventure the divine light is entirely the work of God, implanted into humanity, that provides the context into and from which humanity reasons. Failure to observe this ever-present light is failure to gain wisdom. For Aquinas, the divine illumination is through the use of the gift of natural reason, the divine light in us. In Schumacher's reading, these two options are mutually exclusive.[75]

---

[71] This is also one way in which Thomas departs from Anselm's proposal that God's existence is self-evident within the mind by virtue of illumination. See the discussion in Levering, *Proofs of God*, p. 61. Hence, contra Anselm (and, it seems, Bonaventure) who argued that 'we know truth by knowing God', Levering notes that for Aquinas 'we need not know God before we can know truth about things, even though it is certainly the case that "all our knowledge is caused in us through His influence".' *Proofs of God*, p. 61. The sense of *influentia* is explicit in that account. Levering is quoting Aquinas, *Summa contra gentiles*, 1: 11.

[72] Compare with Muller's comment: 'Where the Thomistic line of thought continues into the Reformation – for example, in the writings of Vermigli, Zanchi, and, to a certain extent, Keckermann – it is modified by a more negative assessment of the powers of reason and by a sense of diastasis between the ways of God and the ways of man that virtually cancels a Thomistic use of the *analgia entis* in theology.' *Post-Reformation Reformed Dogmatics*, vol. 1, *Prolegomena to Theology*, 2nd edn (Grand Rapids: Baker Academic, 2003), p. 65. Cf. Aza Goudriaan, *Reformed Orthodoxy and Philosophy: 1625-1750: Gisbertus Voetius, Petrus van Mastricht, and Anthonius Driessen* (Leiden: Brill, 2006), pp. 29–84.

[73] Levering, *Scripture and Metaphysics*, p. 59.

[74] Thomas is clear on natural reason's insufficiency to lead creatures to eternal blessedness; humanity requires a higher, supernatural light and grace. See especially *ST* I-II, q. 57, a. 1; q. 62 a. 3; II-II, q. 2, a. 3.

[75] See also Therese Scarpelli, 'Bonaventure's Christocentric Epistemology: Christ's Human Knowledge as the Epitome of Illumination in "De Scientia Christi"', *Franciscan Studies* 65 (2007): pp. 68–9, which reinforces the same observation.

How, exactly, does Bavinck mesh Bonaventure's *concursus* model and Aquinas's *influentia* model? In order to see Bavinck's moves, consider Cullen's description of the contrast between Bonaventure and Aquinas:

> Bonaventure is trying to maintain that the intellect knows being not only through the species or likenesses abstracted from sensible things by the action of our active intellect, but also through the intuitive grasp of the Divine Being. Thomas Aquinas, by way of contrast, rejects the position that the mind first knows the Divine Being. … [For Aquinas] the first principles are the 'instruments' of the agent intellect, and it is by means of these that the intellect renders other things actually intelligible. Bonaventure thinks that the condition for the possibility of grasping finite being in the first place is that there is an intuitive grasp of infinite and absolute being. God is the light in which the intellect sees.[76]

As my analysis above has shown, like Bonaventure, Bavinck locates reason within the context of a prior, primordial, knowledge by virtue of revelation such that there is 'an intuitive grasp of the Divine Being'. Revelation precedes and provides the context for the knowledge that is gained by reason – it is *felt* and is thus *known* prior to concepts. Revelation provides the 'atmosphere', both internal and external to the mind, in which human beings come to knowledge. This revelation already sheds a pre-cognitive knowledge for the human knower, and he reasons on that basis, from that embodied and lived reality.

The 'soul's primordial awareness of God', writes Cullen regarding Bonaventure, belongs to 'the tradition of Plato and Augustine'. But rather than rooting this awareness in the soul's reminiscence like Plato, Bonaventure grounds it in the 'presence of God to the soul'.[77] Likewise, Bavinck follows this Augustinian tradition of ascending towards God precisely by looking inward to God's primordial presence in the soul:

> Thus Augustine went back behind thought to the essence of the soul, and found in it not a simple unity but a marvelously rich totality; he found there the ideas, the norms, the laws of the true and the good, the solution of the problem of the certainty of knowledge, of the cause of all things, of the supreme good; he found there the seeds and germs of all knowledge and science and art; he found there even, in the triad of *memoria, intellectus,* and *voluntas* … a reflection (*afdruk*) of the triune being of God. Augustine was the philosopher of self-examination, and in self-consciousness he discovered the starting point of a new metaphysics.[78]

Bavinck, however, does not argue that God's primordial revelation should prevent one from identifying reason as a divine light in us. Like Aquinas, Bavinck also argues in his *Prolegomena* that the faculty of reason in us is the light of the Logos, through which one participates in divine truth. The light of the Logos in revelation, therefore, both

---

[76] Cullen, *Bonaventure*, p. 62.
[77] Cullen, *Bonaventure*, p. 63.
[78] Bavinck, *Philosophy of Revelation*, p. 55. On Bavinck's use of Augustine in conjunction with romantic thought see Brock and Sutanto, 'Herman Bavinck's Reformed Eclecticism'.

precedes the use of reason and is identified with it. Using Cullen's words, Bavinck affirms that the 'action of the active intellect' in the process of abstraction remains a proper mode of knowing, such that the intellect 'renders other things actually intelligible'. By conceiving of revelation as both a pre-cognitive reality (a romantic presence) and something accessed by reason, Bavinck provides resources that bring together the structure of *concursus* and *influentia*: the *agent intellect's work of abstraction is always within the context of a pre-cognitive, primordial knowledge of God, generated by God's ever-present revelation within the psyche.*

III On 'unconscious knowledge' and primordial revelation: A revelational phenomenology as pre-predicative in broader neo-Calvinism

It is interesting that, without carrying the same metaphysical thickness as Bonaventure, various neo-Calvinists have expressed general revelation in a manner that shares conceptual similarity with the *concursus* model. In their account, consistent with what Bavinck says, general revelation is something primordial, located in consciousness, or the heart, in a personal awareness of God that cannot be identified with propositional knowledge. It is even more stimulating to see, as I demonstrate below, that Kuyper would argue that general implanted knowledge of God is an *unconscious* knowledge. Though neo-Calvinists diverge in their affirmations on the role of reason, what can be gathered clearly here is that revelation is a primordial reality within which reason functions as a derivative.[79]

Consider these quotes from two figures before and after Herman Bavinck – his colleague Abraham Kuyper and Bavinck's missiologist nephew, J. H. Bavinck. On the implanted knowledge of God, Kuyper writes this:

> Knowledge of God is implanted, infused into man. It is inseparable from his nature. He cannot shake it off. ... The infused knowledge of God is not something that man possesses. It radiates from God from moment to moment as the steady impression on man's heart of God's omnipresent power. God has made of man's heart a mirror. That mirror may be split and broken but it still reflects God's radiance, though not His true image. The *human heart*, though fallen, remains open to knowledge of God. Our philosophers may talk proudly of our capacity for knowing God, but the Church speaks of the majestic impression of the Lord that bears down on all men.
>
> Thus, the natural knowledge of God is not acquired through training or study. It is infused into all men. That is why all people share in it. It is inseparable from human nature and belongs to man as a human being.[80]

---

[79] For more on this issue, see my 'Neocalvinism on General Revelation'.
[80] Abraham Kuyper, 'The Natural Knowledge of God', Harry van Dyke (trans.), *The Bavinck Review* 6 (2015): p. 75. Emphasis mine.

A little later, he writes:

> In sum, the natural knowledge of God is created into us and therefore part of our nature. It does not radiate from us but is radiating into us. And as a result of sin it bears down on us, being far from destroyed. ... In sensing God's omnipresent power man is *entirely passive*, as passive as our lungs during breathing, our eyes when touched by light, or our eats at the tremor of sound waves. He can neither block nor invite this divine power as it radiates onto him, touches him, and causes his heart to tremble. He can neither prevent God's power from being everywhere nor his own being from being touched by it.[81]

Similarly, J. H. Bavinck wrote this:

> If we wish to use the expression 'general revelation' we must not do so in the sense that one can logically conclude God's existence from it. This may be possible, but it only leads to a philosophical notion of God as the first cause. But that is not the biblical idea of 'general revelation'. When the Bible speaks of general revelation, it means something quite different. There it has a much more personal nature. ... God's deity and eternal power are evident; they overwhelm man; they strike him suddenly. ... They creep up on him; they do not let go of him, even though man does his best to escape them.[82]

The emphases in the above texts by two important neo-Calvinists (especially in the language of infusion and in the explicit denials of the use of inferential reasoning) are that humanity is 'passive' in the reception of divine revelation. There is little to indicate that revelation is essentially or primarily accessed through the creation of rational faculties through which one gains knowledge of God or by which one participates in God's light. 'If you are looking for support of your internal sense of the divine and awareness of God, then look at our *struggle with nature*, not our *intellectual contemplation* of it.'[83] Rather, revelation is a primal and primordial pressure that humanity cannot evade as a work of God. It attends creaturely intelligence in very much the same way as Bonaventure's *concursus* model of divine illumination. As Paul Vissers observes, J. H. Bavinck's doctoral thesis argued that attention to the human's psyche reveals that 'the processes of thinking and learning, far from occurring autonomously, are closely tied to an intuitive apprehension of given reality. It is precisely the operation of this feeling in the process of human reasoning that points to the influence of the human self.'[84] Likewise, rational creatures know God in the very moment that one

---

[81] Kuyper, 'The Natural Knowledge of God', p. 76, emphasis mine.
[82] J. H. Bavinck, *The Church Between Temple and Mosque* (Grand Rapids: Eerdmans, 1966), p. 124.
[83] Kuyper, 'The Natural Knowledge of God', p. 79. Emphasis in original. Notice, too James K. A. Smith's juxtaposition between divine revelation and intellectual arguments for God's existence: 'I am skeptical about arguments for the existence of God – I say we know [God's existence] by means of revelation, which is given to humanity under the conditions of our finitude and social dependence.' 'Echeverria's Protestant Epistemology: A Catholic Response', *Calvin Theological Journal* 49 (2014): p. 288.
[84] Paul Vissers, 'Introduction', in John Bolt, James Bratt and Paul Vissers (eds), James De Jong (trans.), *The J. H. Bavinck Reader* (Grand Rapids: Eerdmans, 2008), p. 8.

knows things in creation or comes to self-consciousness, in a way that seems to curb Aquinas's *influentia* model. In this way of conceiving things, Kuyper's description of natural theology is fitting:

> Natural theology has often been portrayed as a process whereby man calmly contemplates nature, observing its order, regularity and beauty, and from there ascends to a recognition of God's great power. Nothing is further from the truth. For ordinary man, such calm contemplation is an exception. Our constant contact with nature directly affects our life, our body, our struggle for survival. Not abstract reflection but restless, painful experience has acquainted us with the power of nature.[85]

This is not to suggest that for these thinkers there exists a necessarily competitive relationship between divine and human action but rather that there is a distinct construal of the way in which human reason is understood to function. In these contexts, reason is always a response to, and is operative within, the saturation of God's dynamic and ever-present revelation, such that an affirmation of divine revelation does not involve the validation of the use of natural reason as some preamble to attain natural knowledge of God. This brings us to Kuyper's understanding that there is such a thing as *unconscious* knowledge. The conscious reflection of reason on the infused knowledge of God, for Kuyper, is always a second moment:

> Meanwhile, the natural knowledge of God does not remain submerged in our unconscious. It is proper to man to try and account for this sense of the divine. ... Man does not become active until he tries to account for those feelings and wonders what is causing his heart to tremble – in a word – when he tries to become conscious of the sense of the divine that has risen in him.[86]

Knowledge of God is 'submerged' and a 'feeling' located in the 'heart' and again antecedent to any active use of reasoning. It is on the basis of these observations, Kuyper writes, that the church with which he identifies 'makes a sharp distinction between *infused* knowledge of God and *acquired* knowledge of God. Only the latter is conscious.'[87]

---

[85] Kuyper, 'The Natural Knowledge of God', p. 78. Kuyper relates this notion of revelation to science in that it prevents scholars from presuming that academic inquiry is always necessary for human flourishing. 'By means of his revelation', he argues, humanity in every age have 'rich' knowledge 'in their heart' and 'in their soul' that bears the 'mark of the eternal'. Scholars, then, 'must begin by being rich in that faith if they are ever to feel their heart stir with the holy impulse that drives them to engage in true scholarship'. *Scholarship*, p. 9.

[86] Kuyper, 'The Natural Knowledge of God', p. 76. At first glance, this might seem contrary to Schleiermacher's account of feeling, as he wrote, in the *Christian Faith*, §3.2., that 'unconscious states are to be excluded from' his definition. However, Schleiermacher is arguing that feeling cannot include states in which the subject has a *lack* of consciousness, of awareness of oneself as a self (like states of sleeping), whereas Kuyper has a broader definition of the unconscious, which includes any state of the waking consciousness that is *pre-reflective*. Kuyper's unconscious knowledge, that is, is any state of knowing that isn't 'objective' knowing – not having a particular object consciously in mind. Kuyper's claim, then, can be construed as consistent with Schleiermacher's account according to which 'unmediated self-consciousness ... is not a notion but is feeling' (*Christian Faith*, §3.2).

[87] Kuyper, 'The Natural Knowledge of God', p. 77, emphases in original. The language of infused knowledge, as distinct from acquired knowledge, of course, stems from earlier Reformed theology.

Acquired knowledge is an elaboration of and dependent on the primal but pre-cognitive, pre-predicative, knowledge of God: 'The natural knowledge of God does not remain submerged in our unconscious. It is proper to man to try and account for this sense of the divine.'[88] In this way, the neo-Calvinistic construal is not amenable to the characterization of a twofold truth which identifies general revelation with that 'truth about God that can be known by the human mind's own powers' and a distinct 'truth about God that requires divine revelation to be known'.[89] To identify general revelation with predicates that require the operations of thinking is to commit a category mistake. This is not to say that general revelation is not cognizable but that it is irreducible to the level of cognized knowledge. What is known is cognizable and susceptible to articulation, but what is known is known long before it is articulated. Kuyper's claims must not also be construed as if he reckons that the task of scholarship in general is reduced to an unconscious knowledge. Though God infuses knowledge of himself into the consciousness of his image bearers, the task of scholarship remains the searching and finding of the truths that are implanted by the Logos in creation. The conscious use of created reason remains fundamental to scholarship and humanity's proper functioning. It is an 'obligation to investigate the Logos that God has hidden in his creation and to bring it to light'.[90]

What emerges in this discussion is that neo-Calvinism, broadly speaking, generally affirms a positive use of reason within the context of a primordial, romantic, construal of general revelation. Various neo-Calvinists may differ on the relationship between revelation and reason, or how reason can even be used in a fashion that accords with the *influentia* model. Nonetheless, there seems to be a general trend in the tradition to use distinctly Romantic (and phenomenological) language to describe general revelation, which distinguishes it quite sharply from natural theology as an epistemological response to that revelation by unregenerate or regenerate sinners. Provocatively, the early G. C. Berkouwer would characterize objections against Roman Catholicism's view of general revelation as *phenomenological* rather than epistemological. Despite possessing a few 'dangerous' ambiguities, Berkouwer writes that phenomenological concerns have an appropriate place:

> It is striking that the objections to natural theology (as a result of causal conclusions) are raised chiefly by those who have been strongly influenced by *phenomenology*. That is understandable because phenomenology wanted to direct itself, not

---

Calvin says that the sense of divinity 'is engraved upon men's minds ... naturally inborn in all ... the sense of divinity, which [the impious] greatly wished to have extinguished, thrives and presently burgeons. From this we conclude that *it is not a doctrine that must first be learned in school, but one of which each of us is master from his mother's womb and which nature itself permits no one to forget*.' *Institutes of the Christian Religion*, John T. McNeill (ed.), Ford Lewis Battles (trans.), Library of Christian Classics (London: SCM, 1961), I: 3.3. Emphasis mine. It is precisely the immediate language that Calvin deploys here that dissatisfies Plantinga. See the discussion in Kevin Diller, *Theology's Epistemological Dilemma: How Karl Barth and Alvin Plantinga Provide a Unified Response* (Downers Grove: IVP Academic, 2015), pp. 138–43, on Plantinga's apparent identifying of implanted knowledge of God strictly with innate capacity.

[88] Kuyper, 'The Natural Knowledge of God', p. 76.
[89] Levering, *Proofs of God*, p. 60.
[90] Kuyper, *Scholarship*, p. 10. See also his account of 'immediate knowledge' in relation to the sciences on pages 31–8.

simply to the fact of reality, from which a causal argument could be formed, but to the character and nature of this *reality itself*. Over against critical idealism, all emphasis is put up on the *givenness* of reality. Upon the basis of this givenness, this *self-unfolding* of reality, they came to combine this reality with God revealing himself *in* it. ... In spite of the dangers [that might attend phenomenology], we must not forget that the attempt was made to do justice to the idea of revelation.[91]

This reading of Bavinck and the survey of neo-Calvinistic expressions on general revelation suggest at least three generative conclusions. First, their articulation indicates that there is a way to affirm both a radically universal account of general revelation that nevertheless eschews a pre-dogmatic model of natural theology. General revelation is objective in the sense that it is felt, real and universally known, but it is known in the locus of the *psyche* – on an unconscious level that reverberates into the core of one's existential being prior to the mind. Propositional articulations and epistemological inferences as a result of a reflection on that revelation are a response to general revelation, and cannot be identified with it. Sin causes human agents to fail to articulate in propositional form that which is delivered in the psyche. For that reason, Bavinck holds that it is necessary that 'God's revelation in nature' is reproduced explicitly in his word: 'The natural knowledge of God is incorporated and set forth at length in Scripture itself.'[92] This opens up a Reformed account of revelation to philosophical and epistemological resources that emphasize the personal, holistic and existential contours of knowing while suggesting potentially unattended complexities concerning the knowledge of God and the noetic effects of sin. Knowledge of God and its suppression consist less in inferring erroneous propositions about him and more about relationships and dysfunctionality. Suppression and acceptance of the knowledge of God look more like a traumatic relationship and reconciliation, and less about rendering theological beliefs more precise, though, of course, it often includes this latter part. Second, Bavinck specifically provides some inclinations and conceptual resources that resist the pitting of feeling against reasoning. While it may first be thought that Bavinck's emphasis on feeling as a part of the knowing faculty pushes him towards an entirely pragmatic or romantic philosophical programme that sees rationality as second-tier or even an obfuscation of what is primordially most important, his organic account is precisely what resists the binary between an epistemology that prioritizes feelings, on the one hand, and pure rationality, on the other. Indeed, he points towards a holistic epistemology that engages the whole person while standing on divine revelation – an organic account of revelation that couples both non-conceptual and conceptual means of divine revealing, general and special revelation, respectively. Finally, then, these neo-Calvinist accounts suggest a broad-

---

[91] G. C. Berkouwer, *General Revelation* (Grand Rapids: Eerdmans, 1955), p. 82. Emphases in original. Later, on page 166, Berkouwer argued thusly on Kuyper: 'What Kuyper calls the natural knowledge of God is quite other than what Rome understands by this term. In Rome's natural theology we have to do with a true knowledge which is obtained by the natural light of reason.' James K. A. Smith also describes revelation as described in Romans 1 as a 'givenness' suppressed. 'Questions About the Perception of "Christian Truth": On the Affective Effects of Sin', *New Blackfriars* 88 (2007): pp. 585–93 (especially 592).
[92] Bavinck, *RD*, 2: p. 74.

mindedness in the sense that it is not wholly reliant on a correspondist account of knowing that merely connects inner concepts with outer reality – an inner/outer model and representationalistic realist mode of knowing. As such, the neo-Calvinists perform the philosophical flexibility of Christianity. Christian theology is free to adopt philosophical articulations of that theology in an eclectic manner, and is thus not dependent upon a single philosophical handmaiden.

What the previous three chapters show, then, is that Bavinck utilizes his organic motif not simply to organize the structure of knowledge and the relationship between theology and the other fields of science. Rather, Bavinck utilizes the motif to address particular and specific epistemological problems that arise in his day. The motif is not merely a metaphysical principle that organizes the cosmos as a result of the triune life *ad intra*. For Bavinck it is also a fecund theological resource that informs and reshapes the way he thinks Christians should address the intellectual conundrums they face on an academic and philosophical level. The chapters show that he does this by taking seriously a problem taken for granted in the nineteenth to twentieth centuries, especially with respect to the connection of subjects and objects. Reconceptualizing absolute idealism, naive realism and romantic categories, the organic motif is located within a context creatively addressed by Bavinck. In this way, too, he shows that the organic motif allows him to resist false binaries – between realism and idealism, between rationalism and mere emotionalism. His is a theologically principled account that grounds a non-erratic eclecticism.

What emerges throughout this study thus far is an unfolding of the organic motif within the locus of his theological epistemology. Situated within his understanding that creation is marked by unities and diversities because God is an archetypal one-and-three, Bavinck understands the structure of knowledge in a knower's consciousness as a single organism in which there is a unity-in-diversity reflective of creation's organic shape. Christ and the doctrines of faith provide the centre which undergird the diversity. On a broader level, it is the doctrines of the Logos, revelation, creation and providence that provide the grounds on which it can be claimed that subjects and objects correspond with each other, as each participate in a larger organic whole as parts in a creation conceived of as a single organism. Wrestling with the philosophical trends of the unconscious, the romantic emphases on the instinctive and the importance of feeling, Bavinck would deploy resources in both classical and contemporary milieus on theological and organic grounds. With these observations set in place, then, it is appropriate that this study is drawn to a close with a conclusion.

Conclusion

This book has argued that Bavinck's organicism shaped his theological epistemology. The Trinity is an archetypal unity-in-diversity, and creation reflects its creator as an organism filled with unities-in-diversities. The human knower absorbs reality by his or her consciousness, knowledge itself is thus shaped as a single organism and Christian theism provides the grounds for the unity of knowledge. The university and the sciences, when properly construed, are divided into specific fields of knowing that enjoy relative independence with their own methodological concerns and ends, their own *principia*, and yet the whole is greater than the sum of its parts in that all of the fields of knowledge ultimately form a single organism. Specialization can take place as part of the organic process of development if the prior unity is never forgotten. Unity-in-diversity is not merely the shape of the created cosmos: it is the teleological shape, too, of the epistemological reception of that cosmos as worked out in the sciences. It is only the entrance of sin that forces us to dissect and cut apart what is meant to be a singular organism.

In offering this interpretation, Bavinck's epistemology is situated within the Reformed tradition that incorporated both classical and modern sources. As part of his self-conscious eclectic approach, he freely deployed classical and post-Kantian patterns of reasoning, without capitulating to the temptation to endorse or imitate any specific thinker or philosophy wholesale. Past interpretations that characterize Bavinck's epistemology as tethered to a particular '-ism' miss not only his self-consciously eclectic approach but also the substantive way with which he uses the organic motif to structure his epistemology and the deployment of his sources. This reading thus incorporates the many valid insights that have been offered in the secondary literature without succumbing to charging Bavinck with inconsistency, as if he felt the need to make a choice between his classical, Reformed orthodox position and a creative yet critical use of the philosophies prevalent in his day. This study has shown this consistently in showcasing how Bavinck uses Thomas's account of perception and the role of reason with respect to philosophy, Eduard von Hartmann's empiricist absolute idealism, Bavinck's rather romantic approach to the question of whether knowledge can be non-conceptual and the nature of general revelation as being a pre-predicative reality that grounds both innate and acquired knowledge. The organic motif was deployed to answer specific epistemological questions, and there is a holism characteristic of Bavinck's theological epistemology that always stands behind the eclectic deployment of these patterns of reasoning.

This study, then, attempts to put to rest any claims to the effect that there were two Bavincks, and, hopefully, answers the charges that he was inconsistent in his deployment of classical and modern sources. It calls for a reconfiguring of the current discussions around his epistemology: instead of identifying Bavinck with his sources, it focuses on how Bavinck uses his sources with the organic motif in place. Such a reading displays the basic intended coherence of Bavinck's epistemology. Indeed, I contend that it is precisely his desire to produce coherence and develop orthodoxy from such a wide stream of sources that is worthy of emulation.

Given that these conclusions can become starting points for future studies, certain questions do continue to arise as a result of Bavinck's eclecticism and organic vision of knowledge: Can one use such a variety of sources in this way and still remain responsible to the full sense of the works of those authors? Does Bavinck's method produce such mutually exclusive contradictions into a forced unity, when no agreement is really there between the authors and concepts he deploys? Does Bavinck's organicism ultimately hold up under greater critical scrutiny? Or, perhaps more pertinently, is Bavinck's vision of science's unity actually applicable in the present day?

Claims that theology serves as a catalyst for unity, though initially and inherently attractive, become quickly problematic when put into practice. Theoretically, Bavinck's picture of the organism of knowledge as a single unity should generate a culture of fecund learning, as the body of truths that the student learns in one class will coalesce with what she learns in another, and as the research of each department is enriched by interdisciplinary cooperation. Such a vision resists what Alastair Macintyre observes to be the tendency of the modern research university to become a 'multiversity', which eschews the ideal that each discipline should contribute 'to a single shared enterprise'.[1] However, the claim that theology has the capacity to be a servant-queen that serves the other sciences rather than a tyrant that dictates them remains an ideal to be demonstrated rather than a proven axiom. Theology's interaction with the other sciences often goes between facile dismissal of their claims and timid embrace, fearful that scientific conclusions from the other disciplines might threaten accepted boundary lines of orthodoxy. As we saw, Bavinck himself felt those tensions at the Free University of Amsterdam.

Matters are exacerbated when one considers David Kelsey's argument that the ideals of academic freedom and the reality of theological pluralism imply that theological schools 'cannot [assume] at the outset that any one construal (of the Christian thing, social location, way of understanding God, model of excellent schooling, etc.) is the one Christianly correct version'.[2] Indeed, Kelsey is recognizing that different models of theology would produce alternative visions of education and of interdisciplinary engagement, and each theological vision should have a voice in the ongoing pursuit of providing a theological education that is cognizant of the claims of current public knowledge. This challenges directly the Kuyperian and Bavinckian claim that undergird the Free University's creation: that Reformed principles are the starting points for fruitful interdisciplinary research and scientific labour.

These challenges demand a concrete response from those who seek to follow Bavinck's Kuyperian vision of theological schooling. What is needed are not treatises *claiming* that theology – or, more precisely, *Reformed* theology – is a service to the other

---

[1] Alasdair MacIntyre, *God, Philosophy, Universities: A Selective History of the Catholic Philosophical Tradition* (New York: Sheed & Ward, 2009), p. 174.
[2] David Kelsey, *To Know God Truly: What's Theological About a Theological School?* (Eugene: Wipf & Stock, 2011), p. 117.

sciences, but works that concretely *perform* how it might do so. Much like Bonaventure's brief *Reduction of the Arts to Theology*, which performs a Franciscan method of tracing back each art to divine illumination, Bavinck's *Philosophy of Revelation* can be taken as one attempt to do this, showcasing inductively how revelation lies underneath all of the sciences and prevents them from one-sidedness. Scientific labour, however, continues apace, and each generation requires studies that showcase theology's helpfulness in a manner that does not compromise theology's subject matter as a science of God himself. The inherent difficulty of performing these twin tasks of doing justice to theology's subject matter on the one hand and performing a service to the other sciences on the other is demanding, to say the least, especially as theology seems to be further receding into the background in the contemporary day. But pursuing this task is precisely what's needed lest Bavinck's vision remains a merely utopian ideal – pious, yes; comforting, perhaps – but inherently unachievable.

Furthermore, and in anticipation of future studies, it should be made clear that my aims here are not to suggest that Bavinck's epistemology offers definitive answers to all of the questions, nor am I suggesting that one should look to him as an exhaustive guide for all things epistemological. In my attempt to explicate, propel and relate his epistemology to particular contemporary issues and questions, I am suggesting not that his content is wholly to be accepted but that he provides a modus operandi worth emulating for the contemporary theologian in a manner that is sensitive to our own philosophical milieu. That is, I suggest that despite Bavinck's intentions and robustly theological construal of the epistemic situation, his account is still firmly situated within the nineteenth-century philosophical context. Hence, though studying him provides an exemplary test case of how a Reformed theologian should relate to the broader movements of philosophy and epistemology prevalent in one's own time, it does put into question the present or universal applicability of his insights. An example of how this is the case is that his acceptance of the constitutive role of mental representations, the couching of epistemology as a relation between subject and object, the situating of his thinking on the matter between subjective idealism and naive realism, all assume a basic structure of thinking that has been subjected to serious reconsiderations since Bavinck's day. Readers in the twenty-first century have new philosophical questions to ask and resources from which to draw, resources that reject the 'through which' structure of Bavinck's thinking and that seek to go beyond the binaries of realism/idealism, and subject/object. Martin Westerholm recently puts it into sharp focus as he questions the contemporary applicability of Kant's epistemology and the historically situated character of representationalist epistemology, due no less to the influence and significance of Wittgenstein and Martin Heidegger:

> The question of the reality of external objects of experience seemed pressing to those who presumed a representationalism in which cognition is understood in terms of the correspondence between objects and mental images; yet this conception has been marginalized through the critiques of representationalist thinking that have marked twentieth-century philosophy. One of the shared features of the work of Heidegger and Wittgenstein is the notion that representationalism goes astray precisely because it enables human beings to doubt the reality of the external world.

> Where Kant argues that the scandal of philosophy consists in the fact that it has been unable to prove the reality of the external world, Heidegger famously suggests that the true scandal is that such a proof should be thought necessary at all.[3]

Put another way, despite the weight of Bavinck's arguments, his rejection of scepticism, subjective idealism and the confidence with which he purchased the intelligibility of external reality, he still did so *under the categories* of representationalist thinking that was largely ubiquitous in nineteenth-century philosophy. This is not to suggest that one should ignore Kant and the philosophical discourse produced by the impact of his thinking – that is not Westerholm's argument, and in any case it would be a betrayal of Bavinck's convictions concerning the need to engage with the contemporary questions that confront us – but rather, it is to argue that we should take into account the fact that Bavinck's epistemology at this point is a few steps removed from the present epistemological scene.

This observation generates an impetus to ask whether we can preserve the genuine insights provided by Bavinck's organic epistemology in a manner that takes seriously the newer philosophical grammars available in the contemporary context – grammar that pushes beyond the binaries that Bavinck took for granted and from which the particularities of his epistemology were developed. With the emergence of phenomenology, on the one hand, and analytic philosophy, on the other, it is worth exploring what it might mean for the theologian to emulate Bavinck's spirit in bringing about the tradition on which one stands with the contemporary philosophical context in a critical and creative fashion. Bavinck's claim that catholicity involves the rethinking of one's tradition and the desire to move it forward in an attempt to labour for the future does not, after all, demand that one imitates his theology. Rather, he provides a model to follow – and in emulating that model the theologian is required to think within his or her current context afresh. This book, I hope, would stimulate precisely that work.

---

[3] Martin Westerholm, 'Kant's Critique and Contemporary Theological Inquiry', *Modern Theology* 31 (2015): p. 426.

Bibliography

Primary sources

Bavinck, Herman. *Beginselen der psychologie*. Kampen: Bos, 1897.
Bavinck, Herman. 'Calvin and Common Grace'. In *Calvin and the Reformation*, 99–130. Edited by William Park Armstrong. Translated by Geerhardus Vos. New York: Fleming H. Revell, 1909.
Bavinck, Herman. *The Certainty of Faith*. Translated by Harry der Nederlanden. Ontario: Paideia, 1980.
Bavinck, Herman. *Christelijke wereldbeschouwing*. Kampen: Kok, 1904.
Bavinck, Herman. *Christelijke wetenschap*. Kampen: Kok, 1904.
Bavinck, Herman. *The Christian Family*. Translated by Nelson Kloosterman. Grand Rapids: Christian's Library Press, 2012.
Bavinck, Herman. *Christliche Weltanschauung*. Translated by Hermann Cuntz. Heilderberg: Carl Winter, 1907.
Bavinck, Herman. 'Common Grace'. Translated by Raymond C. Van Leeuwen. *Calvin Theological Journal* 24 (1989): 35–65.
Bavinck, Herman. 'The Conscience'. Translated by Nelson Kloosterman. *The Bavinck Review* 6 (2015): 113–26.
Bavinck, Herman. *De katholiciteit van christendom en kerk*. Kampen: Zalsman, 1888.
Bavinck, Herman. *De vrouw in de hedendaagsche maatschappij*. Kampen: Kok, 1918.
Bavinck, Herman. *De welsprekendheid: Eene lezing*. Revised Edition. Kampen: G. Ph. Zalsman, 1901.
Bavinck, Herman. *De wetenschap der H. Godgeleerdheid: Rede ter aanvaarding van het leeraarsambt aan de Theologische School te Kampen*. Kampen: Zalsman, 1883.
Bavinck, Herman. *De zekerheid des geloof*. Kampen: Kok, 1901.
Bavinck, Herman. 'Eene belanrijke apologie van de Christelijke Wereldbeschouwing'. *Theologiesche Studiën* (1894): 142–52.
Bavinck, Herman. *Essays on Religion, Science, and Society*. Edited by John Bolt. Translated by Harry Boonstra and Gerrit Sheeres. Downers Grove: BakersAcademic, 2008.
Bavinck, Herman. 'Foreword to the First Edition (Volume 1) of the *Gereformeerde Dogmatiek*'. Translated by John Bolt. *Calvin Theological Journal* 45 (2010): 9–10.
Bavinck, Herman. 'The Future of Calvinism'. *The Presbyterian and Reformed Review* 5 (1894): 1–24.
Bavinck, Herman. *Gereformeerde dogmatiek*. 4 Volumes. 3rd Edition. Kampen: J.H. Kok, 1918.
Bavinck, Herman. *Gereformeerde dogmatiek*. 4 Volumes. 5th Edition. Kampen: J.H. Kok, 1967.
Bavinck, Herman. 'Godgeleerdheid en godsdienstwetenschap'. *De Vrie Kerk* 18 (1892): 197–225.
Bavinck, Herman. *Godsdienst en godgeleerdheid*. Wageningen: Vada, 1902.

Bavinck, Herman. *Het recht der kerken en de vrijheid der wetenschap*. Kampen: Zalman, 1899.

Bavinck, Herman. *Kennis en leven: Obstellen en artikelen uit vroegere jaren*. Edited by C. B. Bavinck. Kampen: Kok, 1922.

Bavinck, Herman. 'The Kingdom of God, the Highest Good'. Translated by Nelson Kloosterman. *The Bavinck Review* 2 (2011): 133–70.

Bavinck, Herman. *Modernisme en orthodoxie: Rede gehouden bij de overdracht van het Rectoraat aan de Vrije Universiteit op 20 Oktober 1911*. Kampen: Kok, 1911.

Bavinck, Herman. *The Philosophy of Revelation: A New Annotated Edition*. Edited by Cory Brock and Nathaniel Gray Sutanto. Peabody: Hendrickson, 2018.

Bavinck, Herman. *Reformed Dogmatics*. 4 Volumes. Edited by John Bolt. Translated by John Vriend. Grand Rapids: BakerAcademic, 2004.

Bavinck, Herman. 'Religion and Theology'. Translated by Bruce R. Pass. *Reformed Theological Review* 77 (2018): 75–135.

Bavinck, Herman. 'The Pros and Cons of a Dogmatic System'. Translated by Nelson Kloosterman. *The Bavinck Review* 5 (2014): 90–103.

Bavinck, Herman. 'The Theology of Albrecht Ritschl'. Translated by John Bolt. *The Bavinck Review* 3 (2012): 123–63.

Bavinck, Herman and Christiaan Snouch Hurgronje. *Een Leidse Vriendschap: Brieven van Christiaan Snouck Hurgronje aan Herman Bavinck*. Edited by George Harinck and J. Bruijn. Baarn: Ten Have, 1999.

Miscellaneous

Bavinck, Herman. *Het onbewuste*. Manuscript. No date. Historisch Documentatiecentrum voor het Nederlands Protestantisme (1800-heden). Number 346. Folder 413.

Bavinck, Herman. *Notitieboekje met aantekeningen betreffende de zesde druk van Die Welt als Wille und Vorstellung geschreven door Arthur Schopenhauer, en Eduard von Hartman*, Philosophie des Unbewussten. Berlin, 1882. Historisch Documentatiecentrum voor het Nederlands Protestantisme (1800-heden). Number 346. Folder 279.

Bavinck, Herman. *Realism (nature) in de kunst*. No date. Historisch Documentatiecentrum voor het Nederlands Protestantisme (1800-heden). Number 346. Folder 213.

Friesche kerkbode. 1 May 1903. Historisch Documentatiecentrum voor het Nederlands Protestantisme (1800-heden). Number 346. Folder 353.

Minerva: Algemeene Nederlandsch Student Weekblad. 26 March 1903. Historisch Documentatiecentrum voor het Nederlands Protestantisme (1800-heden). Number 346. Folder 353.

Verslag der Handelingen van de Eerste Kamer. 12 March 1913.

Secondary sources

Adams, Nicholas. *The Eclipse of Grace: Divine and Human Action in Hegel*. Hoboken: Blackwell, 2013.

Bibliography

Allen, Michael. 'Knowledge of God'. In *Christian Dogmatics: Reformed Theology for the Church Catholic*, 7-29. Edited by Michael Allen and Scott Swain. Grand Rapids: Baker Academic, 2016.

Allison, Henry. *Kant's Transcendental Idealism: An Interpretation and Defense*. Yale: Yale University Press, 2004.

Aquinas, Thomas. *Commentary on Aristotle Posterior Analytics*. Translated by Richard Berquist. Notre Dame: Dumb Ox Books, 2007.

Aquinas, Thomas. *Commentary on the Gospel of John*. Translated by James A. Weisheipl and Fabrian R. Larcher. Albany: Magi, 1980.

Aquinas, Thomas. *Summa Contra Gentiles*. Edited by Joseph Kenny. New York: Hanover House, 1955-7.

Aquinas, Thomas. *Summa Theologiae*. Translated by Michael Cardinal Browne. London: Eyre & Spottiswoode, 1968.

Aubert, Annette G. *The German Roots of Nineteenth-Century American Theology*. Oxford: Oxford University Press, 2013.

Augustine. *The Trinity*. Translated by Edmund Hill. Brooklyn: New City Press, 1991.

Ayres, Lewis. *Nicaea and Its Legacy: An Approach to Fourth Century Trinitarian Theology*. Oxford: Oxford University Press, 2004.

Bank, Jan and Maarten van Buuren. *Dutch Culture in a European Perspective*, vol. 3: *1900: The Age of Bourgeois Culture*. Translated by Lynn Richards and John Rudge. Hampshire: Palgrave Macmillan, 2004.

Barth, Karl. *Church Dogmatics*. 4 Volumes. 13 Parts. Edited and Translated by G. W. Bromiley, T. F. Torrance, et al. Edinburgh: T&T Clark, 1958.

Barth, Karl. 'Fate and Idea in Theology'. In *The Way of Theology in Karl Barth: Essays and Comments*, 25-63. Edited by H. Martin Rumscheidt. Allison Park: Pickwick, 1986.

Bavinck, J. H. *The Church Between the Temple and the Mosque*. Grand Rapids: Eerdmans, 1966.

Bavinck, J. H. *The J.H. Bavinck Reader*. Edited by John Bolt, James Bratt and Paul Vissers. Translated by James De Jong. Grand Rapids: Eerdmans, 2008.

Beiser, Frederick. 'The Enlightenment and Idealism'. In *The Cambridge Companion to German Idealism*, 18-36. Edited by Karl Emeriks. Cambridge: Cambridge University Press, 2000.

Beiser, Frederick. *The Fate of Reason: German Philosophy from Kant to Fichte*. Cambridge: Harvard University Press, 1987.

Beiser, Frederick. *German Idealism: The Struggle Against Subjectivism 1781-1801*. Cambridge: Harvard University Press, 2002.

Beiser, Frederick. *Late German Idealism: Trendelenburg and Lotze*. Oxford: Oxford University Press, 2013.

Belt, Hank van den. 'An Alternative Approach to Apologetics'. In *The Kuyper Center Review*, vol. 2: *Revelation and Common Grace*, 43-60. Edited by John Bowlin. Grand Rapids: Eerdmans, 2011.

Belt, Hank van den. *The Authority of Scripture in Reformed Theology: Truth and Trust*. Studies in Reformed Theology. Boston: Brill, 2008.

Belt, Hank van den. 'Herman Bavinck and Benjamin B. Warfield on Apologetics and the *Autopistia* of Scripture'. *Calvin Theological Journal* 45 (2010): 32-43.

Belt, Hank van den. 'Herman Bavinck and His Reformed Sources on the Call to Grace: A Shift in Emphasis towards the Internal Work of the Spirit'. *Scottish Bulletin of Evangelical Theology* 29, no. 1 (2011): 41-59.

Belt, Hank van den. 'Religion as Revelation? The Development of Herman Bavinck's View From a Reformed Orthodox to a Neo-Calvinist Approach'. *The Bavinck Review* 4 (2013): 9–31.

Bergmann, Michael. *Justification Without Awareness: A Defense of Epistemic Externalism*. Oxford: Oxford University Press, 2006.

Berkouwer, G. C. *General Revelation*. Grand Rapids: Eerdmans, 1955.

Berlin, Isaiah. *The Roots of Romanticism*. Princeton: Princeton University Press, 2001.

Bolt, John. 'An Adventure in Ecumenicity: A Review Essay of *Berkouwer and Catholicism* by Eduardo Echeverria'. *The Bavinck Review* 5 (2014): 76–89.

Bolt, John. *Bavinck on the Christian Life: Following Jesus in Faithful Service*. Wheaton: Crossway, 2015.

Bolt, John. 'Bavinck's Recipe for Theological Cake'. *Calvin Theological Journal* 45 (2010): 11–17.

Bolt, John. 'Bavinck's Use of Wisdom Literature in Systematic Theology'. *Scottish Bulletin of Evangelical Theology* 29 (2011): 4–24.

Bolt, John. 'Doubting Reformational Anti-Thomism'. In *Aquinas Among the Protestants*, 129–47. Edited by Manfred Svensson and David VanDrunen. Oxford: Wiley-Blackwell, 2017.

Bolt, John. 'Following Bavinck's Lead'. *Comment Magazine* (2012).

Bolt, John. 'Herman Bavinck on Natural Law and Two Kingdoms: Some Further Reflections'. *The Bavinck Review* 4 (2013): 64–93.

Bolt, John. 'An Opportunity Lost and Regained: Herman Bavinck on Revelation and Religion'. *Mid-America Journal of Theology* 24 (2013): 81–96.

Bolt, John. Review of *The Authority of Scripture in Reformed Theology: Truth and Trust*, by Henk van den Belt. *Journal of Reformed Theology* 4 (2010): 75–6.

Bolt, John. 'Sola Scriptura as an Evangelical Theological Method?' In *Reforming or Conforming? Post-Conservative Evangelicals and the Emerging Church*, 63–92. Edited by Gary L. W. Johnson and Ron N. Gleason. Wheaton: Crossway, 2008.

Bolt, John. *A Theological Analysis of Herman Bavinck's Two Essays on the* Imitatio Christi. Lewiston: Edwin Mellen, 2013.

Bonaventure. *Bonaventure: The Soul's Journey into God, the Tree of Life, the Life of St. Francis*. Translated by Ewert Cousins. Mahwah: Paulist Press, 1978.

Bonaventure. *On the Reduction of the Arts to Theology*. Translated by Zachary Hayes. New York: Bonaventure Institute, 1996.

Bowie, Andrew. *Schelling and Modern European Philosophy: An Introduction*. New York: Routledge, 1993.

Bratt, James D. *Abraham Kuyper: Modern Calvinist, Christian Democrat*. Grand Rapids: Eerdmans, 2013.

Bratt, James D. 'The Context of Herman Bavinck's Stone Lectures: Culture and Politics in 1908'. *The Bavinck Review* 1 (2010): 4–24.

Bräutigam, Michael and James Eglinton. 'Scientific Theology? Herman Bavinck and Adolf Schlatter on the Place of Theology in the University'. *Journal of Reformed Theology* 7 (2013): 27–50.

Bremmer, R. H. *Bavinck als Dogmaticus*. Kampen: Kok, 1961.

Brink, Gijsbert van den. 'Reformation Scholasticism and the Trinitarian Renaissance'. In *Scholasticism Reformed: Essays in Honor of Willem J. Van Asselt*, 322–40. Edited by Maarten Wisse, Marcel Sarot and Willemien Otten. Leiden: Brill, 2010.

Brink, Gijsbert van den. 'Social Trinitarianism: A Discussion of Some Recent Theological Criticisms'. *International Journal of Systematic Theology* 16 (2014): 331–50.

Brock, Cory. 'Between Demonization and Dependence: Bavinck's Appropriations of Schleiermacher'. *Ad Fontes* 2 (2018): 1–6.

Brock, Cory and Nathaniel Sutanto. 'Herman Bavinck's Reformed Eclecticism: On Catholicity, Consciousness, and Theological Epistemology'. *Scottish Journal of Theology* 70 (2017): 310–32.

Brown, James. *Subject and Object in Modern Theology: The Croall Lectures Given in the University of Edinburgh 1953*. London: SCM Press, 1953.

Calvin, John. *Institutes of the Christian Religion*. Edited by John T. McNeill. Translated by Ford Lewis Battles. 2 Volumes. The Library of Christian Classics. Philadelphia: Westminster Press, 1960.

Chen, Michael S. 'Herman Bavinck and Augustine on Epistemology'. *The Bavinck Review* 2 (2011): 96–106.

Chiew, Sze Sze. *Middle Knowledge and Biblical Interpretation: Luis de Molina, Herman Bavinck and William Lane Craig*. Frankfurt: Peter Lang, 2016.

Covolo, Robert S. 'Beyond the Schleiermacher-Barth Dilemma: General Revelation, Bavinckian Consensus, and the Future of Reformed Theology'. *The Bavinck Review* 3 (2012): 30–59.

Cowan, Steven, B. and James S. Spiegel, editors. *Idealism and Christianity*. Vol. 2. *Idealism and Christian Philosophy*. London: Bloomsbury, 2016.

Crisp, Oliver. 'On Being a Reformed Theologian'. *Theology* 115 (2012): 14–25.

Crisp, Oliver. 'On Original Sin'. *International Journal of Systematic Theology* 17 (2015): 252–66.

Crisp, Oliver and Michael Rea, editors. *Analytic Theology: New Essays in the Philosophy of Theology*. Oxford: Oxford University Press, 2011.

Cullen, Christopher. *Bonaventure*. Oxford: Oxford University Press.

Davies, Brian. 'Is God Beyond Reason?' *Philosophical Investigations* 32, no. 4 (2009): 338–59.

De Jong, Marinus. 'The Heart of the Academy: Herman Bavinck in Debate with Modernity on the Academy, Theology and the Church'. In *The Kuyper Center Review*, vol. 5: *Church and Academy*, 62–75. Edited by Gordon Graham. Grand Rapids: Eerdmans, 2015.

Deursen, Arie Theodorus van. *The Distinctive Character of the Free University in Amsterdam, 1880–2005: A Commemorative History*. Translated by Herbert Donald Morton. Grand Rapids: Eerdmans, 2008.

Diller, Kevin. 'Can Arguments Boost Warrant for Christian Belief? Warrant Boosting and the Primacy of Divine Revelation'. *Religious Studies* 47 (2011): 185–200.

Diller, Kevin. 'Does Contemporary Theology Require a Postfoundationalist Way of Knowing?' *Scottish Journal of Theology* 60 (2007): 271–93.

Diller, Kevin. 'Karl Barth and the Relationship Between Philosophy and Theology'. *The Heythrop Journal* 51 (2010): 1035–52.

Diller, Kevin. *Theology's Epistemological Dilemma: How Karl Barth and Alvin Plantinga Provide a Unified Response*. Downers Grove: InterVarsity Press, 2014.

Driel, Niels van. 'The Status of Women in Contemporary Society: Principles and Practice in Herman Bavinck's Socio-Political Thought'. In *Five Studies in the Thought of Herman Bavinck, a Creator of Modern Dutch Theology*, 153–95. Edited by John Bolt. Lewiston: Edwin Mellen Press, 2011.

Duby, Steven J. 'Classical Christian Theism and the Criterion of Particularity'. *International Journal of Systematic Theology* 15 (2013): 196–215.

Duby, Steven J. *Divine Simplicity: A Dogmatic Account*. London: T&T Clark, 2016.

Duby, Steven J. 'Scripture as Cognitive Principle of Christian Dogmatics'. *Neue Zeitschrift für Systematische Theologie und Religionsphilosophie* 61 (2019): 223–40.

Duby, Steven J. 'Working with the Grain of Nature: Epistemic Underpinnings for Christian Witness in the Theology of Herman Bavinck'. *The Bavinck Review* 3 (2012): 60–84.

Echeverria, Eduardo J. 'Bavinck on the Family and Integral Human Development'. *Journal of Markets & Morality* 16, no. 1 (2013): 219–37.

Echeverria, Eduardo J. 'The Philosophical Foundations of Bavinck and Dooyeweerd'. *Journal of Markets & Morality* 14, no. 2 (2011): 463–83.

Echeverria, Eduardo J. 'The Reformed Objection to Natural Theology: A Catholic Response to Herman Bavinck'. *Calvin Theological Journal* 45, no. 1 (2010): 87–116.

Eglinton, James. 'Democracy and Ecclesiology: An Aristocratic Church for a Democratic Age?' In *The Kuyper Center Review*, vol. 4: *Calvinism and Democracy*, 134–46. Edited by John Bowlin. Grand Rapids: Eerdmans, 2014.

Eglinton, James. 'To Be or to Become—That Is the Question: Locating the Actualistic in Bavinck's Ontology'. In *The Kuyper Center Review*, vol. 2: *Revelation and Common Grace*, 104–24. Edited by John Bowlin. Grand Rapids: Eerdmans, 2011.

Eglinton, James. 'To Transcend and to Transform: The Neo-Calvinist Relationship of Church and Cultural Transformation'. *The Kuyper Center Review*, vol. 3: *Calvinism and Culture*, 163–97. Edited by John Bowlin. Grand Rapids: Eerdmans, 2013.

Eglinton, James. *Trinity and Organism: Toward a New Reading of Herman Bavinck's Organic Motif*. T&T Clark Studies in Systematic Theology. London: T&T Clark, 2012.

Eglinton, James. '*Vox Theologiae*: Boldness and Humility in Public Theological Speech'. *International Journal of Public Theology* 9 (2015): 5–28.

Elliott, Mark W. 'Bavinck's Use of Augustine as an Antidote to Ritschl'. *Scottish Bulletin of Evangelical Theology* 29, no. 1 (2011): 24–40.

Emery, Giles. 'Trinity and Creation'. In *The Theology of Thomas Aquinas*. Edited by Rik van Nieuwenhove and Joseph Wawrykow. Notre Dame: University of Notre Dame Press, 2005.

Feingold, Laurence. *The Natural Desire to See God according to St. Thomas Aquinas and His Interpreters*. 2nd Edition. Naples: Sapientia, 2010.

Ferrarin, Alfredo. *Hegel and Aristotle*. Cambridge: Cambridge University Press, 2001.

Flipse, Abraham. 'The Origins of Creationism in the Netherlands: The Evolution Debate among Twentieth-Century Dutch Neo-Calvinists'. *Church History* 81 (2012): 104–47.

Fisk, P. J. 'The Unaccommodated Bavinck and Hodge: Prolegomena with Natural Certainty'. *Trinity Journal* 30 (2009): 107–27.

Gaffin, Richard. *God's Word in Servant Form: Abraham Kuyper and Herman Bavinck on the Doctrine of Scripture*. Greenville: Reformed Academic Press, 2008.

Gardner, Sebastian. 'Eduard von Hartmann's *Philosophy of the Unconscious*'. In *Thinking the Unconscious: Nineteenth-Century German Thought*, 173–99. Edited by Angus Nicholls and Martin Liebscher. Cambridge: Cambridge University Press, 2012.

Gerrish, B. A. *The Christian Faith: Dogmatics in Outline*. Louisville: Westminster John Knox, 2015.

Giola, Luigi. *The Theological Epistemology of Augustine's De Trinitate*. Oxford: Oxford University Press, 2008.

Gleason, Ronald. *Herman Bavinck: Pastor, Churchman, Statesman, and Theologian*. Phillipsburg: P&R, 2010.

Goudriaan, Aza. *Reformed Orthodoxy and Philosophy, 1625–1750: Gisbertus Voetius, Petrus van Mastricht, and Anthonius Driessen*. Leiden: Brill, 2006.

Greco, John. 'How to Reid Moore'. *The Philosophical Quarterly* 52 (2002): 544–63.

Grumett, David. 'De Lubac, Grace, and the Pure Nature Debate'. *Modern Theology* 31 (2015): 123–46.
Harinck, George. 'Herman Bavinck and Geerhardus Vos'. *Calvin Theological Journal* 45, no. 1 (2010): 18–31.
Harinck, George. 'The Religious Character of Modernism and the Modern Character of Religion: A Case Study of Herman Bavinck's Engagement with Modern Culture'. *Scottish Bulletin of Evangelical Theology* 29, no. 1 (2011): 60–77.
Harinck, George. '"Something That Must Remain, If the Truth is to be Sweet and Precious to Us": The Reformed Spirituality of Herman Bavinck'. *Calvin Theological Journal* 38 (2003): 248–62.
Harinck, George. 'Why Was Bavinck in Need of a Philosophy of Revelation?' In *The Kuyper Center Review*, vol. 2: *Revelation and Common Grace*, 27–42. Edited by John Bowlin. Grand Rapids: Eerdmans, 2011.
Harinck, George and G. W. Neven, editors. *Ontmoetingen met Herman Bavinck*. Ad Chartas-reeks 9. Barneveld: De Vuurbaak, 2006.
Harinck, George, Cornelis van der Kooi and J. Vree, editors. *'Als Bavinck nu maar eens kleur bekende': Aantekeningen van H. Bavinck over de zaak-Netelenbos, het schriftgezag en de situatie van de gereformeerde kerken, November 1919*. Amsterdam: VU Uitgeverij, 1994.
Hart, Hendrik, Johan van der Hoeven and Nicholas Wolterstorff, editors. *Rationality in the Calvinian Tradition*. Eugene: Wipf & Stock, 2011.
Hartmann, Eduard von. *Philosophie des Unbewussten: Speculatie Resultate nach Inductiv-naturwissenschaftlicher Methode*. 3 Volumes. 10th Edition. Leipzig, Hermann Haacke, 1890.
Hartmann, Eduard von. *Philosophy of the Unconscious*. Translated by William Coupland. London: Trubner, 1884.
Hector, Kevin. *The Theological Project of Modernism: Faith and the Conditions of Mineness*. Oxford: Oxford University Press, 2015.
Hector, Kevin. *Theology Without Metaphysics: God, Language, and the Spirit of Recognition*. Cambridge: Cambridge University Press, 2011.
Hegel, G. W. F. *The Phenomenology of Mind*. Translated by J. B. Bailie. Mineola: Dover, 2004.
Heideman, Eugene P. *The Relation of Revelation and Reason in E. Brunner and H. Bavinck*. Assen: Van Gorcum, 1959.
Helm, Paul. *Calvin at the Centre*. Oxford: Oxford University Press, 2010.
Helm, Paul. *Faith, Form and Fashion: Classical Reformed Theology and Its Postmodern Critics*. Eugene: Cascade Books, 2014.
Helm, Paul. 'Religion and Reason From a Reformed Perspective'. In *Theology and Philosophy: Faith and Reason*, 58–71. Edited by Oliver D. Crisp, Gavin D. Costa, Mervyn Davies and Peter Hampson. New York: T&T Clark, 2012.
Hepp, Valentine. *Dr. Herman Bavinck*. Amsterdam: W. Ten Have, 1921.
Heslam, Peter. *Creating a Christian Worldview: Abraham Kuyper's Lectures on Calvinism*. Grand Rapids: Eerdmans, 1998.
Hoitenga, Jr, Dewey J. *From Plato to Plantinga: An Introduction to Reformed Epistemology*. Albany: State University of New York Press, 1991.
Houlgate, Stephen. *An Introduction to Hegel: Freedom, Truth, and History*. Oxford: Blackwell, 2005.
Howard, Thomas Albert. *Protestant Theology and the Making of the Modern German University*. Oxford: Oxford University Press, 2006.

Huttinga, Wolter. '"Marie Antoinette" or Mystical Depth?: Herman Bavinck on Theology as Queen of the Sciences'. In *Neo-Calvinism and the French Revolution*, 143–54. Edited by James Eglinton and George Harinck. London: Bloomsbury, 2014.

Huttinga, Wolter. *Participation and Communicability: Herman Bavinck and John Milbank on the Relation Between God and the World*. Amsterdam: Buijten & Schipperheijn Motief, 2014.

Inkpin, Andrew. *Disclosing the World: On the Phenomenology of Language*. Cambridge: MIT Press, 2016.

Jaarsma, Cornelius. *The Educational Philosophy of Herman Bavinck: A Textbook in Education*. Grand Rapids: Eerdmans, 1935.

Johnson, Keith. *Karl Barth and the Analogia Entis*. London: T&T Clark, 2010.

Junius, Franciscus. *A Treatise on True Theology*. Translated by David Noe. Grand Rapids: Reformation Heritage, 2014.

Kant, Immanuel. *Critique of Pure Reason*. Translated by Marcus Weigelt. London: Penguin, 2007.

Kant, Immanuel. *Kant: Political Writings*. Edited by H. S. Reiss. Translated by H. B. Nisbet. Cambridge: Cambridge University Press, 1991.

Kelsey, David. *To Understand God Truly: What's Theological about a Theological School?* Eugene: Wipf & Stock, 2011.

Kerr, Fergus. *After Aquinas: Versions of Thomism*. Malden: Blackwell, 2002.

Kilby, Karen. 'Perichoresis and Projection: Problems with Social Doctrines of the Trinity'. *New Blackfriars* 81 (2000): 432–45.

Kilma, Gyula. 'Aquinas on the Materiality of the Human Soul and the Immateriality of the Human Intellect'. *Philosophical Investigations* 32 (2009): 163–82.

Klapwijk, Jacob. 'Abraham Kuyper on Science, Theology, and University'. In *On Kuyper: A Collection of Readings on the Life, Work, and Legacy of Abraham Kuyper*, 221–46. Edited by Steve Bishop and John H. Kok. Sioux Center: Dordt College Press, 2013.

Kolb, Robert. *Martin Luther: Confessor of the Faith*. Oxford: Oxford University Press, 2009.

Komonchak, Joseph. 'Theology and Culture at Mid-Century: The Example of Henry de Lubac'. *Theological Studies* 51 (1990): 579–602.

Kooi, Cornelis van der. 'The Appeal to the Inner Testimony of the Spirit, Especially in H. Bavinck'. *Journal of Reformed Theology* 2 (2008): 103–12.

Kooi, Cornelis van der. 'The Assurance of Faith: A Theme in Reformed Dogmatics in Light of Alvin Plantinga's Epistemology'. *Neue Zeitschrift für Systematische Theologie und Religionsphilosophie* 40 (1998): 91–106.

Kretzmann, Norman. *The Metaphysics of Theism: Aquinas's Natural Theology in Summa Contra Gentiles*. Oxford: Clarendon Press, 2007.

Kuyper, Abraham. *Abraham Kuyper: A Centennial Reader*. Edited by James Bratt. Grand Rapids: Eerdmans, 1998.

Kuyper, Abraham. *Common Grace: God's Gifts for a Fallen World*. Edited by Jordan J. Ballor and Stephen Grabill. Translated by Nelson D. Kloosterman and Edited by M. van der Maas. Bellington: Lexham Press, 2016.

Kuyper, Abraham. *Encyclopedia of Sacred Theology: Its Principles*. Translated by Hendrik de Vries. Norwood: Charles Scribner's Sons, 1898.

Kuyper, Abraham. 'The Natural Knowledge of God'. Translated by Harry van Dyke. *The Bavinck Review* 6 (2015): 73–112.

Kuyper, Abraham. *Ons Instinctieve Leven*. Amsterdam: W. Kirchner, 1908.

Kuyper, Abraham. *Scholarship: Two Convocation Addresses on University Life*. Translated by Harry van Dyke. Grand Rapids: Christian's Library Press, 2014.

Laurentis, Allegra de. 'Absolute Knowing'. In *The Blackwell Guide to Hegel's Phenomenology of Spirit*, 246–64. Edited by Kenneth Westphal. Oxford: Wiley-Blackwell, 2009.
Leithart, Peter. *Athanasius*. Grand Rapids: BakerAcademic, 2011.
Levering, Matthew. *Proofs of God: Classical Arguments from Tertullian to Barth*. Grand Rapids: Baker Academic, 2016.
Levering, Matthew. *Scripture and Metaphysics: Aquinas and the Renewal of Trinitarian Theology*. Oxford: Blackwell, 2004.
Long, Steven A. *Natura Pura: On the Recovery of Nature in the Doctrine of Grace*. New York: Fordham University Press, 2011.
Long, Steven A. 'On Obediential Potency, Human Knowledge, and the Natural Desire for God'. *International Philosophical Quarterly* 37 (1997): 45–63.
MacInerny, Ralph. *Praembula Fidei: Thomism and the God of the Philosophers*. Indiana: Catholic University of America Press, 2006.
MacIntyre, Alasdair. *God, Philosophy, Universities: A Selective History of the Catholic Philosophical Tradition*. New York: Sheed & Ward, 2009.
Macleod, Donald. 'Bavinck's Prolegomena: Fresh Light on Amsterdam, Old Princeton, and Cornelius Van Til'. *Westminster Theological Journal* 68, no. 2 (2006): 261–82.
Martin, Christopher. *Thomas Aquinas: God and Explanations*. Edinburgh: Edinburgh University Press, 1997.
Mattson, Brian. *Restored to Our Destiny: Eschatology and the Image of God in Herman Bavinck's Reformed Dogmatics*. Leiden: Brill, 2011.
Mattson, Brian. 'A Soft Spot for Paganism? Herman Bavinck and "Insider" Movements'. *The Bavinck Review* 4 (2013): 32–43.
Mattson, Brian. 'Van Til on Bavinck: An Assessment'. *Westminster Theological Journal* 70, no. 1 (2008): 111–27.
Mackenzie, J. 'The New Realism and the Old Idealism'. *Mind* 15 (1906): 308–29.
McDowell, John. *Having the World in View: Essays on Kant, Hegel, and Sellars*. Cambridge: Harvard University Press, 2013.
McDowell, John. *Mind and World*. Cambridge: Harvard University Press, 1996.
McFarland, Ian. *From Nothing: A Theology of Creation*. Louisville: Westminster John Knox, 2014.
McGrath, Alister. *Scientific Theology*. Vol 2: *Reality*. London: T&T Clark, 2007.
McInerny, Ralph. *Praembula Fidei: Thomism and the God of the Philosophers*. Indiana: Catholic University of America Press, 2006.
Moore, G. E. 'The Refutation of Idealism'. *Mind* 12 (1903): 433–53.
Mulcahy, Bernard. *Aquinas's Notion of Pure Nature and the Christian Integralism of Henri de Lubac: Not Everything is Grace*. New York: Peter Lang, 2011.
Muller, Richard. *After Calvin: Studies in the Development of a Theological Tradition*. Oxford: Oxford University Press, 2003.
Muller, Richard. *Calvin and the Reformed Tradition: On the Work of Christ and the Order of Salvation*. Grand Rapids: Baker Academic, 2012.
Muller, Richard. *Christ and the Decree: Christology and Predestination in Reformed Theology from Calvin to Perkins*. Grand Rapids: Baker Academic, 1986.
Muller, Richard. *Post-Reformation Reformed Dogmatics: The Rise and Development of Reformed Orthodoxy, ca.1520–1725*. 4 Volumes. 2nd Edition. Grand Rapids: Baker, 2003.
Muller, Richard. *The Unaccommodated Calvin: Studies in the Foundation of a Theological Tradition*. Oxford: Oxford University Press, 2000.
Nichols, Ryan. *Thomas Reid's Theory of Perception*. Oxford: Clarendon Press, 2007.

Nieuwenhove, Rik van. 'Catholic Theology in the Thirteenth Century and the Origins of Secularism'. *Irish Theological Quarterly* 75 (2010): 339–54.
Nieuwenhove, Rik van. *An Introduction to Medieval Theology*. Cambridge: Cambridge University Press, 2012.
O'Donnell, Laurence. '"Bavinck's Bug" or "Van Tillian" Hypochondria?: An Analysis of Prof. Oliphint's Assertion That Cognitive Realism and Reformed Theology are Incompatible'. In *For the Healing of the Nations: Essays on Creation, Redemption and Neo- Calvinism*, 139–72. Edited by Peter Escalante and W. Bradford Littlejohn. Landrum: Davenant Trust, 2014.
O'Donnell, Laurence. *Kees Van Til als Nederlandse-Amerikaanse, Neo-Calvinistisch-Presbyteriaan apologeticus: An Analysis of Cornelius Van Til's Presupposition of Reformed Dogmatics with special reference to Herman Bavinck's Gereformeerde Dogmatiek*. Th.M. Thesis. Grand Rapids: Calvin Theological Seminary, 2011.
O'Donnell, Laurence. 'Neither "Corpernican" nor "Van Tillian": Re-Reading Cornelius Van Til's Reformed Apologetics in Light of Herman Bavinck's Reformed Dogmatics'. *The Bavinck Review* 2 (2011): 71–95.
O'Donovan, Oliver. *Resurrection and the Moral Order: An Outline for Evangelical Ethics*. Grand Rapids: Eerdmans, 1994.
O'Donnell, Laurence. Review of *The Kuyper Center Review*, vol. 2: *Revelation and Common Grace*. Edited by John Bowlin. *The Bavinck Review* 3 (2011): 191–5.
O'Donovan, Oliver. *Self, World, and Time: Ethics as Theology, Volume 1*. Grand Rapids: Eerdmans, 2013.
Oliphint, K. Scott. 'Bavinck's Realism, the Logos Principle, and *Sola Scriptura*'. *Westminster Theological Journal* 72 (2010): 359–90.
Orr, James. *The Christian View of God and the World*. New York: Anson D. F. Randolph and Co., 1898.
Pass, Bruce. 'Herman Bavinck and the Problem of New Wine in Old Wineskins'. *International Journal of Systematic Theology* 17, no. 4 (2015): 432–49.
Pinkard, Terry. *German Philosophy: 1760–1860: The Legacy of Idealism*. Cambridge: Cambridge University Press, 2007.
Plantinga, Alvin. 'Augustinian Christian Philosophy'. *The Monist* 75 (1992): 291–320.
Plantinga, Alvin. *God and Other Minds: A Study of the Rational Justification of Belief in God*. Ithaca: Cornell University Press, 1990.
Plantinga, Alvin. *Warrant and Proper Function*. New York: Oxford University Press, 1993.
Plantinga, Alvin. *Warrant: The Current Debate*. New York: Oxford University Press, 1993.
Plantinga, Alvin. *Warranted Christian Belief*. New York: Oxford University Press, 2000.
Plantinga, Alvin and Nicholas Wolterstorff, editors. *Faith and Rationality: Reason and Belief in God*. Notre Dame: University of Notre Dame Press, 1983.
Rahner, Karl. *The Trinity*. Translated by Joseph Donceel. London: Burns & Oates, 1970.
Redding, Paul. *Analytic Philosophy and the Return of Hegelian Thought*. Cambridge: Cambridge University Press, 2007.
Reid, Thomas. *The Works of Thomas Reid, D.D.: Now Fully Collected, With Selections from His Unpublished Letters*. Edited by William Hamilton. Edinburgh: Maclachlan, Stewart and Co., 1846.
Rogers, Eugene. 'The Narrative of Natural Law in Aquinas' Commentary on Romans 1'. *Theological Studies* 59 (1998): 254–76.
Rota, Michael. 'What Can Aristotelian and Thomistic Philosophy Contribute to Christian Theology?'. In *Theology and Philosophy: Faith and Reason*, 102–15. Edited by Oliver

D. Crisp, Gavin D. Costa, Mervyn Davies and Peter Hampson. New York: T&T Clark, 2012.
Russell, Matheson. 'Phenomenology and Theology: Situating Heidegger's Philosophy of Religion'. *Sophia* 50 (2011): 641–55.
Scarpelli, Therese. 'Bonaventure's Christocentric Epistemology: Christ's Human Knowledge as the Epitome of Illumination in "De Scientia Christi"'. *Franciscan Studies* 65 (2007): 63–86.
Schelling, F. W. J. *First Outline of a System of the Philosophy of Nature*. Translated by Keith R. Peterson. Albany: State University of New York Press, 2004.
Schelling, F. W. J. *Ideas for a Philosophy of Nature*. Translated by Error E. Harris and Peter Heath. Cambridge: Cambridge University Press, 1998.
Schleiermacher, Friederich. *Christian Faith: A New Translation and Critical Edition*. Edited by Catherine L. Kelsey and Terrence N. Tice. Translated by Catherine L. Kelsey, Edwina Lawler and Terrence N. Tice. Louisville: Westminster John Knox, 2016.
Schleiermacher, Friederich. *On Religion: Speeches to its Cultured Despisers*. Translated by John Oman. Louisville: Westminster John Knox, 1994.
Schumacher, Lydia. *Divine Illumination: The History and Future of Augustine's Theory of Knowledge*. Oxford: Wiley & Blackwell, 2011.
Selderhuis, Herman, editor. *A Companion to Reformed Orthodoxy*. Leiden: Brill, 2013.
Shannon, Nathan D. *Shalom and the Ethics of Belief: Nicholas Wolterstorff's Theory of Situated Rationality*. Eugene: Pickwick, 2015.
Siedentop, Larry. *Inventing the Individual: The Origins of Western Liberalism*. United Kingdom: Penguin Books, 2014.
Smith, James K. A. *Awaiting the King: Reforming Public Theology*. Grand Rapids: Baker Academic, 2017.
Smith, James K. A. *Desiring the Kingdom*. Grand Rapids: Baker Academic, 2009.
Smith, James K. A. 'Echeverria's Protestant Epistemology: A Catholic Response'. *Calvin Theological Journal* 49 (2014): 283–92.
Smith, James K. A. *Imagining the Kingdom: How Worship Works*. Grand Rapids: Baker Academic, 2013.
Smith, James K. A. 'Questions About the Perception of "Christian Truth": On the Affective Effects of Sin'. *New Blackfriars* 88 (200): 585–93.
Steinmetz, David. *Calvin in Context*. Oxford: Oxford University Press, 1995.
Strange, Daniel. *Their Rock is Not Like Our Rock: A Theology of Religions*. Grand Rapids: Zondervan, 2014.
Strong, C. A. 'Has Mr. Moore Refuted Idealism?' *Mind* 14 (1905): 174–89.
Swafford, Andrew. *Nature and Grace: A New Approach to Thomistic Ressourcement*. Cambridge: James Clark & Co, 2015.
Swain, Scott and Michael Allen. 'The Obedience of the Eternal Son'. *International Journal of Systematic Theology* 15 (2013): 114–34.
Swinburne, Richard. *The Christian God*. Oxford: Oxford University Press. 1994.
Sutanto, Nathaniel Gray. 'Herman Bavinck on the Image of God and Original Sin'. *International Journal of Systematic Theology* 18 (2016): 177–90.
Sutanto, Nathaniel Gray. 'Herman Bavinck and Thomas Reid on Perception and Knowing God'. *Harvard Theological Review* 111 (2018): 115–34.
Sutanto, Nathaniel Gray. 'Neocalvinism on General Revelation: A Dogmatic Sketch.' *International Journal of Systematic Theology* 20 (2018): 494–516.
Synopsis Purioris Theologiae: Latin Text and English Translation. Volume 1: *Disputations*, 1–23. Edited by Dolf te Velde. Translated by Dolf te Velde and Riemer A. Faber. Leiden: Brill, 2014.

Systma, David S. 'Herman Bavinck's Thomistic Epistemology: The Argument and Sources of his *Principia* of Science'. In *Five Studies in the Thought of Herman Bavinck*, 1–56. Edited by John Bolt. Lewiston, NY: Edwin Mellen Press, 2011.

Taylor, Charles and Hubert Dreyfus. *Retrieving Realism*. Cambridge: Harvard University Press, 2015.

Tillich, Paul. *A History of Christian Thought*. Edited by Carl Braaten. New York: Simon & Schuuster, 1968.

Trendelenburg, Friderich A. *Logische Untersuchungen*. 3rd Edition. Reprint. Hildesheim: Georg Olms Verlagsbuchhandlung, 1964.

Trueman, Carl R. and R. Scott Clark, editors. *Protestant Scholasticism: Essays in Reassessment*. Carlisle: Paternoster Press, 1999.

Turner, James and Mark Noll. *The Future of Christian Learning: An Evangelical and Catholic Dialogue*. Edited by Thomas A. Howard. Grand Rapids: Brazos, 2008.

Turretin, Francis. *Institutes of Elenctic Theology*. 3 Volumes. Edited by James T. Dennison, Jr. Translated by George M. Giger. Philipsburg: Presbyterian & Reformed, 1994.

Van Asselt, Willem J. 'The Fundamental Meaning of Theology: Archetypal and Ectypal Theology in Seventeenth-Century Reformed Thought'. *Westminster Theological Journal* 64 (2002): 319–35.

Van Asselt, Willem J. Martin Bac, Dolf te Velde, editors. *Reformed Thought on Freedom: The Concept of Free Choice in Early Modern Reformed Theology*. Grand Rapids: Baker Academic, 2010.

Van Asselt, Willem J, T. Theo J. Pleitzer, Pieter L. Rouwendal and Maarteen Wisse, editors. *Introduction to Reformed Scholasticism*. Grand Rapids: Reformation Heritage Books, 2011.

Vanderlaan, E. C. *Protestant Modernism in Holland*. New York: Oxford University Press, 1924.

Vanhoozer, Kevin J. *Biblical Authority After Babel: Retrieving the Solas in the Spirit of Mere Protestant Christianity*. Grand Rapids: Brazos, 2016.

Vanhoozer, Kevin J. *Remythologizing Theology: Divine Action, Passion, and Authorship*. Cambridge: Cambridge University Press, 2012.

Van Til, Cornelius. 'Bavinck the Theologian: A Review Article'. *Westminster Theological Journal* 24 (1961): 48–64.

Van Til, Cornelius. *Common Grace and the Gospel*. Edited by K. Scott Oliphint. 2nd Edition. Philipsburg, NJ: Presbyterian & Reformed, 2015.

Van Til, Cornelius. *The Defense of the Faith*. Edited by K. Scott Oliphint. 4th Edition. Philipsburg, NJ: Presbyterian & Reformed, 2008.

Veenhof, Jan. 'De God van de filosofen en de God van de bijbel: Herman Bavinck en de wijsbegeerte'. In *Ontmoetingen met Herman Bavinck*, 219–34. Edited by George Harinck and Gerrit Neven. Barneveld: De Vuurbaak, 2006.

Veenhof, Jan. 'Nature and Grace in Bavinck'. Translated by Albert M. Wolters. *Pro Rege* 34 (June 2006): 10–31.

Veenhof, Jan. 'Revelation and Grace in Herman Bavinck'. In *The Kuyper Center Review*, vol. 2: *Revelation and Common Grace*, 3–13. Edited by John Bowlin. Grand Rapids: Eerdmans, 2011.

Veenhof, Jan. *Revelatie en Inspiratie: De Openbarings- en Schriftbeschouwing van Herman Bavinck in vergelijking met die der ethische theologie*. Amsterdam: Buijten & Schipperheijn N. V., 1968.

Vissers, John. 'Karl Barth's Appreciative Use of Herman Bavinck's Reformed Dogmatics'. *Calvin Theological Journal* 45, no. 1 (2010): 79–86.
Vos, Arvin. *Aquinas, Calvin, and Contemporary Protestant Thought: A Critique of Protestant Views on the Thought of Thomas Aquinas*. Grand Rapids: Eerdmans, 1985.
Vos, Arvin. 'Knowledge According to Bavinck and Aquinas'. *The Bavinck Review* 6 (2015): 9–36.
Vos, Arvin. 'Knowledge According to Bavinck and Aquinas'. *The Bavinck Review* 7 (2017): 8–62.
Vos, Geerhardus. *Redemptive History and Biblical Interpretation: The Shorter Writings of Geerhardus Vos*. Edited by Richard B. Gaffin. Philipsburg, NJ: P&R Publishing, 1980.
Walt, S. P. van der. *Die Wysbegeerte van De. Herman Bavinck*. Potchefstroom: Pro Rege, 1953.
Webster, John. *The Domain of the Word: Scripture and Theological Reason*. London: T&T Clark, 2012.
Webster, John. 'Life in and Out of Himself: Reflections on God's Aseity'. In *Engaging the Doctrine of God: Contemporary Protestant Perspectives*, 107–24. Edited by Bruce McCormack. Grand Rapids: Baker Academic, 2008.
Webster, John. 'Trinity and Creation'. *International Journal of Systematic Theology* 12 (2010): 4–19.
Westerholm, Martin. 'Kant's Critique and Contemporary Theological Inquiry'. *Modern Theology* 31 (2015): 403–27.
White, Thomas Joseph. 'Divine Simplicity and the Holy Trinity'. *International Journal of Systematic Theology* 18 (2016): 66–93.
Wisse, Martin, Marcel Sarot and Willemien Otten, editors. *Scholasticism Reformed: Essays in Honor of Willem J. Van Asselt*. Leiden: Brill, 2010.
Wit, Willem J. De. *On the Way to the Living God: A Cathartic Reading of Herman Bavinck and An Invitation to Overcome the Plausibility Crisis of Christianity*. Amsterdam: VU University Press, 2011.
Wolterstorff, Nicholas. 'Herman Bavinck – Proto Reformed Epistemologist'. *Calvin Theological Journal* 45 (2010): 133–46.
Wolterstorff, Nicholas. 'Is it Possible and Desirable for Theologians to Recover From Kant?' *Modern Theology* 14 (1998): 1–18.
Wolterstorff, Nicholas. *Justice: Rights and Wrongs*. Princeton: Princeton University Press, 2008.
Wolterstorff, Nicholas. *Thomas Reid and the Story of Epistemology*. Cambridge: Cambridge University Press, 2001.
Yadav, Sameer. *The Problem of Perception and the Experience of God: Toward a Theological Empiricism*. Minnesota: Fortress Press, 2015.
Zachhuber, Johannes. *Theology as Science in Nineteenth Century German: From F.C. Baur to Ernst Troeltsch*. Oxford: Oxford University Press, 2013.
Zagzebski, Linda, editor. *Rational Faith: Catholic Responses to Reformed Epistemology*. Notre Dame: University of Notre Dame Press, 1993.

Index

absolute (as a subject)   14, 15, 19 n.11, 21, 26, 29, 119, 121, 125, 126, 127 n.11, 133, 134, 135, 135 n.49, 136, 137, 140, 141, 145, 146
Adams, Nicholas   78 n.9, 115 n.65, 116 n.67
Allen, Michael   26 n.50
Alsted, J.   19
Anselm   169
anthropology   13, 17, 30–7, 40, 43, 45, 55, 56, 120, 163
antithesis   70, 78, 94
Aquinas, Thomas   8, 10, 10 n.51, 11, 14, 15, 23, 27, 31, 46, 75, 76, 77, 78, 80, 81, 82, 83, 84, 85, 86, 87, 88, 89, 90, 101, 142, 143, 144 n.93, 152, 163, 164, 165, 166, 168, 169, 170, 173, 177
Aristotle   32 n.81, 62, 68, 75 n.3, 77, 78 n.9, 82, 86
Augustine   10, 23, 23 n.32, 25, 26, 27, 38, 86 n.55, 89, 153, 157, 165 n.48, 170, 170 n.78
Ayres, Lewis   23 n.31, 29 n.65

Barth, Karl   20, 34 n.94, 81, 84 n.47, 86, 89 n.68, 140 n.7, 174 n.87
Bavinck, Johan   15, 138 n.65, 152, 171–2
Beginselen der psychologie   4, 11 n.56, 15, 29 n.70, 31 n.72, 32 n.81, 63 n.85, 103, 125 n.5, 138 n.63, 151 n.2, 152, 157 n.23, 159, 160, 161 n.34, 162
Beiser, Frederick   11 n.58, 19 n.9, 53 n.36, 128 n.15
Bergmann, Michael   106 n.18
Berkouwer, G. C.   10 n.51, 15, 152, 174, 175 n.91
Bolt, John   3 n.8, 5, 5 n.26, 6 n.33, 7 n.35, 10, 11 n.53, 12, 13, 22 n.27, 32 n.81, 35 n.99, 46 n.3, 52 n.29, 54 n.40, 65 n.95, 67, 83, 87, 91, 93, 94, 95 n.103, 96 n.107, 138 n.65, 159 n.29, 172 n.84
Bonaventure   15, 31, 82, 86, 92, 152, 164, 165, 166, 167, 168, 169, 170, 171, 172, 179
Bratt, James   8 n.40, 120, 121, 138 n.65, 172 n.84
Bräutigam, Michael   2 n.6, 46, 53 n.38, 55 n.42, 57 n.53, 93, 96, 97 n.113
Bremmer, R. H.   94, 95
Brock, Cory   4, 37 n.110, 58 n.58, 77 n.8, 93 n.95, 95 n.104, 137 n.57, 141 n.81, 170 n.78

Cajetan   83–4, 87, 88 n.68
Calvin, John   4, 7, 10 n.51, 14, 38, 66 n.97, 80, 82, 83 n.39, 84, 85, 104, 154
Calvinism   6 n.30, 7, 35 n.101, 50 n.21, 73, 84 n.45, 120 n.88, 152
Catholicism (Roman)   10, 31, 32, 39 n.122, 71, 75–6, 79–81, 83, 100, 174, 175 n.91
catholicity   6, 10, 23 n.32, 66, 79, 180
Christ   1, 14, 20 n.16, 23 n.31, 36, 39, 40–2, 45, 51–2, 58–9, 65, 67 n.101, 76, 90, 91, 164, 168, 176
Christelijke wereldbeschouwing   1 n.2, 4, 14, 18, 19, 20 n.17, 47, 50, 51, 52 n.31, 53, 65, 67, 68 n.108, 77 n.8, 95, 101 n.1, 103, 104 n.9, 109 n.29, 116, 166 n.72, 117, 135, 141, 142, 144, 146, 148 n.104
Christelijke wetenschap   1, 4, 5 n.21, 14, 45 n.1, 47, 49 n.17, 53 n.36, 56 n.46, 57 n.55, 61, 62 n.78, 63 n.90, 64, 71 n.119, 79 n.11, 93 n.94, 95, 96, 97 n.112
common grace   7 n.36, 38 n.115, 58–9, 80, 90, 95–7, 99

Index

Crisp, Oliver 10 n.51, 31 n.76, 85, 86, 98 n.115
Cullen, Christopher 167, 168, 170, 171

decree 134, 136, 140, 141, 144, 145, 146
De Jong, Marinus 60 n.71, 138 n.65, 172 n.84
De Lubac, Henri 10 n.51, 77 n.8, 84, 87, 88, 89, 90, 93
Descartes, René 110-1
Diller, Kevin 81 n.22, 104 n.13, 106 n.18, 107 n.22, 173 n.87
Dreyfus, Hubert 14, 77, 91 n.84, 100, 110 n.30
Duby, Steven J. 10 n.51, 23 n.34, 25 n.42, 82 n.38

eclecticism 30, 75, 77, 137 n.57, 141 n.81, 164, 170 n.78, 176, 178
Eglinton, James 2 n.6, 4 n.13, 7 n.36, 9, 10, 13, 18, 19 n.9, 20, 21, 22 n.27, 23 n.32, 24, 25 n.41, 34, 35 n.101, 36 n.208, 37 n.109, 38 n.113, 40, 41, 46, 53 n.38, 55 n.42, 57 n.53, 75 n.2, 80, 84 n.45, 92 n.85, 93, 96, 97 n.113, 115 n.65, 140 n.76
Emery, Giles 23 n.33
eschatology 20, 33 n.89, 58, 69, 88, 100
externalism 108 n.18, 109 n.29

Feingold, Laurence 88
Fichte, J.G. 62, 63, 128 n.17, 130 n.25

Grumett, David 89

Harinck, George 4 n.12, 8 n.40, 12 n.64, 46 n.4, 73 n.125, 145 n.97
Hector, Kevin 116 n.70, 153 n.9
Hegel, G. W. F. 19, 22, 26, 78, 84 n.48, 111 n.41, 115 n.65, 116, 121, 128 n.17, 133 n.38, 143
Heidegger, Martin 138 n.64, 179-80
Helm, Paul 10, 84, 87, 91, 92, 93
Hepp, Valentine 8 n.41, 72
Higher Education Act 2, 53 n.38
Huttinga, Wolter 7, 8 n.39, 46, 57 n.57, 59 n.63, 87 n.63

idealism 11 n.58, 12, 15, 19, 53 n.36, 75, 102 n.2, 103, 104, 112, 116, 117, 119, 121, 124, 125, 126, 127-34, 135, 139 n.72, 145, 151, 154, 175, 176, 179, 180
 absolute idealism 9, 14, 15, 19, 78 n.9, 102, 121, 126 n.9, 130 n.25, 135, 145, 151, 176. 177
 subjective idealism 15, 112, 119, 121, 124-6, 130 n.25, 145, 154, 179-80
Imago Dei 30, 33, 34 n.94, 35
internalism 106, 109 n.29, 145-7

Johnson, Keith 20 n.19, 89 n.68, 140 n.74
Junius, Franciscus 20 n.21

Kant, Immanuel 3, 6 n.32, 7, 8, 9, 10, 11, 12 n.64, 13, 14, 15, 102, 103, 104, 108, 111, 112, 114, 116, 121, 123, 128 n.15, 133 n.38, 137, 157, 177, 179, 180
Kerr, Fergus 86
Kennis en leven 1 n.1, 14
Kilma, Gyula 143 n.91
Kingdom of God 14, 33, 35 n.99, 47, 55 n.45, 58, 59, 61, 68-71, 76, 100
Klapwijk, Jacob 144 n.93
Kloosterman, Nelson D. 31 n.73, 33 n.85, 34 n.92, 47 n.8, 155 n.15
Kuyper, Abraham 14, 15, 31 n.73, 35 n.101, 41 n.129, 48, 49 n.13, 50, 55 n.42, 64, 68, 71, 72, 77, 84, 91 n.79, 93-7, 100, 101, 105 n.13, 120, 121, 134 n.43, 144 n.93, 152, 161, 163 n.43, 171, 172, 173, 174, 175 n.91, 178

Leithart, Peter 86 n.58, 90, 91
Levering, Matthew 23 n.33, 81 n.27, 86, 87, 169, 174 n.89
Locke, John 111, 118, 121 n.96
Logos 20, 49, 62, 85 n.51, 103 n.8, 142, 144, 145, 152, 154, 163, 164, 166, 167 n.64, 170, 174, 176
Long, Steven A. 87 n.59, 88, 89 n.69

McDowell, John 121 n.96, 133 n.38
McFarland, Ian 28 n.64
Mattson, Brian 8 n.42, 9, 13, 20 n.21, 22 n.27, 31, 33, 75 n.2
metaphysics 3–5, 19, 23, 24 n.35, 26, 42, 51, 54, 85, 88, 90, 96, 118–19, 126, 130, 136 n.51, 144 n.96, 146, 159, 168, 170–1, 176
Moore, G. E. 131
Mulcahy, Bernard 77 n.8, 87
Muller, Richard 4 n.18, 21 n.24, 169 n.72

neo-Calvinism 7, 9, 15, 21, 36, 38 n.115, 46, 47, 57, 72 n.123, 73, 77, 84, 93, 101, 139 n.72, 152, 161, 171–6
nouvelle theologie 83, 84, 90

Opzoomer, Cornelis 2, 3
organism 1, 2, 3, 8, 9, 13, 14, 17, 18, 19, 20, 22, 23, 28, 33, 35, 36, 37, 40, 41 n.129, 42, 43, 45, 47, 48, 49, 51, 59, 60 n.71, 61, 63, 68, 69, 70, 71, 73, 75, 77, 92, 93, 97, 98, 99, 100, 101, 135, 141, 144, 152, 158, 176, 177, 178

Pass, Bruce 4 n.15, 13 n.67
philosophy 53, 57 n.54, 63, 66 n.96, 68–9, 77–9, 81 n.22, 82, 85–7, 91–2, 101, 104, 109–11, 116, 119 n.82, 121 n.95, 126, 129, 133, 134, 136 n.51, 141–2, 143, 161, 167, 177, 179–80
Philosophy of Revelation 4, 6 n.28, 15, 37, 41 n.129, 42, 43, 58, 77 n.8, 78 n.9, 80 n.20, 95, 100, 112, 117, 121, 124, 125, 127–34, 134–45, 147, 151 n.1, 152, 153, 154 n.10, 156, 158, 159 n.28, 162 n.40, 168 n.65, 170 n.78, 179
Plantinga, Alvin 14, 81, 85 n.50, 102, 104–9, 119, 120, 123, 126, 131 n.31, 156 n.19, 174
Plato 7, 26, 32 n.81, 62, 68, 111, 170
principia 14, 46–7, 59–68, 76, 92, 142, 177

realism 6 n.28, 9, 12, 14, 15, 20 n.21, 78 n.9, 88, 91 n.84, 100 n.117, 102, 104, 110 n.30, 114 n.59, 115, 119, 121, 124, 125, 126, 128, 130, 143, 176, 179
Reformed Dogmatics 4, 20, 23–4, 47, 78, 80, 108 n.27, 111, 158

Reformed orthodoxy 4, 6, 8, 12, 62
Reformed theology 30, 37–8, 81 n.28, 85, 173 n.87, 178
Reid, Thomas 14, 102, 106, 108–14, 115, 120, 123
revelation
  general revelation 15, 37–41, 80 n.16, 81, 98–9, 117 n.75, 137, 139, 148, 152, 169, 171–2, 174–5, 177
  special revelation 10, 13, 14, 17, 19 n.14, 21, 37–42, 45, 81, 91, 98–100, 117 n.75, 142, 148, 175
Romanticism 8, 14, 19 n.11, 77–8, 92, 97, 118 n.78, 120, 143, 152–3, 156 n.19, 163–4, 170 n.78, 171, 174–5, 177

Schelling, F. W. J. 19, 78, 128 n.17
Schleiermacher, Friedrich 3, 8, 14, 111 n.41, 137, 138 n.63, 143, 153 n.9, 173 n.86
Schumacher, Lydia 86 n.55, 152, 164–5, 167 n.64, 168–9
sin 31–3, 36, 38–42, 54–5, 58, 68–70, 78, 83, 85, 90, 95, 164, 166, 168, 169, 172, 175, 177
Smith, James K. A. 175 n.91, 67 n.103, 85, 91, 137 n.60
sphere sovereignty 14, 47, 68, 101
Sutanto, Nathaniel Gray 4, 36 n.107, 113 n.49, 137 n.57, 141 n.81, 170 n.78,
Swafford, Andrew 88–9
Sytsma, David 10–11, 80 n.15, 115 n.66, 143, 144 n.92

Taylor, Charles 14, 77, 100, 110 n.30
theology proper 17, 22–30
  natural theology 10, 19 n.14, 21, 38, 75 n.2, 80–1, 148 n.103, 173
  simplicity 13, 17, 23–7
Trendelenburg, F. A. 19, 20 n.17, 22, 53 n.36
Trinity 9, 18, 20–2, 24 n.37, 26–30, 34, 36, 39, 45, 48, 56, 67, 71, 98, 100, 121, 147, 167 n.55, 177
  social Trinitarianism 22–3
Turretin, Francis 24 n.35, 80 n.19

unconscious (the)   15, 18, 102–3, 119, 124–6, 130 n.26, 132–3, 136, 138, 140, 151–2, 157, 158, 160–2, 164, 176
unity-in-diversity   9, 13, 20, 23 n.31, 30, 33–4, 36–7, 45, 47–9, 60, 70–1, 76 n.3, 176, 177

Van Asselt, Willem   20 n.21, 81 n.28
Van den Belt, Henk   11–12, 102–4, 108–9, 119, 123–4, 148
Van den Brink, Gijsbert   23 n.31
Van der Kooi, Cornelis   11, 73 n.125, 102, 104, 108–9, 118 n.78, 119, 123, 148
Van Deursen, Arie   3 n.11, 71–3
Vanhoozer, Kevin   20 n.20, 85, 90–1
Van Nieuwenhove, Rik   23 n.33, 86
Veenhof, Jan   8 n.41, 12 n.64

Von Hartmann, Eduard   14–15, 19 n.11, 22, 102–3, 104, 119–21, 123–45, 177
Vos, Arvin   11, 83–4

Webster, John   26 n.46, 166, 85, 92 n.89
Wetenschap   17, 37, 45–6, 49, 56–68, 70, 71, 75, 78, 94–8, 141
Wolterstorff, Nicholas   14, 75, 86 n.54, 102, 104–8, 110–14, 118–20, 123, 126, 131–2, 156 n.19
worldview   1, 6, 9, 10, 13, 17–19, 31 n.72, 36, 40, 41, 45, 47, 50–6, 59, 67, 80, 91, 93, 95–6, 101, 103, 117 n.75, 135, 142, 144 n.92, 146–8, 159, 164

Zachhuber, Johannes   2 n.6, 54 n.40
Zagzebski, Linda   85, 86 n.54